HOW TO USE THIS INDEX

Placement of marks on the right-hand edge of this page corresponds to the black rules on the page edges throughout the book. To open quickly to any section, flex the pages to expose the page-edge rules and open the book to where the exposed rules align with the mark for that section on this page.

THE ARCHITECT'S STUDIO COMPANION

RULES OF THUMB FOR PRELIMINARY DESIGN

Third Edition

Edward Allen and Joseph Iano

John Wiley & Sons, Inc.

This book is printed on acid-free paper. ∞

Copyright © 2002 by John Wiley & Sons, Inc., New York. All rights reserved.

Published simultaneously in Canada.

No part of this publication may be reproduced, stored in a retrieval system or transmitted in any
form or by any means, electronic, mechanical, photocopying, recording, scanning or otherwise,
except as permitted under Sections 107 or 108 of the 1976 United States Copyright Act, without
either the prior written permission of the Publisher, or authorization through payment of the
appropriate per-copy fee to the Copyright Clearance Center, 222 Rosewood Drive, Danvers, MA
01923, (978) 750-8400, fax (978) 750-4744. Requests to the Publisher for permission should be
addressed to the Permissions Department, John Wiley & Sons, Inc., 605 Third Avenue, New York,
NY 10158-0012, (212) 850-6011, fax (212) 850-6008, E-mail: PERMREQ @ WILEY.COM.

This publication is designed to provide accurate and authoritative information in regard to the
subject matter covered. It is sold with the understanding that the publisher is not engaged in
rendering professional services. If professional advice or other expert assistance is required, the
services of a competent professional person should be sought.

Library of Congress Cataloging-in-Publication Data:

Allen, Edward, 1938–
    The architect's studio companion: rules of thumb for preliminary design / Edward Allen
    and Joseph Iano.— 3rd ed.
        p. cm.
    Includes bibliographical references and index.
    ISBN 0-471-39235-9 (cloth : alk. paper)
        1. Architectural design — Handbooks, manuals, etc.—I. Iano, Joseph. II. Title

NA2750 .A556 2001
721 — dc21

                                                                    2001024235

Printed in the United States of America.
10 9 8 7 6 5 4 3 2 1

ACKNOWLEDGMENTS

We wish to thank the many individuals who contributed so graciously to the making of this book. Among those professionals whom we consulted during its formative stages, special mention goes to Prof. Carl Bovile of the University of Maryland, who strongly influenced the underlying philosophy of the book, and Prof. Stephen Vamosi of the University of Cincinnati, who gave generously of his expertise on mechanical and electrical systems. Robert Heryford, P.E., and Peter S. Watt, P.E., of R. G. Vanderweil Associates and Marvin Mass of Cosentini Associates also shared freely their knowledge in this area. Richard J. Farley of the University of Pennsylvania and Daniel Schodek of Harvard University gave valuable advice on structural matters. Joel Loveland, of the University of Washington Department of Architect and the Seattle Lighting Design Lab, generously provided valuable concepts as well as helpful review for the third edition's chapter on daylighting design. For additional contributions of technical expertise we are indebted to architects Harvey Bryan, Mark Dooling, Jerry Hicks, Douglas Mahone, and Peter Stone.

The first edition of this book was created through an exceptional working relationship with the publisher, John Wiley & Sons, Inc. We thank especially Judith R. Joseph, the editor with whom we began the project, and Claire Thompson, who continued as editor and guided the book through its development with skill and never-ending optimism. We wish to thank Marcia Samuels for an expert job of copyediting and guiding the book through the complexities of production, and Cynthia Zigmund, Erika Levy, and Barbara Tillman for their cheer and professionalism in handling the many administrative difficulties.

For their valuable assistance in reviewing preliminary drafts of the first edition, we thank David Glassner of Temple University, Roger N. Goldstein of Goody, Clancy Associates, Jack Kremers of Kent State University, Sandra Davis Lakeman of California Polytechnic University, Alan Levy of the University of Pennsylvania, John Reynolds of the University of Oregon, Donald Prowler of the University of Pennsylvania, and Marc Schiller of the University of Southern California.

The third edition was produced under the expert care, guidance, and patient encouragement of Wiley senior editor Amanda Miller, with able assistance from Maury Botton. Figaro set the type for the new tables, graphs, and text. Karin Kincheloe, a truly gifted artist, created the designs for all three editions of the book.

We would like, finally, to acknowledge the assistance and support of those closest to our hearts. Edward Allen expresses his gratitude to Mary M. Allen, whose own career is a constant source of inspiration to him, and to Joseph Iano, whose imagination and dedication have greatly enriched their collaborative efforts for the last two decades. Joseph Iano especially thanks Edward Allen for his longstanding friendship and professional encouragement, and Lesley Bain for so many things, but most important to this work, for her patience.

DISCLAIMER

The information in this book has been interpreted from sources that include building codes, industry standards, manufacturers' literature, engineering reference works, and personal contacts with many individuals. It is presented in good faith, but although the authors and the publisher have made every reasonable effort to make this book accurate and authoritative, they do note warrant, and assume no liability for, its accuracy or completeness or its fitness for any particular purpose. The user should note especially that this is a book of first approximations, information that is not intended to be used for final design of any building or structure. It is the responsibility of users to apply their professional knowledge in the use of information contained in this book, to consult original sources for more detailed information as needed, and to seek expert advice as needed, especially in the later stages of the process of designing a building.

CONTENTS

HOW TO USE THIS BOOK

This book is your desktop technical advisor for the earliest stages of building design. It reduces complex engineering and building code information to simple formal and spatial approximations that are readily incorporated into initial design explorations. It does not replace building codes, detailed technical handbooks, and skilled consultants; it simply helps you prepare a buildable preliminary design as a realistic basis for the more detailed design development and consultations that will follow.

After you have used this book on several projects, you will have developed a pattern for its use that suits your own way of going about designing a building. The first time that you use it, there are two approaches you might take. One is simply to enter the book at any point that you wish, using the index tabs and following the logical paths indicated by the cross-references until your need for information is satisfied. Alternatively, you may wish to begin at the beginning, tracing the following steps as a means of finding the information you need while becoming familiar with the layout of the book.

1. Turn to the first section, Designing with Building Codes. Consult the information beginning on page 7 to determine which model building code to use as the basis for your project, and within that code, which Occupancy Group or Groups your building falls within. Make a note of the code and Occupancy Group for ready reference as you progress through the other sections of the book—these pieces of information are your key to unlocking many different kinds of information.

2. Move next to the second section, Designing the Structure. Read the brief passage concerning building code requirements on page 19. Refer to the Height and Area Tables in Designing with Height and Area Limitations that correspond to your building code and Occupancy Groups noted earlier. List from these tables the Construction Types you are permitted to use in your building.

3. Skim the explanation of Construction Types that begins on page 304. Add notes to your list of permitted Construction Types to help you remember which specific structural materials and systems are associated with each Construction Type.

4. Continue the process of selecting a structural system by returning to pages 20–29, which will help you identify one or more specific structural systems that might be appropriate for the building you are designing. Be sure your choices fall within one or another of the Construction Types you previously identified as permitted under the appropriate building code.

5. Follow the page references given with each choice of structural system to learn in detail what each system looks like and what its potentials and limitations are. With the information found here, you can begin adding a structural plan and sections to the design for your building, complete with spacings and approximate sizes of all the members.

6. If you need help in laying out the overall structural system, turn to page 31 and the pages that follow for general advice on configuring a structural system.

7. When you are satisfied that you have a good initial scheme for the structure of your building, move to the third section, Designing Spaces for Mechanical and Electrical Services, which begins on page 137. Decide first whether your building falls into the "large" or "small" category. Follow the references to the pages that correspond to this category, where you will find help in selecting a heating and cooling system. Follow through this section as far as you want to go, learning more about the characteristics of each system that seems appropriate and determining the sizes and configurations of the spaces it requires. Work these spaces for the mechanical and electrical systems into your developing design.

8. Use the information beginning on page 223, Designing with Daylight, to evaluate the suitability of daylight illumination to your project and its potential benefits. If you decide that daylighting is appropriate for your building, this section of the book will help you determine the impact of such systems on your building's form, internal layout, and envelope design.

9. With the help of the fifth section, Designing for Egress, which begins on page 243, modify the circulation scheme of your building to meet code requirements for emergency egress.

10. By this time you should be finding your way through the book with ease, using the index tabs as your primary guideposts and the cross-references as clues to where to look for answers to your next questions.

As you gain experience with this book, developing your own patterns of use and adding notations wherever they are useful to you, it will become a personal handbook uniquely suited to your own way of creating buildings.

DESIGNING WITH BUILDING CODES

1

DESIGNING WITH BUILDING CODES

This section will help you determine which model building code to apply to the project you are designing, and within that code, to which Occupancy Group your project belongs. You will need to know these two facts to have full access to the information throughout this book.

BUILDING CODES AND ZONING ORDINANCES

A designer works under complex legal constraints that exert a powerful influence on the form a building may take. Local zoning ordinances control building uses, heights, areas, distances from property lines, and on-site parking capacities. Building codes enacted at the local, county, state, or provincial level regulate everything from building heights and areas to the types of interior finish materials that may be used. Further constraints are often imposed by local fire districts, by state regulations pertaining to particular uses, and by national regulations governing equal access to public facilities.

Zoning laws and use-specific codes are most often promulgated at the local or state level and do not lend themselves to simple generalization from one jurisdiction to the next. For this reason, this book does not attempt to address these requirements, and the designer should consult local regulations for guidance in these areas. On the other hand, although building codes are also enacted at local levels, the vast majority of North American building codes are derived from a handful of nationally recognized "model codes." The use of model codes as the basis for the majority of local building codes results in sufficient standardization that these regulations can be simplified and generalized in a meaningful way. Thus, preliminary guidelines can be provided for incorporating building code requirements into your project.

This book provides building code information based on two model building codes, the International Code Council's *International Building Code,* and the National Research Council of Canada, Institute for Research in Construction's *National Building Code of Canada.* The International Building Code is the joint creation of three model code organizations in the United States, each of which previously published its own model code. Although at the time of this writing, the International Building Code is still quite new, it has widespread support within the design and construction industry and its adoption by regulatory jurisdictions continues to grow. Currently it represents the best national code standard available in the United States. Likewise, the National Building Code of Canada is the model on which most local Canadian codes are based. This book condenses, from these two model codes, the provisions that have the most direct and important effects on building form: height and area limitations, beginning on page 295, and requirements for the design of egress systems, starting on page 243. Code requirements having to do with the detailed design of structural and mechanical components of buildings are reflected here indirectly through the preliminary sizing charts for structural elements (pages 47–135) and the rules of thumb for providing space for mechanical and electrical systems (pages 137–220).

To make use of the information provided in this book, start by selecting the model code appropriate to your project: for projects in the United States, the International Building Code, and for projects in Canada, The National Building Code of Canada. Next, consult the appropriate code-specific index that follows to ascertain the Occupancy Group (or Groups) of the building you are designing. These two pieces of information—model code and occupancy—are the keys that will unlock code-related information throughout other sections of this book.

Some large cities, states, and counties have written their own building codes, and some jurisdictions continue to base their codes on any of a number of earlier model codes. Some of these codes are sufficiently similar to one of the model codes presented here that once you have determined the similarity, you may use the information in this book as a reasonable approximation during the early stages of design. Others are too dissimilar to permit use of the code guidance given here. Before becoming too deeply immersed in a design, be sure exactly which codes and regulations govern your project and verify that the information you use accurately reflects the requirements for your project, whether that information comes from this book or other sources.

WHICH BUILDING CODE TO CONSULT

If your project is in the United States, use the International Building Code, starting on this page, as the basis for determining preliminary code requirements for your project. See page 5 for more information about model building codes and their applicability to your project.

OCCUPANCY CLASSIFICATION

Buildings, or portions of buildings, are classified by the activities for which they are used, termed *Occupancy Groups.* These group classifications reflect the relative life-safety hazard associated with the activities and occupant characteristics. In general, buildings intended for larger numbers of occupants, for public use, and for inherently hazardous activities are afforded greater levels of protection than those planned for smaller groups, private uses, or nonhazardous activities. Use the following two tables to determine which occupancy groups most appropriately describe your project.

If your building contains multiple uses, determine the occupancy classification for each. Later in this book you will find more detailed information on the how to apply the various code requirements to such mixed-use facilities; if you would like to learn more about mixed-use buildings right now, you may turn to pages 300–301.

GENERAL DESCRIPTION OF OCCUPANCY GROUPS

The following table describes each occupancy group according to the classifications of the International Building Code.

Occupancy	General Description
A ASSEMBLY	Assembly uses include social, recreational, and civic gatherings of 50 or more persons. Assembly includes five subgroups: A-1: This group includes theaters for the viewing of motion pictures, dramatic arts, and performances, usually with fixed seating. A-2: This group includes food and drink establishments. A-3: This group includes recreational, amusement, and worship uses not specifically falling under other Assembly groups, including, for example, galleries, auditoriums, churches, community halls, courtrooms, dance halls, gymnasiums, lecture halls, libraries, museums, passenger station waiting areas, and the like. A-4: This group includes indoor sports arenas with spectator seating. A-5: This group includes outdoor sports arenas.
B BUSINESS	Business uses include office, professional, and service activities, and storage of related records and accounts. Business use also includes education facilities past the 12th grade, but does not include retail or wholesale sales, which are classified as Group M, Mercantile.
E EDUCATIONAL	Educational uses include schools for grades K through 12 and day care for children older than 2½ years of age, with 6 or more occupants. Day care for no more than 100 children 2½ years of age or less may also be classified as an Educational use when each day care room is located on the level of exit discharge and has an exit door opening directly to the exterior. For day care facilities with 5 or fewer occupants, use Group R-3, Residential. For educational uses above the 12th grade, use Group B, Business.

(continued)

OCCUPANCY GROUPS: INTERNATIONAL BUILDING CODE

Occupancy	General Description
F FACTORY	Factory uses include manufacturing and industrial processes, except those considered highly hazardous, which are classified as Group H, Hazardous. Factory use has two subgroups:

F-1: This group includes moderate-hazard manufacturing processes and materials, such as those involving aircraft, appliances, automobiles, machinery, electronics, plastics, printing, and woodworking.

F-2: This group includes low-hazard manufacturing processes and materials, such as those involving nonalcoholic beverages, brick and masonry, ceramics, glass, gypsum, ice, and metal fabrication.

H HAZARDOUS	Hazardous uses include manufacturing, processing, and storage of materials with a high potential for health or physical safety hazard. Hazardous use classifications are specific and detailed about the amounts and types of explosive, flammable, corrosive, or toxic materials involved. If you are considering design of such a facility, you should consult the building code from the very outset of the project to verify requirements.
I INSTITUTIONAL	Institutional uses include facilities where occupants cannot fully care for themselves, including residential care, day care, assisted living, health care, and correctional facilities. Institutional uses are divided into four subgroups:

I-1: This group includes 24-hour residential care facilities for 17 or more occupants, in which occupants are capable of responding to an emergency without physical assistance from facility staff. A facility such as this with 5 or fewer occupants may be classified as Group R-3, Residential, or, with between 6 and 16 occupants, Group R-4.

I-2: This group includes 24-hour medical, psychiatric, and custodial care facilities with 6 or more occupants, in which occupants are not capable of self-preservation in an emergency. A facility such as this with 5 or fewer occupants may be classified as Group R-3, Residential. Group I-2 also includes 24-hour care for 6 or more infants $2\frac{1}{2}$ years of age or less.

I-3: This group includes facilities whose occupants are under restraint or security, including prisons, correctional centers, and the like.

I-4: This group includes custodial care on less than a 24-hour basis for 6 or more occupants of any age. Facilities with 5 or fewer occupants may be classified as Group R-3, Residential. Day care for children older than $2\frac{1}{2}$ may also be categorized as Group E, Educational. In some cases, day care for up to 100 children $2\frac{1}{2}$ years of age or less may also be classified as Group E. See Group E in this table for more information.

M MERCANTILE	Mercantile uses include the display and sale of retail and wholesale merchandise and the related stocking of such goods.
R RESIDENTIAL	Residential uses include facilities where people live and sleep when not in a supervised setting that would be classified as an Institutional use. Residential uses are subdivided into four subgroups:

R-1: This group includes all residential facilities where the occupants are primarily transient, including hotels, motels, and the like.

R-2: This group includes primarily permanent residential occupancies that contain three or more dwelling units, such as apartment houses, dormitories, fraternities, sororities, and the like.

R-3: This group includes one- and two-family residential occupancies. It also includes adult or child care facilities for 5 or fewer persons.

R-4: This group includes residential care or assisted living facilities for between 6 and 16 occupants.

S STORAGE	This group includes storage not classified as H, Hazardous, and is divided into two subgroups:

S-1: This group includes storage of moderate-hazard items such as books and paper, furniture, grain, lumber, tires, and other materials, as well as motor vehicle repair facilities.

S-2: This group includes parking garages and the storage of goods considered low hazard and nonflammable.

U UTILITY	Utility uses include agricultural buildings and other miscellaneous uses such as aircraft hangers, barns, carports, private garages, greenhouses, livestock shelters, retaining walls, sheds, stables, tanks, towers, and the like.

OCCUPANCY GROUPS: INTERNATIONAL BUILDING CODE

INDEX OF OCCUPANCIES

You may use the following index of uses to determine the Occupancy Group classification for your project. If the specific use for your project is not listed, choose the most similar use based on comparisons of number and density of occupants, nature of the activity, and any associated fire- or life-safety risks.

WHERE DO I GO FROM HERE?

Once you have determined the building code Occupancy Group classifications for your project, you can use this information throughout the other sections of this book. If you are unsure of where to go next, see page xi, How to Use This Book, for suggestions on how proceed.

Building Use	Occupancy
Agricultural buildings, barns, livestock shelters	U
Aircraft hangers	S-1
Aircraft hangers, accessory to one- or two-family residences	U
Airport traffic control towers	B
Alcohol and drug centers, 24-hour, 17 or more persons	I-1
Amusement arcades	A-3
Amusement park structures	A-5
Animal hospitals, kennels, pounds	B
Apartment houses	R-2
Art galleries	A-3
Assisted living, 17 or more persons	I-1
Assisted living, 5 or fewer persons	R-3
Assisted living, between 6 and 16 persons	R-4
Auditoriums	A-3
Banks	B
Banquet halls	A-2
Barber and beauty shops	B
Barns	U
Bleachers, outdoors	A-5
Boarding houses, not transient	R-2
Boarding houses, transient	R-1
Bowling alleys	A-3
Car washes	B
Carports	U
Child care, 5 or fewer children, any age	R-3
Child care, places of worship during religious functions	Included with primary use, usually B

Building Use	Occupancy
Child care, 6 or more children 2½ years of age or less, less than 24-hour	I-4, or E with certain occupant number and egress restrictions
Childcare, 6 or more children 2½ years of age or less, 24-hour	I-2
Childcare, 6 or more children older than 2½ years of age	E or I-4
Churches	A-3
Civic administration	B
Clinic, outpatient	B
Community halls	A-3
Congregate care facilities, 24-hour, 17 or more persons	I-1
Convalescent facilities, 24-hour, 17 or more persons	I-1
Convents	R-2
Correctional centers	I-3
Courtrooms	A-3
Dance halls	A-3
Day care, 5 or fewer adults of any age, less than 24-hour (for children, see Child care)	R-3
Day care, 6 or more adults of any age, less 24-hour (for children, see Child care)	I-4
Department stores	M
Detention centers	I-3
Detoxification facilities, 24-hour	I-2
Drug stores	M
Dry cleaning and laundries	B
Educational occupancies above the 12th grade	B
Educational occupancies K through 12	E

OCCUPANCY GROUPS: INTERNATIONAL BUILDING CODE

Building Use	Occupancy	Building Use	Occupancy
Electronic data processing	B	Post offices	B
Exhibition halls	A-3	Prisons	I-3
Factories depending on hazard	F-1 or F-2,	Professional services	B
Fences, more than 6 ft (2 m) high	U	Radio and television stations, without audience facilities	B
Fire and police stations	B	Radio and television studios, admitting an audience	A-1
Fraternities, sororities	R-2	Reformatories	I-3
Funeral parlors	A-3	Rehabilitation facilities, 17 or more persons, 24-hour	I-1
Grandstands, outdoors	A-5		
Greenhouses	U	Residences, single- or two-family	R-3
Group homes, 17 or more persons	I-1	Residential care, 17 or more persons, 24-hour	I-1
Gymnasiums	A-3		
Halfway houses, 17 or more persons	I-1	Residential care, between 6 and 16 persons, 24-hour	R-4
Hazardous materials processing and storage	H-1 through H-5; consult the code for more information	Residential care, 5 or fewer persons, 24-hour	R-3
Hospitals	I-2	Restaurants	A-2
Hotels	R-1	Retail or wholesale stores	M
Jails	I-3	Retaining walls	U
Laboratories, testing and research	B	Sales rooms	M
Lecture halls	A-3	Sheds	U
Libraries	A-3	Skating rinks with spectator seating, indoor	A-4
Markets	M		
Medical care, 24-hour, with 5 or fewer persons	R-3	Sports arenas, indoor	A-4
		Stadiums, outdoors	A-5
Medical care, 24-hour, with 6 or more persons	I-2	Storage	S-1 or S-2, depending on hazard
Monasteries	R-2	Swimming pools, indoor, with spectator seating	A-4
Motels	R-1		
Motion picture theaters	A-1	Swimming pools, indoor, without spectator seating	A-3
Motor vehicle repair	S-1		
Motor vehicle service stations	M	Tanks	U
Motor vehicle showrooms	B	Taverns and bars	A-2
Museums	A-3	Telephone exchanges	B
Night clubs	A-2	Tennis courts, indoors, with spectator seating	A-4
Nursing homes	I-2		
Parking garages, open or closed	S-2	Tennis courts, indoors, without spectator seating	A-3
Passenger station waiting areas	A-3	Theaters	A-1
Pool and billiard halls	A-3	Towers	U

WHICH BUILDING CODE TO CONSULT

If your project is in Canada, use the National Building Code of Canada, starting on this page, as the basis for determining preliminary code requirements for your project. See page 5 for more information about model building codes and their applicability to your project.

OCCUPANCY CLASSIFICATION

Buildings, or portions of buildings, are classified by the activities for which they are used, termed Use or Occupancy Groups. These group classifications reflect the relative life-safety hazard associated with the activities and occupant characteristics. In general, buildings intended for larger numbers of occupants, for public use, and for inherently hazardous activities are afforded greater levels of protection than those planned for smaller groups, private uses, or nonhazardous activities. Use the following two tables to determine what Occupancy Group classifications most appropriately describe your project.

If your building contains multiple uses, determine the occupancy classification for each. Later in this book you will find more detailed information on the how to apply the various code requirements to such mixed-use facilities; if you would like to learn more about mixed-use buildings right now, you can turn to pages 300–301.

GENERAL DESCRIPTION OF OCCUPANCIES

The following table describes each Occupancy Group according to the classifications of the National Building Code of Canada.

DESIGNING WITH BUILDING CODES

11

Occupancy	General Description
A ASSEMBLY	Assembly uses include social, recreational and civic gatherings. Assembly includes four subdivisions:
	A-1: This division includes facilities for the production and viewing of the performing arts.
	A-2: This division includes recreational, amusement, and worship uses not specifically falling under other Assembly groups, including, for example, auditoriums, churches, community halls, courtrooms, dance halls, gymnasiums, lecture halls, libraries, museums, passenger stations and depots, nonresidential schools and colleges, and the like.
	A-3: This division includes arena-type facilities.
	A-4: This division includes outdoor gatherings.
B CARE OR DETENTION	Care or Detention uses include facilities where occupants cannot fully care for themselves, including residential care, assisted living, health care, and correctional facilities. Care or Detention includes two subdivisions:
	B-1: This division includes facilities where occupants are under restraint or are rendered incapable of self-preservation by facility security systems.
	B-2: This division includes facilities where occupants have cognitive or physical limitations requiring special care.
C RESIDENTIAL	Residential uses include all kinds of residential occupancies not classified as Care or Detention, such as apartments, boarding houses, residential colleges and schools, hotels, single-family houses, and the like.
D BUSINESS AND PERSONAL SERVICES	Business and Personal Services uses include office, professional, and service activities, but does not include retail or wholesale sales, which are classified as E Mercantile.
E MERCANTILE	Mercantile uses include the display and sale of retail and wholesale merchandise and the related stocking of such goods.
F INDUSTRIAL	Industrial uses include manufacturing and industrial processes. Industrial includes three subdivisions:
	F-1: This group includes high-hazard manufacturing processes.
	F-2: This group includes medium-hazard manufacturing processes and materials.
	F-3: This division includes low-hazard manufacturing processes and materials.

INDEX OF OCCUPANCIES

You may also use the following index of uses to determine the Occupancy Group classification for your project. If the specific use for your project is not listed, choose the most similar use based on comparisons of number and density of occupants, nature of the activity, and any associated fire- or life-safety risks.

WHERE DO I GO FROM HERE?

Once you have determined the building code Occupancy Group classifications for your project, you can use this information throughout the other sections of this book. If you are unsure of where to go next, see page xi, How to Use This Book, for suggestions on how proceed.

Building Use	Occupancy
Aircraft hangars	F-2
Amusement park structures	A-4
Apartments	C
Arenas	A-3
Art galleries	A-2
Auditoriums	A-2
Banks	D
Barber and hairdressing shops	D
Beauty parlors	D
Beverage establishments	A-2
Bleachers, outdoors	A-4
Boarding houses	C
Bowling alleys	A-2
Children's custodial homes	B-2, except as noted below
Children's custodial homes, not more than 10 ambulatory persons living in a dwelling unit as a single housekeeping unit	C
Churches, places of worship	A-2
Clubs, nonresidential	A-2
Clubs, residential	C
Cold-storage plants	F-2
Colleges, nonresidential	A-2
Colleges, residential	C
Community halls	A-2
Convalescent homes	B-2, except as noted below
Convalescent homes, not more than 10 ambulatory persons living in a dwelling unit as a single housekeeping unit	C
Convents, residential	C
Courtrooms	A-2

Building Use	Occupancy
Creameries	F-3
Dance halls	A-2
Dental offices	D
Department stores	E
Distilleries	F-1
Dormitories	C
Dry cleaning establishments, self-service	D
Dry cleaning plants	F-1
Electrical substations	F-2
Exhibition halls, mercantile	E
Exhibition halls, other than mercantile	A-2
Factories	F-1, F-2, or F-3, depending on hazard
Farm buildings	Must conform to the National Farm Building Code, not covered in this publication
Freight depots	F-2
Garages, including open-air parking	F-3
Grain elevators	F-1
Grandstands, outdoors	A-4
Gymnasiums	A-2
Helicopter rooftop landing areas	F-2
Hospitals	B-2
Hotels	C
Houses	C
Infirmaries	B-2
Jails	B-1
Laboratories	F-2 or F-3, depending on hazard
Laundries, self-service	D

OCCUPANCY GROUPS: NATIONAL BUILDING CODE OF CANADA

Building Use	Occupancy
Lecture halls	A-2
Libraries	A-2
Lodging houses	C
Manufacturing or processing plants for chemicals, paint, varnish, lacquer, rubber, waste paper	F-1
Markets	E
Medical offices	D
Mills for cereal, feed, grain	F-1
Monasteries	C
Motels	C
Motion picture theaters	A-1
Museums	A-2
Nursing homes	B-2
Offices	D
Opera houses	A-1
Orphanages	B-2
Passenger stations and depots	A-2
Penitentiaries	B-1
Police stations, with detention quarters	B-1
Police stations, with detention quarters, not more than 1 story in height or 600 m² (6460 ft²) in area	B-2
Police stations, without detention quarters	D
Power plants	F-3
Prisons	B-1
Psychiatric hospitals, with detention quarters	B-1
Psychiatric hospitals, without detention quarters	B-2
Radio stations	D
Recreational piers	A-2

Building Use	Occupancy
Reformatories, with detention quarters	B-1
Reformatories, without detention quarters	B-2
Restaurants	A-2
Reviewing stands, outdoors	A-4
Rinks, indoors	A-3
Sanatoriums, without detention quarters	B-2
Schools and colleges, nonresidential	A-2
Schools and colleges, residential	C
Service stations	F-2
Shops	E
Spray painting operations	F-1
Stadiums	A-4
Storage	F-1, F-2, or F-3, depending on hazard
Stores	E
Supermarkets	E
Swimming pools, indoors, with or without spectator seating	A-3
Television studios, admitting a viewing audience	A-1
Television studios, not admitting a viewing audience	F-2
Theaters, including experimental theaters	A-1
Tool and appliance rental and service establishments, small	D
Undertaking premises	A-2
Warehouses	F-1, F-2, or F-3, depending on hazard
Woodworking factories	F-2
Workshops	F-2 or F-3, depending on hazard

DESIGNING THE STRUCTURE

■■ SELECTING THE STRUCTURAL SYSTEM

This section will help you select a structural system for the preliminary design of a building.

BUILDING CODE CRITERIA FOR THE SELECTION OF STRUCTURAL SYSTEMS

When choosing a structural system for a building, you must first determine the range of structural systems that the relevant building code allows. Each of the model building codes requires you to do this by determining first the Occupancy Group into which a building falls, then consulting tables, formulas, and numerous detailed provisions of the code that prescribe the maximum height and floor area to which a building of a given Occupancy Group may be built using each of a range of code-defined Construction Types. To streamline this laborious process for purposes of preliminary design, simplified tables of height and area limitations for each of the model building codes included in this book are compiled on pages 317–401. You should consult the indexes on pages 7–13 first to determine which code governs in the area where your building will be built and the Occupancy Group into which that code places your building. The Construction Type or Types into which each structural system falls are identified on pages 304–315.

DESIGN CRITERIA FOR THE SELECTION
OF STRUCTURAL SYSTEMS

If you wish to create a building with a highly irregular form:	Choose systems with simple floor and roof framing that are fabricated mostly on-site, such as Sitecast concrete using any slab system without beams or ribs (pages 107–123) Light gauge steel framing (pages 88–91) Platform frame (pages 49–65) Masonry construction with either concrete slab or wood light floor framing (pages 71–85)
If you wish to leave the structure exposed while retaining a high fire-resistance rating:	Choose structural systems that are inherently resistant to fire and heat, including All concrete systems (although ribbed systems may require added thickness in the ribs or slab, or an applied fireproofing) (pages 107–135) Heavy timber frame (pages 49–69) Mill construction (pages 71–85) Structural steel is highly susceptible to loss of strength in a fire and usually must be protected with a fire-resistive finishing system. For further information on the fire resistance of various structural systems and uses for which they are permitted, see pages 304–315.
If you wish to allow column placements that deviate from a regular grid:	Use systems that do not include beams or joists in the floor and roof structure, such as Sitecast concrete two-way flat plate or flat slab (pages 118–121) Metal space frame
If you wish to minimize floor thickness to reduce total building height or to reduce floor spandrel depth on the building facade:	The thinnest floor systems are concrete slabs without ribs, preferably prestressed, such as Sitecast concrete two-way flat plate or flat slab, especially when posttensioned (pages 118–121) Precast prestressed hollow core or solid slab (pages 132–133) Posttensioned one-way solid slab (pages 114–115)
If you wish to minimize the area occupied by columns or bearing walls:	Consider long-span structural systems, such as Heavy wood trusses (pages 66–67) Glue laminated wood beams (pages 62–63) Glue laminated wood arches (pages 68–69) Conventional steel frame (pages 87–105) Open-web steel joists (pages 100–101) Single-story rigid steel frame (pages 102–103) Steel trusses (pages 104–105) Sitecast concrete waffle slab, particularly when posttensioned (pages 122–123) Precast concrete single or double tees (pages 134–135) You may also wish to consider other long-span systems, such as specially fabricated steel beams, suspended systems, arches, vaults, and shells.

20

DESIGN CRITERIA FOR THE SELECTION
OF STRUCTURAL SYSTEMS

If you wish to allow for changes to the building over time:

Consider short-span one-way systems that permit easy structural modification, such as

Light gauge or conventional steel frame (pages 87–105)
Any wood system, including those incorporating masonry construction (pages 49–79)
Sitecast concrete one-way solid slab or one-way joist construction, excluding posttensioned (pages 114–117)
Precast concrete solid or hollow core slab (pages 132–133)

If you wish to permit construction under adverse weather conditions:

Select a system that does not depend on on-site chemical processes (such as the curing of concrete or mortar) and that can be erected quickly, such as

Any steel system (pages 87–105)
Any wood system (pages 49–69)
Precast concrete systems, particularly those that minimize the use of sitecast concrete toppings and grouting (pages 125–135)

If you wish to minimize off-site fabrication time:

Consider systems in which the building is constructed on-site from easily formed, relatively unprocessed materials, such as

Any sitecast concrete system (pages 107–123)
Light gauge steel framing (pages 88–91)
Platform frame (pages 49–65)
Any masonry system (pages 72–79)

If you wish to minimize on-site erection time:

Consider systems using highly preprocessed, prefabricated, or modular components, such as

Single-story rigid steel frame (pages 102–103)
Conventional steel frame, particularly with hinge connections (pages 87–105)
Any precast concrete system (pages 125–135)
Heavy timber frame (pages 49–69)

If you wish to minimize construction time for a one- or two-story building:

Consider systems that are lightweight and easy to form, or prefabricated and easy to assemble, such as

Any steel system (pages 87–105)
Heavy timber frame (pages 49–69)
Platform frame (pages 49–65)

(continued)

DESIGN CRITERIA FOR THE SELECTION
OF STRUCTURAL SYSTEMS

If you wish to minimize construction time for a 4- to 20-story building:

Choose from the following systems

    Precast concrete (pages 125–135)
    Conventional steel frame (pages 87–105)

Once the structural components for either of the above systems are prefabricated, on-site erection proceeds quickly.

    Any sitecast concrete system (pages 107–123)

The absence of lead time for the prefabrication of components in these systems allows construction of the building to begin on-site at the earliest time.

If you wish to minimize construction time for a building 30 stories or more in height:

Choose a system that is strong, lightweight, prefabricated, and easy to assemble

    Steel frame (pages 87–105)

Systems of precast and sitecast concrete are also becoming economical alternatives to steel frame construction in some regions.
The structural design of high-rise buildings is a specialized task, and the necessary consultants should be sought out as early as possible in the design process.

If you wish to minimize the need for diagonal bracing or shear walls:

Choose a system that is capable of forming rigid joints, such as

    Any sitecast concrete system, particularly those with beams or deepened slabs around the columns (pages 107–123)
    Steel frame with welded rigid connections (pages 87–105)
    Single-story rigid steel frame (pages 102–103)

When depending on a rigid frame for lateral stiffness, the sizes of the framing members often must be increased to resist the added bending stresses produced in such systems.

If you wish to minimize the dead load on the building foundation:

Consider lightweight or short span systems, such as

    Any steel system (pages 87–105)
    Any wood system (pages 49–69)

If you wish to minimize structural distress due to unstable foundation conditions:

Frame systems without rigid joints are recommended, such as

    Steel frame, with bolted connections (pages 87–105)
    Heavy timber frame (pages 60–63)
    Precast concrete systems (pages 125–135)
    Platform framing (pages 49–65)

Welded steel frame, masonry bearing wall, and sitecast concrete frame are particularly to be avoided.

DESIGN CRITERIA FOR THE SELECTION
OF STRUCTURAL SYSTEMS

If you wish to minimize the number of separate trades and contracts required to complete the building:

Consider systems that incorporate many of the functions of a complete wall system in one operation, such as

Masonry construction, including Mill or Ordinary construction (pages 72–85)

Precast concrete loadbearing wall panel systems (pages 128–129)

If you wish to provide concealed spaces within the structure itself for ducts, pipes, wires, and other building mechanical systems:

Consider systems that naturally provide convenient hollow spaces, such as

Truss and open-web joist systems (pages 64–67, 100–101, 104–105)

Light gauge steel framing (pages 88–91)

Platform frame (pages 49–65)

Light gauge steel framing and platform frame construction are often applied as finish or infill systems in combination with other types of building structure to provide such spaces. For more information on the integration of building services and the structural system, see pages 170–189 and 202–221.

DESIGN CRITERIA: SUMMARY CHART

	WOOD AND MASONRY				STEEL			
	Pages 49–65	Pages 49–69	Pages 71–85	Pages 71–85	Pages 88–91	Pages 102–103	Pages 87–105	Pages 87–105
GIVE SPECIAL CONSIDERATION TO THE SYSTEMS INDICATED IF YOU WISH TO:	Platform Frame	Timber Frame	Ordinary Construction	Mill Constrction	Light Gauge Steel Framing	Single-Story Rigid Steel Frame	Steel Frame—Hinged Connections	Steel Frame—Rigid Connections
Create a highly irregular building form	●		●		●			
Expose the structure while retaining a high fire-resistance rating		●		●				
Allow column placements that deviate from a regular grid								
Minimize floor thickness								
Minimize the area occupied by columns or bearing walls						●	●	●
Allow for changes in the building over time	●	●	●	●	●		●	●
Permit construction under adverse weather conditions	●	●			●	●	●	●
Minimize off-site fabrication time	●		●	●	●			
Minimize on-site erection time		●				●	●	●
Minimize construction time for a one- or two-story building	●	●			●	●	●	●
Minimize construction time for a 4- to 20-story building							●	●
Minimize construction time for a building 30 stories or more in height							●	
Avoid the need for diagonal bracing or shear walls						●		●
Minimize the dead load on a foundation	●	●			●	●	●	●
Minimize structural distress due to unstable foundation conditions	●	●					●	
Minimize the number of separate trades needed to complete a building			●	●				
Provide concealed spaces for ducts, pipes, etc.	●		●		●			

DESIGN CRITERIA: SUMMARY CHART

	SITECAST CONCRETE										PRECAST CONCRETE			
	One-Way Solid Slab (Pages 114–115)	Posttensioned One-Way Solid Slab (Pages 114–115)	One-Way Joist (Pages 116–117)	Posttensioned One-Way Joist (Pages 116–117)	Two-Way Flat Plate (Pages 118–119)	Posttensioned Two-Way Flat Plate (Pages 118–119)	Two-Way Flat Slab (Pages 120–121)	Posttensioned Two-Way Flat Slab (Pages 120–121)	Waffle Slab (Pages 122–123)	Posttensioned Waffle Slab (Pages 122–123)	Solid Slab (Pages 132–133)	Hollow Core Slab (Pages 132–133)	Double Tee (Pages 134–135)	Single Tee (Pages 134–135)
	●	●			●	●	●	●						
	●	●	●	●	●	●	●	●	●	●	●	●	●	●
			●		●	●	●	●						
		●			●		●				●	●		
									●	●			●	●
	●		●								●	●		
											●	●	●	●
	●	●	●	●	●	●	●	●	●	●				
											●	●	●	●
	●	●	●	●	●	●	●	●	●	●	●	●	●	●
	●	●	●	●	●	●	●	●	●	●				
											●	●	●	●

PRACTICAL SPAN RANGES FOR STRUCTURAL SYSTEMS

This chart gives practical ranges for various structural systems. Greater or lesser spans may be possible in some circumstances. Page references are included where a system is covered in greater detail elsewhere in this book.

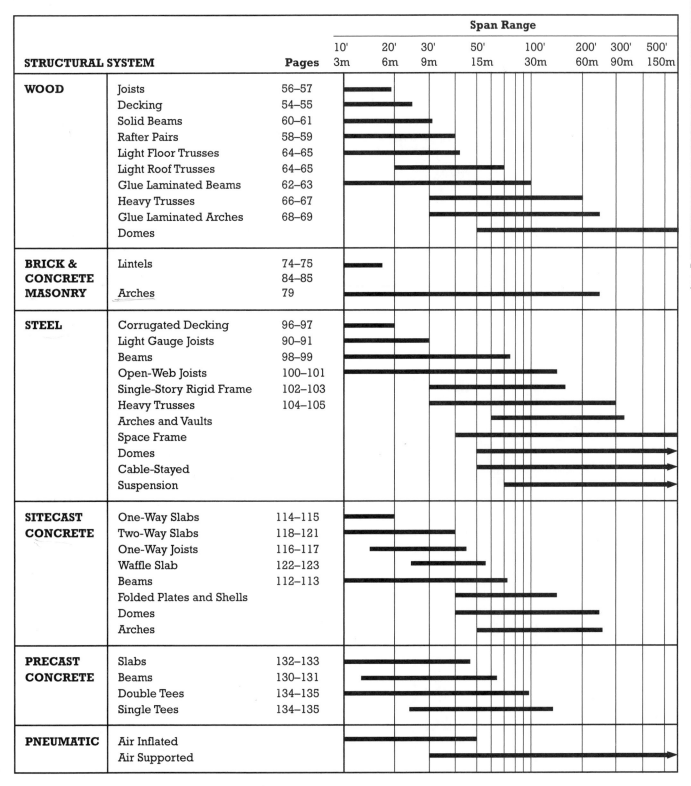

STRUCTURAL SYSTEM		Pages	Span Range
WOOD	Joists	56–57	
	Decking	54–55	
	Solid Beams	60–61	
	Rafter Pairs	58–59	
	Light Floor Trusses	64–65	
	Light Roof Trusses	64–65	
	Glue Laminated Beams	62–63	
	Heavy Trusses	66–67	
	Glue Laminated Arches	68–69	
	Domes		
BRICK & CONCRETE MASONRY	Lintels	74–75 84–85	
	Arches	79	
STEEL	Corrugated Decking	96–97	
	Light Gauge Joists	90–91	
	Beams	98–99	
	Open-Web Joists	100–101	
	Single-Story Rigid Frame	102–103	
	Heavy Trusses	104–105	
	Arches and Vaults		
	Space Frame		
	Domes		
	Cable-Stayed		
	Suspension		
SITECAST CONCRETE	One-Way Slabs	114–115	
	Two-Way Slabs	118–121	
	One-Way Joists	116–117	
	Waffle Slab	122–123	
	Beams	112–113	
	Folded Plates and Shells		
	Domes		
	Arches		
PRECAST CONCRETE	Slabs	132–133	
	Beams	130–131	
	Double Tees	134–135	
	Single Tees	134–135	
PNEUMATIC	Air Inflated		
	Air Supported		

Span Range scale: 10' (3m), 20' (6m), 30' (9m), 50' (15m), 100' (30m), 200' (60m), 300' (90m), 500' (150m)

LIVE LOAD RANGES FOR BUILDING OCCUPANCIES

OCCUPANCY	Light Loads 20 psf / 1.0 kPa	60 psf / 2.9 kPa	Medium Loads 100 psf / 4.8 kPa	Heavy Loads 150 psf / 7.2 kPa	Very Heavy Loads 250 psf / 12.0 kPa
Assembly Areas			Fixed seats — Movable seats; Stage areas		
Building Corridors		Private	Public		
Garages		Passenger cars		Trucks and buses	
Hospitals		Private rooms	Operating rooms; Laboratories		
Hotels and Multifamily Housing		Private rooms	Public rooms		
Libraries			Reading rooms	Stacks	
Manufacturing				Light	Heavy
Office Buildings		Offices	Lobbies		
One- and Two-Family Dwellings	Attics — Bedrooms	Living spaces			
Outdoor Areas				Pedestrian	Vehicular
Roof Loads	No snow	Moderate snow	High mountains; Pedestrian		
Storage Areas				Light	Heavy
Schools		Classrooms	Assembly	Shops	
Stores			Retail	Wholesale	
Miscellaneous Public Facilities	Penal institutions; Cell blocks	Bowling alleys; Poolrooms	Gymnasium; Dance halls; Dining rooms; Restaurants; Stadiums; Skating rinks	Armories; Drill rooms	

LIVE LOAD RANGES FOR STRUCTURAL SYSTEMS

LIVE LOAD RANGES FOR STRUCTURAL SYSTEMS

STRUCTURAL SYSTEM		Pages	Light Loads	Medium Loads	Heavy Loads	Very Heavy Loads
WOOD	Platform Frame	49–65	■	■		
	Timber Frame	49–69	■	■	■	■
MASONRY	Ordinary Construction	71–85	■	■		
	Mill Construction	71–85		■	■	■
STEEL	Light Gauge Steel Framing	88–91	■	■		
	Single-Story Rigid Steel Frame	102–103	■	■	■ (Roof loads only)	
	Conventional Steel Frame	87–105		■	■	■
SITECAST CONCRETE	One-Way Solid Slab	114–115	■	■	■	
	One-Way Beam and Slab	114–115			■	■
	One-Way Joists	116–117		■	■	■
	Two-Way Flat Plate	118–119	■	■	■	
	Two-Way Flat Slab	120–121		■	■	■
	Waffle Slab	122–123		■	■	■
	Two-Way Beam and Slab	118–119			■	■
PRECAST CONCRETE	Solid Slab	132–133	■	■	■	
	Hollow Core Slab	132–133	■	■	■	
	Double Tee	134–135		■	■	■
	Single Tee	134–135		■	■	■

Use the charts on these two pages to identify appropriate structural systems based on the activities planned within the building. Read the chart on the facing page first to determine the approximate live load range associated with the expected building use. Once a load range has been determined, consult the chart on this page to select systems that are recommended within that range. Roof loads are also covered to aid in the selection of roof structural systems.

If a building will have multiple uses, read from the chart for the higher load range. Or, if the different uses will be physically separate within the building, the load ranges for each use may be applied to the appropriate areas.

CONFIGURING THE STRUCTURAL SYSTEM

This section will aid you in making a preliminary layout of the structural system of a building.

LATERAL STABILITY AND STRUCTURAL SYSTEMS

STABILIZING ELEMENTS

All buildings must be designed to resist lateral forces such as wind and earthquake. Three basic structural configurations may be used, either singly or in combination: the shear wall, the braced frame, and the rigid frame. The choice of lateral force resisting system and location of its elements will have a fundamental influence on the form of the building and the arrangement of its interior space.

Shear Walls

In tall buildings, shear walls are most commonly constructed of reinforced concrete, 12 to 18 in. (300 to 500 mm) or more in thickness. They may also be constructed of masonry, wood, or in very tall buildings, even steel. In comparison to other systems, shear walls are extremely stiff, making them a good choice wherever a relatively compact arrangement of stabilizing elements is desired. They are also relatively heavy, and must be mostly solid, with only limited openings through the wall. To minimize interference with floor plans, shear walls are often incorporated into the building core, stair tower enclosures, or other vertical structures. Shear walls can also be part of the exterior wall, though at some loss of access to daylight and exterior views.

Braced Frames

Braced frames are composed of open, triangulated frameworks, most often constructed of steel or wood. In terms of strength per weight, they are the most efficient lateral force stabilizing system. Like shear walls, braced frames are often incorporated into the building core or other vertical structures. They can also be part of exterior wall systems, where in comparison to shear walls, their greater degree of openness results in less of an impact on daylight access and views.

Rigid Frames

Rigid frames depend on extra stiff connections in the structural framework to resist the effects of lateral forces. The rigid joints required in this system are most easily constructed in steel, though at added cost in comparison to other systems, or in sitecast concrete where they are formed as a natural part of concrete's internal reinforcing. Rigid joints may also occasionally be constructed in precast concrete, though with greater difficulty. The absence of solid panels or diagonal bracing makes this system attractive where the greatest flexibility in plan configuration is desired. However, rigid frame is the most structurally inefficient of the lateral force resisting systems. It is most suitable for low or broad structures requiring relatively modest resistance. Or, in taller buildings, it may be used in combination with another system. In addition, rigid frame also places greater stresses on the structural framework, and as a result, columns and beams may be heavier, and column spacing may be less than in a structure relying on some other lateral force resisting system.

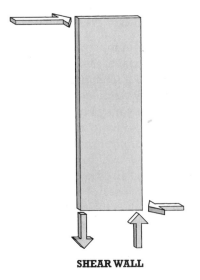

SHEAR WALL

BRACED FRAME

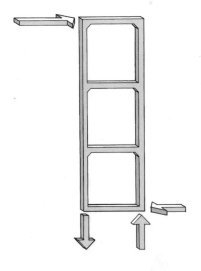

RIGID FRAME

CONFIGURING STABILIZING ELEMENTS

The arrangement of shear walls, diagonal braces, or rigid joints in a structure is crucial to their effectiveness in resisting lateral forces acting on the building. As illustrated in the adjacent schematic floor plans, these elements may be placed within the interior of the building or at the perimeter, and they may be combined in a variety of ways. However, they must be arranged so as to resist lateral forces acting from all directions. This is usually accomplished by aligning one set of stabilizing elements along each of the two perpendicular plan axes of a building. Stabilizing elements must also be arranged in as balanced a fashion as possible in relation to the mass of the building. Unbalanced arrangements of these elements result in the displacement of the center of resistance of the building away from its center of mass. Such a condition causes unusual building movements under lateral loads that may be difficult to control.

In general, lateral force resisting elements are heaviest and most extensive at the base of a building where the accumulated forces are greatest, and diminish in weight and extent as they approach the top of the building. In addition, considerations of lateral stability become increasingly important as the height of the building increases. The configuration of stabilizing elements is discussed in more detail on the following pages.

Stabilizing elements may be placed within the interior or at the perimeter of a building.

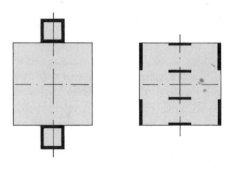

Stabilizing elements should be arranged in a balanced fashion.

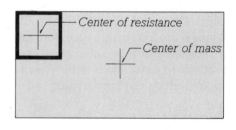

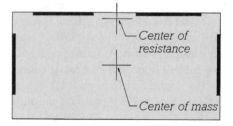

Unbalanced arrangements of stabilizing elements result in the displacement of the center of resistance of the building away from its center of mass. Such arrangements shoul be avoided.

LATERAL STABILITY AND STRUCTURAL SYSTEMS

This chart indicates the methods of resisting lateral forces most appropriate to each structural system. More detailed information on the individual systems can be found on the pages noted in the chart.

STRUCTURAL SYSTEM		Pages	Rigid Frame	Semi-Rigid Joints w/Supplemental Braced Frame or Shear Wall	Braced Frame	Shear Wall
WOOD	Platform Frame	49–65			● Let-in bracing	● Panel sheathing
	Timber Frame	49–69			● Timber bracing	● Diagonal or panel sheathing
MASONRY	Ordinary Construction	71–85				● Masonry walls
	Mill Construction	71–85				● Masonry walls
STEEL	Light Gauge Steel Framing	88–91			● Strap bracing	● Panel sheathing
	Single-Story Rigid Steel Frame	102–103	● Parallel to frames only		● Perpendicular to frames	
	Conventional Steel Frame	87–105	● Requires welded connections	●	●	● Sitecast concrete
SITECAST CONCRETE	One-Way Solid Slab	114–115	○ May require added structure	●		
	One-Way Beam and Slab	114–115	●	●		
	One-Way Joist	116–117	●	●		
	Two-Way Flat Plate	118–119	○ May require added structure	●		
	Two-Way Flat Slab	120–121	○ May require added structure	●		
	Waffle Slab	122–123	●	●		
	Two-Way Beam and Slab	118–119	●	●		
PRECAST CONCRETE	Solid Slab	132–133	○		○ Uncommon	●
	Hollow Core Slab	132–133	○		○ Uncommon	●
	Double Tee	134–135	○		○ Uncommon	●
	Single Tee	134–135	○		○ Uncommon	●

● Recommended
○ Possible in some circumstances

WALL AND SLAB SYSTEMS

VERTICAL LOAD RESISTING ELEMENTS

Wall and slab systems are composed of loadbearing walls spanned by horizontal slabs. The placement of walls in this system is restricted by their role as structural elements, as they must be located to support the loads from slabs and walls above. Due to the significant presence of the walls in the plan of the building, the use of a wall and slab system generally implies a close correspondence between the structural module and the planning of building functions. Furthermore, economic considerations usually dictate that the arrangement of walls be as uniform as possible, making this system particularly attractive for building types that require regular arrangements of uniformly sized spaces, such as apartments, schools, and hotels.

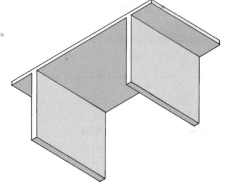

WALL AND SLAB SYSTEMS
(shown from below)

LATERAL LOAD RESISTING ELEMENTS

The regularly placed structural walls used in this system are well suited to act as shear walls for lateral stability. They may be used alone or combined with rigid frames or braced frames, for instance, where structural walls run in only one direction in a building.

    When used alone, shear walls must be arranged to resist lateral forces in all directions, such as in some variation of a complete or partial box form. Shear walls should always be placed as symmetrically as possible in the building plan, particularly in taller buildings. The sizes and spacing of openings in shear walls may need to be restricted as well.

Shear walls may be arranged in a box form to resist lateral forces from all directions.

SYSTEMS WELL SUITED TO WALL AND SLAB FRAMING

Bearing walls of any type may be used to create wall and slab structural systems. See the following sections for more information:

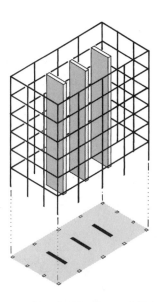

When combined with other stabilizing mechanisms, shear walls may be arranged so as to resist forces in only one direction of a building.

WALL AND SLAB SYSTEMS

WALL AND SLAB SYSTEM LAYOUTS

The distance between walls is equal to the span of the slab. Walls can be any length but are required wherever slabs are supported. Where necessary, openings in walls can be made by including beams over such openings to carry loads from above. In multistory buildings the locations of bearing walls should coincide from floor to floor. However, where it is desirable to omit bearing walls from a lower floor, it may be possible to design the wall above as a deep beam supported at its ends only.

Wall and slab systems can be combined with column systems to permit greater open areas in a plan. Wherever possible, keep walls in locations that are most desirable for lateral load resistance.

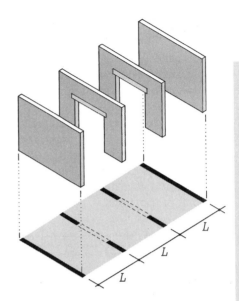

In wall and slab systems, the distance between walls is equal to the span of the slab. Openings in walls may be made when beams are added to carry loads from above.

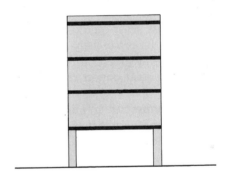

Bearing walls may act as deep beams to span across openings below, as shown in this schematic cross section.

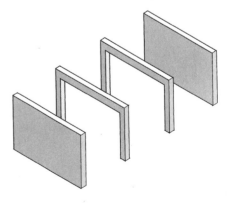

Bearing wall and column systems may be combined for more flexibility in plan layouts.

COLUMN AND BEAM SYSTEMS

VERTICAL LOAD RESISTING ELEMENTS

Column and beam systems are composed of vertical columns, horizontally spanning girders and beams, and a slab spanning between the beams. The columns in this system have less impact than loadbearing walls on the planning of spaces within a building. Where the sizes of interior spaces of a building do not correspond with a structural module or are irregular in shape or size, where maximum open space is desired, or where a high degree of flexibility in the use of space over time is desired, column and beam systems are a good choice. Compared to column and slab systems, column and beam systems are also practical over a greater range of spans and bay proportions.

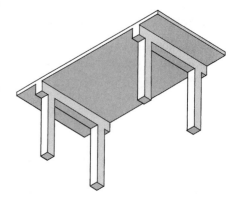

COLUMN AND BEAM SYSTEMS
(shown from below)

LATERAL LOAD RESISTING ELEMENTS

Column and beam systems of steel frame or sitecast concrete construction are well suited to rigid frame action. When used in this way, rigid joints are required at some or all column to beam connections. In sitecast concrete, rigid joints are produced as a normal feature of the system. In steel, rigid connections must be welded and are generally more expensive to construct. Rigid joints are difficult to construct and are rarely used in precast concrete. Because no added braces or walls are required, rigid frame systems are often preferred for their minimal interference with the plan of a building. However, the use of rigid frames generally restricts column placements to regular, orthogonal layouts, and often requires deeper beams and more closely spaced and larger columns than would otherwise be required with either braced frame or shear walls. Rigid frames are normally not well suited for structures with unusually long spans or tall columns.

When braced frames or shear walls are used for lateral stability, columns and beams may be joined with simpler, hinged connections, such as the bolted connections normally used in steel and timber structures or the flexible welded connections used in precast concrete. The stabilizing braces or walls may be located within the interior of the building or at the perimeter, but they must be placed so as to resist lateral forces in all directions. Building cores or stair towers housing vertical circulation or other systems often can be easily designed to incorporate such elements, thus eliminating their intrusion from the remainder of the building floor plan. When located at the perimeter of the structure, these elements may influence the design of the building facade.

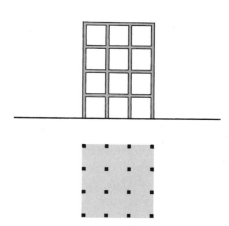

Rigid frame structures require no additional bracing or shear walls, as shown in this elevation and plan.

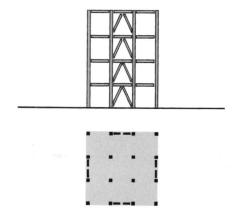

The locations of braced frames or shear walls must be considered in relation to the elevation and plan of the building.

COLUMN AND BEAM SYSTEMS

SYSTEMS WELL SUITED TO COLUMN AND BEAM FRAMING

Information on column and beam systems may be found in the following sections:

Systems	Pages
Wood Beams	60–63
Steel Beams and Girders	98–99
Sitecast Concrete Beams and Girders	112–113
Precast Concrete Beams and Girders	130–131

COLUMN AND BEAM SYSTEM LAYOUTS

Columns are located on the lines of the beams above. Although column spacings may vary within the limits of the spanning capacity of the beams, for reasons of economy, columns are typically restricted to some regular gridded arrangement.

Various combinations of beams and slabs are possible. Beams can span in one direction only, with slabs spanning perpendicular to them. With this arrangement, column spacing in one direction is equal to the span of the beams; in the other direction, it is equal to the span of the slabs.

More flexibility in the location of columns can be achieved with beams spanning in both directions. Deeper beams, termed girders, span the columns. The girders in turn support shallower, secondary beams, spanning perpendicular to them. Finally, the distance between the secondary beams is spanned by the slab. Column spacings with such beam and girder arrangements are limited only by the spanning capacity of the beams in either direction. The choice of the direction of the span of the girders and beams in such a structure can be influenced by a variety of factors, including the particular structural systems involved, the relative structural efficiency of either arrangement, the lateral stability requirements for the overall structure, and the integration of the floor structure with other building systems such as electrical wiring in the slab or ducts and piping running beneath the floor framing. These considerations are covered in more detail in the sections of this book covering specific structural or mechanical systems.

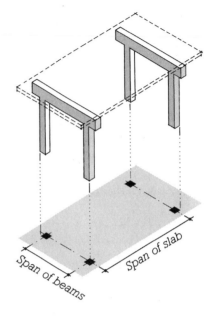

In column and beam systems, columns are located on beam lines.

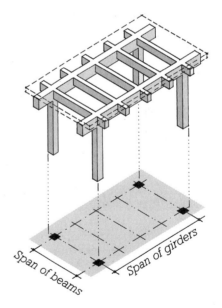

Beams span both directions in beam and girder systems.

COLUMN AND SLAB SYSTEMS

VERTICAL LOAD RESISTING ELEMENTS

Column and slab systems are composed of vertical columns directly supporting horizontally spanning slabs without the use of beams. As with column and beam systems, the reliance on columns for carrying vertical loads permits greater independence between the building plan and the structural system. The absence of beams in column and slab systems may permit even greater flexibility in column placements than with column and beam systems, because columns are not restricted to beam lines. Column and slab systems may also be attractive economically due to the simplification of construction techniques and the reduction in total floor depths that they make possible.

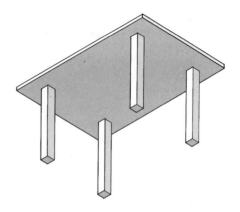

COLUMN AND SLAB SYSTEMS
(shown from below)

LATERAL LOAD RESISTING ELEMENTS

Rigid frame action is possible in column and slab systems, although its effectiveness depends on the depth of the slab, particularly in the areas close to the columns. Where large lateral forces are expected with systems with shallow slabs, a deepening of the slab or the addition of structural beams between columns may be required to achieve sufficient lateral resistance.

Shear walls or braced frames may also be used to develop lateral resistance in column and slab systems. These elements may be used either as the sole means of lateral bracing, or as enhancements to the rigid frame action of the system. They may be located within the interior of the building or at the perimeter, but they must be placed so as to resist lateral forces in all directions. The locations of interior elements must be coordinated with the building plan. Building cores housing vertical circulation or other systems can often be easily designed to incorporate such elements, thus eliminating their intrusion from the remainder of the floor plan. When located at the perimeter of the structure, shear walls or braces may influence the design of the building facade.

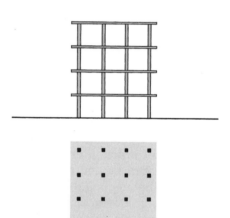

As shown in this elevation and plan, rigid frame action is possible with column and slab systems, although its effectiveness may be limited.

SYSTEMS WELL SUITED TO COLUMN AND SLAB FRAMING

Conventional structural systems that are configured as column and slab systems are metal space frame, or sitecast concrete systems, including two-way flat plate, two-way flat slab, and either one-way joist or waffle slab construction (when these two systems are used with shallow beams that do not extend below the surface of the ribs). For further information, see the following pages:

Systems	Pages
Sitecast Concrete Two-Way Flat Plate	118–119
Sitecast Concrete Two-Way Flat Slab	120–121
Sitecast Concrete One-Way Joists	116–117
Sitecast Concrete Waffle Slab	122–123

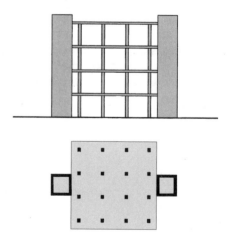

Shear walls are commonly used with column and slab systems. In this elevation and plan, the shear walls are shown incorporated into a pair of vertical cores.

40

COLUMN AND SLAB SYSTEMS

COLUMN AND SLAB SYSTEM LAYOUTS

Column spacing in either direction is equal to the span of the slab. For maximum economy and structural efficiency, column bays should be approximately square in proportion, and column displacements from regular lines should be minimized. However, column layouts are more flexible in column and slab systems because columns are not restricted to beam lines. Variations in column placements, changes in bay sizes, and irregular plan shapes may be more easily accommodated than in other framing systems.

STRUCTURAL LIMITATIONS OF COLUMN AND SLAB SYSTEMS

The absence of beams in sitecast concrete flat plate and flat slab construction may limit the structural performance of these systems. The relatively shallow depth of the joint between the columns and slabs can restrict their capacity to carry heavy loads on the slab and can limit their resistance to lateral forces. Though the addition of beams to these systems adds substantially to construction costs, it may be a practical alternative where longer spans are required, very heavy loads must be carried, or additional lateral resistance is needed and the use of shear walls or braced frames is undesirable. Such configurations are covered in more detail in the sections describing these structural systems.

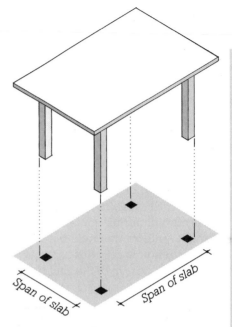

In column and slab systems, the span of the slab is equal to the column spacing in either direction.

The absence of beams in column and slab systems may facilitate irregular column layouts or plan shapes.

HIGH-RISE STRUCTURAL CONFIGURATIONS

THE DESIGN OF HIGH-RISE STRUCTURES

As the height of a building increases, the design of its structural system becomes increasingly specialized and complex. A variety of factors, many of them difficult to characterize at the schematic level, can have a major influence on the selection and design of a structural system. The great vertical loads on the structure, the character of wind and earthquake forces specific to the building site, the local foundation conditions, the relative costs of various construction systems within the region, unusual structural conditions within the building, and the particular expertise of the structural engineer are all important factors. For these reasons no serious attempt at the design of a high-rise structure should be made without the participation of a qualified structural engineer, even in the early phases of design. Within this context, however, the information in this section may serve to inform the architect of the basic structural systems available for tall buildings and to describe the relationship of these structural systems to the total design of the building.

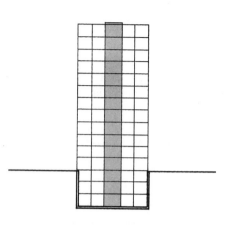

Major loadbearing elements should be continuous vertically to the foundations of the building.

VERTICAL LOAD RESISTING SYSTEMS

The vertical load resisting systems for high-rise buildings are essentially the same as those for low-rise structures discussed on the previous pages. In the tallest buildings, column and beam systems are predominant due to their efficient use of space, versatility as structural systems, and ease of construction. Because of the large gravity loads associated with tall buildings, special care should be taken that major structural elements are not interrupted vertically. Whenever possible, building cores, columns, and loadbearing walls should not shift laterally from floor to floor and should be continuous from the roof to the foundation of the building.

However, configurations may occur in which all loads do not have direct and continuous paths to the foundation. In some cases it is desirable to redistribute vertical loads in a structure outward toward the corners of the building to increase its resistance to overturning. Unique spaces in the lower portions of tall buildings, such as auditoriums, lobbies, atriums, or other public facilities, often require longer span systems that must interrupt the paths of loadbearing elements from above. Any changes in the massing of a building or in programmed uses at different levels within the building may dictate changes in the arrangement or spacing of structural elements for these different areas. Where such changes in structural configuration must occur, the effects may range from the use of transfer beams or trusses designed to redistribute vertical loads horizontally to, in extreme cases, the reconsideration of the basic structural configuration or programmatic organization of the building.

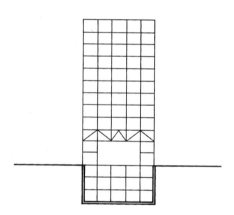

Transfer beams or trusses may be used to interrupt vertical loadbearing elements where necessary.

HIGH-RISE STRUCTURAL CONFIGURATIONS

LATERAL LOAD RESISTING SYSTEMS

Increasing the height of a building increases its sensitivity to both wind and earthquake forces. The taller the building, the more these forces will dominate the design of the entire structure, and the more attention should be given to designing for them. The following guidelines are particularly important in the design of high-rise buildings.

Tall, narrow buildings are more difficult to stabilize against lateral forces than broader buildings. In such instances more effective stabilizing mechanisms may be required, and their elements may assume more prominence in the final design of the building.

Especially in areas of high seismic activity, tall buildings that are non-symmetrical or unbalanced in either massing or the arrangement of stabilizing elements can experience forces that may be difficult to control. Such conditions should be avoided whenever possible.

Parts of a building that are independent in massing can be expected to move differently under the dynamic loads associated with earthquakes. The leg of an L-shaped building, the stem of a T-shaped building, a wide base with a narrow tower, or other forms composed of discrete masses may interact in adverse ways. Under such conditions, masses should be designed as separate structures, with independent vertical and lateral load resisting systems, to minimize these effects.

Buildings of inherently unstable massing should be avoided. Discontinuities in the stiffness of a structure at different levels may lead to excessive deflections or other unfavorable responses to lateral loads. For instance, an open space with long horizontal spans at the base of a tall building may produce excessive flexibility at that level. If such a "soft story" cannot be avoided, the addition of special bracing elements at that level may be required.

Tall buildings may interact with winds in unpredictable ways. With buildings of irregular form, or on sites where adjacent structures or other features may produce unusual air movements, specialized studies of the building's response to local wind pressures and fluctuations may be required.

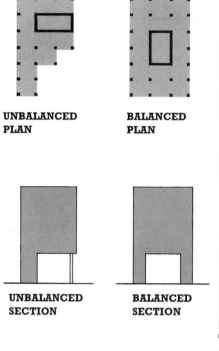

UNBALANCED PLAN **BALANCED PLAN**

UNBALANCED SECTION **BALANCED SECTION**

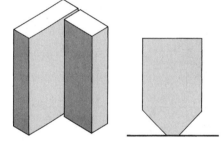

Discrete building masses should be structurally independent. Inherently unstable building masses should be avoided.

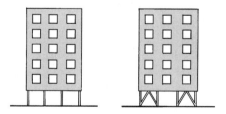

Discontinuities in the stiffness of structures at different levels should be avoided, or additional stabilizing elements may be required.

HIGH-RISE STRUCTURAL CONFIGURATIONS

The three mechanisms of shear wall, braced frame, and rigid frame can be configured in specialized ways for use in high-rise structures. The following systems are presented in order of increasing resistance to lateral forces. The adjacent diagrams illustrate these systems schematically in elevation above and plan below.

CONVENTIONAL CONFIGURATIONS

The conventional arrangements of stabilizing elements used in low-rise buildings may be extended for use in buildings up to 20 to 25 stories in height. The same considerations that apply to low-rise buildings apply to taller buildings as well. Stabilizing elements should be arranged so as to resist lateral forces along all major axes of the building. These elements should be arranged in a balanced manner either within the building or at the perimeter. And such elements must be integrated with the building plan or elevation.

Shear walls and braced frames are the stabilizing elements most commonly used in buildings of this height, due to their structural efficiency. They may be used either separately or in combination. The use of rigid frames as the sole means of stabilizing structures of this height is possible, although it may be less desirable because of the increased size of the beams and columns that it necessitates. For steel structures, the fabrication of welded joints required with rigid frames also becomes increasingly uneconomical as the number of these connections multiplies. Rigid frames may also be used in combination with either shear walls or braced frames to enhance the total lateral resistance of a structure.

CORE STRUCTURES

Core structures constitute the system most commonly used to stabilize all but the tallest buildings. In these structures, stabilizing elements are integrated into the vertical cores that house circulation and mechanical systems in tall buildings. One of the principal advantages of core structures is that with the incorporation of the resisting elements into the building core, interference with the surrounding usable space in the building is minimized. In concrete construction, core walls already intended to enclose these other building systems can easily be designed to also act as shear walls, in many cases with no increase in size. In steel construction, core structures are usually designed as braced frames.

A single core servicing an entire building should be located at the center of the building. In buildings with more than one core, the cores should be located symmetrically in the building plan so as to provide balanced resistance under lateral loads from any direction. Cores typically comprise approximately 20%–25% of the total floor area of a high-rise building. They should be formed as closed elements, approximately square or cylindrical, with openings into the core kept to a minimum.

Simple core structures can be used in buildings as high as 35 to 40 stories. Core structures can also be enhanced structurally with the addition

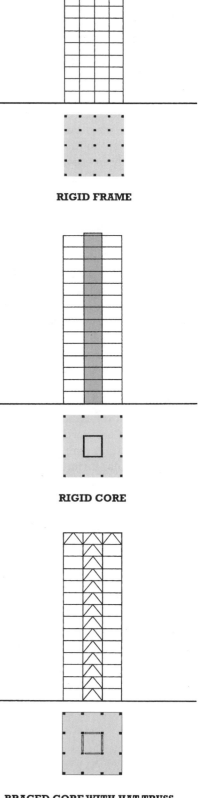

RIGID FRAME

RIGID CORE

BRACED CORE WITH HAT TRUSS

HIGH-RISE STRUCTURAL CONFIGURATIONS

of bracing in the form of "hat" trusses. Hat trusses involve the perimeter columns of the building in resisting lateral loads, thus improving the overall performance of the building. Such trusses may influence the design of the building facade or the location of mechanical floors. Columns at the perimeter of the building may also increase in size with this system. These core-interactive structures are suitable for buildings up to approximately 55 stories in height.

For further information on the design of building cores to accommodate mechanical and circulation systems, see pages 170–184.

TUBE STRUCTURES

The tallest buildings are most often designed as tube structures. In this system stabilizing elements are located at the perimeter of the structure, leaving the layout of the interior of the building virtually unrestricted by considerations of lateral stability. Either braced frame or rigid frame elements, constructed from either steel or concrete, may be used. Simple tube structures and their variations are generally used for buildings approximately 50 to 55 stories or greater in height.

The use of rigid frame tubes may affect the size and spacing of framing elements at the perimeter of the building. Beams may need to be deeper and columns may need to be larger and more closely spaced than would otherwise be required. When building in steel, the welded joints required in this system may be more costly to construct, although construction systems have been developed that allow the off-site fabrication of these joints, thus minimizing this disadvantage.

Braced frame tubes are one of the most structurally efficient lateral load resisting configurations. When built in steel, these structures also rely on more easily constructed bolted connections. The diagonal braces that are an integral part of this system often have a significant impact on the appearance of the building facade.

The performance of rigid frame tube structures may be enhanced with the addition of belt trusses located at the perimeter of the structure. These trusses may be located at various levels in the structure, and as with hat trusses, they may influence the location of mechanical floors and overall facade design.

Variations on the tube structure are also possible. "Tube-in-tube" structures, in which perimeter tubes interact with rigid cores, may be designed for enhanced structural performance. "Bundled tube" structures permit greater variation in the massing of a structure and can enhance the overall performance of the structure as well.

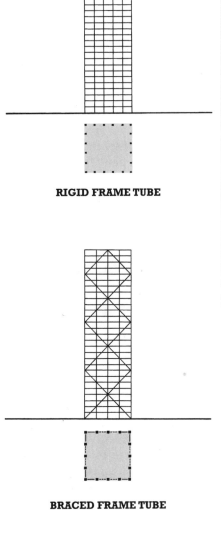

RIGID FRAME TUBE

BRACED FRAME TUBE

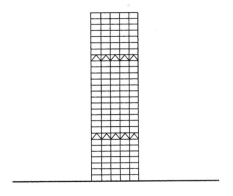

RIGID FRAME TUBE WITH BELT TRUSSES

THE DESIGN OF LARGE BUILDINGS FOR EARTHQUAKES

Particularly in areas of high seismic risk, the design of the structural system for a tall building will be strongly influenced by the behavior of the structure under the dynamic loads of an earthquake. The final selection of a structural system and material should be based on a detailed engineering analysis, as well as the recommendations of the structural engineer. The following guidelines may be useful for preliminary considerations.

Steel

Structural steel frames are particularly well suited to withstanding the forces associated with major earthquakes. The light weight of steel reduces overall building mass, thereby minimizing the forces experienced by the structure under dynamic conditions. And the high ductility of steel allows the design of a structure capable of dissipating the great amounts of energy imparted to it during a major earthquake. Designing steel structures that take full advantage of these characteristics results in a building frame that is flexible but highly resilient and capable of withstanding extreme forces without collapse.

Relying on structures that are flexible as a strategy for withstanding the destructive effects of earthquakes is the predominant approach used for the design of tall buildings on the North American continent. However, the large movements that can be expected in such a structure during a major

earthquake present difficulties in the design of nonstructural elements and their connections to the building frame. As much as possible, elements such as external cladding or interior partitions must be isolated from the structural frame so as to minimize damage to them during an earthquake and so that they do not restrict the movements of the structure itself under dynamic conditions.

Concrete

Concrete is, in contrast to steel, more massive and less ductile. The high mass of concrete is generally disadvantageous under dynamic conditions, as greater loads will be experienced by the structure. And the more brittle character of concrete lessens its capacity to absorb dynamic energy, although adequate ductility in concrete frame structures can be achieved with careful design of the steel reinforcing. These characteristics of concrete result in building frames that are relatively stiff and that depend much more on the brute strength of the frame to resist the forces of earthquakes.

The relative stiffness of concrete structures may be preferable where earthquake loads are not as severe or for buildings that are less tall. Concrete structures may also be desirable for building sites where the ground movements associated with earthquakes are such that the shorter period of vibration of a stiffer structure may be advantageous. Because building movements in concrete structures are significantly less than in steel structures, the detailing of nonstructural elements and their

connections to the building frame may also be simplified.

Dampers and Base Isolators

A building's earthquake resistance can be enhanced with devices that specifically target an earthquake's dynamic effects. Dampers are shock absorber like devices that dissipate the energy imparted into a building structure during an earthquake. Dampers may be incorporated into the framing of a building, or may be combined with a system of base isolators. Base isolators are devices installed at the foundation level of a building that allow a degree of separation between the building and the ground it rests on. With base isolation, some portion of the ground movements experienced during an earthquake are never imparted to the building at all. From a preliminary design point of view, the impact of these systems is to reduce the forces a building structure must itself resist, thereby lessening the extent or size of its own lateral force resisting elements. In addition, buildings with base isolation must be designed to allow for the relative displacements that will occur when the ground underneath moves differently from the building above. Utility lines must be provided with flexible connections where they exit the building, and connections to structures at the building perimeter such as stairs, walkways, and adjacent buildings must be able to accommodate significant differential movements. In severe earthquake zones, displacements of up to 30 in. (760 mm) may be expected.

■■ SIZING THE STRUCTURAL SYSTEM

This section will assist you in assigning approximate sizes to structural elements. Additional information on designing and building with each structural system is also provided.

WOOD STRUCTURAL SYSTEMS

Wood construction typically takes one of two distinct forms: Wood Light Frame construction uses relatively thin, closely spaced members to form walls, floors, and roofs in a system called Platform Frame construction. Heavy Timber construction uses larger members configured as a post and beam system. Both of these systems are fully treated in this section.

Either Wood Light Frame or Heavy Timber construction can be combined with masonry construction for increased fire resistance and load capacity. These systems are more fully described under Masonry Structural Systems, beginning on page 71.

PLATFORM FRAME CONSTRUCTION

Platform frame construction is an economical and flexible building system. It is used extensively for single-family and multifamily housing, as well as for low-rise apartment buildings and small commercial structures.

Because this system is largely fabricated on-site and the individual framing members are small, it is particularly well suited for use where unusual layouts or irregular forms are desired. Where economy is a primary concern, the use of a 2- or 4-ft (0.6- or 1.2-m) modular plan dimension may be desirable. Platform frame construction easily and unobtrusively incorporates mechanical systems and other building services.

Platform framing is a wall and slab system. Lateral bracing may be supplied either by shear wall or braced frame action of the load-bearing walls.

HEAVY TIMBER CONSTRUCTION

Heavy Timber construction is characterized by high fire resistance (it has a substantially higher fire rating than unprotected steel), high load capacity, and the unique aesthetic qualities of the exposed wood frame. The framing members for Heavy Timber construction may

be either solid wood or glue laminated. Heavy timber frames are used for low-rise commercial and industrial buildings and in residential construction. Because the framing members are typically prefabricated, on-site erection times can be rapid with this system. However, the larger sizes of the framing members make this system less suitable than platform framing for structures that are highly irregular in form or layout. Special provisions may also be required for the integration of mechanical and electrical systems into heavy timber framing.

As in platform framing, economy of construction may be maximized with the use of a 2- or 4-ft (0.6- or 1.2-m) design module when planning a timber frame structure.

Timber frames may be stabilized laterally by the shear resistance of the walls or panels used to enclose the frame, or with the use of diagonal bracing. The masonry bearing walls of Ordinary or Mill construction are also well suited to acting as shear walls.

FIRE-RESISTANCE RATINGS FOR WOOD COLUMNS

To qualify as components of Mill construction as defined by most building codes, wood columns supporting floor loads must have a nominal size of at least 8 × 8 in. (191 × 191 mm). Columns supporting roof and ceiling loads only may be as small as 6 × 8 in. (140 × 191 mm). Columns of lesser dimension may be used in Ordinary construction and Wood Light Frame construction.

WOOD COLUMNS

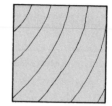

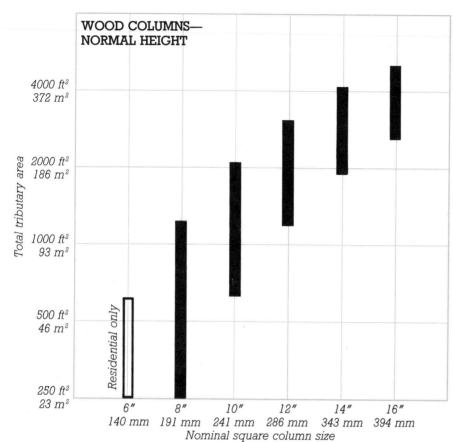

WOOD COLUMNS— NORMAL HEIGHT

Total tributary area

4000 ft²
372 m²

2000 ft²
186 m²

1000 ft²
93 m²

500 ft²
46 m²

250 ft²
23 m²

Residential only

| 6″ | 8″ | 10″ | 12″ | 14″ | 16″ |
| 140 mm | 191 mm | 241 mm | 286 mm | 343 mm | 394 mm |

Nominal square column size

The top chart is for wood columns of up to 12 ft (3.7 m) in height between floors. For strong woods or low loads, read toward the top of the indicated areas. For heavy loads, or for columns resisting lateral or other bending forces, read toward the bottom.

■ Strong woods include Douglas Fir, Larch, Southern Pine, and Oak.

■ For rectangular columns, read from the square column with equivalent area.

■ Actual column size is ½ in. (13 mm) less than nominal in each di-rection.

■ Total *tributary area* is the total area of roofs and floors supported by the column.

For columns taller than 12 ft (3.7 in) between floors, read both charts on this page. Use the larger of the two sizes indicated.

■ When reading the bottom chart for light loads or strong woods, decrease column size by one size (less 2 in. or 50 mm). For heavy loads, or for columns resisting lateral or other bending forces, in crease column' size by one size (add 2 in. or 50 mm).

■ For rectangular columns, read from the square column the same size as the least dimension of the rectangular column.

WOOD COLUMNS—TALL

Height

48′
14.6 m

36′
11.0 m

24′
7.3 m

12′
3.7 m

0

16 × 16
394 × 394 mm

14 × 14
343 × 343 mm

12 × 12
286 × 286 mm

10 × 10
241 × 241 mm

8 × 8
191 × 191 mm

6 × 6
140 × 140 mm

| 0 | 400 ft² | 800 ft² | 1200 ft² | 1600 ft² |
| | 37.2 m² | 74.3 m² | 111.5 m² | 148.6 m² |

Total tributary area

ACTUAL SIZES OF WALL STUDS

Nominal Size	Actual Size
2×4	1½" × 3½" (38 × 89mm)
2×6	1½" × 5½" (38 × 140mm)
2×8	1½" × 7¼" (38 × 184mm)

SPACING OF WALL STUDS

Wall studs are most commonly spaced 16 in. (406 mm) center-to-center. A 12-in. (305-mm) spacing may be used where greater strength and stiffness are required. Where the structural requirements are less, a 24-in. (610-mm) spacing may also be used so long as the applied sheathing or finishing panels are sufficiently stiff to span the greater distance between studs. In all cases studs must fall on a 4-ft (1219-mm) module in order to coordinate with the standard width of various panel products that are used as an integral part of this system.

FIRE-RESISTANCE RATINGS OF WOOD STUD WALLS

Wood stud walls are classified as Wood Light Frame construction and may qualify for a 1-hour fire rating when covered on both sides with ⅝-in. (16-mm) Type X gypsum board or its equivalent.

WOOD STUD WALLS

WOOD STUD WALLS—NORMAL HEIGHT

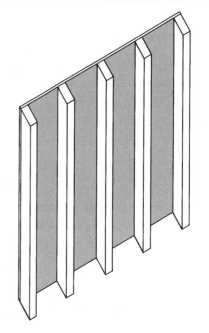

Studs supporting roof only:
2 ×4 @ 24"o.c. (38 × 89 mm @ 610 mm o.c.)
2 ×6 @ 24" o.c. (38 × 140 mm @ 610 mm o.c.)

Studs supporting one floor and roof:
2 ×4 @ 16" o.c. (38 × 89 mm @ 406 mm o.c.)
2 ×6 @ 24" o.c. (38 × 140mm @ 610 mm o.c.)

Studs supporting two floors and roof:
2 ×6 @ 16" o.c. (38 × 140 mm @ 406 mm o.c.)

Studs supporting three floors and roof:
2 ×8 @ 16" o.c. (38 × 406 mm @ 184 mm o.c.)

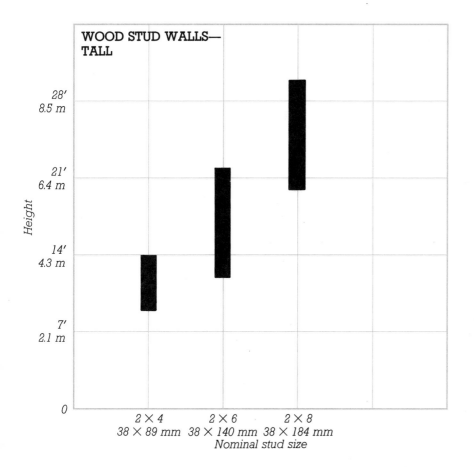

The table above is for wood stud walls up to 9 ft (2.7 m) tall between floors. Minimum combinations of stud size and spacing are given based on the total number of floors of building.

For walls taller than 9 ft (2.7 m) between floors, consult both the table above and the chart below. Use the larger of the two sizes indicated.

■ When reading the bottom chart for light loads, 12-in. (305-mm) stud spacings, or strong woods, read toward the top in the indicated areas. For heavy loads or 24-in. (610-mm) stud spacings, read toward the bottom.

■ Strong woods include Douglas Fir, Larch, Southern Pine, and Oak.

■ Wall heights may be increased with the addition of intermediate bracing perpendicular to the wall plane.

FIRE-RESISTANCE RATINGS FOR WOOD DECKING

To qualify for Mill construction as defined by the building codes, wood floor decking must be at least 3 in. (64 mm) in nominal thickness, with minimum 1-in. nominal (19-mm) wood finish flooring laid over it at right angles. Roof decking for Mill construction must be at least 2 in. (38 mm) in nominal thickness. Decking of lesser thickness may he used in Ordinary construction and Wood Light Frame construction.

WOOD DECKING

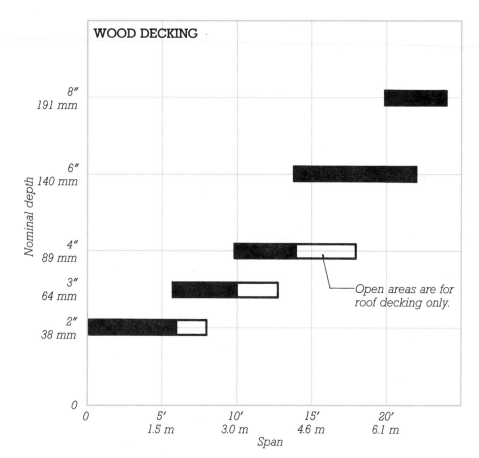

WOOD DECKING

Nominal depth

8″ / 191 mm
6″ / 140 mm
4″ / 89 mm
3″ / 64 mm
2″ / 38 mm
0

Open areas are for roof decking only.

Span

0
5′ / 1.5 m
10′ / 3.0 m
15′ / 4.6 m
20′ / 6.1 m

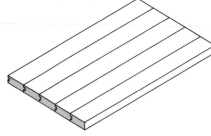

This chart is for solid or laminated wood decking. For light loads or strong woods, read toward the right in the indicated areas. For large loads or normal woods, read toward the left.

■ Strong woods include Douglas Fir, Larch, Southern Pine, and Oak.

■ Decking comes in various nominal widths, 6 and 8 in. (150 and 200 mm) being the most common. Actual depth is ½ in. (13 mm) less than nominal.

■ Allow approximately ¾ in. (19 mm) for the depth of finish flooring.

WOOD FLOOR JOISTS

ACTUAL SIZES OF FLOOR JOISTS

Nominal Size	Actual Size	
2 × 6	1½" × 5½"	(38 × 140 mm)
2 × 8	1½" × 7¼"	(38 × 184 mm)
2 × 10	1½" × 9¼"	(38 × 235 mm)
2 × 12	1½" × 11¼"	(38 × 286 mm)

TOTAL FINISHED FLOOR THICKNESS

To estimate total finished floor thickness, add 2 in. (50 mm) to actual joist size for finish ceiling, subflooring, and finish flooring.

BEAMS SUPPORTING FLOOR FRAMING

Wood Beams

For sizing wood beams, see the chart on page 61. To determine clearance under a wood beam, assume the top of the beam is level with the top of the floor joists.

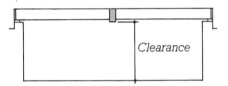

JOISTS WITH WOOD FLOOR BEAM

Steel Beams

Beam Size	Approximate Depth of Beam		Span of Beam	
W8	8"	(203 mm)	8'–13'	(2.4–4.0 m)
W10	10"	(254 mm)	10'–16'	(3.0–4.9 m)
W12	12"	(305 mm)	12'–18'	(3.7–5.5 m)

For lightly loaded beams, use the longer spans indicated. For heavily loaded beams, use the shorter spans.

To determine clearance under a steel beam, assume the top of the beam is level with the top of the foundation wall.

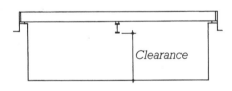

JOISTS WITH STEEL FLOOR BEAM

FIRE-RESISTANCE RATINGS FOR WOOD LIGHT FRAME JOISTS

Wood light frame floors with nominal 1-in. (19-mm) subflooring and finish flooring can have a 1-hour fire-resistance rating when the underside of the framing is finished with ⅝-in. (16-mm) Type X gypsum board or its equivalent.

WOOD FLOOR JOISTS

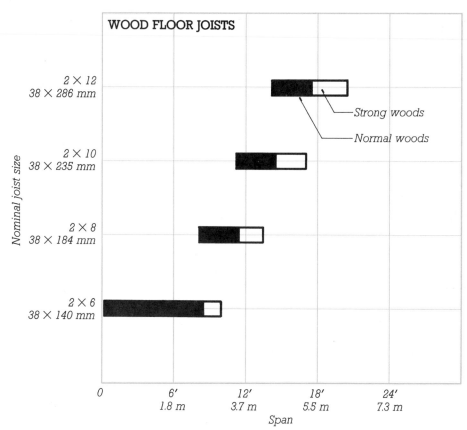

WOOD FLOOR JOISTS

Nominal joist size

- 2 × 12
  38 × 286 mm
  - *Strong woods*
  - *Normal woods*
- 2 × 10
  38 × 235 mm
- 2 × 8
  38 × 184 mm
- 2 × 6
  38 × 140 mm

| 0 | 6' | 12' | 18' | 24' |
| | 1.8 m | 3.7 m | 5.5 m | 7.3 m |

Span

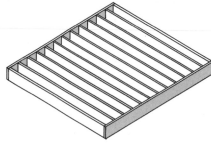

The top chart is for wood floor joists with residential floor loads. For larger loads, increase the indicated joist size by one size (plus 2 in., or 50 mm). For ceiling joists supporting only residential attic loads, decrease the indicated joist size by one size (less 2 in., or 50 mm).

■ Strong woods include Douglas Fir, Larch, Southern Pine, and Oak.

■ For 12-in. (305-mm) joist spacings, increase allowable spans 1 to 2 ft (0.3 to 0.6 in). For 24-in. (610-mm) joist spacings, decrease allowable spans 1 to 2 ft (0.3 to 0.6 in).

■ Most often wood floor joists are spaced 16 in. (406 mm) center-to-center. Spacings of 12 and 24 in. (305 and 610 mm) are also used. In all cases members should fall on a 4-ft. (1219-mm) module to coordinate with the standard width of various panel products that are used as an integral part of this system.

■ The bottom table is for wood I-joists. Consisting of top and bottom flanges of solid wood or laminated veneer lumber and webs of plywood or oriented strand board, these manufactured framing components can span further than conventional solid wood joists. Spans shown in the table are for normal residential floor loads.

WOOD I-JOIST SPANS

I-Joist Depth	I-Joist Spacing O. C.			
	24" (610 mm)	19.2" (488 mm)	16" (406 mm)	12" (305 mm)
16" (406 mm)	21'-5" (6.5 m)	23'-2" (7.1 m)	24'-8" (7.5 m)	27'-1" (8.3 m)
14" (356 mm)	19'-4" (5.9 m)	20'-11" (6.4 m)	22'-3" (6.8 m)	24'-6" (7.5 m)
11⅞" (295 mm)	15'-10" (4.8 m)	17'-1" (5.2 m)	18'-2" (5.5 m)	20'-0" (6.1 m)
9½" (241 mm)	13'-4" (4.1 m)	14'-5" (4.4 m)	15'-4" (4.7 m)	16'-10" (51 m)

WOOD ROOF RAFTERS

ACTUAL SIZES OF ROOF RAFTERS

Nominal Size	Actual Size	
2 × 4	1½" × 3½"	(38 × 89 mm)
2 × 6	1½" × 5½"	(38 × 140 mm)
2 × 8	1½" × 7¼"	(38 × 184 mm)
2 × 10	1½" × 9¼"	(38 × 235 mm)

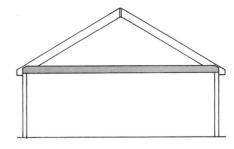

RAFTERS WITH RAFTER TIES

TIES OR BEAMS SUPPORTING ROOF RAFTERS

Rafter ties connecting rafters at their bases may be sized either as floor joists, if they are intended to support habitable space, or as ceiling joists, if they are supporting attic loads only. See the chart on the facing page.

Structural ridge beams can eliminate the need for ties at the base of the rafters. See page 97 for sizing wood beams.

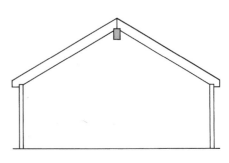

RAFTERS WITH RIDGE BEAM

FIRE-RESISTANCE RATINGS FOR WOOD LIGHT FRAME RAFTERS

Wood light frame roofs can have a 1-hour fire-resistance rating when the underside of the framing is finished with ⅝-in. (16-mm) Type X gypsum board or its equivalent.

WOOD ROOF RAFTERS

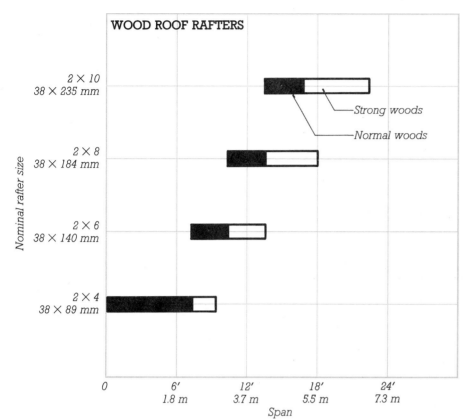

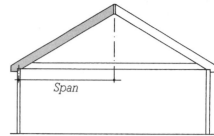

This chart is for wood rafters with a pitch of at least 3:12 and no finish ceiling attached to the underside of the rafters.

■ For rafters with lower slopes (including flat roofs) or with attached finish ceilings, reduce allowable spans by 1 to 2 ft (0.3 to 0.6 m).

■ For unusually heavy roof loads, increase rafter size by one size (plus 2 in., or 50 mm).

■ Strong woods include Douglas Fir, Larch, Southern Pine, and Oak.

■ Most often wood roof rafters are spaced 16 in. (406 mm) center-to-center. Spacings of 12 and 24 in. (305 and 610 mm) are also used. In all cases members should fall on a 4-ft. (1219-mm) module to coordinate with the standard width of various panel products that are used as an integral part of this system.

WOOD BEAMS

SIZES OF SOLID WOOD BEAMS

Nominal Depth	Actual Depth
4"	3½" (89 mm)
6"	5½" (140 mm)
8", 10", 12"	¾" (19 mm) less than nominal for beam widths of 2", 3", and 4", and
	½" (13 mm) less than nominal for beam widths greater than 4"
14" or greater	½" (13 mm) less than nominal

The actual widths of solid beams are ½ in. (13 mm) less than nominal.

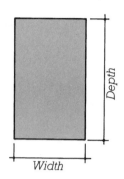

FRAMING FOR HEAVY TIMBER CONSTRUCTION

A heavy timber framing system that uses both beams and girders allows for a great range of bay sizes and proportions. The beam spacing is determined by the allowable span of the floor or roof decking as tabulated on page 55. For preliminary design, limit beam and girder spans to a maximum of 20 ft (6 m) for solid wood, or 24 ft (7.3 m) for laminated wood.

FIRE-RESISTANCE RATINGS FOR WOOD BEAMS

To qualify for Mill construction as defined by most building codes, wood floor beams must have a nominal size of at least 6 × 10 (140 × 241 mm). If supporting a roof and ceiling only, they may be no smaller than 4 × 6 (89 × 140 mm). Beams of lesser dimension may be used in Ordinary construction and Wood Light Frame construction.

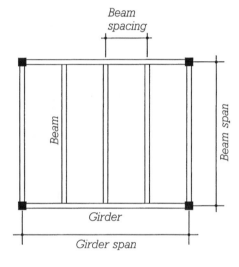

HEAVY TIMBER FLOOR FRAMING

WOOD BEAMS

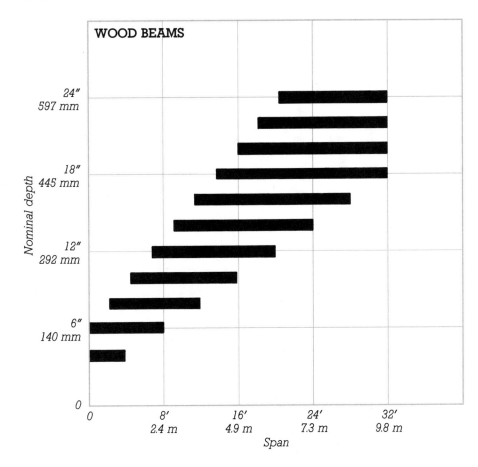

WOOD BEAMS

Nominal depth

24″
597 mm

18″
445 mm

12″
292 mm

6″
140 mm

0

Span

0   8′   16′   24′   32′
    2.4 m   4.9 m   7.3 m   9.8 m

SOLID BEAM   **BUILT-UP BEAM**

This chart is for solid or built-up beams as shown. For girders, or for beams carrying large loads, read toward the left in the indicated areas. For light loads or strong woods, read toward the right.

■ Strong woods include Douglas Fir, Larch, Southern Pine, and Oak.

■ Practical widths for solid beams range from one-fourth of the depth of the beam to equal to the depth of the beam.

■ A girder should be at least 2 in. (50 mm) deeper than the beams it supports.

GLUE LAMINATED WOOD BEAMS

SIZES OF GLUE LAMINATED BEAMS

Glue laminated beams are specified by their actual size. Depths must be a multiple of $1\frac{1}{2}$ in. (38 mm), the thickness of one lamination.

Width	Depth	
$3\frac{1}{8}$" (79 mm)	3"–24"	(76–610 mm)
$5\frac{1}{8}$" (130 mm)	$4\frac{1}{2}$"–36"	(114–914 mm)
$6\frac{3}{4}$" (171 mm)	6"–48"	(152–1219 mm)
$8\frac{3}{4}$" (222 mm)	9"–63"	(229–1600 mm)
$10\frac{3}{4}$" (273 mm)	$10\frac{1}{2}$"–75"	(267–1905 mm)

CONTINUOUS SPAN GLUE LAMINATED BEAMS

For maximum efficiency, glue laminated beams may be configured with continuous spans. For such configurations, read toward the right in the indicated area on the chart on the facing page. Practical spans for continuous span beam systems range from 25 to 65 ft (7.5 to 20.0 m).

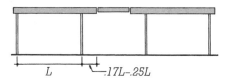

CONTINUOUS SPAN GLUE LAMINATED BEAMS

FIRE-RESISTANCE RATINGS FOR GLUE LAMINATED WOOD BEAMS

The model building codes do not distinguish between glue laminated and solid wood beams. To quality for Mill construction as defined by most building codes, wood floor beams must have a nominal size of at least 6 × 10 (140 × 241 mm). If supporting a roof and ceiling only, they may be no smaller than 4 × 6 (89 × 140 mm). Beams of lesser dimension may be used in Ordinary construction and Wood Light Frame construction.

GLUE LAMINATED WOOD BEAMS

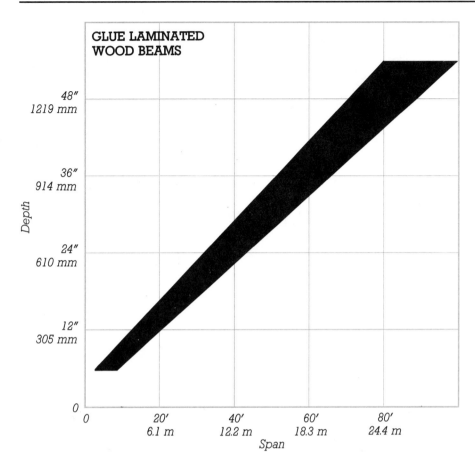

This chart is for glue laminated beams.

■ Normal spacings for glue laminated beams range from 4 ft (1.2 m) for small beams supporting decking to 24 ft (7.3 m) for larger beams supporting joists or purlins.

■ Typical widths for glue laminated beams are one-fourth to one-seventh of the depth, rounded to the nearest standard width as shown on the facing page.

■ For girders, read depths from the extreme lefthand edge of the indicated area. A girder should be at least 1½ in. (38 mm) deeper than the beams it supports.

WOOD FLOOR AND ROOF TRUSSES — LIGHT

Light wood floor and roof trusses are commonly used in place of conventional wood joists and rafters in platform frame construction. These prefabricated elements permit quicker erection in the field, greater clear spans, simplified framing due to the lack of interior loadbearing walls, and easier running of electrical and mechanical services due to the open spaces within the trusses.

FIRE-RESISTANCE RATINGS FOR LIGHT WOOD TRUSSES

These trusses are classified as Wood Light Frame construction. They can have a 1-hour fire-resistance rating when covered with nominal 1-in. (19-mm) subflooring and finish flooring and when the underside of the framing is finished with ⅝-in. (16-mm) Type X gypsum board or its equivalent.

WOOD FLOOR AND ROOF TRUSSES—LIGHT

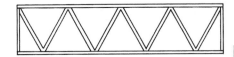

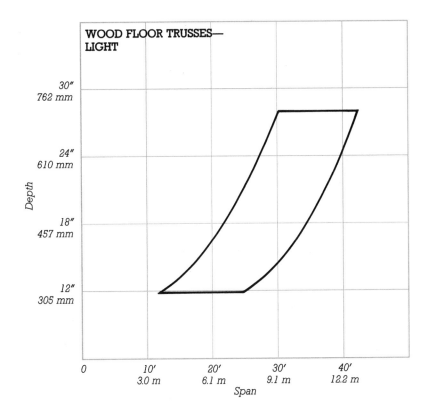

WOOD FLOOR TRUSSES— LIGHT

Depth

- 30″ / 762 mm
- 24″ / 610 mm
- 18″ / 457 mm
- 12″ / 305 mm

Span

- 0
- 10′ / 3.0 m
- 20′ / 6.1 m
- 30′ / 9.1 m
- 40′ / 12.2 m

The top chart is for wood floor trusses constructed from light members (up to 6 in., or 140 mm, deep). For heavy loads, read toward the left in the indicated area. For light loads, read toward the right. For preliminary design, use depths in even 2-in. (50-mm) increments. The sizes available may vary with the manufacturer.

■ Typical truss spacing is 16 to 48 in. (406 to 1219 mm).

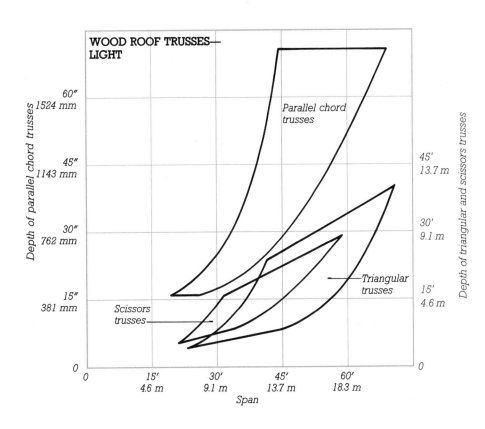

WOOD ROOF TRUSSES— LIGHT

Depth of parallel chord trusses

- 60″ / 1524 mm
- 45″ / 1143 mm
- 30″ / 762 mm
- 15″ / 381 mm
- 0

Parallel chord trusses

Triangular trusses

Scissors trusses

Depth of triangular and scissors trusses

- 45′ / 13.7 m
- 30′ / 9.1 m
- 15′ / 4.6 m
- 0

Span

- 0
- 15′ / 4.6 m
- 30′ / 9.1 m
- 45′ / 13.7 m
- 60′ / 18.3 m

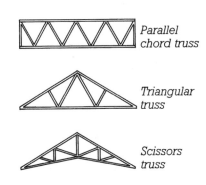

Parallel chord truss

Triangular truss

Scissors truss

The bottom chart is for wood roof trusses constructed from light members (up to 6 in., or 140 mm, deep). Read depths of parallel chord trusses from the left-hand scale, and depths of other trusses from the right-hand scale. For heavy loads, read toward the left in the indicated area. For light loads, read toward the right. Triangular or scissors trusses are commonly available with top chord slopes in whole number pitches from 2:12 to 7:12. Available sizes may vary with the manufacturer.

■ Typical truss spacing is 16 to 48 in. (406 to 1219 mm).

WOOD TRUSSES — HEAVY

SPACING OF HEAVY WOOD ROOF TRUSSES

Roof trusses spaced no greater than 4 to 8 ft (1.2 to 2.4 m) require no additional joists or purlins. The maximum practical spacing of trusses with joists or purlins is approximately 20 ft (6.1 in).

FIRE-RESISTANCE RATINGS FOR HEAVY WOOD TRUSSES

To qualify for Mill construction as defined by most building codes, truss members may be no smaller in nominal dimension than 8 × 8 in. (191 × 191 mm) for floor trusses. Roof truss members may be as small in nominal dimension as 4 × 6 in. (89 × 140 mm).

WOOD TRUSSES — HEAVY

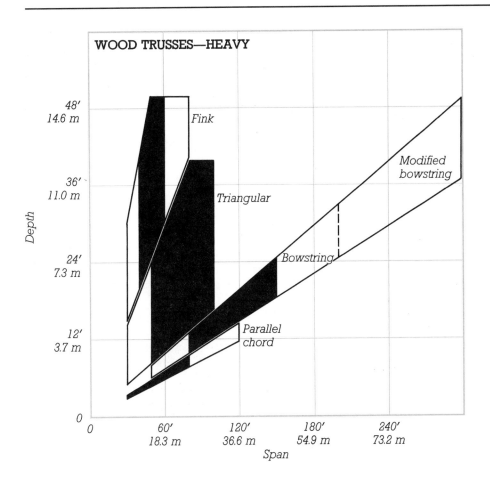

WOOD TRUSSES—HEAVY

Depth
- 48' / 14.6 m
- 36' / 11.0 m
- 24' / 7.3 m
- 12' / 3.7 m
- 0

Fink

Triangular

Modified bowstring

Bowstring

Parallel chord

Span
- 0
- 60' / 18.3 m
- 120' / 36.6 m
- 180' / 54.9 m
- 240' / 73.2 m

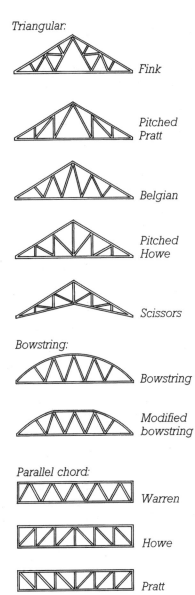

Triangular:
- Fink
- Pitched Pratt
- Belgian
- Pitched Howe
- Scissors

Bowstring:
- Bowstring
- Modified bowstring

Parallel chord:
- Warren
- Howe
- Pratt

This chart is for wood trusses constructed from heavy members (a minimum of 4 × 6 in., or 89 × 140 mm, in nominal size).

■ The most economical span ranges for each truss type are indicated with the solid tone.

GLUE LAMINATED WOOD ARCHES

DIMENSIONS FOR POINTED ARCHES

LOW- TO MEDIUM-PITCH ARCHES (3:12 TO 8:12)

Wall Height	Thickness of Arch	Depth of Base	Depth of Crown
10'–18' (3.0–5.5 m)	3⅛", 5⅛", 6¾" (79, 130, 171 mm)	7½"–18" for short spans (191–457 mm) 8"–30" for medium spans (203–762 mm) 8½"–35" for long spans (216–889 mm)	7½"–27" (191–686 mm)

HIGH-PITCH ARCHES (10:12 TO 16:12)

Wall Height	Thickness of Arch	Depth of Base	Depth of Crown
8'–12' (2.4–3.7 m)	5⅛" (130 mm)	7½" for short spans (191 mm) 7¾" for medium spans (197 mm) 9½"–10" for long spans (241–254 mm)	7¾"–24½" (197–622 mm)

FIRE-RESISTANCE RATINGS FOR GLUE LAMINATED ARCHES

Glue laminated arches supporting only a roof and ceiling qualify as components of Mill construction under most building codes if they are no smaller than nominal 4 × 6 in. (89 × 140 mm) at any point.

GLUE LAMINATED WOOD ARCHES

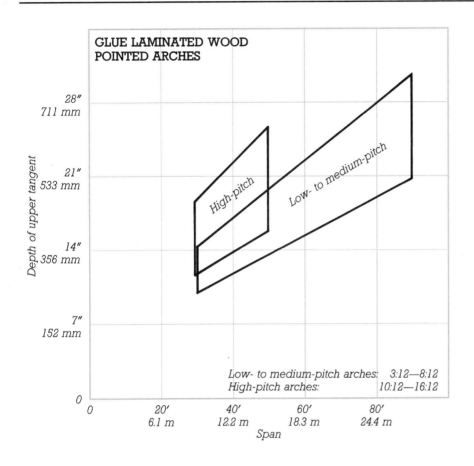

GLUE LAMINATED WOOD POINTED ARCHES

Depth of upper tangent

28″ / 711 mm
21″ / 533 mm
14″ / 356 mm
7″ / 152 mm
0

High-pitch

Low- to medium-pitch

Low- to medium-pitch arches: 3:12—8:12
High-pitch arches: 10:12—16:12

Span

0
20′ / 6.1 m
40′ / 12.2 m
60′ / 18.3 m
80′ / 24.4 m

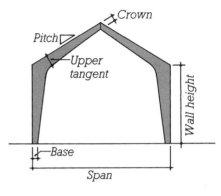

Crown

Pitch

Upper tangent

Wall height

Base

Span

The top chart is for glue laminated pointed arches. For low pitches, high loads, and high side walls, read toward the top in the indicated areas. For high pitches, low loads, and low side walls, read toward the bottom.

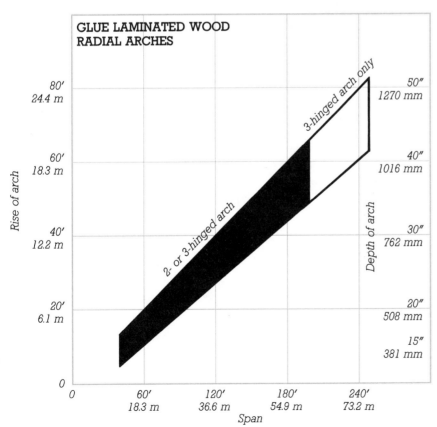

GLUE LAMINATED WOOD RADIAL ARCHES

Rise of arch

80′ / 24.4 m
60′ / 18.3 m
40′ / 12.2 m
20′ / 6.1 m
0

3-hinged arch only

2- or 3-hinged arch

Depth of arch

50″ / 1270 mm
40″ / 1016 mm
30″ / 762 mm
20″ / 508 mm
15″ / 381 mm

Span

0
60′ / 18.3 m
120′ / 36.6 m
180′ / 54.9 m
240′ / 73.2 m

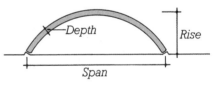

Depth

Rise

Span

2-HINGE RADIAL ARCH

3-HINGE RADIAL ARCH

The bottom chart is for glue laminated radial arches. Read the rise of the arch from the left-hand scale, and the depth of the arch from the right-hand scale.

■ The thickness of a radial arch should be at least one-fifth of its depth.

MASONRY STRUCTURAL SYSTEMS

Masonry construction rarely forms a complete building system by itself. Nonbearing masonry walls can be combined with other structural systems either in the form of infill between framing elements or as a veneer applied over wall or frame systems. Loadbearing masonry walls and columns can be combined with various spanning elements to form complete structural systems.

Masonry walls may be constructed in a great variety of ways. Use the following guidelines for preliminary design: Single-wythe walls are generally limited to nonbearing applications or as a veneer over other wall systems. Cavity wall construction is a preferred choice for exterior walls because of its high resistance to water penetration and its improved thermal performance. Concrete block construction is generally more economical than brick because of the reduced labor of laying the larger units and the lower material costs. Loadbearing masonry walls and columns must be steel reinforced in all but the smallest structures.

Since masonry construction takes place on-site and utilizes elements of small size, it is well suited for use in the construction of buildings of irregular form. Modular dimensions should be used, however, to minimize the need for partial units in construction. Use a module of one-half the nominal length of a masonry unit in plan, and the height of one brick or block course in elevation.

MASONRY AND WOOD CONSTRUCTION

Masonry can form the exterior (and sometimes interior) loadbearing walls for either Wood Light Frame construction or Heavy Timber construction, systems named Ordinary construction and Mill construction, respectively. Both of these systems have higher fire-resistance ratings than all-wood construction and are permitted for use in larger and taller buildings. For more information on the fire resistance of these systems and the building types for which their use is permitted, see pages 312–313. For sizing the wood elements of Ordinary or Heavy Timber construction, see the appropriate pages under Wood Structural Systems beginning on page 49.

MASONRY AND STEEL CONSTRUCTION

Open-web joists are the steel spanning elements most commonly used with loadbearing masonry construction because of the rela-tively small concentrated loads produced where the joists bear on the walls. Where steel beams and girders bear upon masonry walls, pilasters may be required at points of support. For economy and strength, interior columns in such systems are typically structural steel rather than masonry. See pages 87–105 for information on steel construction.

MASONRY AND CONCRETE CONSTRUCTION

The sitecast and precast concrete spanning elements most commonly used with loadbearing masonry walls are shorter span slabs without ribs or beams. These systems are often highly economical due to the minimal floor depths associated with these spanning elements, the absence of any requirement for added fire-resistive finishes, and the acoustical and energy performance of these high-mass materials. See pages 107–123 for information on sitecast concrete construction and pages 125–135 for information on precast concrete construction.

BRICK MASONRY COLUMNS

RECTANGULAR COLUMNS

For the design of rectangular columns or pilasters, read from the top chart on the facing page using a square column of equivalent area. For columns or pilasters over 12 ft (3.7 m) tall, read from the bottom chart using the lesser dimension of a column, or the greater dimension of a pilaster.

    The widths of two sides of a rectangular column should not exceed a ratio of 3:1; those of a pilaster should not exceed 4:1.

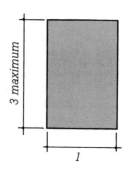

RECTANGULAR COLUMNS

FIRE-RESISTANCE RATINGS FOR BRICK MASONRY COLUMNS

Brick columns 12 in. (305 mm) square have a fire-resistance rating of 4 hours.

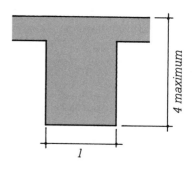

RECTANGULAR PILASTERS

BRICK MASONRY COLUMNS

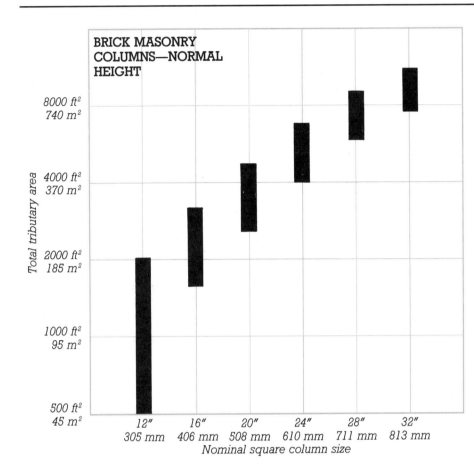

BRICK MASONRY
COLUMNS—NORMAL
HEIGHT

Total tributary area

8000 ft²
740 m²

4000 ft²
370 m²

2000 ft²
185 m²

1000 ft²
95 m²

500 ft²
45 m²

| 12″ | 16″ | 20″ | 24″ | 28″ | 32″ |
| 305 mm | 406 mm | 508 mm | 610 mm | 711 mm | 813 mm |

Nominal square column size

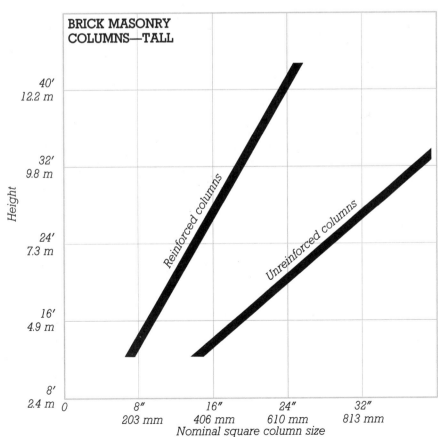

BRICK MASONRY
COLUMNS—TALL

Height

40′
12.2 m

32′
9.8 m

24′
7.3 m

16′
4.9 m

8′
2.4 m

Reinforced columns

Unreinforced columns

| 0 | 8″ | 16″ | 24″ | 32″ |
| | 203 mm | 406 mm | 610 mm | 813 mm |

Nominal square column size

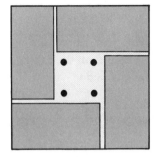

The top chart is for reinforced brick masonry columns or pilasters up to 12 ft (3.7 m) in height between floors.

■ For low loads or high-strength bricks, read toward the top in the solid areas. For high loads or low-strength bricks, read toward the bottom.

■ For unreinforced masonry, increase indicated column dimensions by 30%.

■ Columns less than 12 in. (305 mm) square are restricted to supporting minor loads only. They may not be used to carry floor loads or concrete roof loads.

■ Actual column size is equal to nominal size less ½ in. (13 mm).

■ Total tributary area is the total area of roofs and floors supported by the column.

The bottom chart is for columns with unbraced heights greater than 12 ft (3.7 in). Read along the solid line for the appropriate type. Use the larger of the two sizes indicated by both charts on this page.

CAVITY WALLS

For cavity walls, use only the net width of the structural wythe when reading the charts on the facing page. For structural wythes of concrete block, see pages 82–83.

MASONRY BEARING WALLS

Brick masonry bearing walls are commonly used for a variety of low-rise structures and in high-rise structures of up to approximately 20 stories in height. The cellular nature of high-rise bearing wall configurations makes this system well suited to building types such as apartments, hotels, dormitories, etc. In all but the smallest structures, masonry walls should be steel reinforced.

For structures of up to approximately 6 stories in height, the interior crosswalls and corridor walls typical of masonry structures are usually sufficient to provide the required lateral bracing for the structure. This permits the design of the exterior walls to remain relatively open. At greater heights, lateral stability requirements will increasingly dictate a more complete cellular configuration of walls. In this case the sizes and distribution of openings in the exterior walls may be more restricted.

Loadbearing walls should be aligned consistently from floor to floor and should be continuous from the roof to the building foundation. Where it is desirable to omit walls on a lower floor, it may be possible to design the wall above to act as a deep beam spanning between columns at each end. Such wall-beams may span 20 to 30 ft (6 to 9 m).

WALL PILASTERS

Pilasters are used both to carry concentrated vertical loads and to brace a wall against lateral forces and buckling.

When designing for vertical loads, locate the pilaster directly below the point of load application, and size the pilaster using the charts on pages 72–73.

Pilasters are used to brace walls laterally when the distance between other supports such as floor slabs or crosswalls is insufficient for this purpose. Use the bottom chart on the facing page to determine the maximum permissible spacing between such supports for any particular wall type and thickness. If the spacing is too great, the wall thickness may be increased, or pilasters may be added at the required spacing.

FIRE-RESISTANCE RATINGS FOR BRICK

Brick masonry walls 6 in. (152 mm) thick have a fire-resistance rating of 2 hours. At a thickness of 8 in. (203 mm), a 4-hour rating is achieved.

74

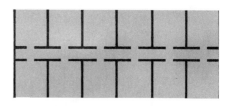

LOW-RISE BEARING WALL CONFIGURATION (*shown in plan*)

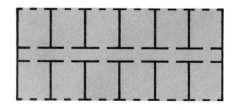

HIGH-RISE BEARING WALL CONFIGURATION (*shown in plan*)

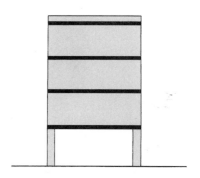

Bearing walls may act as deep beams to span across openings below, as shown in this schematic cross section.

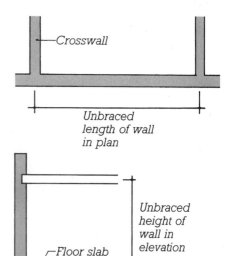

Crosswall

Unbraced length of wall in plan

Unbraced height of wall in elevation

Floor slab

UNBRACED HEIGHT OR LENGTH OF MASONRY WALLS

BRICK MASONRY WALLS

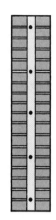

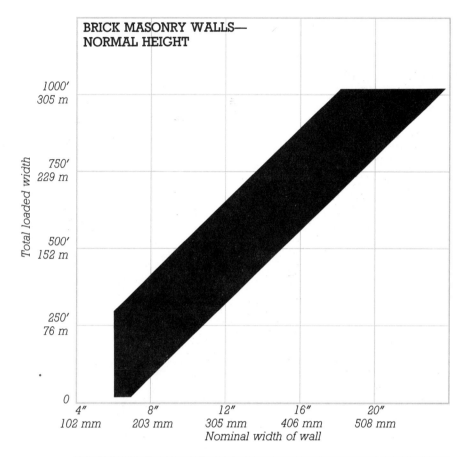

BRICK MASONRY WALLS—NORMAL HEIGHT

Total loaded width

- 1000' / 305 m
- 750' / 229 m
- 500' / 152 m
- 250' / 76 m
- 0

Nominal width of wall

- 4" / 102 mm
- 8" / 203 mm
- 12" / 305 mm
- 16" / 406 mm
- 20" / 508 mm

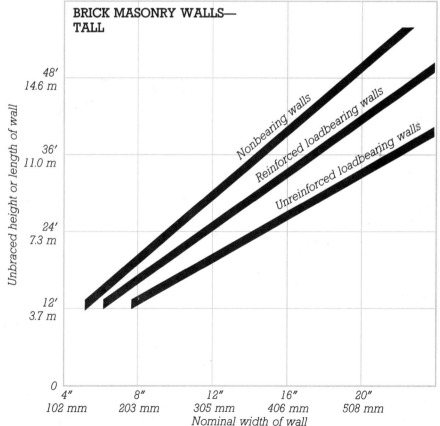

BRICK MASONRY WALLS—TALL

Unbraced height or length of wall

- 48' / 14.6 m
- 36' / 11.0 m
- 24' / 7.3 m
- 12' / 3.7 m
- 0

Nonbearing walls

Reinforced loadbearing walls

Unreinforced loadbearing walls

Nominal width of wall

- 4" / 102 mm
- 8" / 203 mm
- 12" / 305 mm
- 16" / 406 mm
- 20" / 508 mm

The top chart is for reinforced brick masonry loadbearing walls up to 12 ft (3.7 m) in height between floors. For light loads or high-strength bricks, read toward the top in the indicated area. For high loads or low-strength bricks, read toward the bottom.

■ For unreinforced walls, increase the indicated wall thickness by 25%. Unreinforced bearing walls less than 12 in. (305 mm) thick are recommended for low-rise residential construction only.

■ Nominal wall thickness may be any even number of inches. Actual wall thickness is equal to nominal thickness less ½ in. (13 mm).

■ *Total loaded width* is one-half the span of one floor supported by the wall multiplied by the number of floors and roof above the wall.

The bottom chart is for bearing walls taller than 12 ft (3.7 m) between floors and for all nonbearing walls. Read along the solid line for the appropriate wall type. For tall bearing walls, use the larger of the sizes indicated by both charts on this page. For nonbearing walls, refer to this chart only.

■ *Unbraced height or length of wall* is the vertical distance between floors or the horizontal distance between pilasters or crosswalls, whichever is less. (See the illustration on the facing page.)

STEEL ANGLE LINTELS

The chart below is for steel angle lintels. The spans indicated are for lintels carrying wall loads only. Heavier structural shapes, such as channels or wide flange sections combined with plates, may be used where longer spans or greater load capacities are required.

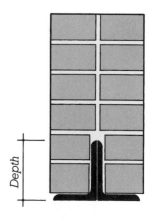

Depth of Angle	Maximum Span
3" (76 mm)	5' (1.5 m)
4" (102 mm)	6' (1.8 m)
5" (127 mm)	7' (2.1 m)
6" (152 mm)	8' (2.4 m)

FIRE-RESISTANCE RATINGS FOR BRICK MASONRY LINTELS

Brick masonry lintels not less than 8 in. (203 mm) in nominal dimension may be assumed to have a fire-resistance rating of 3 hours.

BRICK MASONRY LINTELS

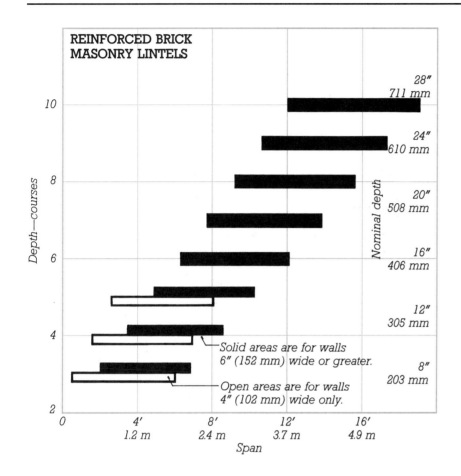

REINFORCED BRICK
MASONRY LINTELS

Depth—courses

Nominal depth

28″
711 mm

24″
610 mm

20″
508 mm

16″
406 mm

12″
305 mm

8″
203 mm

*Solid areas are for walls
6″ (152 mm) wide or greater.*

*Open areas are for walls
4″ (102 mm) wide only.*

Span

0   4′   8′   12′   16′
     1.2 m   2.4 m   3.7 m   4.9 m

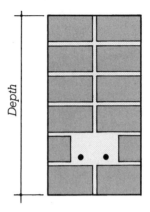

Depth

This chart is for steel reinforced brick masonry lintels. For lintels carrying only wall loads, read toward the right in the indicated areas. For additional superimposed loads, such as floor loads, read toward the left. For most applications, lintel depths of 4 to 7 courses are sufficient.

■ Depths for this chart are based on modular brick coursing: 3 courses = 8 in. (203 mm). For other sizes, read depths in inches from the right-hand scale, and round up to a whole course height.

■ Actual depth is the thickness of one mortar joint less than the nominal depth (approximately $\frac{1}{2}$ in., or 13 mm).

BRICK MASONRY ARCHES

MINOR BRICK ARCHES

The following rules apply to arches with spans of up to 6 to 8 ft (1.8 to 2.4 m): Almost any shape of arch will work at these spans, particularly when the arch is embedded in a wall. Depths of arches typically range from 4 to 16 in. (102 to 406 mm). Thicknesses of minor arches should be at least 4 to 8 in. (102 to 203 mm). Concentrated loads bearing directly on minor brick arches, especially jack arches, should be avoided. The thrusts produced by any arch must be resisted at its supports. This resistance can be provided by buttressing from an adjacent arch or an adjacent mass of masonry, or by an arch tie.

Segmental arches are most efficient when the rise of the arch is between 0.08 and 0.15 times the span of the arch.

Apply the following rules for jack arches:

Camber	Depth	Skewback
⅛" per foot of span (1:100)	8" (203 mm) minimum	½" per foot of span for every 4" of arch depth (40 mm per meter of span for every 100 mm of arch depth)

MAJOR BRICK ARCHES

Major brick arches can span to approximately 250 ft (75 m). Parabolic shapes are recommended for long span arches. The most efficient rise is approximately 0.20 to 0.25 times the span of the arch.

FIRE-RESISTANCE RATINGS FOR BRICK MASONRY ARCHES

Brick masonry arches not less than 8 in. (203 mm) in nominal dimension may be assumed to have a fire-resistance rating of 3 hours.

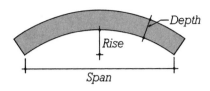

SEGMENTAL ARCH

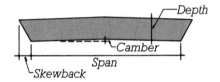

JACK ARCH

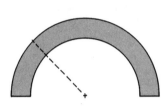

SEMICIRCULAR ARCH

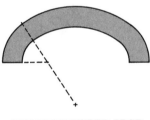

MULTI-CENTERED ARCH

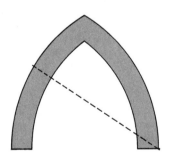

POINTED ARCH

PARABOLIC ARCH

CONCRETE BLOCK COLUMNS

RECTANGULAR COLUMNS

For the design of rectangular columns or pilasters, read from the top chart on the facing page using a square column of equivalent area. For columns or pilasters over 12 ft. (3.7 m) tall, read from the bottom chart using the lesser dimension for a column, the greater dimension for a pilaster.

   The ratio of the widths of two sides of a column or pilaster should not exceed 3:1.

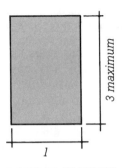

RECTANGULAR COLUMNS

FIRE-RESISTANCE RATINGS OF CONCRETE BLOCK COLUMNS

The fire resistance of concrete masonry units varies with the composition and type of unit. For preliminary design, columns at least 12 in. (305 mm) square may be assumed to have a 4-hour fire-resistance rating.

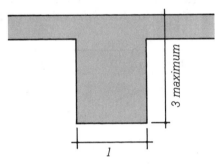

RECTANGULAR PILASTERS

CONCRETE BLOCK COLUMNS

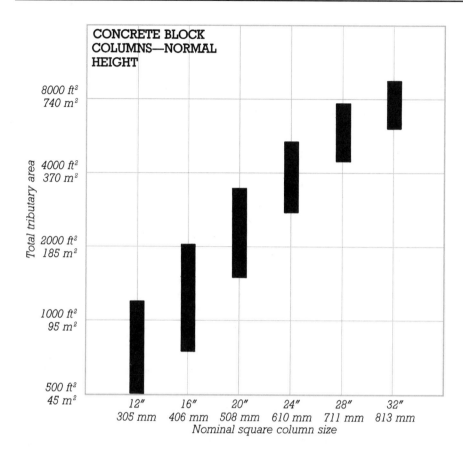

CONCRETE BLOCK COLUMNS—NORMAL HEIGHT

Total tributary area

- 8000 ft² / 740 m²
- 4000 ft² / 370 m²
- 2000 ft² / 185 m²
- 1000 ft² / 95 m²
- 500 ft² / 45 m²

Nominal square column size:
- 12" / 305 mm
- 16" / 406 mm
- 20" / 508 mm
- 24" / 610 mm
- 28" / 711 mm
- 32" / 813 mm

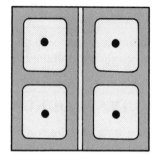

The top chart is for reinforced concrete block columns or pilasters up to 12 ft (3.7 m) in height between floors. For low loads or high-strength blocks, read toward the top in the indicated areas. For high loads or low-strength blocks, read toward the bottom.

■ For unreinforced solid masonry, increase the indicated column size by 50%.

■ Columns less than 12 in. (305 mm) square are not permitted, except for the support of minor loads.

■ Actual column size is equal to nominal size less $\frac{3}{8}$ in. (10 mm).

■ *Total tributary area* is the total area of roofs and floors supported by the column.

The bottom chart is for columns with unbraced heights greater than 12 ft (3.7 m). Read along the solid line for the appropriate type. Use the larger of the two sizes indicated by both charts on this page.

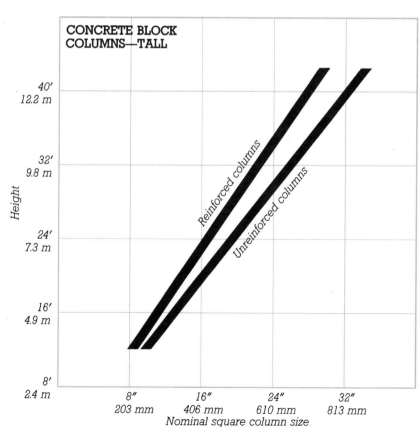

CONCRETE BLOCK COLUMNS—TALL

Height

- 40' / 12.2 m
- 32' / 9.8 m
- 24' / 7.3 m
- 16' / 4.9 m
- 8' / 2.4 m

Reinforced columns

Unreinforced columns

Nominal square column size:
- 8" / 203 mm
- 16" / 406 mm
- 24" / 610 mm
- 32" / 813 mm

CONCRETE BLOCK WALLS

CAVITY WALLS

For cavity walls, use only the net width of the structural wythe when reading the charts on the facing page.

MASONRY BEARING WALLS

Concrete masonry bearing walls are commonly used for low-rise structures and in high-rise structures of up to approximately 20 stories in height. The cellular nature of high-rise bearing wall configurations makes this system well suited to building types such as apartments, hotels, dormitories, etc. In all but the smallest structures, masonry walls should be steel reinforced.

For structures of up to approximately 6 stories in height, the interior crosswalls and corridor walls typical of masonry structures are usually sufficient to provide the required lateral bracing for the structure. This permits the design of the exterior walls to remain relatively open. At greater heights, lateral stability requirements will increasingly dictate a more complete cellular configuration of walls, and the sizes and distribution of openings in the exterior walls may be more restricted.

Loadbearing walls should be aligned consistently from floor to floor and be continuous from the roof to the building foundation. Where it is desirable to omit walls on a lower floor, it may be possible to design the wall above to act as a deep beam spanning between columns at each end. Such wall-beams may span 20 to 30 ft (6 to 9 m).

WALL PILASTERS

Pilasters are used both to carry concentrated vertical loads and to brace a wall against lateral forces and buckling. When designing for vertical loads, locate the pilaster directly below the point of load application, and size the pilaster using the charts on pages 80–81.

Pilasters are used to brace walls laterally when the distance between other supports such as floor slabs or crosswalls is insufficient for this purpose. Use the bottom chart on the facing page to determine the maximum permissible spacing between such supports for any particular wall type and thickness. If the spacing is too great, the wall thickness may be increased, or pilasters may be added at the indicated spacing.

FIRE-RESISTANCE RATINGS FOR CONCRETE MASONRY WALLS

The fire resistance of concrete masonry walls varies with the composition and design of the masonry units themselves. For preliminary design, assume that a concrete masonry wall at least 8 in. (203 mm) thick can achieve a fire-resistance rating of 3 to 4 hours. A 2-hour rating is achieved at a thickness of 6 in. (152 mm), a 1-hour rating at 4 in. (102 mm).

82

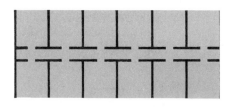

LOW-RISE BEARING WALL CONFIGURATION (*shown in plan*)

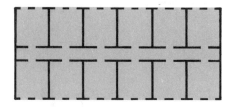

HIGH-RISE BEARING WALL CONFIGURATION (*shown in plan*)

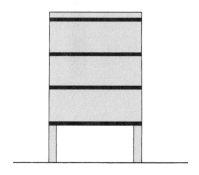

Bearing walls may act as deep beams to span across openings below, as shown in this schematic cross section.

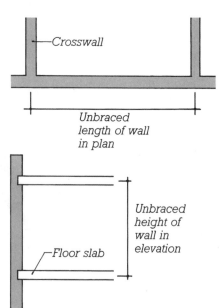

UNBRACED HEIGHT OR LENGTH OF MASONRY WALLS

CONCRETE BLOCK WALLS

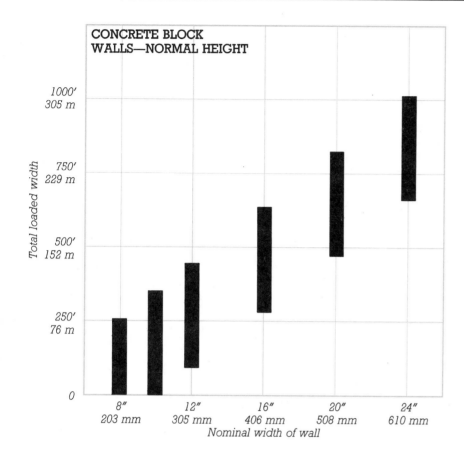

CONCRETE BLOCK WALLS—NORMAL HEIGHT

Total loaded width

- 1000' / 305 m
- 750' / 229 m
- 500' / 152 m
- 250' / 76 m
- 0

Nominal width of wall
- 8" / 203 mm
- 12" / 305 mm
- 16" / 406 mm
- 20" / 508 mm
- 24" / 610 mm

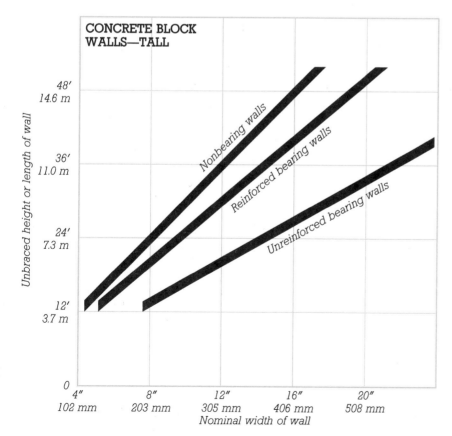

CONCRETE BLOCK WALLS—TALL

Unbraced height or length of wall

- 48' / 14.6 m
- 36' / 11.0 m
- 24' / 7.3 m
- 12' / 3.7 m
- 0

Nonbearing walls

Reinforced bearing walls

Unreinforced bearing walls

Nominal width of wall
- 4" / 102 mm
- 8" / 203 mm
- 12" / 305 mm
- 16" / 406 mm
- 20" / 508 mm

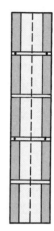

The top chart is for reinforced concrete block loadbearing walls up to 12 ft (3.7 m) in height between floors. For light loads or high-strength block, read toward the top in the solid areas. For high loads or low-strength block, read toward the bottom.

■ For unreinforced walls, increase the indicated wall thickness by 25%. Unreinforced bearing walls less than 12 in. (305 mm) thick are recommended for residential construction only.

■ Actual wall thickness is equal to nominal thickness less ⅜ in. (10 mm).

■ *Total loaded width* is one-half the span of one floor supported by the wall multiplied by the number of floors and roof above the wall.

The bottom chart is for bearing walls taller than 12 ft (3.7 m) between floors and for all nonbearing walls. Read along the solid line for the appropriate wall type. For tall bearing walls, use the larger of the sizes indicated by both charts on this page. For nonbearing walls, refer to this chart only.

■ *Unbraced height or length of wall* is the vertical distance between floors or the horizontal distance between pilasters or crosswalls, whichever is less. (See illustration on facing page.)

PRECAST CONCRETE AND STRUCTURAL STEEL LINTELS

Precast concrete lintels that are 8 in. (203 mm) deep can span up to approximately 8 ft (2.4 m). Lintels 16 in. (406 mm) deep can span up to approximately 16 ft (4.9 m).

Lintels made of combinations of steel angles can span up to approximately 8 ft (2.4 m). Greater spans are possible with heavier structural steel shapes, such as channels or wide flange sections combined with plates.

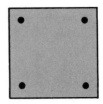

PRECAST CONCRETE LINTELS

FIRE-RESISTANCE RATINGS FOR CONCRETE BLOCK LINTELS

The fire resistance of concrete masonry construction varies with the composition and design of the masonry units themselves. For preliminary design, concrete masonry lintels not less than 8 in. (203 mm) in nominal dimension may be assumed to have a fire-resistance rating of 3 hours.

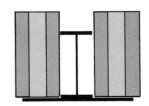

STRUCTURAL STEEL LINTELS

CONCRETE BLOCK LINTELS

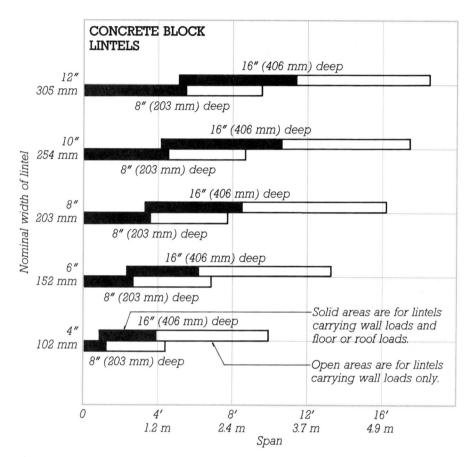

CONCRETE BLOCK LINTELS

Nominal width of lintel

12″
305 mm
16″ (406 mm) deep
8″ (203 mm) deep

10″
254 mm
16″ (406 mm) deep
8″ (203 mm) deep

8″
203 mm
16″ (406 mm) deep
8″ (203 mm) deep

6″
152 mm
16″ (406 mm) deep
8″ (203 mm) deep

4″
102 mm
16″ (406 mm) deep
8″ (203 mm) deep

Solid areas are for lintels carrying wall loads and floor or roof loads.

Open areas are for lintels carrying wall loads only.

| 0 | 4′ 1.2 m | 8′ 2.4 m | 12′ 3.7 m | 16′ 4.9 m |

Span

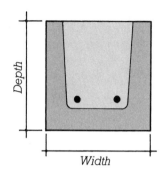

Depth

Width

This chart is for steel reinforced concrete block lintels. Open areas are for lintels carrying wall loads only. Solid areas are for lintels carrying wall loads and floor or roof loads. For light loads, read toward the right in the indicated areas. For heavy loads, read toward the left.

■ Actual sizes are equal to nominal size less ⅜ in. (10 mm).

STEEL STRUCTURAL SYSTEMS

Steel elements are of two basic types: *Structural steel* shapes are formed into their final shapes by hot-rolling. This method produces such common elements as wide flange sections, angles, channels, bars, and plates. *Lightweight steel* members are cold-formed from thin sheets or rods. Such elements include roof and floor decking and a variety of light framing members such as channels, studs, and joists.

STRUCTURAL STEEL FRAMING

Conventional hot-rolled structural steel is a versatile, strong material that has applications ranging from single-story structures to the tallest buildings. The high level of prefabrication normally used with structural steel results in a system that is precise and fast to erect.

Structural steel elements are normally configured as a post and beam frame, with other materials or systems added to make a complete building. The slab system most commonly used with structural steel framing is a sitecast concrete slab poured over corrugated steel decking. Other sitecast or precast concrete systems are also used. Steel frames can support a great variety of cladding systems, with curtain walls of steel, aluminum, glass, masonry, and stone being the most common.

Due to the rapid loss of the strength of steel at elevated temperatures, special measurements must be taken in most circumstances to protect the structural elements in a steel frame from the heat of fire. The required fire-resistive assemblies or coatings may have a significant impact on the architectural use of structural steel. See pages 304–311 for more information on the requirements for fire protection of structural steel.

LIGHTWEIGHT STEEL

Lightweight steel framing finds applications in low-rise structures where the light weight and ease of assembly of these elements are an advantage. Many of the details of this system and the sizes of the structural elements are similar to those used in Wood Light Frame construction, a system lightweight steel framing often competes with. However, the noncombustibility of steel allows this system to be used in building types where wood construction is not permitted. (See pages 310–311 and 314 for more information on building types permitted using lightweight steel framing.) The small size of the individual structural elements and the reliance on on-site fabrication and erection also make this system a good choice where buildings of irregular or unusual form are desired.

STEEL LIGHTWEIGHT WALL STUDS

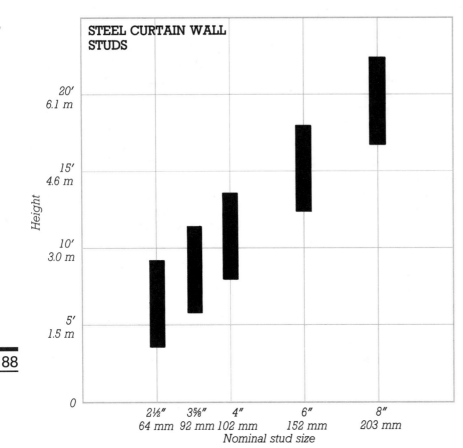

This chart is for curtain wall studs—nonbearing studs resisting wind loads only. For light loads, close stud spacings, or heavy-gauge studs, read toward the top in the indicated areas. For heavy loads, wide stud spacings, or light-gauge studs, read toward the bottom.

■ For brittle facings such as a masonry veneer which requires increased stiffness, read toward the bottom in the indicated areas.

■ Typical stud spacings are 12, 16, and 24 in. (305, 406, and 610 mm).

■ Stud widths vary from 1 to 2½ in. (25 to 64 mm) or more.

■ Actual stud size is usually equal to nominal size. Availability of sizes varies with the manufacturer.

■ Stud heights may be increased with the addition of intermediate bracing perpendicular to the wall plane.

FIRE-RESISTANCE RATINGS FOR LIGHTWEIGHT STEEL FRAMING

Lightweight steel construction may be used without fire protection in Unprotected Noncombustible construction, but this is seldom practical, because an interior surface material generally must be attached to the studs and joists to stabilize them against buckling.

Gypsum board or gypsum veneer plaster base, the most common interior finishes, can be applied in thicknesses sufficient to achieve up to a 4-hour fire-resistance rating.

STEEL LIGHTWEIGHT WALL STUDS

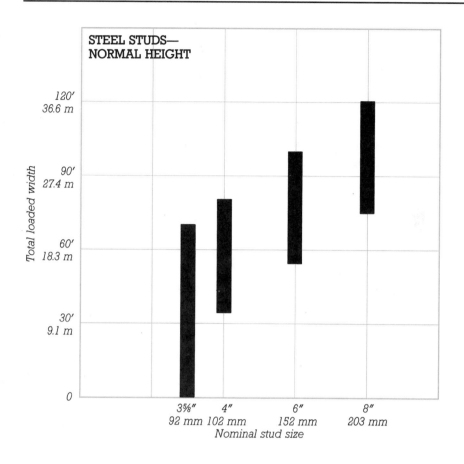

STEEL STUDS— NORMAL HEIGHT

Total loaded width

120'
36.6 m

90'
27.4 m

60'
18.3 m

30'
9.1 m

0

Nominal stud size

3⅝"
92 mm

4"
102 mm

6"
152 mm

8"
203 mm

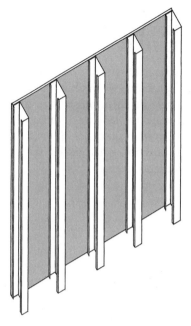

The top chart is for lightweight steel loadbearing studs up to 9 ft (2.7 m) tall between floors. For light loads, close stud spacings, or heavy-gauge studs, read toward the top in the indicated areas. For heavy loads, wide stud spacings, or light-gauge studs, read toward the bottom.

■ Typical stud spacings are 12, 16, and 24 in. (305, 406, and 610 mm).

■ Stud widths vary from 1 to 2½ in. (25 to 64 mm) or more.

■ Actual stud size is usually equal to nominal size. Availability of sizes varies with the manufacturer.

■ *Total loaded width* is the width of one floor supported by the wall multiplied by the number of floors and roof above the wall.

■ For stud walls taller than 9 ft (2.7 m) between floors, read both charts on this page. Use the larger of the two sizes indicated.

■ For light loads, close stud spacings, or heavy-gauge studs, read toward the top in the indicated areas. For heavy loads, wide stud spacings, or light-gauge studs, read toward the bottom.

■ Stud heights may be increased with the addition of intermediate bracing perpendicular to the wall plane.

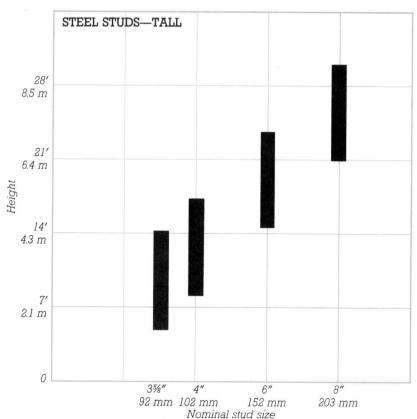

STEEL STUDS—TALL

Height

28'
8.5 m

21'
6.4 m

14'
4.3 m

7'
2.1 m

0

Nominal stud size

3⅝"
92 mm

4"
102 mm

6"
152 mm

8"
203 mm

FIRE-RESISTANCE RATINGS FOR LIGHTWEIGHT STEEL FRAMING

Lightweight steel construction may be used without fire protection in Unprotected Noncombustible construction, but this is seldom practical, because an interior surface material generally must be attached to the studs and joists to stabilize them against buckling.

Gypsum board or gypsum veneer plaster base, the most common interior finishes, can be applied in thicknesses sufficient to achieve up to a 3-hour fire-resistance rating.

STEEL LIGHTWEIGHT FLOOR JOISTS

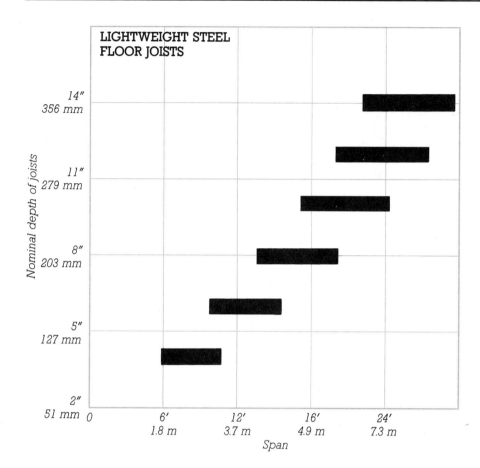

LIGHTWEIGHT STEEL FLOOR JOISTS

Nominal depth of joists:
- 14″ / 356 mm
- 11″ / 279 mm
- 8″ / 203 mm
- 5″ / 127 mm
- 2″ / 51 mm

Span:
- 0
- 6′ / 1.8 m
- 12′ / 3.7 m
- 16′ / 4.9 m
- 24′ / 7.3 m

This chart is for lightweight steel floor joists. For light loads, close joist spacings, or heavy-gauge steel, read toward the right in the indicated areas. For heavy loads, wide spacings, or light-gauge steel, read toward the left.

■ Actual size is equal to nominal size less from 0 to ¾ in. (19 mm), depending on the manufacturer.

■ Typical joist widths are 1⅝, 2, and 2½ in. (41, 51, and 64 mm).

COLUMN LAYOUT

All columns at the perimeter of a building should be oriented with their flanges facing outward to facilitate the attachment of cladding to the structural frame of the building. Elsewhere, columns should be oriented with their webs parallel to the short axis of a building whenever possible. This permits the maximum contribution from the columns to the stability of the building in the direction in which the building is most susceptible to lateral forces.

Columns above and below each other at the perimeter of a multistory building are also often aligned on their outer faces. Despite the misalignment of column centers that occurs as the column size reduces on upper floors, this arrangement is desirable for the consistent curtain-wall fastening detail that it produces.

See pages 98–99 for additional information on the sizing of column bays.

FINAL DIMENSIONS OF STEEL COLUMNS

The finish dimension of a steel column must be increased from the actual size of the section to account for applied fireproofing, protective cover or other finishes, and the added depth of connecting plates and protruding bolt heads where column sections are joined. The total finish dimension may range from 2 to 8 in. (50 to 200 mm) greater than the actual column size.

92

FIRE-RESISTANCE RATINGS FOR STEEL COLUMNS

Exposed steel columns may be used in Unprotected Noncombustible construction. Fire-resistance ratings of up to 4 hours are easily achieved with applied fireproofing.

STEEL COLUMNS

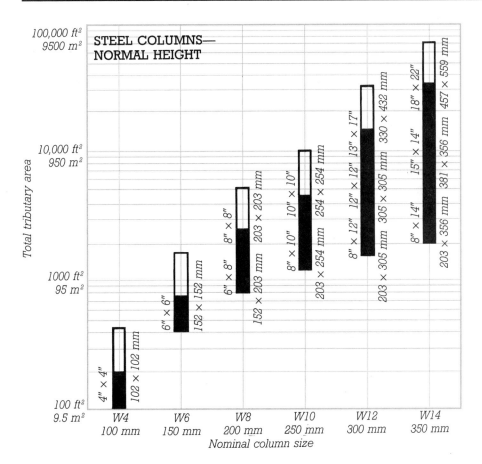

STEEL COLUMNS—
NORMAL HEIGHT

The top chart is for steel wide flange section columns up to 12 ft (3.7 m) tall between floors.

■ For normal loads, read high in the solid areas. For heavy loads, read lower in the solid areas. For light loads, read in the open areas.

■ Approximate actual column sizes are shown to the sides of the bars.

■ For high-strength (50 ksi or 345 MPa) steel columns, sizes W8 or larger, increase the indicated tributary area by 30%.

■ For columns that are at the perimeter of a building, or that are part of a rigid frame system, select one nominal column size larger than shown by this chart.

■ W14 sections are the largest standard rolled sizes commonly used as columns. Larger built-up sections capable of carrying greater loads may be shop-fabricated.

■ *Total tributary area* is the total area of roofs and floors supported by the column.

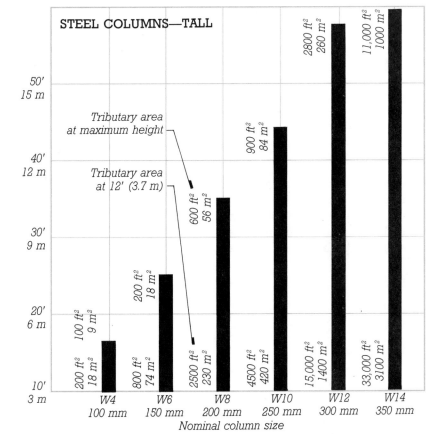

STEEL COLUMNS—TALL

The bottom chart shows the maximum height permitted for each nominal column size. The tributary areas for average loads, at the maximum height and at 12 ft (3.7 m), are shown next to the bars. (The area that can be supported decreases with increasing column height). For intermediate heights, the tributary area may be interpolated between these two values.

■ Maximum column height must be decreased for columns that are part of a rigid frame system.

■ Column height may be increased with the use of intermediate bracing or with rigid end connections that restrain buckling.

STRUCTURAL STEEL TUBING

Standard shapes for structural steel tubing include square tubes, rectangular tubes, and round pipes. Compared to wide flange sections or other shapes of similar size, tubes and pipes are more resistant to buckling forces, making them good choices for columns and compressive struts in all types of steel systems. They are employed as columns in long-span steel structures for their greater efficiency, and because they are available in lighter weights than other standard shapes, they are frequently used in one- or two-story steel structures as well. Tube and pipe sections are popular choices for use in the fabrication of steel trusses and space frames, and their high torsional resistance makes them excellent choices for single post supports such as for signs or platforms.

The simple profiles and clean appearance of steel tubes and pipes also make them popular for use where the steel may remain visible in the finished structure, or for structures exposed to the weather where the absence of moisture- and dirt-trapping profiles and ease of maintenance are desirable characteristics.

SIZES FOR STEEL TUBES AND PIPES

Tubes and pipes are generally available in whole-inch (25-mm) sizes up to 6 or 8 in. (152 or 203 mm). Greater sizes are available in even-inch (51-mm) increments.

Shape	Width of Tube or Diameter of Pipe	Thickness of Wall
Square tubes	3" × 3"–16" × 16" (76 × 76 mm–406 × 406 mm)	0.188"–0.625" (5–16 mm)
Rectangular tubes	3" × 2"–16" × 12" (76 × 51 mm–406 × 305 mm)	0.188–0.625" (5–16 mm)
Pipes	3"–12" (76–305 mm)	0.216"–0.875" (5–22 mm)

FINISH DIMENSIONS OF STEEL COLUMNS

The finish dimension of a steel column must be increased from the actual size of the section to account for applied fireproofing, protective cover or other finishes, and the added depth of connecting plates and protruding bolt heads where column sections are joined. The total finish dimension may range from 2 to 8 in. (50 to 200 mm) greater than the actual column size.

STEEL TUBE COLUMNS

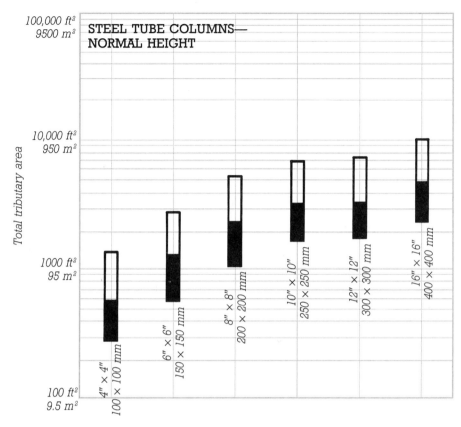

STEEL TUBE COLUMNS—
NORMAL HEIGHT

Total tributary area

100,000 ft²
9500 m²

10,000 ft²
950 m²

1000 ft²
95 m²

100 ft²
9.5 m²

4" × 4"
100 × 100 mm

6" × 6"
150 × 150 mm

8" × 8"
200 × 200 mm

10" × 10"
250 × 250 mm

12" × 12"
300 × 300 mm

16" × 16"
400 × 400 mm

Nominal column size

This chart is for square tube steel columns up to 12 ft (3.7 m) tall between floors.

■ For normal loads, read high in the solid areas. For heavy loads, read lower in the solid areas. For light loads, read in the open areas.

■ For columns at the perimeter of a building, or that are part of a rigid frame system, select one nominal column size larger than shown by this chart, or consider rectangular tubes larger in one axis only.

■ Actual column size is equal to the nominal size.

■ *Total tributary area* is the total area of roofs and floors supported by the column.

■ Tributary area will be less for taller columns.

FIRE-RESISTANCE RATINGS FOR STEEL TUBE AND PIPE COLUMNS

Exposed steel columns or other framing elements may be used in Unprotected Noncombustible construction. Fire-resistance ratings of up to 4 hours are easily achieved with applied fireproofing.

STEEL FLOOR AND ROOF DECKING

STEEL FLOOR DECKING

Corrugated steel floor decking with a sitecast concrete topping is the slab system most commonly used over structural steel framing. Typical span ranges for steel floor decking when used with structural steel framing are from 6 to 15 ft (1.8 to 4.6 m). Longer spans or shallower depths than those indicated on the chart on the facing page may be possible, although increased construction costs may result from the need for additional temporary shoring of the decking during erection.

CELLULAR FLOOR DECKING

The use of cellular decking to provide protected spaces within the floor slab for the running of electrical and communications wiring may influence the overall framing plan for the building. The layout of such a distribution system can determine the direction in which the decking cells will run in various areas of the building plan. The orientation of the beams or joists carrying the decking will be determined from this in turn, as in all cases these elements must run perpendicular to the cells in the decking. See page 187 for additional information on the planning of such systems. When reading from the chart for cellular deck on the facing page, read toward the bottom in the indicated area.

STEEL ROOF DECKING

Steel roof decking may have a sitecast concrete or gypsum topping or may be covered directly with a variety of board or roofing products. A common and economical configuration for roof decking is $1\frac{1}{2}$ in. (38-mm) decking spanning up to approximately 8 ft (2.4 m). Many proprietary metal roof decking systems, with a wide variety of performance characteristics, are also available. For information on such systems, consult individual manufacturers

FIRE-RESISTANCE RATINGS FOR STEEL DECKING

Steel roof decking without a concrete topping may be used in Unprotected Noncombustible construction.

The fire resistance of roof or floor decking with a concrete topping varies with the configuration of the decking and the thickness of the topping. Though resistance ratings of as high as 3 hours may be possible, for preliminary design, assume that decking must be protected with applied fireproofing or an appropriately fire-resistive ceiling to achieve ratings of more than 1 hour.

STEEL FLOOR AND ROOF DECKING

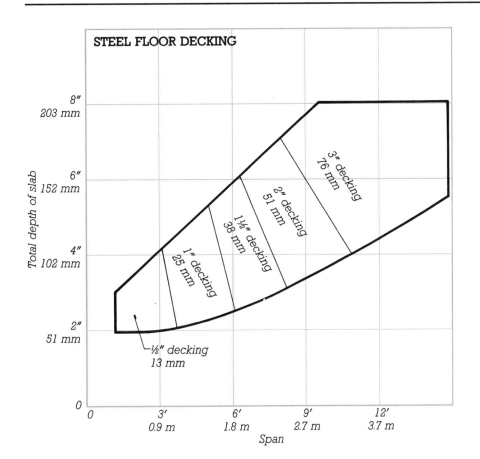

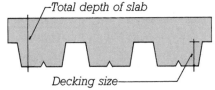

The top chart is for corrugated or cellular steel floor decking with concrete slab topping. For light loads, read toward the bottom in the indicated areas. For heavy loads, read toward the top.

■ *Total depth of slab* is the depth of the decking and the concrete topping. Approximate sizes for the steel decking alone are shown within the chart.

■ Deeper deck sections with spans of up to approximately 25 ft (7.6 m) may be available from some manufacturers.

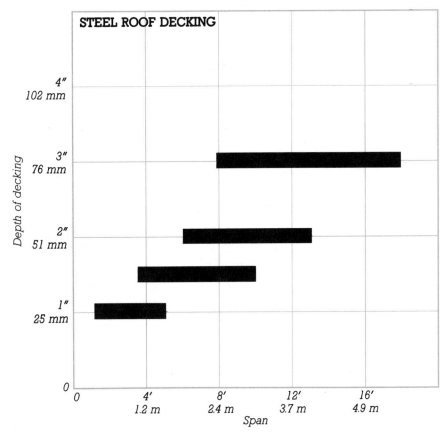

The bottom chart is for corrugated steel roof decking. For light loads, read toward the right in the indicated areas. For heavy loads, read toward the left.

■ Deeper deck sections with spans of up to approximately 25 ft (7.6 m) may be available from some manufacturers.

STEEL BEAMS AND GIRDERS

Structural steel is a versatile building material. While it can be used in a great variety of ways, consider the following guidelines for what is most economical in common practice.

FLOOR AND ROOF FRAMING

The most economical span range for conventional steel floor and roof framing is from 25 to 40 ft (8 to 12 m). Individual column bays should be approximately 1,000 square feet (95 m²) in area, and rectangular in shape, with the long side 1.25 to 1.5 times as long as the shorter side. Above spans of approximately 40 feet (12 m), consider open-web steel joists for their lighter weight and greater economy (see pages 100–101).

The spacing between individual beams depends on the applied loads and the decking system. Spacings from 6 to 15 ft (1.8 to 4.6 m) are common with corrugated steel and concrete slab decking. Spacings up to approximately 8 ft (2.4 m) are typical for roof decking systems.

BEAM AND GIRDER CONFIGURATION

The orientation of beams and girders in a floor or roof framing system may depend on a variety of factors. In relation to the building at large, it may be advantageous to run girders parallel to the building's shorter axis, the direction most susceptible to lateral forces. In this way, these stronger members can contribute additional lateral resistance to the building through rigid frame action.

Within individual column bays, it is usually more economical to run girders in the shorter direction of a rectangular bay, allowing the lighter beams to span the longer way. However, when cellular decking is used as part of a wiring system, beam and girder directions may be set so that the wire conduits within the decking run in preferred directions as required by communications or power distribution plans (see page 187).

COMPOSITE BEAMS

In composite construction, shear studs are added to the top of the floor beams. This causes the concrete deck and steel framing to act as a unified structural element and results in reduced beam depths. Composite construction can be more economical, particularly at longer spans. However, a thicker concrete deck may be required. In some cases "partial" composite design, where fewer studs are used and less than full composite action is achieved, proves to be the most economical solution.

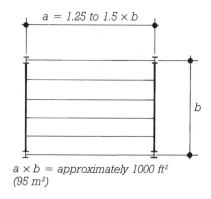

a × b = approximately 1000 ft²
(95 m²)

For economical framing of steel bays, the lighter beams should span 1.25 to 1.5 times the span of the heavier girders. Bay area should equal approximately 1000 ft² (95 m²).

STEEL BEAMS AND GIRDERS

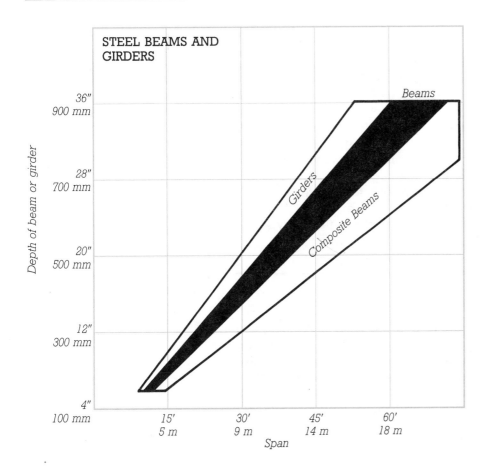

This chart is for steel wide-flange beams and girders. For average and light loads, read toward the right in the indicated areas. For heavy loads, read toward the left.

■ For beams acting as girders or as composite beams, read in the open areas indicated.

■ Beams or girders also acting as part of a rigid frame for lateral stability may be deeper than indicated by this chart.

■ Typical widths of beams and girders range from approximately one-third to one-half the depth of the member. Heavy sections used for heavy loads or to conserve depth may be wider.

■ Depths of up to 36 in. (914 mm) are available as standard rolled sections. Greater depth beams capable of longer spans may be shop fabricated.

FIRE-RESISTANCE RATINGS FOR STEEL BEAMS AND GIRDERS

Exposed steel beams and girders may be used in Unprotected Noncombustible construction. Fire-resistance ratings of as high as 4 hours are easily achieved with applied fireproofing or an appropriately fire resistive ceiling. Some building codes also allow reduced fire protection or exposed steel for roof structures that are 15 to 25 ft (4.6 to 7.6 m) or more above the floor.

OPEN-WEB JOIST FRAMING

The light weight of open-web steel joists makes them an economical alternative to conventional structural steel members for spans greater than 30 to 40 ft (9 to 12 m). Where significant concentrated loads exist, open-web joists may need to be supplemented with additional structural members.

Girders used with open-web joists may be joist girders (a heavier version of an open-web joist) or conventional structural steel members. For greater loads and spans, heavy steel trusses may also be used. For rectangular bays, the joists usually span the longer direction. (See pages 98–99 for structural steel beams and girders and pages 104–105 for heavy steel trusses.)

A variety of proprietary composite systems are also available. Such systems are particularly effective at overcoming the excessive flexibility sometimes encountered with long-span joist systems.

FIRE-RESISTANCE RATINGS
FOR OPEN-WEB STEEL JOISTS

Exposed open-web joists and joist girders may be used in Unprotected Noncombustible construction. Fire-resistance ratings of as high as 3 hours are easily achieved with applied fireproofing or an appropriately fireresistive ceiling. The fire-resistive ceiling is used more commonly, due to the difficulty of applying fireproofing directly to the complex surfaces of an open-web joist. Some building codes also permit reduced fire protection or exposed steel for roof structures that are 15 to 25 ft (4.6 to 7.6 m) or more above the floor.

STEEL OPEN-WEB JOISTS

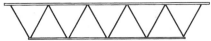

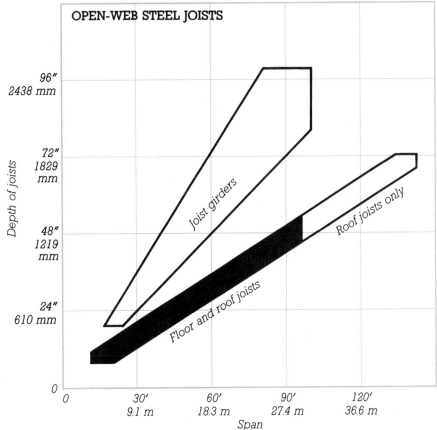

This chart is for open-web steel joists and joist girders for floors and roofs. For light loads or close joist spacings, read toward the right in the indicated areas. For heavy loads or large joist spacings, read toward the left.

■ Joist spacings range from 2 to 10 ft (0.6 to 3.0 m) or more, depending on the floor loads and the decking system applied over the joists.

■ Joists generally come in depths of 8 to 32 in. in 2-in. increments (from 203 to 813 mm in 51-mm increments) and from 32 to 72 in. in 4-in. increments (from 813 to 1829 mm in 102-mm increments). Availability of sizes varies with the manufacturer.

■ Joist girders come in depths of 20 to 96 in. in 4-in. increments (from 508 to 2438 mm in 102-mm increments).

RELATED DIMENSIONS FOR SINGLE-STORY RIGID STEEL FRAMES

For the span ranges indicated on the chart on the facing page, the following dimensions may be used:

Wall Height	Depth at Base	Roof Pitch
8'–30' (2.4–9.1 m)	7"–21" (178–533 mm)	1:12–4:12

Typical spacing of frames is 20 or 25 ft (6.1 or 7.6 m).

For variations on the rigid frame system, or for sizes outside the range of those shown in the chart, consult with individual manufacturers.

FIRE-RESISTANCE RATINGS FOR SINGLE-STORY RIGID STEEL FRAMES

Exposed steel frames may be used in Unprotected Noncombustible construction. Fire-resistance ratings of as high as 4 hours are easily achieved with applied fireproofing or an appropriately fire-resistive ceiling. Some building codes also allow reduced fire protection or exposed steel for roof structures that are 15 to 25 ft (4.6 to 7.6 m) or more above the floor.

SINGLE-STORY RIGID STEEL FRAMES

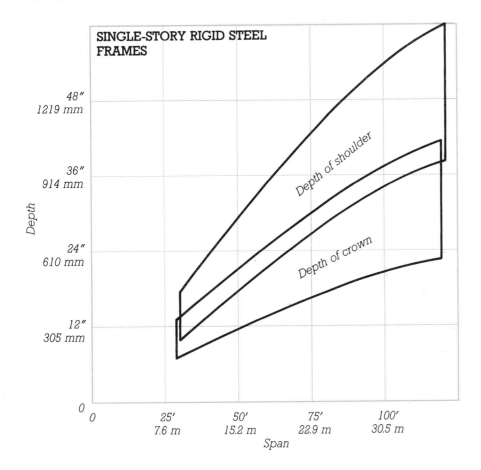

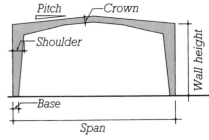

This chart is for single-story rigid steel frame structures. For heavy loads, read toward the top in the indicated areas. For light loads, read toward the bottom.

■ Spans as great as 200 ft (61.0 m) or more may be available from some manufacturers. Greater spans are also available with the use of intermediate columns.

ECONOMICAL SPAN RANGES FOR PARALLEL CHORD TRUSSES

Parallel chord trusses are most economical for spans up to 120 to 140 ft (35 to 45 m), due to the increased difficulty of shipping elements greater than 12 ft (3.7 m) deep. Triangular and bowstring trusses can be shipped at slightly greater depths. Trusses spanning 300 ft (90 m) or more may be fabricated on-site.

FIRE-RESISTANCE RATINGS FOR STEEL TRUSSES

Exposed steel trusses may be used in Unprotected Noncombustible construction. Fire-resistance ratings of as high as 4 hours are easily achieved with applied fireproofing or an appropriately fire-resistive ceiling. Some building codes also allow reduced fire protection or exposed steel for roof structures that are 15 to 25 ft (4.6 to 7.6 m) or more above the floor.

STEEL TRUSSES

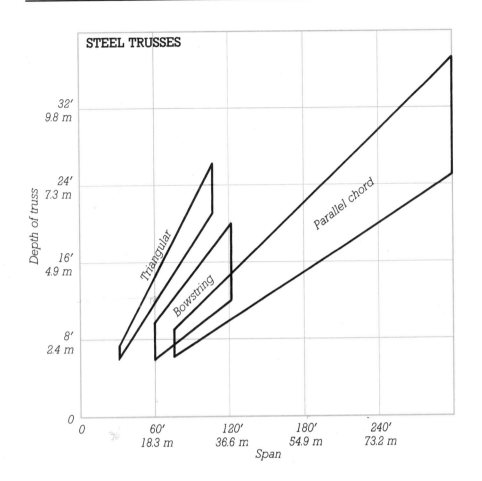

STEEL TRUSSES

Depth of truss

- 32' / 9.8 m
- 24' / 7.3 m
- 16' / 4.9 m
- 8' / 2.4 m
- 0

Triangular

Bowstring

Parallel chord

Span

- 0
- 60' / 18.3 m
- 120' / 36.6 m
- 180' / 54.9 m
- 240' / 73.2 m

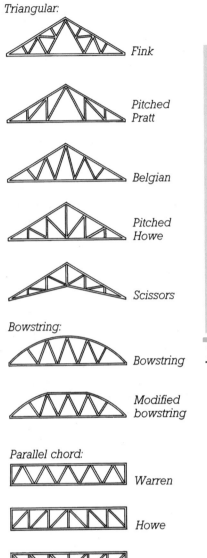

Triangular:

Fink

Pitched Pratt

Belgian

Pitched Howe

Scissors

Bowstring:

Bowstring

Modified bowstring

Parallel chord:

Warren

Howe

Pratt

This chart is for steel trusses fabricated from structural steel members. Because these trusses are custom designed and fabricated, a great variety of shapes and configurations are possible.

SITECAST CONCRETE STRUCTURAL SYSTEMS

The initial choice of a sitecast concrete framing system is most often based on the desired spans or column spacings of the structure and on the expected magnitude of the in-service loads on the building. The following systems are listed in order of increasing spans, load capacity, and cost:

- One-Way Solid Slab
- Two-Way Flat Plate
- Two-Way Flat Slab
- One-Way Joist
- Waffle Slab
- One-Way Beam and Slab
- Two-Way Beam and Slab

For short-span, light-load conditions, systems from the top of this list are the most economical. For long spans and heavy loads, systems from the bottom of the list may be required.

POSTTENSIONING

The span ranges of sitecast concrete systems can be increased by the use of posttensioned reinforcing. Charts for the sizing of posttensioned systems are included in this section. Posttensioning also substantially reduces the depth of spanning members and may be desirable where total floor-to-floor heights must be kept to a minimum. The extensive use of posttensioning in a concrete structure may limit the ease with which such a structure can be modified in the future, since penetrations in slabs and beams must not interrupt the continuity of the reinforcing or surrounding concrete. This may make posttensioning an undesirable choice for buildings where significant change in program or structure must be anticipated.

ARCHITECTURAL SITECAST CONCRETE CONSTRUCTION

The inherent fire-resistive qualities of concrete construction allow concrete systems to remain wholly or partially exposed in a finished building. Furthermore, the process by which concrete is formed on-site and its monolithic and plastic qualities as a finished product give this material unique architectural potential. For these reasons, the choice of a concrete framing system may have significant architectural implications that should be considered early in the design process. Factors to consider in the architectural use of sitecast concrete include the added cost and difficulty of achieving acceptable levels of finish quality and dimensional accuracy with exposed concrete, the ease of integrating building mechanical and electrical services into the exposed structure, and the potential aesthetic qualities of the various construction elements and systems. If an extensive use of architectural concrete is being considered for a project, the necessary consultants should be sought out at the earliest possible time, as the use of architectural concrete will have a major impact on the design and construction of the building.

CONCRETE STRENGTH AND COLUMN SIZE

The top chart on the facing page is based on a concrete strength of 5000 psi (35 MPa). Higher-strength concretes may be used to reduce the required column size. For other concrete strengths, multiply the indicated column size by the amount in the table to the right.

Concrete Strength		Multiply Column Size by
3000 psi	(21 MPa)	1.20
7000 psi	(48MPa)	0.95
9000 psi	(62 MPa)	0.80
11,000 psi	(76 MPa)	0.75

COLUMN SIZE AND CONCRETE SLAB SYSTEMS

For the two-way slab systems in the table to the right, column size may be limited by the depth of the slab. For further information see the pages indicated.

Systems	Pages
Sitecast Concrete Two-Way Flat Plate	118–119
Sitecast Concrete Two-Way Flat Slab	120–121
Sitecast Concrete Waffle Slab	122–123

ECONOMICAL CONCRETE COLUMN DESIGN

Column sizes should change as little as possible throughout a building. Column strength can be varied where required by changing the strength of the concrete mix or by adjusting the amount of steel reinforcing. Where size increases cannot be avoided, increasing only one dimension of a column at a time, in even 2-in. (50-mm) increments, is usually preferred.

Column locations should be continuous to the building foundation. Where columns on floors above cannot be supported directly below, large transfer beams are required.

Column placements should be as uniform and ordered as possible. Irregular column placements prevent the use of the most economical forming methods. Rectangular or square columns should conform to standard orthogonal alignments. Deviations from the normal complicate formwork where the column and the slab meet. See the diagrams to the right.

VARIATIONS IN COLUMN SIZE

FIRE-RESISTANCE RATINGS FOR SITECAST CONCRETE COLUMNS

Fire-resistance ratings for concrete construction vary with the type and density of concrete used. Use the following guidelines for preliminary design:

To achieve a 4-hour rating, a concrete column must be at least 14 in. (356 mm) in minimum dimension. For a 3-hour rating, the minimum dimension is 12 in. (305 mm). For 2 hours, a column must be at least 10 in. (254 mm) on a side, and for 1 hour, 8 in. (203 mm).

VARIATIONS IN COLUMN PLACEMENTS

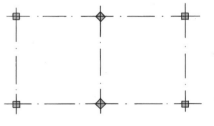

VARIATIONS IN COLUMN ALIGNMENTS

SITECAST CONCRETE COLUMNS

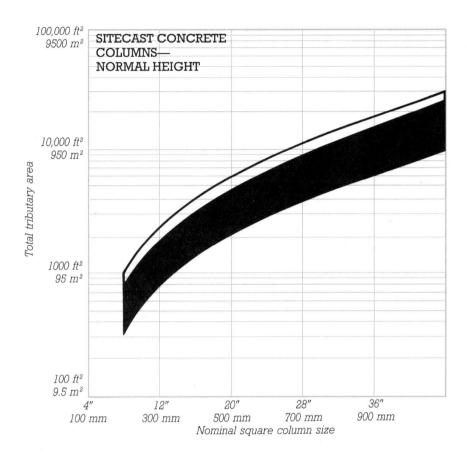

SITECAST CONCRETE
COLUMNS—
NORMAL HEIGHT

Total tributary area

100,000 ft²
9500 m²

10,000 ft²
950 m²

1000 ft²
95 m²

100 ft²
9.5 m²

4"
100 mm

12"
300 mm

20"
500 mm

28"
700 mm

36"
900 mm

Nominal square column size

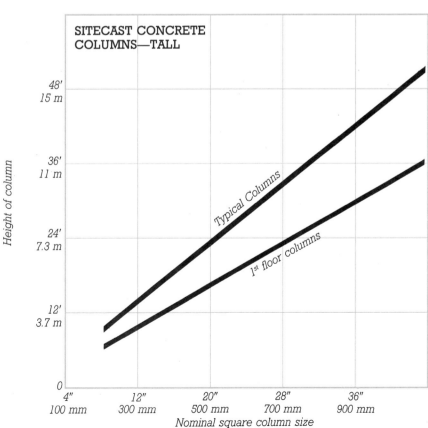

SITECAST CONCRETE
COLUMNS—TALL

Height of column

Typical Columns

1st floor columns

48'
15 m

36'
11 m

24'
7.3 m

12'
3.7 m

0

4"
100 mm

12"
300 mm

20"
500 mm

28"
700 mm

36"
900 mm

Nominal square column size

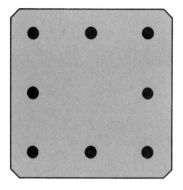

The top chart is for sitecast concrete columns up to 12 ft (3.7 m) tall. For normal loads, read toward the top in the solid area. For heavy loads, read toward the bottom. For light loads, read in the open area.

■ Measure the height of the column from the top of the floor below to the underside of the beam or slab above (not floor-to-floor).

■ For rectangular columns, select a column of equal area. For round columns, use a column diameter 25% greater than the square size.

■ For columns that are located at the perimeter of a building or that are part of a rigid frame system, read toward the bottom in the solid area.

■ Actual column size is equal to the nominal column size less ½ in. (13 mm).

■ *Total tributary area* is the total area of roofs and floors supported by the column.

The bottom chart is for columns with unbraced heights greater than 12 ft (3.7 m). Use the larger of two sizes indicated by both charts on this page. For typical columns, read on the upper curve. For columns at the first floor of a building, where the lower ends are unrestrained, read on the lower curve.

■ For rectangular columns, read from this chart using the least dimension of the column. For round columns, read from this chart using the column diameter and reduce the indicated height by 15%.

SITECAST CONCRETE WALLS

Sitecast concrete bearing walls may be used as the primary loadbearing element in a structural system or may be an integrated part of many other systems. Some of the most common uses for concrete walls include construction below grade, building structural cores, and shear walls in steel or concrete frame construction.

ECONOMICAL DESIGN OF SITECAST CONCRETE WALLS

Vary wall thicknesses as little as possible. Where necessary, changes in thickness should be in 2- or 4-in. (50- or 100-mm) increments.

Loadbearing wall locations should be consistent from floor to floor and continuous to the building foundation. Where it is desirable to omit bearing walls on a lower floor, an economical alternative may be to design the wall above to act as a deep beam spanning between columns at each end. The space between the columns may then remain open. Such wall-beams may economically span up to 20 to 30 ft (6 to 9 m).

Concrete building cores should be symmetrical and rectilinear in shape and should vary as little as possible in shape or size from floor to floor. The locations and sizes of openings in core walls and the floor should also be as consistent as possible. See pages 170–184 for additional information on the design of building cores.

The use of pilasters should be avoided. Where required, they should be regularly spaced and of consistent, standard dimensions.

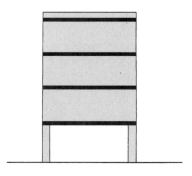

Bearing walls may act as deep beams to span across openings below.

FIRE-RESISTANCE RATINGS FOR SITECAST CONCRETE WALLS

Fire-resistance ratings for concrete construction vary with the type and density of concrete used. Use the following guidelines for preliminary design:

For a fire-resistance rating of 4 hours, sitecast concrete loadbearing walls must be at least 6.5 in. (165 mm) thick. A 3-hour rating is achieved at a thickness of 6 in. (152 mm), a 2-hour rating at 5 in. (127 mm), and a 1-hour rating at 3.5 in. (89 mm).

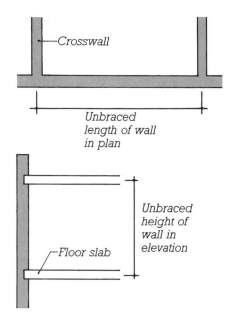

UNBRACED HEIGHT OR LENGTH OF CONCRETE WALLS

SITECAST CONCRETE WALLS

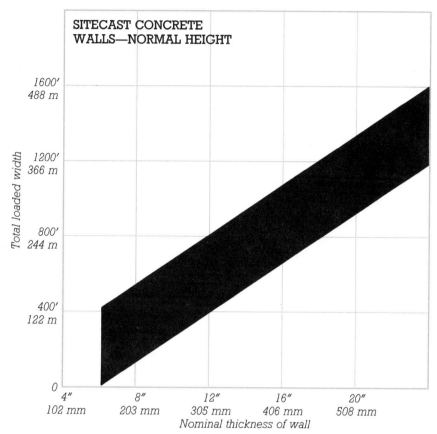

SITECAST CONCRETE WALLS—NORMAL HEIGHT

Total loaded width

1600'
488 m

1200'
366 m

800'
244 m

400'
122 m

0

4"
102 mm

8"
203 mm

12"
305 mm

16"
406 mm

20"
508 mm

Nominal thickness of wall

The top chart is for concrete load-bearing walls up to 12 ft (3.7 m) in height between floors. For normal loads, read toward the top in the indicated area. For high loads, read toward the bottom.

■ Actual wall thickness is equal to the nominal thickness less ½ in. (13 mm).

■ *Total loaded width* is one-half the span of one floor supported by the wall multiplied by the number of floors and roof above the wall.

The bottom chart is for bearing walls taller than 12 ft (3.7 m) between floors and for nonbearing walls. Read along the solid line for the appropriate wall type. For tall bearing walls, use the larger of the sizes indicated by both charts on this page. For nonbearing walls, refer to this chart only.

■ *Unbraced height or length of wall* is the vertical distance between floors or the horizontal distance between pilasters or crosswalls, whichever is less. (See the lower diagram on the facing page.)

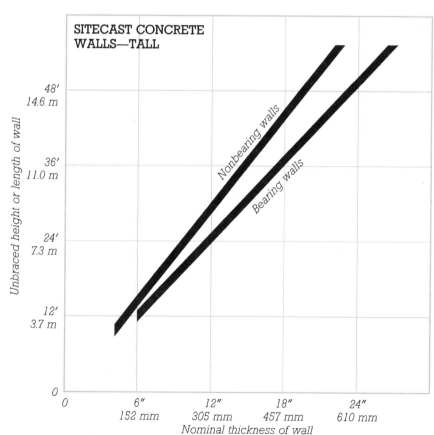

SITECAST CONCRETE WALLS—TALL

Unbraced height or length of wall

48'
14.6 m

36'
11.0 m

24'
7.3 m

12'
3.7 m

0

Nonbearing walls

Bearing walls

0

6"
152 mm

12"
305 mm

18"
457 mm

24"
610 mm

Nominal thickness of wall

ECONOMICAL BEAM DESIGN

Vary the sizes of beams throughout the building as little as possible. Size the beam with the longest span, using the chart on the facing page. Beams with shorter spans can often be the same size with reduced reinforcement.

Use beam widths equal to or greater than the widths of the columns supporting them.

In some systems an economical alternative to conventionally sized beams and girders are wide, shallow beams called either slab bands (for solid slab construction), or joist bands (for one-way joist construction). Savings in total floor-to-floor heights are possible with the reduced beam depths, and formwork costs are reduced. The depth of the slab itself may be reduced as well, since with the broader beams, the span of the slab between beams is lessened. See pages 114–115 for slab bands and pages 116–117 for joist bands.

FIRE-RESISTANCE RATINGS FOR
SITECAST CONCRETE BEAMS AND GIRDERS

Fire-resistance ratings for concrete beams and girders vary with the type and density of concrete used, as well as with the proximity of the steel reinforcing to the surface of the beam. Use the following guidelines for preliminary design:

Concrete beams and girders with a minimum width of 9.5 in. (241 mm) may have a fire-resistance rating of up to 4 hours.

SITECAST CONCRETE BEAMS AND GIRDERS

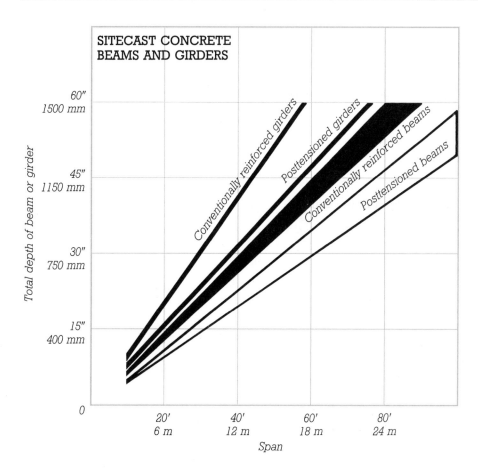

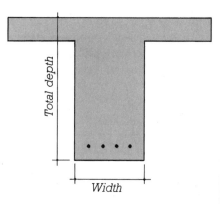

This chart is for sitecast concrete beams and girders, either conventionally reinforced or posttensioned. For lightly to moderately loaded beams, read toward the right in the indicated areas. For heavy loads or simple spans, read toward the left.

■ For girders, read on the lines indicated.

■ Size beam depths in even 2-in. (50 mm) increments.

■ *Total depth of beam or girder* is measured from the bottom of the beam to the top of the slab.

■ Normal beam widths range from one-third to one-half of the beam depth. Use beam widths in multiples of 2 or 3 in. (50 or 75 mm).

SITECAST CONCRETE ONE-WAY SOLID SLAB

One-way solid slab construction supported by bearing walls is the least expensive sitecast concrete framing system for short spans and light loads. It is a popular concrete system for multiple dwelling building types such as apartments or hotels, where the regular spacing of bearing walls is easily coordinated with the layout of the small, uniformly arranged rooms typical of these buildings.

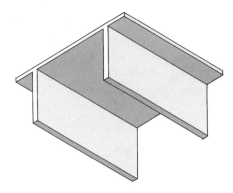

ONE-WAY SOLID SLAB WITH BEARING WALLS

ONE-WAY BEAM AND SLAB SYSTEMS

The addition of beams and girders to one-way solid slab construction can increase the load capacity and span range of the system and eliminate the need for regularly spaced walls in the building plan. The increased complexity of a beam and girder system, however, makes this one of the most expensive of all sitecast concrete systems to construct. One-way beam and slab construction is usually economical only where long spans or high loads must be accommodated, such as with industrial uses or in areas of high seismic risk.

Slab bands can be an economical alternative to conventional deeper beams when beams are used. Savings in total floor-to-floor heights are possible with the reduced beam depths, and formwork costs are reduced. The depth of the slab itself may be reduced as well, since with the broader beams, the span of the slab between the beams is lessened.

Maximum repetition of standard sizes increases the economy of slab and beam systems. Wherever possible, beam depths should be sized for the longest spans, and then the same depths should be used throughout. Beam widths and spacings, slab depths, and column sizes and spacings should also vary as little as possible within the structure.

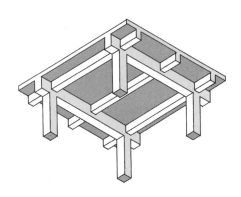

ONE-WAY SOLID SLAB WITH BEAMS

FIRE-RESISTANCE RATINGS FOR ONE-WAY SOLID SLAB CONSTRUCTION

Fire-resistance ratings for concrete construction vary with the type and density of concrete used. Use the following guidelines for preliminary design:

To achieve a 3-hour fire-resistance rating, a solid slab must be at least 6.5 in. (165 mm) thick. For a 2-hour rating, the minimum thickness is 5 in. (127 mm), for 1½ hours, 4.5 in. (114 mm), and for 1 hour, 3.5 in. (89 mm).

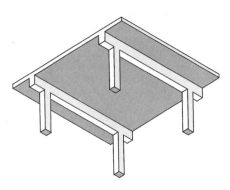

ONE-WAY SOLID SLAB WITH BEAMS AND GIRDERS

114

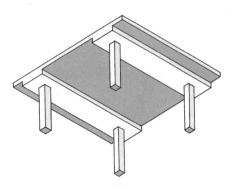

ONE-WAY SOLID SLAB WITH SLAB BANDS

SITECAST CONCRETE ONE-WAY SOLID SLAB

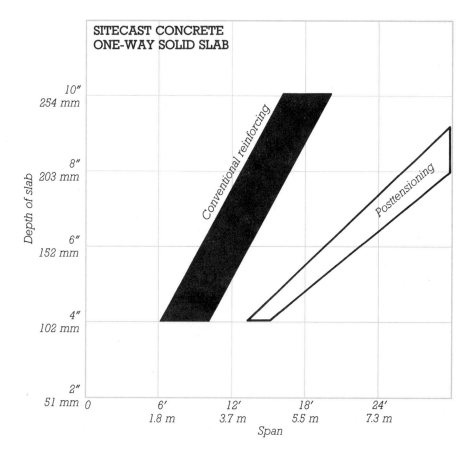

SITECAST CONCRETE ONE-WAY SOLID SLAB

Depth of slab — Conventional reinforcing / Posttensioning

Span

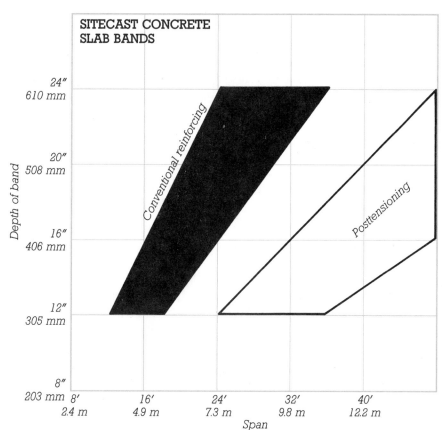

SITECAST CONCRETE SLAB BANDS

Depth of band — Conventional reinforcing / Posttensioning

Span

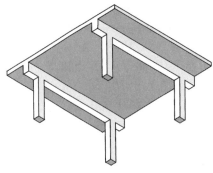

The top chart is for sitecast concrete one-way solid slab construction, either conventionally reinforced or posttensioned. For light to medium loads, read toward the right in the indicated areas. For heavy loads, read toward the left.

■ Size slab depth up to the nearest ½ in. (10 mm).

■ For the sizing of concrete beams, see pages 112–113.

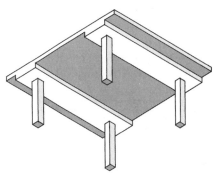

The bottom chart is for concrete slab bands—deep, wide beams that can be used with one-way solid slab construction. For light loads, read toward the right in the indicated areas. For heavy loads, read toward the left.

■ Size beam depths to the nearest inch (25 mm) and widths to the nearest foot (300 mm).

■ Typical widths for slab bands range from one-sixth to one-third of the span of the slab between the beams. For slab bands that are relatively deep or that span short distances, choose a narrow width. For those that are relatively shallow or that span long distances, choose a wide width.

SITECAST CONCRETE ONE-WAY JOISTS

One-way joist construction is an economical system for heavy loads or relatively long spans. This system is also sometimes desirable for the distinctive appearance of the underside of the slab, which may be left exposed in finished construction.

JOIST LAYOUT

The spacing of joists depends on the widths of the pans and the joists. Standard pan widths are 20 and 30 in. (508 and 762 mm). Joists typically range in width from 5 to 9 in. (127 to 229 mm). A 6-in. (152-mm) wide joist may be assumed for preliminary purposes.

In medium- and light-load applications, alternate joists may be omitted for greater economy. This system, called wide module or skip joist construction, is economical for spans of up to approximately 40 ft (12 m). In some instances, joist spacing may be increased to as much as 9 ft (2.7 m).

In long-span or heavy-load applications, joists may be broadened 2 to 2½ in. (50 to 65 mm) over the last 3 ft (1 m) toward their ends for increased capacity.

For joist spans of greater than 20 ft (6.1 m), distribution ribs running perpendicular to the joists are required. These ribs are 4 in. (102 mm) wide and the same depth as the joists. For longer spans, allow a maximum of 15 ft (4.6 m) between evenly spaced lines of ribs.

The economy of this system depends on the maximum repetition of standard forms and sizes. Depths, thicknesses, and spacings should vary as little as possible.

JOIST BANDS

The use of joist bands the same depth as the joists is a highly economical alternative to conventional deeper beams. This system reduces building height, speeds construction, and simplifies the installation of building utilities. In some instances it may even prove economical to use a joist system deeper than otherwise necessary in order to match the required depth of the joist bands.

With rectangular column bays and normal to heavy loads, joist bands should usually run in the shorter direction.

FIRE-RESISTANCE RATINGS FOR ONE-WAY JOIST CONSTRUCTION

Fire resistance ratings for concrete construction vary with the type and density of concrete used. Use the following guidelines for preliminary design:

A slab that is 3 in. (76 mm) deep between joists has a fire-resistance rating of from 0 to 1½ hours. A 4½-in. (114-mm) deep slab provides from 1½ to 3 hours of fire protection. For higher fire-resistance ratings, the slab thickness may be increased, fireproofing materials may be applied to the underside of the joists and slab, or an appropriately fire-resistive ceiling may be used.

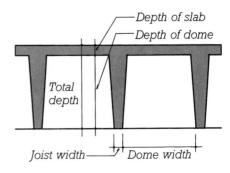

ONE-WAY JOISTS

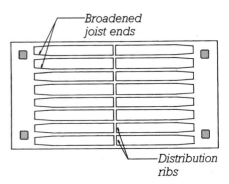

Joist bands usually run the shorter direction in rectangular bays.

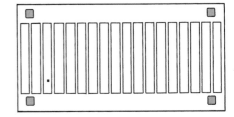

With light loads, it may be more economical to run joist bands in the long direction in a rectangular bay.

SITECAST CONCRETE ONE-WAY JOISTS

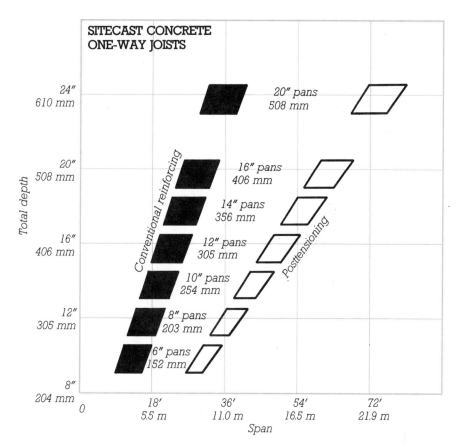

SITECAST CONCRETE ONE-WAY JOISTS

Total depth / Span

- 24″ / 610 mm
- 20″ / 508 mm
- 16″ / 406 mm
- 12″ / 305 mm
- 8″ / 204 mm

Conventional reinforcing

Posttensioning

- 20″ pans / 508 mm
- 16″ pans / 406 mm
- 14″ pans / 356 mm
- 12″ pans / 305 mm
- 10″ pans / 254 mm
- 8″ pans / 203 mm
- 6″ pans / 152 mm

Span: 0 — 18′ / 5.5 m — 36′ / 11.0 m — 54′ / 16.5 m — 72′ / 21.9 m

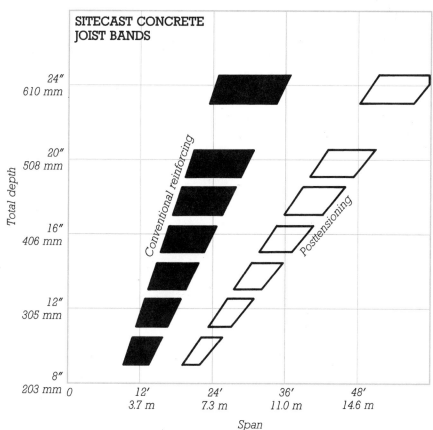

SITECAST CONCRETE JOIST BANDS

Total depth / Span

- 24″ / 610 mm
- 20″ / 508 mm
- 16″ / 406 mm
- 12″ / 305 mm
- 8″ / 203 mm

Conventional reinforcing

Posttensioning

Span: 0 — 12′ / 3.7 m — 24′ / 7.3 m — 36′ / 11.0 m — 48′ / 14.6 m

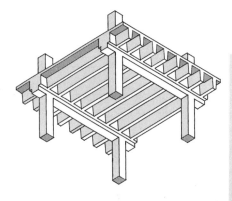

The top chart is for sitecast concrete one-way joist construction, either conventionally reinforced or posttensioned. For light loads, read toward the right in the indicated areas. For heavy loads, read toward the left.

■ *Total depth* is measured from the bottom of the joist to the top of the slab. (See the diagram on the facing page.) Depths are indicated on the chart for slabs of 3 to 4½ in. (76 to 114 mm) deep with standard pan sizes. The choice of the slab depth usually depends on the required fire-resistance rating for the system.

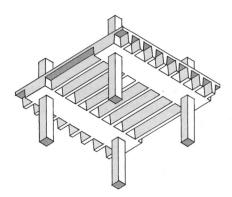

The bottom chart is for concrete joist bands—deep, wide beams used with the one-way joist system. For light loads, read toward the right in the indicated areas. For heavy loads, read toward the left.

■ For economy of form, use a joist band of the same depth as the joists.

■ Typical widths for joist bands range from ito 6 ft (0.3 to 1.8 m).

SITECAST CONCRETE TWO-WAY FLAT PLATE

Two-way flat plate construction is one of the most economical concrete framing systems. This system can span farther than one-way slabs, and the plain form of the slab makes it simple to construct and easy to finish. This system is commonly used in apartment and hotel construction, where it is well suited to the moderate live loads, it is economical to construct, and the flexibility of its column placements permits greater ease of unit planning and layout.

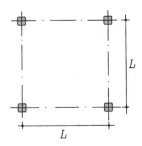

SQUARE BAYS

COLUMN LAYOUTS FOR FLAT PLATE CONSTRUCTION

For maximum economy and efficiency of the two-way structural system, the following guidelines on column placement should be followed whenever possible:

Column bays are most efficient when square or close to square. When rectangular bays are used, the sides of the bays should differ in length by a ratio of no more than 2:1.

Individual columns may be offset by as much as one-tenth of the span from regular column lines. (Columns on floors above and below an offset column must also be equally offset to maintain a vertical alignment of columns.)

Successive span lengths should not differ by more than one-third of the longer span. Slabs should also span over at least three bays in each direction.

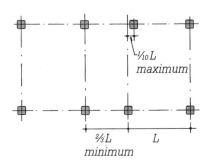

RECTANGULAR BAYS

TWO-WAY SLAB AND BEAM CONSTRUCTION

Two-way slab and beam construction uses beams to support the slab between columns. The high construction costs of this system make it economical only for long spans and heavy loads, such as in heavy industrial applications, or where high resistance to lateral forces is required. For preliminary sizing of slab depths, read from the area for posttensioned construction in the chart on the facing page.

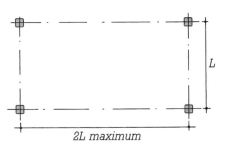

COLUMN OFFSETS AND BAY SIZE VARIATIONS

FIRE-RESISTANCE RATINGS FOR TWO-WAY FLAT PLATE CONSTRUCTION

Fire-resistance ratings for concrete construction vary with the type and density of concrete used. Use the following guidelines for preliminary design:

To achieve a 3-hour fire-resistance rating, the slab must be at least 6.5 in. (165 mm) thick. For a 2-hour rating, the minimum thickness is 5 in. (127 mm), for 1½ hours, 4.5 in. (114 mm), and for 1 hour, 3.5 in. (89 mm).

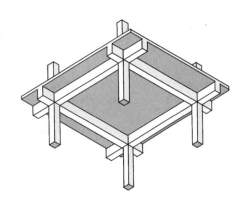

TWO-WAY SLAB AND BEAM CONSTRUCTION

SITECAST CONCRETE TWO-WAY FLAT PLATE

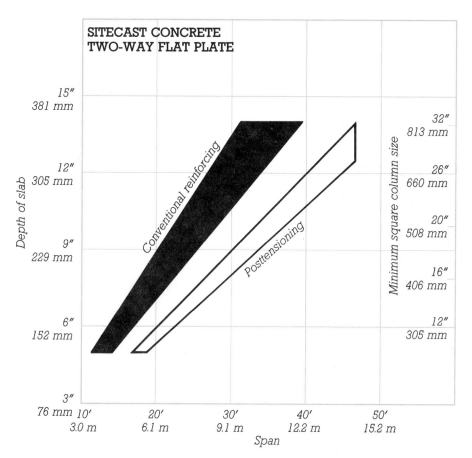

SITECAST CONCRETE
TWO-WAY FLAT PLATE

Depth of slab

15" 381 mm

12" 305 mm

9" 229 mm

6" 152 mm

3" 76 mm

Conventional reinforcing

Posttensioning

Minimum square column size

32" 813 mm

26" 660 mm

20" 508 mm

16" 406 mm

12" 305 mm

Span

10' 3.0 m   20' 6.1 m   30' 9.1 m   40' 12.2 m   50' 15.2 m

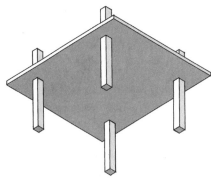

This chart is for sitecast concrete flat plate construction, either conventionally reinforced or posttensioned. For medium to light loads, read toward the right in the indicated areas. For heavy loads, read toward the left.

■ For rectangular column bays, use the span of the longer of the two sides of the bay in reading from this chart.

■ Size slab depth to the nearest ½ in. (10 mm).

COLUMN SIZES FOR FLAT PLATE CONSTRUCTION

The shallow depth of the junction between the slab and the column in flat plate construction restricts the minimum column size in this system. The right-hand scale on the chart above provides minimum square column sizes for various slab thicknesses. The required minimum column sizes for this system also depend on the applied loads on the structure. For light loads, reduce the indicated column size by 2 in. (50 mm). For heavy loads, increase the column size by 2 to 4 in. (50 to 100 mm).

■ For rectangular columns, use a column whose area is equal to that of the square column indicated. For round columns, use a column diameter one-third greater than the square column size indicated. Column sizes may also need to be increased at the edges of a slab.

■ For columns in multistory buildings, or for columns over 12 ft (3.7 m) tall, column size should also be checked using the charts on pages 108–109.

■ If smaller column sizes are desired, consider two-way flat slab construction as an alternative construction system. See pages 120–121.

SITECAST CONCRETE TWO-WAY FLAT SLAB

The two-way flat slab system is distinguished from flat plate construction by the strengthening of the column-to-slab junction, usually in the form of drop panels and/or column caps. Flat slab construction is an economical alternative to flat plate construction for heavier loads and longer spans. It also has increased resistance to lateral forces and often requires smaller columns than flat plate construction. However, the drop panels and column caps used in this system result in increased construction costs and greater overall floor depths than with flat plate construction.

DROP PANELS, COLUMN CAPS, AND SHEARHEADS

All flat slab construction requires some form of strengthening at the column-to-slab junction. Most commonly this is accomplished with the addition of drop panels, a deepening of the slab in the column region.

There are a number of alternatives to the exclusive use of drop panels in flat slab construction. Column caps, a widening of the columns toward their tops, may be used in place of drop panels where the loads on the slab are light, or in conjunction with drop panels where loads are very high. Where all such formed elements are considered undesirable, special arrangements of steel reinforcing in the slab, termed shearheads, may be an acceptable alternative to these methods.

The minimum size for drop panels is a width of one-third the span of the slab and a total depth of one and one-fourth times the depth of the slab. For heavy loads, panels may increase in width and depth.

For maximum economy, keep all drop panels the same dimensions throughout the building. The difference in depth between the slab and the drop panels should be equal to a standard lumber dimension. The edges of drop panels should be a minimum of 16 ft 6 in. (5.0 m) apart to utilize standard 16-ft (4.9-m) lumber in the formwork.

When column caps are used, their overall width should be eight to ten times the slab depth. Column caps are commonly either tapered or rectangular in profile, but should be approximately half as deep as their width at the top.

The addition of beams to flat slab construction can increase the load capacity and span range of the system, though with increased costs.

FIRE-RESISTANCE RATINGS
FOR TWO-WAY FLAT SLAB CONSTRUCTION

Fire-resistance ratings for concrete construction vary with the type and density of concrete used. Use the following guidelines for preliminary design:

To achieve a 3-hour fire-resistance rating, the slab must be at least 6.5 in. (165 mm) thick. For a 2-hour rating, the minimum thickness is 5 in. (127 mm), for 1½ hours, 4.5 in. (114 mm), and for 1 hour, 3.5 in. (89 mm).

120

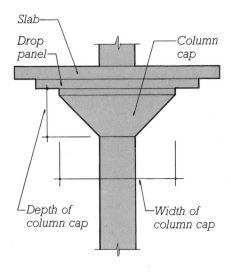

DROP PANELS AND COLUMN CAPS

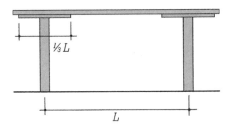

DROP PANEL WIDTH

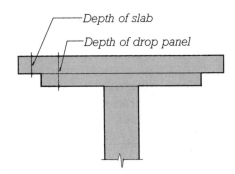

DROP PANEL DEPTH

SITECAST CONCRETE TWO-WAY FLAT SLAB

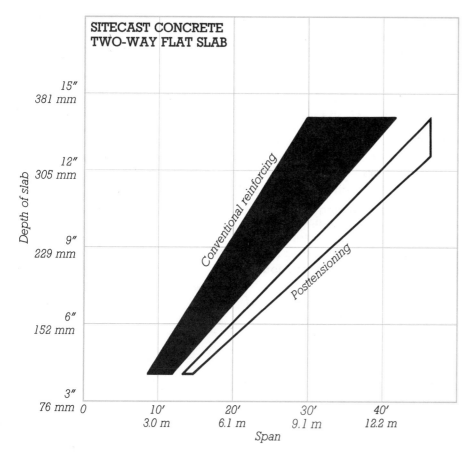

SITECAST CONCRETE TWO-WAY FLAT SLAB

Depth of slab

15″ / 381 mm
12″ / 305 mm
9″ / 229 mm
6″ / 152 mm
3″ / 76 mm

Conventional reinforcing

Posttensioning

0   10′ / 3.0 m   20′ / 6.1 m   30′ / 9.1 m   40′ / 12.2 m

Span

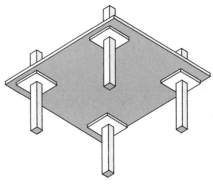

This chart is for concrete two-way flat slab construction, either conventionally reinforced or posttensioned. For light loads, read toward the right in the indicated areas. For heavy loads, read toward the left.

■ For rectangular column bays, use the span of the longer of the two sides of the bay in reading from this chart.

■ Size slab depth to the nearest ½ in. (10 mm).

COLUMN SIZES AND LAYOUTS FOR FLAT SLAB CONSTRUCTION

For light to moderate loads, use a minimum square column size of 12 in. (300 mm) for preliminary design. For heavier loads, larger columns or the addition of column caps may be required. Column size may be increased by 4 to 12 in. (100 to 300 mm) for extremely heavy loads.

For rectangular columns, use a column whose area is equal to that of the recommended square column size. For round columns, use a column diameter one-third greater than the recommended square column size. Column sizes may also need to be increased in multistory buildings or for columns taller than 12 ft (3.7 m). See pages 108–109 for checking column sizes for these conditions.

For maximum economy and efficiency of the two-way structural system, column layouts for flat slab construction should adhere to the same guidelines as those described for flat plate construction. Column bays should be approximately square, and column offsets from regular lines should be minimized. See page 118 for a complete discussion of these guidelines.

SITECAST CONCRETE WAFFLE SLAB

The waffle slab (or two-way joist) system is an economical system for long spans or heavy loads. This system is often desirable for the distinctive appearance of the underside of the slab, which may be left exposed in finished construction.

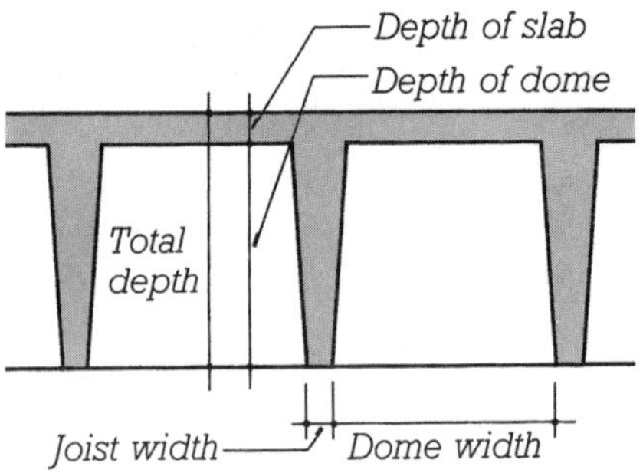

RIB LAYOUT FOR WAFFLE SLAB CONSTRUCTION

Standard 19-in (483-mm) domes are used with ribs that are 5 in. (127 mm) wide to create a 24-in. (610-mm) module. Domes of 30 in. (762 mm) are used with 6-in. (152-mm) ribs to create a 36-in. (914-mm) module. Standard domes are also available for 4- and 5-ft (1.2- and 1.5-m) modules, and other square or rectangular sizes can be specially ordered.

Solid heads must be created over all columns by omitting domes in the vicinity of each column and pouring the slab flush with the bottom of the ribs. The number of domes omitted varies, increasing with longer spans and heavier loads. In some cases solid strips may extend continuously between columns in both directions.

The economy of this system depends on the maximum repetition of standard forms and sizes. Depths, thicknesses, and spacings should vary as little as possible.

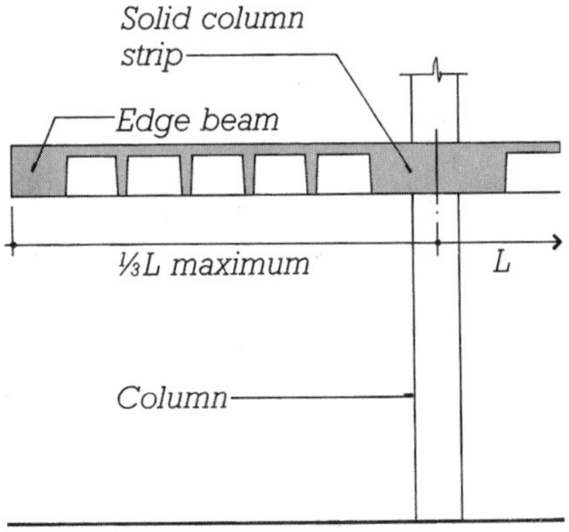

WAFFLE SLAB

EDGE CONDITIONS

When the slab ends flush with the edge columns, the area between the outermost rib and the slab edge is filled solid to create an edge beam. The slab may also cantilever beyond the columns by as much as one-third of a full span. In this case, both an edge beam and a solid strip running between the edge columns may be required.

EDGE BEAMS AND CANTILEVERS

FIRE-RESISTANCE RATINGS FOR WAFFLE SLAB CONSTRUCTION

Fire-resistance ratings for concrete construction vary with the type and density of concrete used. Use the following guidelines for preliminary design:

A 3-in. (76-mm) slab thickness between ribs gives a fire-resistance rating of 0 to 1 hour. A 3½-in. (89-mm) thickness gives 1 hour, a 4½-in. (114-mm) thickness gives 1½ hours, and a 5-in. (127-mm) thickness gives 2 hours. For higher fire-resistance ratings, the slab thickness may be increased further, fireproofing materials may be applied to the underside of the ribs and slab, or an appropriately fire-resistive ceiling may be used.

SITECAST CONCRETE WAFFLE SLAB

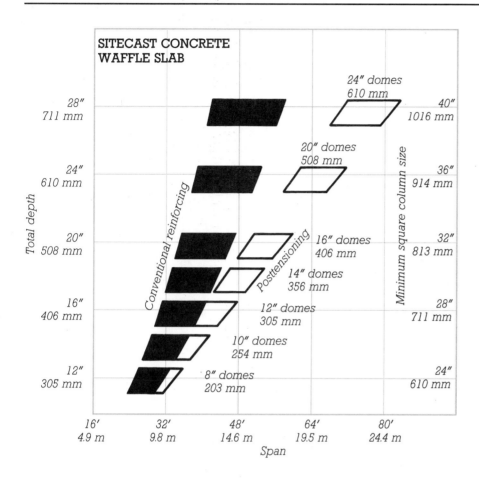

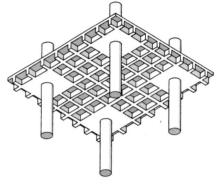

This chart is for concrete waffle slab construction, either conventionally reinforced or posttensioned. For light loads, read toward the right in the indicated areas. For heavy loads, read toward the left.

■ For rectangular bays, use the average of the spans of the two sides of the bay when reading from this chart.

■ *Total depth* is the sum of the depth of the ribs and the slab. (See the diagram on the facing page.) Depths are indicated on the chart for slabs from 3 to 4½ in. (76 to 114 mm) deep with standard pan sizes. The choice of the slab depth usually depends on the required fire-resistance rating for the system. See the facing page for fire-resistance information.

COLUMN SIZES AND LAYOUTS FOR WAFFLE SLAB CONSTRUCTION

In waffle slab construction, minimum column size is dependent on the overall thickness of the slab. The right-hand scale on the chart above provides minimum square column sizes for various slab thicknesses. For light loads, reduce the indicated column size by 2 to 4 in. (50 to 100 mm). For heavy loads, increase the indicated column size by 4 to 12 in. (100 to 300 mm).

For rectangular columns, use a column whose area is equal to that of the square column indicated. For round columns, use a column diameter one-third greater than the square column size indicated.

For columns in multistory buildings or for columns over 12 ft (3.7 m) tall, column size should also be checked using the charts on pages 108–109.

For maximum economy and efficiency of the two-way structural system, column layouts for waffle slab construction should adhere to the same guidelines as those described for flat plate construction. Column bays should be approximately square, and column offsets from regular lines should be minimized. See page 118 for a complete discussion of these guidelines.

PRECAST CONCRETE STRUCTURAL SYSTEMS

Precast prestressed concrete framing systems are characterized by reduced depths and deflections for spanning members, faster construction, and increased quality and durability of the concrete itself as compared to conventional sitecast concrete. Where future changes to a structure are anticipated, precast concrete may be a preferred choice for the ease with which individual elements in the system may be removed or replaced. The difficulty of fabricating rigid joints in these systems leads to a greater reliance on shear walls or cross bracing to achieve lateral stability than in sitecast concrete structures, and makes them potentially more sensitive to vibrations produced by heavy machinery or other sources. Precast concrete spanning elements are also often used in combination with other site-fabricated vertical systems such as sitecast concrete, masonry, or steel.

SELECTING A PRECAST CONCRETE FRAMING SYSTEM

The initial choice of a framing system should be based on the desired spanning capacity or column spacings of the system and the magnitude of the expected loads on the structure. The following precast concrete systems are listed in order of increasing spans, load capacity, and cost:

- Solid Flat Slab
- Hollow Core Slab
- Double Tee
- Single Tee

For short spans and light loads, select a system from the top of the list. For longer spans and heavier loads, systems toward the bottom of the list are required.

As with sitecast concrete, the inherent fire-resistive qualities of precast concrete construction allow these systems to remain wholly or partially exposed in the finished building. For this reason, the choice of a concrete framing system often has significant architectural implications that should be considered early in the design process. Thus the designer may also wish to consider the following factors in the choice of a precast concrete system:

- The ease of integration of building services into the system.
- The possible use of the underside of the slab as a finish ceiling.
- The aesthetic qualities of the system.

LAYING OUT A PRECAST CONCRETE SYSTEM

The economy of precast concrete construction depends on the maximum repetition of standard elements and sizes. Use the following guidelines for preliminary layout of a precast concrete structure to ensure maximum economy:

- In the direction of the span of the deck members, use a modular dimension of 1 ft (0.3 m). If a wall panel has been selected, use the width of the panel as the modular dimension.
- In the direction transverse to the span of the deck members, use a module of 8 ft (2.4 m). If a deck member has been selected, use the width of the member as the modular dimension.

- Floor-to-floor heights need not be designed to any particular module, though the maximum repetition of the dimension chosen is desirable. Where precast wall panels are used, floor-to-floor heights should be coordinated with the height of the wall panel.
- Restrictions due to shipping and handling of members usually limit span lengths to 60 to 80 ft (18 to 24 m) maximum. Further transportation restrictions on depths of elements usually limit bay widths to between 24 and 40 ft (7 and 12 m) where girders are used.

In general, any design features that require unique structural elements, excessive variations in the sizes of elements, alterations in structural configuration, or deviation from the standard dimensions of the system should be avoided. Where the maximum flexibility of layout with precast concrete elements is desired, solid flat slabs or hollow core slabs may be preferred for their shorter spans and the greater ease with which they may be sawn after casting to conform to irregular conditions.

PROJECT SIZE

The economy of precast concrete construction also depends on the size of the construction project. The following figures are approximate minimum project sizes for which the production of precast concrete elements may be economical:

- 10,000 ft^2 (1000 m^2) of architectural wall panels, or
- 15,000 ft^2 (1500 m^2) of deck or slab members, or
- 1000 linear feet (300 m) of girders, columns, or pilings.

PRECAST CONCRETE COLUMNS

Precast concrete columns are typically combined with precast concrete beams in a post and beam configuration. Unlike with sitecast concrete construction, the fabrication of rigid joints in a precast concrete frame is difficult and rarely done. Instead, shear walls or diagonal bracing are normally incorporated into the framing system in order to stabilize the structure against lateral forces.

Precast concrete columns are usually reinforced conventionally. Prestressing may be used to reduce stresses on the column during transportation and handling or when significant bending or buckling stresses may be expected in service.

**PRECAST CONCRETE COLUMN
WITH TWO CORBELS**

STANDARD SIZES AND SHAPES OF PRECAST CONCRETE COLUMNS

Precast concrete columns are commonly available in square sizes from 10 to 24 in. (254 to 619 mm). Rectangular sections are also produced, although available sizes will vary with the supplier. For projects using over approximately 1000 linear feet (300 meters) of columns, a greater range of cross sections and sizes may be produced economically.

Columns in lengths up to approximately 60 ft (18 m) can be transported easily. Columns up to approximately 100 ft (30 m) in length can be shipped with special arrangements that may affect the overall economy of the system.

For ease of casting, columns with corbels should be restricted to corbels on two opposite sides, or at most, on three sides.

As with all precast concrete elements, precast columns should be as consistent as possible in dimensions and layout in order to achieve maximum economy.

CONCRETE STRENGTH AND COLUMN SIZE

The top chart on the facing page is based on a concrete strength of 5000 psi (34.5 MPa). Higher-strength concretes may be used to reduce the required column size. For higher concrete strengths, multiply the indicated column size by the amount in the table to the right:

Concrete Strength		Multiply Column Size by
7000 psi	(48MPa)	0.95
9000 psi	(62 MPa)	0.80
11,000 psi	(76 MPa)	0.75

FIRE-RESISTANCE RATINGS FOR PRECAST CONCRETE COLUMNS

Fire-resistance ratings for concrete construction vary with the type and density of concrete used. Use the following guidelines for preliminary design:

Precast columns must be at least 14 in. (356 mm) in minimum dimension to achieve a 4-hour fire-resistance rating. For a 3-hour rating, the minimum dimension is 12 in. (305 mm). For 2 hours, a column must be at least 10 in. (254 mm) on a side.

PRECAST CONCRETE COLUMNS

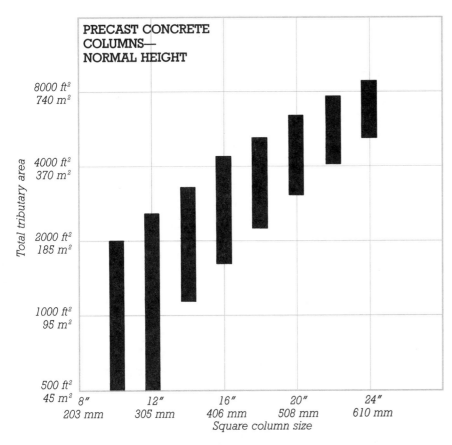

PRECAST CONCRETE COLUMNS— NORMAL HEIGHT

Total tributary area

8000 ft² / 740 m²
4000 ft² / 370 m²
2000 ft² / 185 m²
1000 ft² / 95 m²
500 ft² / 45 m²

8" / 203 mm — 12" / 305 mm — 16" / 406 mm — 20" / 508 mm — 24" / 610 mm

Square column size

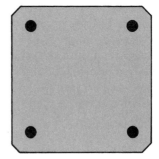

The top chart is for square precast concrete columns up to 12 ft (3.7 m) in height between floors. For normal loads, read toward the top in the indicated areas. For high loads, read toward the bottom.

■ For rectangular columns, select a column of equivalent area.

■ Actual column size is equal to the nominal column size.

■ *Total tributary area* is the total area of roofs and floors supported by the column.

The bottom chart is for columns with unbraced heights of greater than 12 ft (3.7 m). Use the larger of the two sizes indicated by both charts on this page.

■ For rectangular columns, read from this chart using the least dimension of the column.

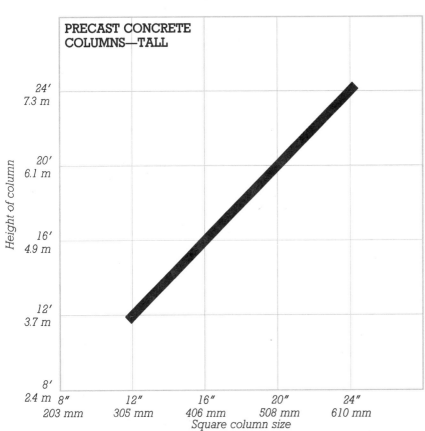

PRECAST CONCRETE COLUMNS—TALL

Height of column

24' / 7.3 m
20' / 6.1 m
16' / 4.9 m
12' / 3.7 m
8' / 2.4 m

8" / 203 mm — 12" / 305 mm — 16" / 406 mm — 20" / 508 mm — 24" / 610 mm

Square column size

PRECAST CONCRETE WALL PANELS

There is great variety in precast concrete wall panel types and applications. Panels may be prestressed or conventionally reinforced; they may be loadbearing or nonbearing; they may or may not contribute to the lateral stability of a building; they may be flat, ribbed, or more intricately shaped; and they may be solid, hollow, or a sandwich of concrete with an insulating core. Precast concrete wall panels may be used in conjunction with a precast concrete framing system or with other framing systems, such as steel or concrete.

PANEL TYPES

Flat panels may be one to two stories high. Ribbed panels may be one to four stories high.

Wall panels may also be formed in a great variety of original shapes. The design of such panels depends on specialized knowledge of precasting methods. When the use of such panels is planned, the necessary consultants should be sought out early in the design process. For the preliminary sizing of these panels, use the chart for ribbed panels on the facing page. Loadbearing wall panels such as these may be used in buildings up to approximately 16 to 20 stories in height.

Panels with openings usually may not be prestressed. Panels without openings may be prestressed to reduce thickness or to limit stresses in the panels during transportation and handling.

128

SIZES OF PRECAST CONCRETE WALL PANELS

Solid panels are commonly available in thicknesses of from $3\frac{1}{2}$ to 10 in. (89 to 254 mm). Sandwich or hollow core panels range in thickness from $5\frac{1}{2}$ to 12 in. (140 to 305 mm). Ribbed wall panels are commonly available in thicknesses of 12 to 24 in. (305 to 610 mm).

For preliminary design, assume an 8-ft (2.4-m) width for all panel types. With special provisions, panels in widths of up to approximately 14 ft (4.3 m) may be transported without excessive economic penalty.

FIRE-RESISTANCE RATINGS FOR PRECAST CONCRETE WALL PANELS

Fire-resistance ratings will vary with the density of concrete used in the panel, and in sandwich panels, with the type of core insulation as well. The following guidelines may be used for preliminary design:

Panels must be at least 6.5 in. (165 mm) thick to achieve a fire-resistance rating of 4 hours. A 3-hour rating is achieved at a thickness of 6 in. (152 mm), a 2-hour rating at 5 in. (127 mm), and a 1-hour rating at 3.5 in. (89 mm).

PRECAST CONCRETE WALL PANELS

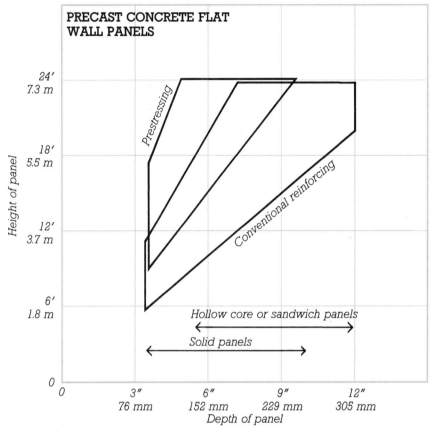

PRECAST CONCRETE FLAT WALL PANELS

Height of panel

- 24′ / 7.3 m
- 18′ / 5.5 m
- 12′ / 3.7 m
- 6′ / 1.8 m
- 0

Prestressing

Conventional reinforcing

Hollow core or sandwich panels

Solid panels

Depth of panel

- 0
- 3″ / 76 mm
- 6″ / 152 mm
- 9″ / 229 mm
- 12″ / 305 mm

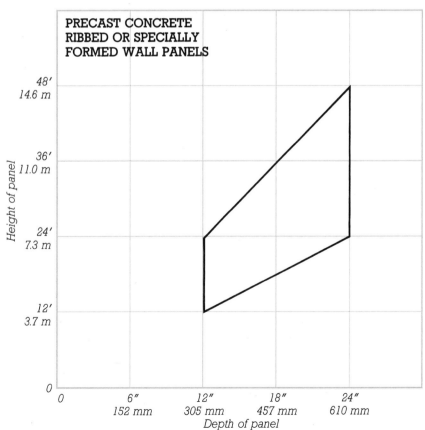

PRECAST CONCRETE RIBBED OR SPECIALLY FORMED WALL PANELS

Height of panel

- 48′ / 14.6 m
- 36′ / 11.0 m
- 24′ / 7.3 m
- 12′ / 3.7 m
- 0

Depth of panel

- 0
- 6″ / 152 mm
- 12″ / 305 mm
- 18″ / 457 mm
- 24″ / 610 mm

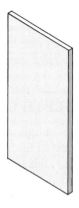

The top chart is for flat precast concrete wall panels, either prestressed or conventionally reinforced. For nonbearing panels, read toward the left in the indicated areas. For loadbearing panels, read toward the right.

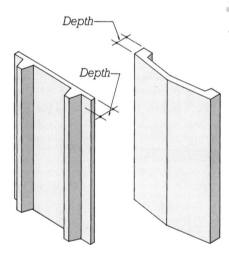

Depth

Depth

The bottom chart is for precast concrete wall panels formed with ribs, stems, or other stiffening features. For nonbearing or prestressed panels, read toward the left in the indicated area. For loadbearing panels, conventionally reinforced panels, or panels with integral window openings, read toward the right.

■ *Depth of panel* is the total depth of the panel and any stiffening features.

■ For the preliminary design of spandrel panels, use the distance between columns for the height indicated on either chart.

PRECAST CONCRETE BEAMS AND GIRDERS

Precast prestressed concrete girders are commonly used to carry all varieties of precast concrete decking elements between columns or bearing walls. They can be used in any building type where precast concrete construction is to be considered.

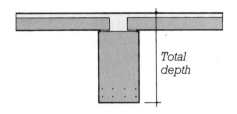

RECTANGULAR BEAM WITH SOLID OR HOLLOW CORE SLABS

TOTAL DEPTH OF FLOOR SYSTEMS

Rectangular beams are commonly used with solid or hollow core slabs resting on top of the beam. Total floor depth at the beam is the sum of the depths of the slab (and topping, if any) and the beam.

Inverted T- and L-beams are commonly used with double and single tees. When erected, the top of the tees should be level with or slightly above the top of the beam. When the tees rest directly on the beam ledge, the total floor depth at the beam is the depth of the tee (and topping, if any) plus the depth of the ledge. Deeper tees may have their ends notched or "dapped" so as to rest lower on the beam. The use of dapped tees may result in total floor depths of as little as the depth of the tee itself plus any topping.

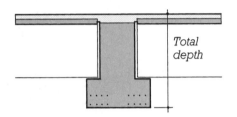

INVERTED T-BEAM WITH SINGLE OR DOUBLE TEES

FIRE-RESISTANCE RATINGS FOR PRECAST BEAMS AND GIRDERS

Fire-resistance ratings will vary with the density of concrete used in the beams. The following guidelines may be used for preliminary design:

A prestressed concrete beam not smaller than 9.5 in. (241 mm) in width has a fire-resistance rating of 3 hours. For a 2-hour rating, the minimum width is 7 in. (178 mm), and for 1 hour, 4 in. (102 mm).

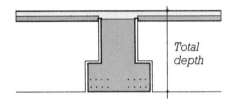

INVERTED T-BEAM WITH DAPPED TEES

PRECAST CONCRETE BEAMS AND GIRDERS

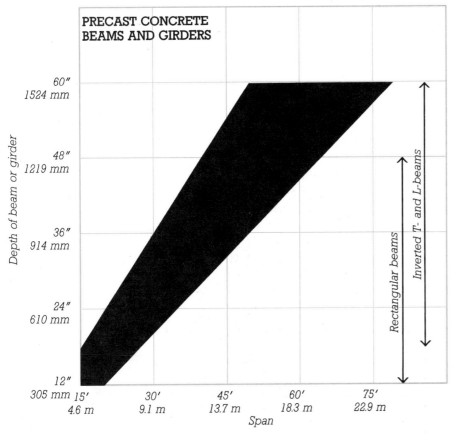

PRECAST CONCRETE
BEAMS AND GIRDERS

Depth of beam or girder

60″ / 1524 mm
48″ / 1219 mm
36″ / 914 mm
24″ / 610 mm
12″ / 305 mm

15′ / 4.6 m — 30′ / 9.1 m — 45′ / 13.7 m — 60′ / 18.3 m — 75′ / 22.9 m

Span

Rectangular beams

Inverted T- and L-beams

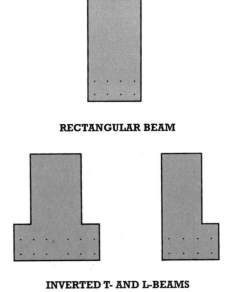

RECTANGULAR BEAM

INVERTED T- AND L-BEAMS

This chart is for precast concrete beams and girders. For light loads or close beam spacings, read toward the right in the indicated area. For heavy loads and large beam spacings, or for girders, read toward the left.

COMMON SIZES OF PRECAST CONCRETE BEAMS AND GIRDERS

Rectangular beams commonly range in depth from 18 to 48 in. (457 to 1219 mm). Widths range from 12 to 36 in. (305 to 914 mm).

Inverted T- and L-beams commonly range in depth from 18 to 60 in. (457 to 1524 mm), although sections deeper than 48 in. (1219 mm) may be subject to shipping or handling restrictions. Widths of the beam stem (not including the ledges) range from 12 to 30 in. (305 to 762 mm).

Standard dimensions for beam ledges are 6 in. (152 mm) wide and 12 in. (305 mm) deep.

Beam sizes typically vary in increments of 2 or 4 in. (50 or 100 mm). Availability of sizes varies with suppliers.

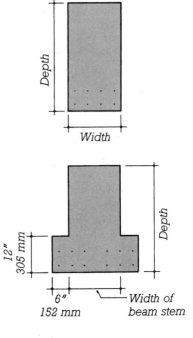

Depth

Width

12″ / 305 mm

Depth

6″ / 152 mm

Width of beam stem

PRECAST CONCRETE SLABS

Precast prestressed concrete solid and hollow core slabs are commonly used in hotels, multifamily dwellings, commercial structures, hospitals, schools, and parking structures.

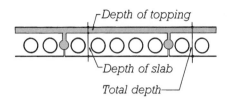

**HOLLOW CORE SLABS WITH
SITECAST TOPPING**

CONCRETE TOPPING ON PRECAST SLABS

Sitecast concrete topping is often applied over precast concrete slabs to increase the structural performance of the slab, to increase the fire resistance of the floor system, to allow the integration of electrical and communications services into the floor, or to provide a more level and smoother floor surface in preparation for subsequent finishing. In buildings such as hotels, housing, and some parking structures, where these requirements may not exist, the use of untopped slabs may be an acceptable and economical system choice.

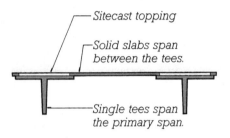

**SPREAD TEE SYSTEM WITH
SOLID SLABS**

SPECIAL SYSTEMS

Both solid and hollow core slabs may be combined with other spanning elements to create several variations of floor systems referred to as spread systems. These systems can provide increased economy and may allow greater flexibility in the choice of building module.

- Either slab type may be used as a secondary element spanning transversely between longer spanning single tees, double tees, or channels.

- Hollow core slabs can be spread from 2 to 3 ft (0.6 to 0.9 m), with corrugated steel decking spanning between the slabs. This system is usually topped. Where many floor penetrations are expected, this is an especially attractive system due to the ease of creating openings through the steel decking.

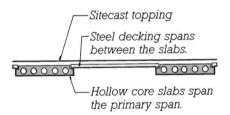

HOLLOW CORE SLAB SPREAD SYSTEM

FIRE-RESISTANCE RATINGS FOR SOLID FLAT SLABS AND HOLLOW CORE SLABS

Fire-resistance ratings will vary with the density of concrete used in the slabs and the topping. Use the following guidelines for preliminary design:

Solid slab floors must be at least 5.5 in. (140 mm) thick to have a fire resistance rating of 3 hours. For a 2-hour rating, the required thickness is 4.5 in. (114 mm). A 1½-hour rating requires a minimum thickness of 4 in. (102 mm), and a 1-hour rating, 3.5 in. (89 mm). These thicknesses include the depth of any topping.

Hollow core slabs at least 8 in. (203 mm) deep achieve a fire-resistance rating of 2 hours without a concrete topping. With the addition of a 2-in. (50-mm) topping, the rating rises to 3 hours.

PRECAST CONCRETE SLABS

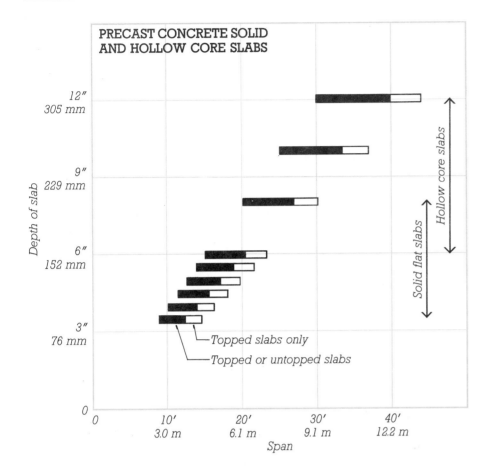

SOLID FLAT SLAB

HOLLOW CORE SLAB

This chart is for precast concrete solid flat slabs and hollow core slabs. For light loads, read toward the right in the indicated areas. For heavy loads, read toward the left.

■ The open areas indicated on the chart are for slabs with an added sitecast concrete topping only. The solid areas are for either topped or untopped slabs. The depths indicated on the chart are for the slabs alone, without any additional topping. Where a topping is used, add 2 in. (50 mm) to the indicated depths for preliminary design. See the facing page for further information on the use of concrete toppings.

COMMON SIZES OF SOLID AND HOLLOW CORE SLABS

Solid flat slabs come in depths of 3½ to 8 in. (89 to 203 mm). For depths of 6 in. (152 mm) and above, however, hollow core slabs are usually more economical. Typical widths are 8 to 12 ft (2.4 to 3.7 m).

Hollow core slabs come in depths of 6 to 12 in. (152 to 305 mm). Typical widths are 2 ft, 3 ft 4 in., 4 ft, and 8 ft (0.6, 1.0, 1.2, and 2.4 m). Availability of sizes varies with suppliers.

PRECAST CONCRETE SINGLE AND DOUBLE TEES

Precast prestressed single and double tees can span farther than precast slabs and are commonly used in such building types as commercial structures, schools, and parking garages.

SPREAD TEE SYSTEMS

Single and double tees may be combined with other spanning elements to create framing systems referred to as *spread systems.* In these systems, the tees are erected with spaces between. These gaps are then bridged with precast solid or hollow core slabs, or with sitecast concrete that is poured as part of the topping. These systems can increase the economy of long-span structures and may allow greater flexibility in the choice of building module.

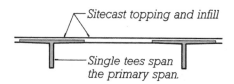

Sitecast topping and infill

Single tees span the primary span.

SPREAD TEE SYSTEM WITH SITECAST CONCRETE TOPPING AND INFILL

FIRE-RESISTANCE RATINGS FOR SINGLE AND DOUBLE TEES

Fire resistance will vary with the density of concrete used in the slabs and topping. Use the following guidelines for preliminary design:

For a fire-resistance rating of 3 hours, single and double tees require applied fire-protection materials or an appropriately fire-resistive ceiling. For ratings of 2 hours and less, protection may be achieved by regulating the thickness of the concrete topping: 3.5 in. (90 mm) for 2 hours, 3.0 in. (75 mm) for 1½ hours, and 2.0 in. (50 mm) for 1 hour.

PRECAST CONCRETE SINGLE AND DOUBLE TEES

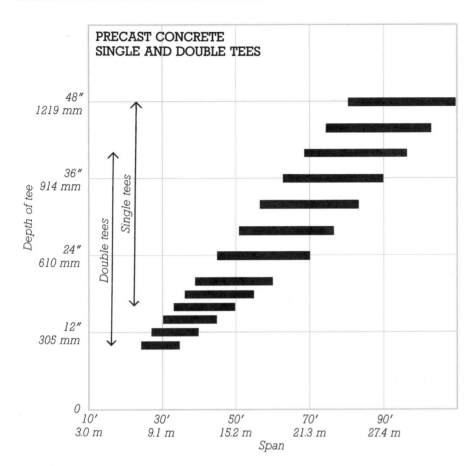

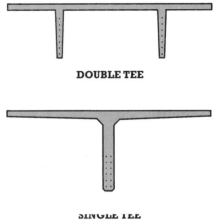

DOUBLE TEE

SINGLE TEE

This chart is for precast concrete single and double tees. For light loads, read toward the right in the indicated areas. For heavy loads, read toward the left.

■ Because they do not require temporary support against tipping, double tees are easier and more economical to erect than single tees. Their use is preferred wherever possible.

■ Double tees are most commonly used with a concrete topping. For preliminary purposes, add 2 in. (50 mm) to the depths indicated on the chart. Roof slabs and deep single tees may not need to be topped.

COMMON SIZES OF PRECAST SINGLE AND DOUBLE TEES

Double tees come in widths of 4, 8, 10, and 12 ft (1.2, 2.4, 3.0, and 3.7 m). Common depths are from 10 to 40 in. (254 to 1016 mm). Single tees come in widths of 6, 8, 10, and 12 ft (1.8, 2.4, 3.0, and 3.7 m). Common depths are from 16 to 48 in. (406 to 1219 mm). Tees longer than 60 to 80 ft (18 to 24 m) may be less economical because of increased transportation and handling costs. Availability of sizes varies with suppliers.

■■■
DESIGNING SPACES FOR MECHANICAL AND ELECTRICAL SERVICES

■■■
SELECTING HEATING AND COOLING SYSTEMS FOR LARGE BUILDINGS

This section will help you select a heating and cooling system for the preliminary design of a large building.

DESIGN CRITERIA FOR THE SELECTION OF HEATING AND COOLING SYSTEMS FOR LARGE BUILDINGS

If you wish to minimize first cost of the heating and cooling system:	Choose the simplest possible all-air system:
	
	    Single duct, constant air volume (pages 150–151)
	
	or choose a system that involves no ductwork or piping:
	
	    Through-the-wall and packaged terminal units (page 158)

If you wish to minimize operating cost:	Choose systems that convert fuel to heating and cooling energy with maximum efficiency:
	
	    Variable air volume (pages 148–149)
	    Single duct, constant air volume (pages 150–151)
	    Hydronic convectors (pages 156–157)
	
	or choose a system that uses ambient heat from the surrounding environment:
	
	    Closed-loop heat pump system (page 155)

If you wish to maximize control of air quality and air velocity:	Choose one of the all-air heating systems:
	
	    Variable air volume (VAV) (pages 148–149)
	    VAV reheat (page 149)
	    VAV induction (page 149)
	    Dual-duct VAV (page 149)
	    Single duct, constant air volume (pages 150–151)
	    Multizone (page 151)

If you wish to maximize individual control over temperature in a number of rooms or zones:	Choose a system that can react separately to a number of thermostats:
	
	    Variable air volume (VAV) (pages 148–149)
	    VAV reheat (page 149)
	    VAV induction (page 149)
	    Dual-duct VAV (page 149)
	    Constant air volume reheat (page 151)
	    Multizone (page 151)
	    Air-water induction (pages 152–153)
	    Fan-coil terminals (page 154)
	    Through-the-wall and packaged terminal units (page 158)

If you wish to minimize system noise:	Choose a system that operates at low air velocities and whose moving parts are distant from the occupied spaces, such as:
	
	    Any all-air system other than an induction system (pages 148–151)
	    Hydronic convectors (pages 156–157)

DESIGN CRITERIA FOR THE SELECTION OF HEATING AND COOLING SYSTEMS FOR LARGE BUILDINGS

If you wish to minimize the visual obtrusiveness of the heating and cooling system:	Choose a system that has minimal hardware in the occupied spaces of the building, such as: Any all-air system (pages 148–151)
If you wish to minimize the floor space used for the mechanical system, or the floor-to-floor height of the building:	Choose a local system that has no ductwork or piping, such as: Through-the-wall and packaged terminal units (page 158) or a system that minimizes the size of the ductwork or piping, such as: Induction systems (pages 149, 152–153) Hydronic convectors (pages 156–157)
If you wish to minimize maintenance requirements of the heating and cooling system:	Choose systems that are very simple and have few moving parts in the occupied spaces of the building: Variable air volume (pages 148–149) Single duct, constant air volume (pages 150–151) Hydronic convectors (pages 156–157)
If you wish to avoid having a chimney in the building:	Choose systems that are electrically powered: Electric boilers (pages 148–157) Through-the-wall and packaged terminal units (page 158) Closed-loop heat pumps (page 155)
If you wish to maximize the speed of construction:	Choose systems that can be installed by a single trade, such as: Through-the-wall and packaged terminal units (page 158)

HEATING AND COOLING SYSTEMS FOR LARGE BUILDINGS: SUMMARY CHART

GIVE SPECIAL CONSIDERATION TO THE SYSTEMS INDICATED IF YOU WISH TO:	Variable Air Volume (VAV) (page 148)	VAV Reheat (page 149)	VAV Induction (page 149)	Dual-Duct VAV (page 149)	Single Duct, Constant Air Volume (CAV) (page 150)
Minimize first cost					●
Minimize operating cost	●				●
Maximize control of air velocity and air quality	●	●		○	●
Maximize individual control over temperature	●	●	○	○	
Minimize system noise	●	●		○	●
Minimize visual obtrusiveness	●	●	○	○	●
Maximize flexibility of rental space	●	●	○	○	●
Minimize floor space used for the heating and cooling system			○		
Minimize floor-to-floor height			○		
Minimize system maintenance	●				●
Avoid having a chimney					
Maximize the speed of construction					

● Frequently used
○ Infrequently used
† System for heating only

HEATING AND COOLING SYSTEMS FOR LARGE BUILDINGS: SUMMARY CHART

CAV Reheat (page 151)	Multizone (page 151)	Air-Water Induction (page 152)	Fan-Coil Terminals (page 154)	Closed-Loop Heat Pumps (page 155)	Hydronic Convectors† (page 156)	Packaged Terminal Units or Through-the-Wall Units (page 158)
						●
				●	●	
○	○					
○	○	○	●	●		●
○	○				●	
○	○				●	
○	○	○	●		●	●
		○	●	●	●	●
		○	●	●	●	●
					●	
						●
						●

SOME TYPICAL CHOICES OF HEATING AND COOLING SYSTEMS FOR LARGE BUILDINGS

OCCUPANCY	Variable Air Volume (VAV) (page 148)	VAV Reheat (page 149)	VAV Induction (page 149)	Dual-Duct VAV (page 149)	Single Duct, Constant Air Volume (CAV) (page 150)
Apartments					
Arenas, Exhibition Halls	●*				●*
Auditoriums, Theaters*	●				●
Factories	●*	●			●*
Hospitals	●	●		●	
Hotels, Motels, Dormitories	●				
Laboratories	●	●		●	●
Libraries	●				
Nursing Homes	●				
Offices	●*		●		
Places of Worship	●				●
Schools	●*	●			
Shopping Centers	●*				
Stores	●*				

● Frequently used
○ Infrequently used
* Sometimes installed as packaged systems
† System for heating only

SOME TYPICAL CHOICES OF HEATING AND COOLING SYSTEMS FOR LARGE BUILDINGS

CAV Reheat (page 151)	Multizone (page 151)	Air-Water Induction (page 151)	Fan-Coil Terminals (page 154)	Closed-Loop Heat Pumps (page 155)	Hydronic Convectors† (page 156)	Packaged Terminal Units or Through-the-Wall Units (page 158)
			●	●	●	●
			●			
	●					
	●*	○	●		●	
●	●	○	●			
		○	●	●		●
●						
	●					
			●			●
	●*	○			●	
	●				●	
			●			
	●*					
	●*					

ZONING A BUILDING FOR HEATING AND COOLING

Before attempting to select a heating and cooling system, rough out a zoning scheme for the building, establishing separately controlled zones so that thermal comfort can be achieved throughout a building despite conditions that differ between one space and another. Sometimes a zone should be no larger than a single room (a classroom, a hotel room). Sometimes a number of spaces with similar thermal requirements can be grouped into a larger zone (a group of offices that are occupied during the day but not at night; a group of galleries in a museum). Sometimes rooms must be put in separate zones because they have differing requirements for air quality or temperature (locker rooms in a gymnasium complex, cast dressing rooms in a theater). Sometimes different zones must be established to deal effectively with different rates of internal generation of heat (a kitchen in a restaurant or dining hall, a computer room in a school, a metal casting area in an industrial building).

Buildings in which solar heat gain through windows is a major component of the cooling load need to be zoned according to the various window orientations of the rooms. In commercial buildings where each tenant will be billed separately for heating and cooling costs, each tenant space will constitute a separate zone. A large business or mercantile building might be divided into several large zones of approximately equal size to fit the capacities of the fans and ductwork or the capacities of packaged air conditioning systems. A multi-use building may incorporate parking, retail shops, lobbies, offices, and apartments, each requiring a different type of heating and cooling system.

The zoning of a building is significant in the early stages of design because it may suggest a choice of heating and cooling system: Room-by-room zoning suggests an all-water fan coil system or packaged terminal units for an apartment building, for example, meaning that the building does not have to be designed to accommodate major ductwork. Zoning may also have an impact on where the major equipment spaces are placed. It often makes sense to put major equipment on the "seam" between two zones. An example of this might be placing the major heating and cooling equipment on the second or third floor of a multi-use downtown building, above retail and lobby spaces and below multiple floors of office space.

CENTRAL SYSTEMS VERSUS LOCAL SYSTEMS

In a *central system,* heat is supplied to a building or extracted from it by large equipment situated in one or several large mechanical spaces. Air or water is heated or cooled in these spaces and distributed to the inhabited areas of the building by ductwork or piping to maintain comfortable temperatures.

In a *local system,* independent, self-contained pieces of heating and cooling equipment are situated throughout the building, one or more in each room.

Central systems are generally quieter and more energy efficient than local systems and offer better control of indoor air quality. Central equipment tends to last longer than local equipment and is more convenient to service. Local systems occupy less space in a building than central systems because they do not require central mechanical spaces, ductwork, or piping. They are often more economical to buy and install. They can be advantageous in buildings that have many small spaces requiring individual temperature control.

Pages 148–157 describe alternative choices of central heating and cooling systems for large buildings. Local systems are described on page 158.

FUELS

Heating and cooling equipment in large buildings may be powered by oil, gas, electricity, steam, or hot water. In central areas of many large cities, utility-generated pipeline steam is available. In some large complexes of buildings, such as university campuses, steam or hot water is furnished to each structure, along with chilled water for cooling, via underground pipelines from a single central boiler/chiller plant. Steam and hot water, where available, are ideal energy sources for heating and cooling, because no chimney is needed and the necessary heat exchange equipment for steam or hot water is more compact than the fuel-burning boilers that would otherwise be required. Electricity is also an ideal energy source, because it is clean, it is distributed through compact lines, and electrical equipment tends to be quieter and smaller than fuel-burning equipment. In most geographic areas, however, electricity converted directly into heat is a very costly fuel as compared to oil or gas. Gas burns cleanly and requires no on-site storage of fuel. In areas where it is more economical than gas, fuel oil is favored despite its need for on-site storage tanks.

MEANS OF DISTRIBUTION

The distribution of heating and cooling energy in central systems involves the circulation of air or water or both to the inhabited spaces.

• In *all-air systems,* central fans circulate conditioned air to and from the spaces through long runs of ductwork.

• In *air and water systems,* air is ducted to each space. Heated water and chilled water are also piped to each space, where they are used to modify the temperature of the circulated air at each outlet to meet local demands. Air and water systems circulate less air than all-air systems, which makes them somewhat more compact and easier to house in a building.

• In *all-water systems,* air is circulated locally rather than from a central source, so ductwork is eliminated. Only heated water and chilled water are furnished to each space. The water piping is much smaller than equivalent ductwork, making all-water systems the most compact of all.

All-air systems offer excellent control of interior air quality. The central air-handling equipment can be designed for precise control of fresh air, filtration, humidification, dehumidification, heating, and cooling. When the outdoor air is cool, an all-air system can switch to an economizer cycle, in which it cools the building by circulating a maximum amount of outdoor air. All-air systems concentrate maintenance activities in unoccupied areas of the building because there are no water pipes, condensate drains, valves, fans, or filters outside the mechanical equipment rooms.

Air-and-water and all-water systems, besides saving space, can offer better individual control of temperature in the occupied spaces than some all-air systems, but they are inherently more complicated, and much of the maintenance activity must be carried out in the occupied spaces.

SELECTING HEATING AND COOLING SYSTEMS FOR LARGE BUILDINGS

The next few pages summarize the choices of heating and cooling systems for large buildings. To determine the space required by any system, look first at the list of major components that is included with each system description. The dimensions of any components that are unique to the system are given immediately following this list. Components that are common to more than one system may be sized using the charts on pages 190–193.

CENTRAL ALL-AIR SYSTEMS: SINGLE DUCT, VARIABLE AIR VOLUME (VAV)

Description

Air is conditioned (mixed with a percentage of outdoor air, filtered, heated or cooled, and humidified or dehumidified) at a central source. Supply and return fans circulate the conditioned air through ducts to the occupied spaces of the building. At each zone, a thermostat controls room temperature by regulating the volume of air that is discharged through the diffusers in the zone.

Typical Applications

VAV is the most versatile and most widely used system for heating and cooling large buildings.

Advantages

This system offers a high degree of local temperature control at moderate cost. It is economical to operate and virtually self-balancing.

Disadvantages

VAV is limited in the range of heating or cooling demand that may be accommodated within a single system. When one area of a building needs heating while another needs cooling, a VAV system cannot serve both areas without help from a secondary system (see *Variations*, following).

Major Components

Boilers and chimney, chilled water plant, cooling tower, fan room, outdoor fresh air and exhaust louvers, vertical supply and return ducts,

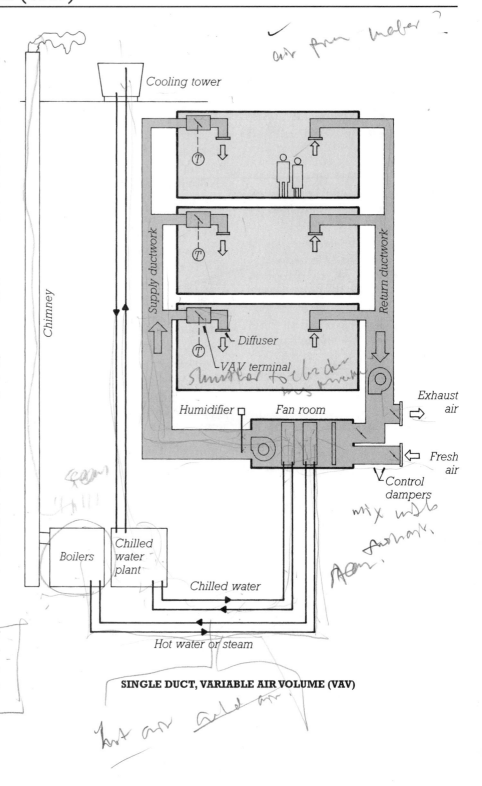

SINGLE DUCT, VARIABLE AIR VOLUME (VAV)

148

CENTRAL ALL-AIR SYSTEMS: SINGLE DUCT, VARIABLE AIR VOLUME (VAV)

horizontal supply and return ducts, VAV control box for each zone, supply diffusers, return grilles. (For an illustration of typical diffusers and grilles, see page 189.)

Alternately, in buildings of moderate size, a *packaged system* may be used in place of all components other than ducts, VAV control boxes, diffusers, and grilles. A *single-packaged system,* incorporating all central components in a single metal box, may be installed on the roof or outside an exterior wall, or a *split-packaged system* may be installed, with a compressor and condensing unit in an outdoor box and an air handling unit in an indoor box. Multiple packaged systems are often used to serve buildings that are large in horizontal extent. For more detailed information on packaged units, see pages 166–167.

Sizing the Components

The VAV control box is usually concealed above a suspended ceiling. It is approximately 8 to 11 in. (200 to 280 mm) high for zones up to 1500 sq ft (150 m²) in area, and up to 18 in. (460 mm) high for zones up to 7000 sq ft (700 m²). Its horizontal dimensions vary with its capacity, up to a maximum length of about 5 ft (1.5 m). To size the other components of a VAV system, use the charts on pages 190–193.

Variations

1. In buildings with large areas of windows, VAV is often combined with a second system around the perimeter of the building to deal with the large differences in heating and cooling demand between interior and perimeter rooms. The second system is most commonly either an induction system (see variation 3, following) or hydronic convectors (see pages 156–157).

2. A single duct *variable air volume reheat system* is identical to the basic VAV system, up to the point at which the air enters the local ductwork for each zone. In a reheat system, the air then passes through a reheat coil before it is distributed to the local diffusers. The reheat coil may be either an electric resistance coil or a pipe coil that carries hot water circulated from the boiler room. A local thermostat controls the flow of water or electricity through the reheat coil, allowing for close individual control of room temperature. This variation can overcome the inability of VAV systems to cope with a wide range of heating and cooling demands. VAV reheat systems are more energy-efficient than constant air volume reheat systems (page 151) because in the VAV systems the reheat coil is not activated unless the VAV system is incapable of meeting the local requirement for temperature control, and a much smaller amount of tempered air is circulated.

3. In the *variable air volume induction system,* a smaller volume of conditioned air is circulated through small high-velocity ducts from a central source. Each outlet is designed so that the air discharging from the duct continually pulls air from the room into the outlet, mixes it with air from the duct, and discharges the mixture into the room. This variation is used where limited space is available for ducts. It is also used to maintain a sufficient level of air movement in spaces that do not have a high demand for heating or cooling.

4. In a *dual-duct variable air volume system,* paired side-by-side ducts carry both heated and cooled air to each zone in the building. At each zone, the two airstreams are proportioned and mixed under thermostatic control to achieve the desired room temperature. This variation gives excellent local temperature control, but it requires an expensive and space-consuming dual system of ductwork, and it is not energy-efficient.

CENTRAL ALL-AIR SYSTEMS: SINGLE DUCT, CONSTANT AIR VOLUME (CAV)

Description

Air is conditioned (mixed with a percentage of outdoor air, filtered, heated or cooled, and humidified or dehumidified) at a central source. Supply and return fans circulate the air through ducts to the occupied spaces of the building. A master thermostat controls the central heating and cooling coils to regulate the temperature of the building.

Typical Applications

Spaces that have large open areas, few windows, and uniform loads, such as lobbies, department stores, theaters, auditoriums, and exhibition halls.

Advantages

This system offers a high degree of control of air quality. It is comparatively simple and easy to maintain.

Disadvantages

The entire area served by the system is a single zone, with no possibility for individual temperature control.

Major Components

Boilers and chimney, chilled water plant, cooling tower, fan room, outdoor fresh air and exhaust louvers, vertical supply and return ducts, horizontal supply and return ducts, supply diffusers, and return grilles. (For an illustration of typical diffusers and grilles, see page 189.)

Alternately, in buildings of moderate size, a *packaged system* may be used in place of all components other than ducts, diffusers, and grilles. A *single-packaged system,* incorporating all central components in a single metal box, may be installed on the roof or outside an exterior wall, or a *split-packaged system* may be installed, with a compressor and a condensing unit in an outdoor box and an air

handling unit in an indoor box. Multiple packaged systems are often used to serve buildings that are large in horizontal extent. For more detailed information on packaged units, see pages 166–167.

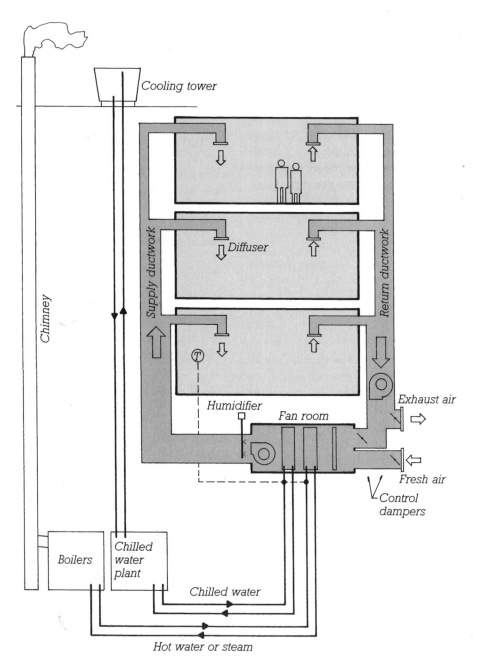

SINGLE DUCT, CONSTANT AIR VOLUME (CAV)

Sizing the Components

For the dimensions of these components, see the charts on pages 190–193.

150

CENTRAL ALL-AIR SYSTEMS: SINGLE DUCT, CONSTANT AIR VOLUME (CAV)

Variations

1. A *furnace* is an indoor unit that incorporates a source of heat and an air circulating fan into a single metal box. The source of heat may be a gas burner, an oil burner, an electric resistance coil, or a heat pump coil. Cooling coils may also be incorporated if desired. The capacity of furnaces is limited to such an extent that they are used mostly in single-family houses and other very small buildings; multiple furnaces are sometimes used to heat and cool somewhat larger buildings. For a more extended discussion of furnaces, see pages 203–205.

2. A single duct, *constant volume reheat system* is identical to the CAV system first described, up to the point at which the air enters the local ductwork for each zone. In reheat systems, the air then passes through a reheat coil. The reheat coil may carry hot water or steam piped from the boiler room, or it may be an electric resistance coil. A local thermostat controls the temperature of the reheat coil, allowing for close individual control of room temperature. Reheat systems are typically used in situations requiring precise temperature control and constant airflow, such as laboratories, hospital operating rooms, or specialized industrial processes. Because constant air volume reheat systems are inherently wasteful of energy, first cooling air and then heating it, they are not often specified for new buildings.

3. In the *multizone system,* several ducts from a central fan serve several zones. In one type of multizone system, dampers blend hot and cold air at the fan to send air into each duct at the temperature requested by the thermostat in that zone. In another type (the one illustrated here), reheat coils in the fan room regulate the temperature of the air supplied to each zone. Multizone systems require a large amount of space for ductwork in the vicinity of the fan, so they are generally restricted to a small number of zones with short runs of ductwork. Packaged multizone units are available.

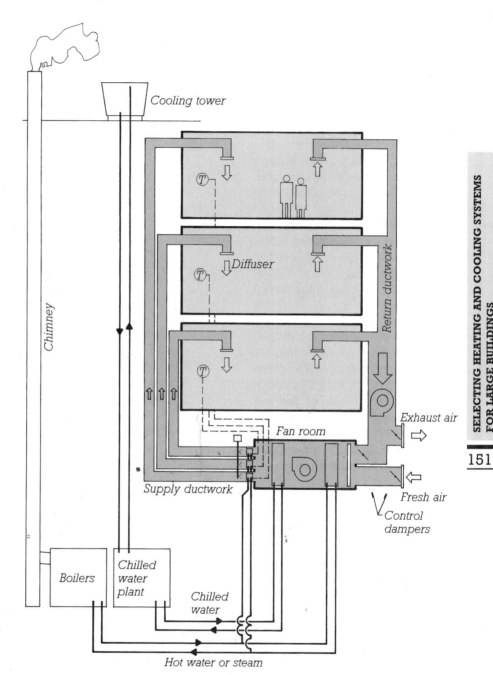

MULTIZONE SYSTEM

CENTRAL AIR AND WATER SYSTEMS: AIR-WATER INDUCTION SYSTEM

Description

Fresh air is heated or cooled, filtered, and humidified or dehumidified at a central source and circulated in small high-velocity ducts to the occupied spaces of the building. Each outlet is designed so that the air discharging from the duct (called *primary air*) draws a much larger volume of room air through a filter. The mixture of primary air and room air passes over a coil that is either heated or cooled by *secondary water* piped from the boiler room and chilled water plant. The primary air (about 15% to 25% of the total airflow through the outlet) and the heated or cooled room air that has been induced into the outlet (75% to 85% of the total airflow) are mixed and discharged into the room. A local thermostat controls water flow through the coil to regulate the temperature of the air. Condensate that drips from the chilled water coil is caught in a pan and removed through a system of drainage piping (not shown in the accompanying diagram).

Typical Applications

Exterior spaces of buildings with a wide range of heating and cooling loads where close control of humidity is not required, especially office buildings.

Advantages

This system offers good local temperature control. Space requirements for ductwork and fans are less than for all-air systems. There are no fans in the occupied spaces.

152

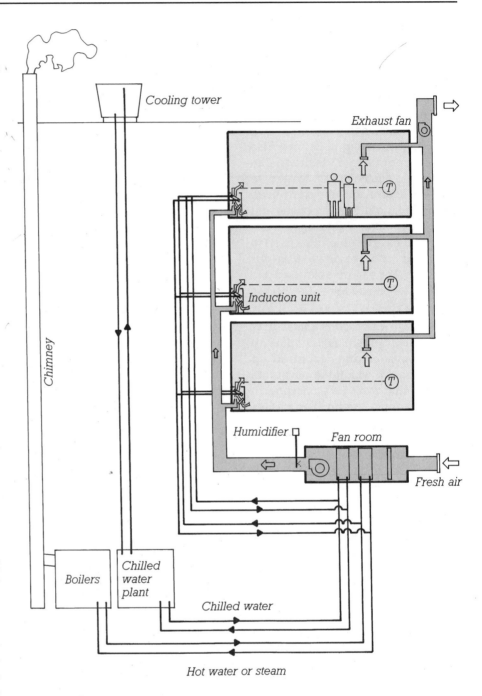

AIR-WATER INDUCTION SYSTEM

CENTRAL AIR AND WATER SYSTEMS: AIR-WATER INDUCTION SYSTEM

Disadvantages

This is a relatively complicated system to design, install, maintain, and manage. It tends to be noisy, and it is very inefficient in its use of energy. Humidity cannot be closely controlled. It is rarely designed or specified today.

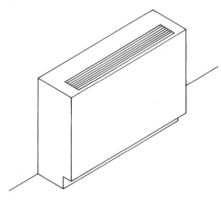

AIR-WATER INDUCTION UNIT

Major Components

Boilers and chimney, chilled water plant, cooling tower, fan room, outdoor fresh air and exhaust louvers, vertical supply and return ducts, horizontal supply and return ducts, vertical supply and return piping, horizontal supply and return piping, condensate drainage piping, air-water induction units. The water piping to each unit may consist of two, three, or four pipes, depending on whether a single coil is used for both heating and cooling or separate coils are provided for each. An additional pipe is required for condensate drainage.

Sizing the Components

Induction units are usually sized to fit beneath a window. Heights range from 25 to 28 in. (635 to 710 mm), depths from 9 to 12 in. (230 to 305 mm), and lengths from 30 to 84 in. (760 to 2130 mm). For the dimensions of the other components of the system, see the charts on pages 190–193.

Variations

Fan-coil units with primary air supply are similar to induction units, but use a fan to blow air through the coils instead of relying on the induction action of the primary airstream to circulate air from the room. The advantage of the fan-coil unit is that it can continue to circulate air even when the primary air is turned off. The primary air can be supplied through either the fan-coil unit or a separate diffuser.

CENTRAL ALL-WATER SYSTEMS: FAN-COIL TERMINALS

Description

Hot and/or chilled water are piped to fan-coil terminals. At each terminal, a fan draws a mixture of room air and outdoor air through a filter and blows it across a coil of heated or chilled water and then back into the room. A thermostat controls the flow of hot and chilled water to the coils to control the room temperature. Condensate that drips from the chilled water coil is caught in a pan and removed through a system of drainage piping (not shown in this diagram). In most installations the additional volume of air brought from the outdoors is used to pressurize the building to prevent infiltration or is exhausted through toilet exhaust vents.

Typical Applications

Buildings with many zones, all located on exterior walls, such as schools, hotels, motels, apartments, and office buildings.

Advantages

No fan rooms or ductwork spaces are required in the building. The temperature of each space is individually controlled.

Disadvantages

Humidity cannot be closely controlled. This system requires considerable maintenance, most of which must take place in the occupied space of the building.

Major Components

Boilers and chimney, chilled water plant, cooling tower, vertical supply and return piping, horizontal supply and return piping, condensate drainage piping, fan-coil terminals, outside air grilles.

Sizing the Components

Fan-coil terminals are usually sized to fit beneath a window. Heights range from 25 to 28 in. (635 to 710 mm), depths from 9 to 12 in. (230 to

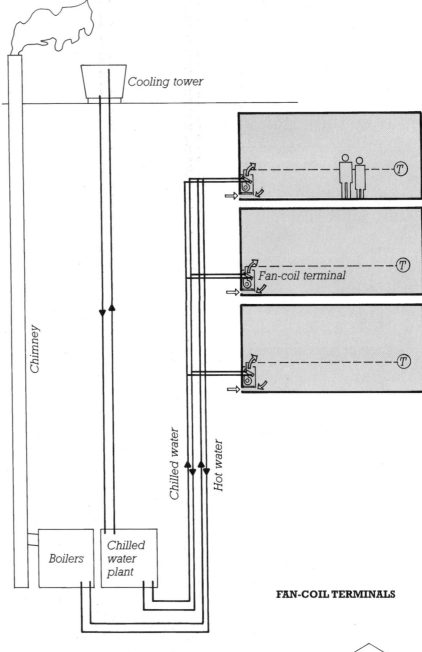

FAN-COIL TERMINALS

305 mm), and lengths from 30 to 84 in. (760 to 2130 mm). For the dimensions of the other components of the system, see the chart on pages 190–191.

Variations

Fan-coil terminals are also manufactured in a horizontal ceiling-hung configuration and in a tall, slender configuration for mounting in vertical chases.

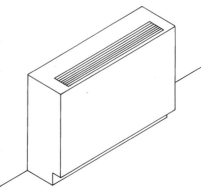

FAN-COIL TERMINAL

CENTRAL ALL-WATER SYSTEMS: CLOSED-LOOP HEAT PUMPS

Description

A water-to-air heat pump unit in each space provides heating, cooling, and fresh air. The water source for all the heat pumps in the building circulates in a closed loop of piping. Control valves allow the water source to circulate through a cooling tower in the summer and a boiler in the winter and to bypass both the boiler and the cooling tower in spring and fall and at any other time when the heating and cooling needs of the various rooms in the building balance one another.

Typical Applications

Hotels containing chronically overheated areas (kitchens, laundry, assembly rooms, restaurants).

Advantages

This is an efficient system in which heat extracted from chronically overheated areas can be used to heat underheated areas (guest rooms).

Disadvantages

This is an expensive system to install, and careful economic analysis is needed to determine if the high installation costs can be balanced by energy savings. The heat pumps require that much of the routine maintenance take place in the occupied spaces.

Major Components

Heat pump units, boiler room, cooling tower.

Sizing the Components

The heat pumps may be located above a dropped ceiling over the bathroom and dressing areas in hotel rooms, or below windows. A typical under-window heat pump unit is approximately 30 in. (760 mm) high, 12 in. (305 mm) deep, and 60 in. (1525 mm) long. An above-ceiling unit has approximately the same dimensions, with the 12-in. (305-mm) dimension vertical. For the dimensions of the other components of the system, see the chart on pages 190–191.

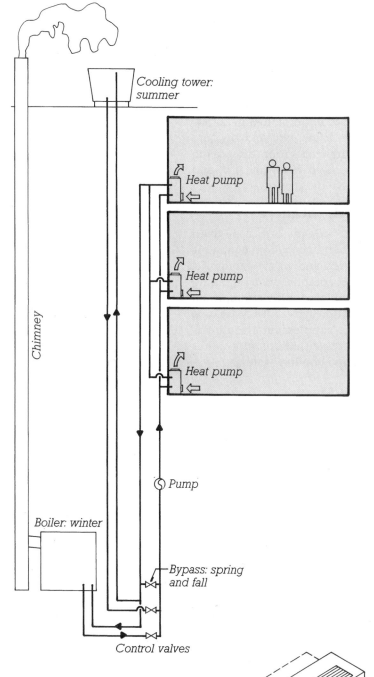

CLOSED-LOOP HEAT PUMPS

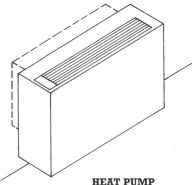

HEAT PUMP

CENTRAL ALL-WATER SYSTEMS: HYDRONIC CONVECTORS

Description

Hot water from the boiler room is circulated through fin-tube convectors, which are horizontal pipes with closely spaced vertical fins, usually mounted in a simple metal enclosure with an air inlet opening below and outlet louvers above. The heated fins, working by convection, draw cool room air into the enclosure from below, heat it, and discharge it out the top.

Typical Applications

Hydronic convectors are used alone in buildings where cooling is not required and where ventilation may be accomplished by opening windows or through a supplemental ventilation system. They are also used as a supplemental source of heat in combination with other heating and cooling systems.

Advantages

This is an economical system to install and operate. It provides excellent comfort during the heating season. Convectors are available in configurations ranging from continuous horizontal strips to cabinet units, either recessed or surface-mounted. Local control of temperature is possible through thermostatically controlled zone pumps or zone valves, through self-contained, thermostatically controlled valves at each convector or, in some types of convectors, through manually controlled dampers.

(continued)

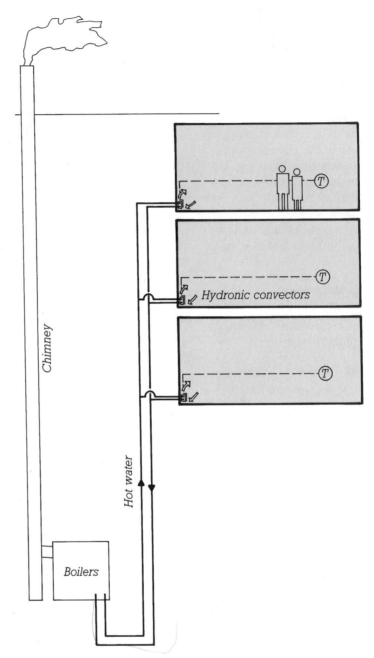

HYDRONIC CONVECTORS

CENTRAL ALL-WATER SYSTEMS: HYDRONIC CONVECTORS

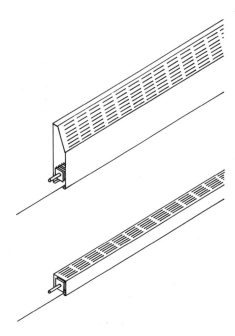

HYDRONIC FIN-TUBE CONVECTORS

Disadvantages

This is a system for heating only. Cooling, humidity control, and ventilation must be provided by separate means.

Major Components

Boilers and chimney, vertical supply and return piping, horizontal supply and return piping, convectors.

Sizing the Components

Hydronic convectors usually run continuously around the perimeter of a building. Each contains one or sometimes two continuous fin-tubes. The sheet metal enclosures for the fin-tubes are available in a variety of configurations: The smallest is about 5 in. (127 mm) square in cross section and should be mounted at least 4 in. (100 mm) above the floor. Enclosures up to 28 in. (710 mm) high and 6 in. (152 mm) deep are often used for improved thermal performance. The top of the enclosure contains small louvers and may be sloping or flat. For the dimensions of the other components of a hydronic heating system, see the chart on pages 190–191.

Variations

1. Hydronic heating is useful in buildings down to the scale of single-family residences. See pages 206–207.

2. In spaces where insufficient perimeter is available for convectors, or where the presence of convectors is undesirable, fan-forced unit heaters may be used. These are housed in metal cabinets that may be recessed in a wall, mounted on the surface of a wall, or suspended from the ceiling structure. Each heater contains a hot-water coil fed from the boiler room and an electric fan to circulate air across the coil. Unit heaters are very compact in relation to their heating capacity as compared to convectors.

LOCAL SYSTEMS: PACKAGED TERMINAL UNITS AND THROUGH-THE-WALL UNITS

Description

One or several through-the-wall units or packaged terminal units are mounted on the exterior wall of each room. Within each unit, an electric-powered compressor and evaporator coil provide cooling capability. Heating is supplied either by electric resistance coils or by utilizing the compressor in a reversible cycle as a heat pump. A fan draws indoor air through a filter, adds a portion of outdoor air, passes the air across the cooling and heating coils, and blows it back into the room. Another fan circulates outdoor air independently through the unit to cool the condensing coils (and, in a heat pump cycle, to furnish heat to the evaporator coils). A control thermostat is built into each unit.

There are several alternative types of equipment that fit into this category. *Packaged terminal units* are contained primarily in an indoor metal cabinet that fits beneath a window; they are connected to outdoor air with a wall box and an outdoor grille. *Through-the-wall* units are contained in a rectangular metal box that is mounted directly in an opening in the exterior wall of the building. A variation of the through-the-wall unit is the familiar *window-mounted unit,* used only for low-cost retrofitting of existing buildings. The only service distribution to any of these types of units is an electric cable or conduit.

Typical Applications

Apartments, dormitories, motels, hotels, office buildings, schools, nursing homes.

TYPICAL DIMENSIONS OF PACKAGED TERMINAL UNITS AND THROUGH-THE-WALL UNITS

	Width	Depth	Height
Packaged Terminal Units	43" (1100 mm)	14"–20" (360–510 mm)	16" (410 mm)
Through-the-Wall Units	24–26" (610–660 mm)	17"–30" (430–760 mm)	16"–18" (410–460 mm)

Advantages

Units are readily available and easily installed. Initial costs are often lower than for central systems. Each room has individual control of temperature. No building space is utilized for central equipment, ductwork, or piping. Operating costs may be lower than for central systems in buildings in which not all spaces need to be heated or cooled all the time, such as motels.

Disadvantages

Maintenance costs are high and equipment life is relatively short. Maintenance must be carried out in the occupied spaces. The equipment is often noisy and inefficient. Air distribution can be uneven. Wintertime humidification is not possible. Operating costs are high in areas with very cold winters and costly electricity. Through-the-wall and window-mounted units can be unsightly.

Major Components

Packaged terminal units or through-the-wall units. Typical dimensions of these units are given in the table above.

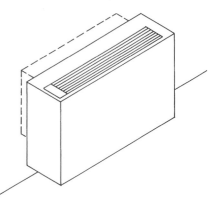

PACKAGED TERMINAL UNIT

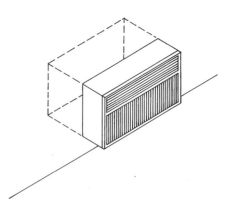

THROUGH-THE-WALL UNIT

158

■■■ CONFIGURING AND SIZING MECHANICAL AND ELECTRICAL SERVICES FOR LARGE BUILDINGS

This section will help you lay out the necessary spaces for mechanical and electrical equipment in a preliminary design for a large building.

The major equipment spaces for a large building are discussed in alphabetical order on the pages that follow.

BOILER ROOM AND CHIMNEY

The boiler room produces hot water or, less commonly, steam, to heat the building and to heat domestic water. Sometimes steam is also used to power absorption chilling equipment. A boiler room for a large building normally contains at least two boilers so that one may be in service even if the other is being cleaned or repaired. All boilers are connected to a single chimney. The boiler room may be placed anywhere in a building; common locations are a basement, a mechanical room on grade, a mechanical floor, or the roof. It should be on an outside wall because it needs an intake grille for combustion air and a door or removable panel to allow for removal and replacement of boilers. Because of the noise and heat it gives off, a boiler room should be placed below or adjacent to areas such as loading docks and lobbies that will not be adversely affected. It is helpful to locate the boiler room next to the chilled water plant; the two facilities are often combined in a single room. Hot water supply and return pipes run from the boilers through vertical shafts to reach the other floors of the building.

Boilers and their associated equipment create very heavy floor loadings that need to be taken into account when designing the supporting structure.

Boilers may be fueled by gas, electricity, or oil. Electric boilers, which generally are economical only in areas where electricity costs are very low, eliminate the need for combustion air inlets and a chimney. Generally, a two-week supply of fuel for an oil-fired boiler is stored in tanks in or near the building. The filler pipes must be accessible to oil delivery vehicles. These tanks are usually buried next to the building if space permits. If the tanks are inside the building, they must be installed in a naturally ventilated room that is designed so that it can contain the full contents of a tank and keep the contents from escaping into the building if the tank should leak. A basement location on an outside wall is preferred. Oil for a boiler on an upper floor of a building is pumped up a shaft through a pipe from the tanks below.

An approximate floor area for a boiler room may be determined using the chart on pages 190–191. In larger buildings, a long, narrow room is usually preferable to a square one. The ceiling height of a boiler room varies from a minimum of 12 ft (3.66 m) for a building of moderate size to a maximum of 16 ft (4.88 m) for a large building.

The size of the chimney that is associated with fuel-burning boilers varies with the type of fuel, the height of the chimney, the type of draft (natural, forced, or induced) that is employed, and other factors. For preliminary design purposes, allow a floor area of 2 ft × 2 ft (610 mm square) for a chimney in a very small building, and 6 ft × 6 ft (1.83 m square) in a very large building, interpolating between these extremes for buildings of other sizes. Keep in mind that the chimney runs through every floor of the building above the boiler room.

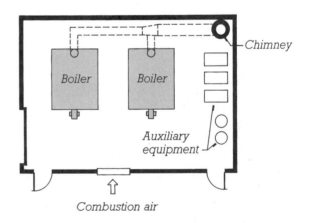

TYPICAL LAYOUT OF BOILER ROOM

160

CHILLED WATER PLANT

The chilled water plant produces cold water (usually 42° to 45°F, or 5° to 6°C) that is used for cooling the building. The chillers are fueled by electricity, gas, or steam. The chillers give off heat, noise, and vibration, and should not be located near spaces they will adversely affect. They may be placed anywhere in the building from basement to roof, but they are heavy and require deeper-than-normal structural members for support. An outside wall location is desirable to allow for the necessary ventilation and maintenance access. Ideally the chilled water plant should be adjacent to the boiler room; the two are often housed in the same room in a building of moderate size. Chilled water supply and return pipes run from the chilled water pumps to the fan rooms or terminals that they serve. Condenser water supply and return pipes run between the chillers and the cooling towers.

An approximate floor area for a chilled water plant may be determined using the chart on pages 190–191. In larger buildings a long, narrow room is usually preferable to a square one. The ceiling height of a chilled water plant varies from a minimum of 12 ft (3.66 m) for a building of moderate size to a maximum of 16 ft (4.88 m) for a very large building.

COOLING TOWERS

Cooling towers extract heat from the water that is used to cool the condenser coils of the chilled water plant. In effect, the cooling towers are the mechanism by which the heat removed from a building by the air conditioning system is dissipated into the atmosphere. Most cooling towers are "wet," meaning that the hot water from the condensers splashes down through the tower, giving off heat by evaporation and convection to a stream of air that is forced through the tower by fans. The cooled water is collected in a pan at the bottom of the tower and circulated back to the chillers.

The size and number of cooling towers are related to the cooling requirements of the building. Cooling towers may be located on the ground if they are at least 100 ft (30 m) from any building or parking lot, to avoid property damage and unhealthful conditions from the splash, fog, and microorganisms given off by the towers. An alternate location is the roof of the building, but because of the noise and vibration they generate, the towers should be isolated acoustically from the frame of the building, and noise-sensitive areas such as auditoriums and meeting rooms should not be located directly below them. Rooftop cooling towers must be located well away from windows and fresh air louvers.

A preliminary estimate of the roof or ground area occupied by cooling towers may be obtained from the chart on pages 190–191. Cooling towers range between 13 and 40 ft (4 and 12 m) in height; the height for a given building can be estimated by interpolating between these two extremes. The towers usually have a 4-ft (1.2-m) crawlspace beneath. For free airflow, they should be located one full width apart and at least 10 to 15 ft (3 to 5 m) from any screen wall or parapet wall unless the wall has very large louvers at the base to allow for intake air.

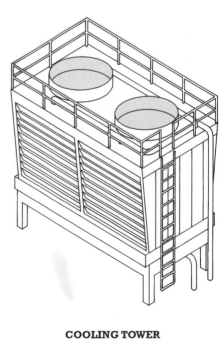

COOLING TOWER

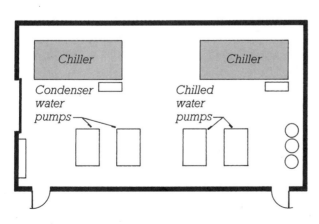

TYPICAL LAYOUT OF CHILLED WATER PLANT

ELECTRICAL SERVICE ENTRANCE, TRANSFORMERS, SWITCHGEAR, AND EMERGENCY POWER SUPPLY

Every building has an electrical transformer or transformers, a meter or meters, and a panel or switchgear that distributes the power to the interior wiring that services the building. The locations and sizes of these elements vary considerably, depending on the size and purpose of the building, the type of electric service provided by the local utility, the standards and practices of the utility company, the preferences of the building owner, the judgment of the electrical engineer, and local electrical codes.

For reasons of efficiency, electric utilities transmit electricity at high voltages. Transformers reduce this to lower voltages that can be utilized directly in the building—typically 120/208 volts or 115/230 volts in wall and floor receptacles, and up to 480/277 volts in some types of machinery and lighting fixtures. A commercial building of up to 25,000 sq ft (2500 m²) or a residential building up to twice this size will most often buy its electricity at these lower voltages. For buildings in this size range, the transformer is provided by the utility company and may be mounted overhead on a transmission pole, on the ground (especially where transmission lines are underground), or, in some dense urban situations, in a nearby building or underground vault. A meter or meters belonging to the utility company are installed on or in the building where the service wires enter, and distribution within is usually by means of panels of circuit breakers that are located in an adjacent utility space or a small electrical closet.

Owners of larger buildings will sometimes prefer to buy electricity at these lower voltages, but they can obtain energy more economically by providing their own transformers and purchasing electricity at the higher transmission voltage. One typical pattern is to bring electricity to the building at 13,800 volts and then to step down to 480/277 volts with a large primary transformer or transformers at the service entrance. The 277-volt electricity is used directly in many types of commercial and industrial lighting, and at 480 volts, electricity can be distributed efficiently to electrical closets in various parts of the building. Each electrical closet houses one or more small secondary transformers to step down from 480 volts to the lower voltages needed for convenience receptacles and machinery.

Primary transformers may be located either outside or inside the building. Where space is available, an outdoor transformer mounted on a ground-level concrete pad is preferred to an indoor transformer, because it is less expensive, cools better, is easier to service, transmits less noise to the building, and is safer against fire. Some common dimensions of pad-mounted transformers are shown in the upper table on the facing page. A trans-

former of this type does not need to be fenced unless for visual concealment, in which case there must be a clear space of 4 ft (1.2 m) all around the pad for ventilation and servicing. The pad should be within 30 ft (9 m) of a service road and requires a clear service lane 6 ft (1.83 m) wide between the transformer and the road. Multiple outdoor transformers are often used to serve larger buildings and are usually placed at intervals around the perimeter of the building to supply electricity as close as possible to its point of final use.

In a dense urban situation, or where the building owner finds outdoor placement objectionable, the primary transformer or transformers must be located within the building. Oil-filled transformers of the type the utility company provides for large buildings must be placed in a transformer vault, which is a fire-rated enclosure with two exits. In a few large cities, it is customary to place the transformer vault under the sidewalk, covered with metal gratings for ventilation. Dry-type transformers of the kind usually bought by owners of small- and medium-sized buildings do not need a vault; they may be placed in the main electric room. The transformer vault or main electric room is often placed in the basement or on the ground floor, but may be located on higher floors. Primary transformers are very heavy and require a heavier, deeper supporting structure than the rest of the building.

In buildings with dry-type transformers, the switchgear, consisting of disconnect switches, secondary switches, fuses, and circuit breakers, may be housed in the same enclosure with the transformers in a configuration known as a unit substation. In large buildings with oil-filled transformers, the switchgear is located in a room adjacent to the transformer vault.

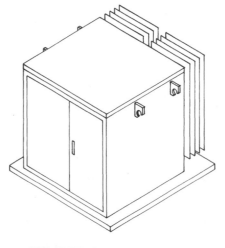

PAD-MOUNTED TRANSFORMER

MAJOR EQUIPMENT SPACES FOR LARGE BUILDINGS

Transformers and switchgear must be ventilated because they give off large quantities of heat. It is best to locate them against an outside wall so that high and low convective ventilation openings can be provided. If this is not possible, ventilation can be accomplished by ductwork and fans connected to outdoor air louvers. Access panels or doors must be provided for servicing and replacing switchgear and transformers. Some examples of sizes of transformer vaults and switchgear rooms are given in the lower table on this page.

Note also that where a high priority is placed on maintaining a continuous supply of electrical power, power may be brought to the building from two or more independent electric substations. In this way, a failure at any single substation will not interrupt power to the building.

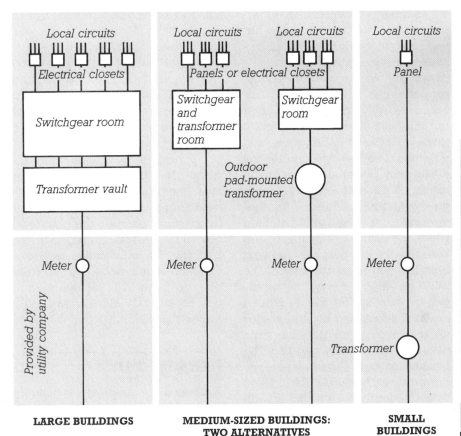

LARGE BUILDINGS   MEDIUM-SIZED BUILDINGS: TWO ALTERNATIVES   SMALL BUILDINGS

TYPICAL DIMENSIONS OF PAD-MOUNTED TRANSFORMERS

Floor Area of Commercial Building in Ft² (m²)	Number of Residential Units	Pad Size in Inches (m)
18,000 (1,700)	50	52 × 44 (1.3 × 1.2)
60,000 (5,700)	160	52 × 50 (1.3 × 1.3)
180,000 (17,000)	—	96 × 96 (2.4 × 2.4)

TYPICAL SIZES OF TRANSFORMER VAULTS AND SWITCHGEAR ROOMS

Floor Area of Commercial Building in Ft² (m²)	Floor Area of Residential Building in Ft² (m²)	Size of Combined Room for Transformers and Switch gear in Ft (m)	Size of Transformer Vault in Ft (m)	Size of Switchgear Room in Ft (m)
150,000 (15,000)	300,000 (30,000)	30 × 30 × 11 (9.14 × 9.14 × 2.44)		
100,000 (10,000)	200,000 (20,000)		20 × 20 × 11 (6.0 × 6.0 × 3.35)	30 × 20 × 11 (9.0 × 6.0 × 3.35)
300,000 (30,000)	600,000 (60,000)		20 × 40 × 11 (6.0 × 12.0 × 3.35)	30 × 40 × 11 (9.0 × 12.0 × 3.35)
1,000,000 (100,000)	2,000,000 (200,000)		20 × 80 × 11 (6.0 × 24.0 × 3.35)	30 × 80 × 11 (9.0 × 24.0 × 3.35)

In many buildings an emergency generator is required to furnish electricity during power outages. The emergency generator is driven by an engine fueled with propane gas or diesel oil. This engine needs large quantities of air for combustion and cooling, and it gives off exhaust gases, noise, and vibration. The best location for the emergency power supply is on the ground outside the building, near the switchgear room. Engine-generator sets in prefabricated weather-resistant housings are available for this purpose. The next best location is on the roof of the building; alternatively, the emergency power supply may be placed inside the building on an exterior wall, as remote as possible from occupied areas of the building. The housing or room for an emergency power supply is usually 12 ft (3.66 m) wide. A length of 18 ft (5.5 m) will accommodate an emergency power supply for an average commercial building of up to 150,000 sq ft (14,000 m^2); 22-ft (6.7-m) length will accommodate the supply for a building of up to 400,000 sq ft (37,000 m^2). Where a building owner requires emergency power for other than life-safety loads, these space requirements can grow very rapidly.

There is a loss of power for a period of up to 10 seconds between the time a power interruption occurs and the time the emergency generator takes over. This is usually acceptable, but in some buildings with specialized medical equipment, computers, communications equipment, certain types of lighting, or an extraordinary need for security, an uninterruptible power supply (UPS) is needed to keep electricity flowing during the brief transition from utility electricity to that generated on-site. Where a UPS is needed, it requires, in addition to the emergency power supply, a room for batteries and an adjacent room for specialized circuit breakers and electronic controls. These should be located close to the area that utilizes the UPS power. A typical computer room of 10,000 sq ft (1000 m^2) requires an outside-ventilated battery room of 500 sq ft (47 m^2), and a room of 200 sq ft (19 m^2) for electronic equipment. Both these rooms require air conditioning.

Several large conductors run from the transformers to the switchgear and from the switchgear to the vertical and horizontal distribution components that feed electrical closets throughout the building. For information on vertical distribution and electrical closets, see page 173. For information on horizontal distribution, see pages 185–189.

EXHAUST FANS

Exhaust fans draw air constantly from toilet rooms, locker rooms, bathrooms, janitor closets, storage rooms, corridors, and kitchens and deliver it to the outdoors to keep the air fresh in these spaces. Exhaust fans are also used to evacuate air from laboratory fume hoods and many industrial processes. The fans are usually housed in small mushroom ventilators on the roof and are connected to the spaces they serve by ducts that run through the vertical shafts in the cores of the building. It is extremely difficult to generalize about the sizes of exhaust ducts and fans; they tend not to be extremely large, so it is usually sufficient to allow a small amount of shaft space and roof space that can later be adjusted in consultation with the mechanical engineer.

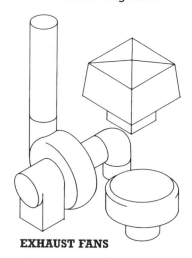

EXHAUST FANS

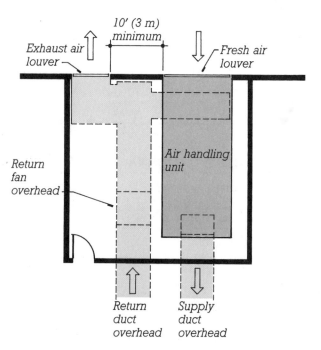

TYPICAL LAYOUT OF FAN ROOM

164

MAJOR EQUIPMENT SPACES FOR LARGE BUILDINGS

FAN ROOMS AND OUTDOOR AIR LOUVERS

In an all-air system, an air handling unit in a fan room circulates air through a filter and thermostatically controlled hot water and chilled water coils to condition it. The conditioned air is ducted to the occupied spaces of the building. A return fan draws air from the occupied spaces into return grilles and back to the fan room through return ducts. Just before it passes through the heating and cooling coils again, a portion of the air is diverted by a damper and exhausted through a louver to the outdoors. An equal portion of fresh air is drawn in through another outdoor louver and added to the stream of return air.

Fan rooms may be located anywhere in the building; they are supplied with hot and chilled water through insulated pipes from the boiler room and chilled water plant. A floor plan of a typical fan room is shown on the facing page. If only a single fan room is used, it may be placed in the basement, on the ground floor, on the roof, or on any intermediate floor, as close to the vertical distribution shafts as possible. It is convenient to locate this room near an outside wall, but if an outside wall location is not possible, ducts to the outdoors are used to convey fresh air and exhaust air to and from the fan. These ducts may run horizontally, above a ceiling, or vertically, in a shaft.

The maximum vertical "reach" of a fan room is approximately 25 stories up and/or down; more typically, fan rooms are located so none needs to circulate air more than 11 to 13 stories in each direction.

Multiple fans distributed throughout the building are often desirable because they allow the building to be zoned for better local control and they reduce the total volume of ductwork in the building. It can be advantageous to

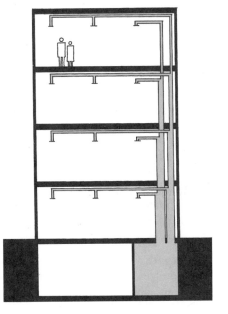

FAN ROOM IN BASEMENT

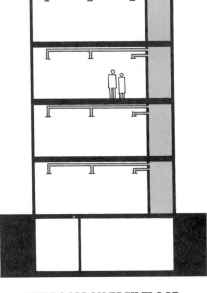

FAN ROOM ON EACH FLOOR

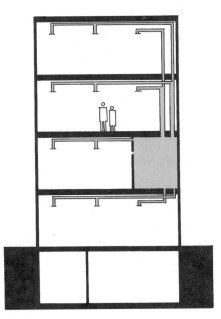

FAN ROOM ON INTERMEDIATE FLOOR

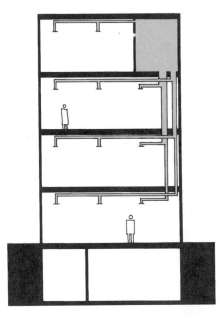

FAN ROOM AT TOP OF BUILDING

have a separate fan room for each floor of a building, because this saves floor space by eliminating most or all of the vertical runs of ductwork. Separate fan rooms are used in buildings that bill tenants individually for heating and cooling costs. Again, it is preferable to locate each fan room at the perimeter of the building.

Fan room equipment is often heavy enough to require stronger structural support than the surrounding areas of the building. Noise-sensitive areas such as meeting rooms and auditoriums should not be located adjacent to fan rooms, which produce vibration and noise.

(continued)

The fresh air and exhaust air louvers associated with a fan room are noisy and create local winds. They need to be located a short distance apart, usually at least 10 ft (3 m), on the exterior wall, so that the outgoing and incoming air will not mix. Louvers for small pieces of equipment such as fan-coil units are very small. With careful design work, they can be integrated unobtrusively into the fabric of the wall. Louvers for larger pieces of equipment grow progressively larger with the floor area each serves. They are large and conspicuous for central fans serving a number of floors and require special attention on the part of the architect.

Use the graph on pages 192–193 as a means of determining the approximate sizes of outdoor louvers for preliminary design purposes. The same graph gives information on sizing fan rooms as a function of floor area served. Using this graph, one may quickly evaluate a number of schemes for air distribution, using one fan room or many, to determine the effect of each scheme on the space planning and exterior appearance of the building.

LOADING DOCK AND ASSOCIATED SPACES

Every large building needs at least a single loading dock and freight room for receiving and sending mail and major shipments, moving tenant furniture in and out, removing rubbish, and facilitating the servicing of mechanical and electrical equipment. The dock needs to be situated so that trucks may back up to it easily without obstructing traffic on the street. The freight room inside the dock area should open directly to the rubbish compactor and the freight elevators and should be connected to the major mechanical equipment

spaces and the mail room. It is often appropriate to locate the oil filler pipes next to the truck ramp that leads to the loading dock. If possible, the access doors to the major equipment spaces should also open to the dock or ramp area. For dimensional information on truck ramps and loading docks, consult *Architectural Graphic Standards.*

PACKAGED CENTRAL HEATING AND COOLING EQUIPMENT

Packaged central heating and cooling equipment comes in two different configurations:

■ *Single-packaged* heating and cooling equipment combines the functions of a boiler room and chimney, a chilled water plant, and a fan room into a compact, rectangular, weatherproof unit that is specified, purchased, and installed as a single piece of equipment. The supply and return ducts from the building are connected through the roof or the wall of the building to the fan inside the packaged unit.

■ *Split-packaged* units are furnished in two parts, an outdoor package that incorporates the compressor and condensing coils, and an indoor package that contains the cooling and heating coils and

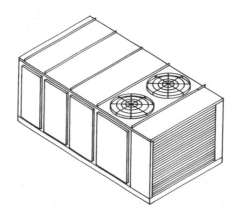

SPLIT-PACKAGED UNIT

the circulating fan. The two packages are connected by insulated refrigerant tubing and control wiring. Split-packaged units cost slightly more than single-packaged units, but they are slightly more energy efficient because none of their ductwork is located outside the insulated shell of the building.

Packaged units, whether single or split, are fueled entirely by electricity or by a combination of electricity and gas. Packaged equipment is simple for the designer to select and specify and is easy to purchase and install because it is supplied as off-the-shelf units that need only external connections to fuel, electricity, control wiring, and air ducts.

Packaged units are available in single-zone and multizone configurations in a variety of sizes to serve a wide range of demands for cooling and heating. They can be purchased as variable air volume or constant air volume (VAV or CAV) systems (see pages 148–151).

Single-packaged units are generally located either on the roof or on a concrete pad alongside the building. If alongside, the supply and return ducts are connected to the end of the unit and pass through the side wall of the building before branching out to the spaces inside. In a rooftop installation, the ducts pass through the bottom of the unit and into the building. The ducts from single-packaged units can serve low multistory buildings through vertical shafts that connect to above-ceiling branch ducts on each floor. Rooftop units may be placed at intervals to serve a building of any horizontal extent. The same is true of units located alongside the building, although the depth of the building is somewhat restricted by the maximum practical reach of the ducts. Using the chart on pages 192–193, you may select a combination of

MAJOR EQUIPMENT SPACES FOR LARGE BUILDINGS

unit size and numbers of units to serve any desired size and shape of building. For buildings taller than four or five stories, or large buildings where only one central plant may be installed, conventional central equipment assembled from components must be used because of the relatively limited capacity range of packaged units.

The table below will help to determine preliminary sizes for split-packaged equipment. The inside package may be obtained as a horizontal unit that hangs from the roof structure, or as a vertical unit that stands on the floor. The outside package may be located on the roof or on a concrete pad next to the building.

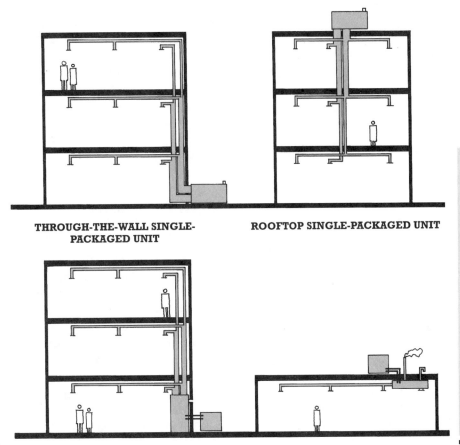

THROUGH-THE-WALL SINGLE-PACKAGED UNIT

ROOFTOP SINGLE-PACKAGED UNIT

SPLIT-PACKAGED UNITS

TYPICAL DIMENSIONS OF SPLIT-PACKAGED COMPONENTS

COOLING CAPACITY IN TONS (MCAL/SEC)		10 (35)	20 (70)	30 (106)	40 (141)	50 (176)
Outdoor Unit	Length	6'-4" (1.93 m)	12'-11" (3.94 m)	12'-11" (3.94 m)	12'-11" (3.94 m)	12'-11" (3.94 m)
	Width	3'-8" (1.12 m)	4'-0" (1.22 m)	4'-10" (1.47 m)	7'-1" (2.16 m)	7'-1" (2.16 m)
	Height	3'-4" (1.02 m)	2'-4" (0.71 m)	3'-2" (0.97 m)	4'-9" (1.45 m)	5'-8" (1.73 m)
Indoor Ceiling-Suspended Unit	Length	8'-3" (2.51 m)	7'-10" (2.39 m)	9'-0" (2.74 m)	9'-8" (2.95 m)	9'-8" (2.95 m)
	Width	5'-3" (1.60 m)	6'-8" (2.03 m)	7'-10" (2.39 m)	10'-7" (3.23 m)	10'-7" (3.23 m)
	Height	2'-2" (0.66 m)	2'-6" (0.76")	3'-0" (0.91")	3'-10" (1.17 m)	3'-10" (1.17 m)
Indoor Floor-Mounted Unit	Length	5'-3" (1.60 m)	6'-8" (2.03 m)	7'-10" (2.39 m)	10'-7" (3.23 m)	10'-7" (3.23 m)
	Width	2'-2" (0.66 m)	2'-6" (0.76 m)	3'-0" (0.91 m)	3'-10" (1.17 m)	3'-10" (1.17 m)
	Height	8'-3" (2.51 m)	7'-10" (2.39 m)	9'-0" (2.74 m)	9'-8" (2.95 m)	9'-8" (2.95 m)

Use the chart on pages XXX–XXX to estimate the required cooling capacity.

SEWAGE EJECTOR PIT

If the lowest level of a building lies below the level of the sewer or septic tank, sewage is collected in an underfloor pit and pumped up to the sewer. The pumps do not necessarily occupy floor space, because they are usually contained within the pit, but the pit must lie beneath unobstructed floor space so it can be inspected and serviced through a removable cover.

TELECOMMUNICATIONS ROOM

A central room for telephone and data systems should be located in the basement or on the ground floor as close to the telecommunications service entrance as possible. Where telecommunications distribution closets are stacked on floors above, this room should be located directly below these closets as well. Equipment needs in this room will vary depending on the particular systems to be installed, and are also likely to vary significantly over time. For this reason, this room, and all other components of the telecommunications distribution system in the building, should be configured with ease of access and maximum flexibility in mind. For preliminary purposes, the service entrance room should be no smaller than 60 sq ft (6 m^2), and may be 400 sq ft (40 m^2) in size or larger for a large commercial office building. The room should be free of plumbing, steam or other piping, and should be in a separate cooling zone to allow independent temperature control. From this room, telecommunications wiring extends to distribution closets on each floor (see page 173).

WASTE COMPACTOR

A waste compactor is necessary in most large buildings. It may be coupled with a container system to facilitate the trucking of the compacted rubbish.

The compactor is often served by a vertical refuse chute from the upper floors of the building. The chute must be placed in a fire-rated enclosure and must be provided with an automatic sprinkler head above the top opening. Some codes also require the provision of a 2-hour enclosed chute room outside the chute opening at each floor. Inside diameters of chutes range from 15 to 30 in. (380 to 760 mm), with 24 in. (610 mm) being a typical dimension.

The waste compactor should be located directly beneath the refuse chute and adjacent to the loading dock. The size and shape of the compactor itself vary widely with the manufacturer and the capacity of the unit. A compactor room of 60 sq ft (5.6 m²) is sufficient for a small apartment building. A larger building will require 150 to 200 sq ft (14.0 to 18.6 m²) and industrial waste compacting facilities can be much larger.

WATER PUMPS

Where the water service enters the building, a room is required to house the water meter and the sprinkler and standpipe valves. In a building taller than three or four stories, a suction tank and a pair of water pumps are needed to boost the water pressure in the domestic water system. A similar pair of pumps are required for a sprinkler system. A chiller for drinking water and a heat exchanger to heat domestic hot water are often located in the same area. The table below will assist in determining the necessary floor areas for water pumps.

In a few large cities, local codes require the provision of a large gravity tank on the roof of the building to furnish a reserve of water in case of fire. In most areas, however, the pumps alone are sufficient.

WORKROOMS, CONTROL ROOMS, AND OFFICES

Operating and maintenance personnel in large buildings need space in which to work. Offices should be provided for operating engineers and maintenance supervisors. A room is required to house the control console for a large-building heating and cooling system. Lockers and workrooms are needed for mechanics, plumbers, electricians, and custodial workers. Storage facilities should be provided near the loading dock and service elevator for tools, spare parts, and custodial equipment and supplies.

SPACE REQUIREMENTS FOR WATER PUMPS

Domestic Water Pumps	
Area Served	Room Dimensions
Up to 200,000 ft² (Up to 18,600 m²)	8' × 12' (2.44 × 3.66 m)
200,000 to 1,000,000 ft² (18,600 to 93,000 m²)	16' × 12' (4.88 × 3.66 m)

Fire Pumps (assuming sprinklers)	
Area Served	Room Dimensions
Up to 100,000 ft² (Up to 9300 m²)	8' × 12' (2.44 × 3.66 m)
100,000 to 200,000 ft² (9300 to 18,600 m²)	20' × 12' (6.1 × 3.66 m)
1,000,000 ft² (93,000 m²)	30' × 24' (9.15 × 7.32 m)

CONFIGURING AND SIZING MECHANICAL AND ELECTRICAL SERVICES FOR LARGE BUILDINGS

169

VERTICAL DISTRIBUTION OF SERVICES FOR LARGE BUILDINGS

PLANNING SERVICE CORES

Spaces for the vertical distribution of mechanical and electrical services in a large building need to be planned simultaneously with other building elements that are vertically continuous or that tend to occur in stacks—principally the structural columns, bearing walls, shear walls, and wind bracing; exit stairways; elevators and elevator lobbies; and rooms with plumbing: toilet rooms, bathrooms, kitchens, and janitor closets. These elements tend to coalesce into one or more core areas where the vertically continuous elements are concentrated into efficient, neatly packaged blocks of floor space, leaving most of each floor open for maximum flexibility of layout.

Different types of buildings call for different sorts of core arrangements. In high-rise office buildings, where a maximum amount of unobstructed, rentable area is the major criterion for floor layout, a single central core is almost universal. In low-rise commercial and institutional buildings, horizontal distances are often great enough that a single core would be inefficient, and vertical elements are divided into several cores of varied internal composition. These are likely to be located asymmetrically in response to particular requirements relating to the servicing and circulation patterns of the building. In a dormitory, apartment building, or hotel, a common pattern of vertical services features slender shafts sandwiched between the units. Shafts next to the interior corridor carry the plumbing for the bathrooms and kitchens that back up to them. If the heating and cooling equipment for the units is located over the bathrooms and kitchens, the hot and chilled water piping and ductwork may share these same shafts. If the heating and cooling are done

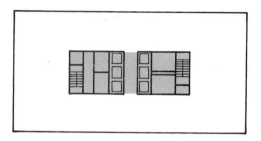

HIGH-RISE OFFICE BUILDING: VERTICAL SERVICES IN A CONCENTRATED CORE

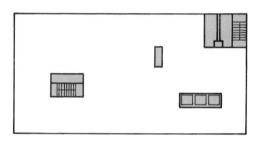

LOW-RISE BUILDING: VERTICAL SERVICES IN SCATTERED LOCATIONS

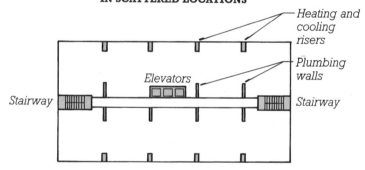

HOTEL OR APARTMENT BUILDING: VERTICAL SERVICES BETWEEN UNITS

along the outside walls, another set of shafts may be created between units around the perimeter of the building to serve this equipment.

Vertical distribution shafts need to connect directly with the major equipment spaces that feed them and the horizontal distribu-tion lines they serve. The boiler room, chilled water plant, central fan room, exhaust fans, water pumps, sewage ejector, waste compactor, and cooling towers need to cluster closely around the vertical distribution

shafts. The electric and telecommunications switchgear should not be far away. The electrical and telecommunications closets must stack up along the wiring shafts at each floor. The toilet rooms, bathrooms, kitchens, and janitor closets must back up to plumbing walls. Horizontal supply and return ducts need to join easily with the vertical ducts in the shafts, and horizontal piping for hot and chilled water distribution must branch off conveniently from the riser pipes.

VERTICAL DISTRIBUTION OF SERVICES FOR LARGE BUILDINGS

LOCATING THE CORES IN THE BUILDING

A centrally located core leaves the daylit perimeter area of the building open for use. It also works efficiently with a scheme that distributes services horizontally from one set of shafts, because it minimizes duct and pipe sizes. The central location can be undesirable, however, because it interrupts the open space of the floor. A core at one edge of the building does not have this problem, but it may not be able to incorporate exit stairways that are separated widely enough (see page 245), and it obstructs a portion of the daylit perimeter. Either of these core locations connects well to major equipment at the ground, the roof, and any intermediate mechanical floors.

A core located in a corner, on the other hand, is undesirable because horizontal distribution lines from the core are long, exit stairways are too close together, and connections to major equipment are congested. Two or more corner cores used in combination can overcome some of these problems.

Multiple cores often work well, particularly in broad, low-rise buildings. Exit stairways can be widely separated and connected to a simple, clear system of corridors and elevators. Vertical risers for mechanical services can be located where they work best, minimizing the congestion of ducts and pipes at points of connection to horizontal networks.

Core locations may also be dictated in part by the structural scheme that provides lateral stability to the building. A large, centrally located core or two symmetrically placed cores can furnish ideal locations for wind bracing. A core at the edge of the building or a detached core cannot house all the wind bracing for the building because it is located asymmetrically with respect to one of the principal axes of the building (see pages 33–35). Scattered cores and corner cores may not be large enough to develop the required depth of wind trusses.

The chart below summarizes some of the advantages and disadvantages of different options for core placement.

CHARACTERISTICS OF CORE PLACEMENTS

1 = Best 5= Worst	Edge	Detached	Central	Two	Corners	Scattered
Flexibility of typical rental areas	2	1	3	4	2	5
Perimeter for rental areas	4	3	1	1	5	2
Ground floor high-rent area	3	1	3	4	2	5
Typical distance of travel from core	4	5	2	1	3	3
Clarity of circulation	3	4	2	1	3	5
Daylight and view for core spaces	2	1	5	5	1	4
Service connections at roof	3	4	2	1	5	3
Service connections at ground	3	4	2	1	5	3
Suitability for lateral bracing	4	5	1	1	2	3

PLANNING THE INTERNAL ARRANGEMENT OF THE CORES

The ratio of the total floor area of the core or cores of a building to the floor area served varies widely from one building to the next. The average total area of the cores in 40- to 70-story New York City office buildings, including the stairways, toilets, elevators, and elevator lobbies, is approximately 27% of the open area of each floor served by the core. This ratio runs as high as 38% in some older buildings, but ranges around 20% to 24% in office towers of recent design. At the other extreme, the total core area of a three-story suburban office building is likely to be in the range of 7% of the floor area served, because there are few elevators, much less lobby space for elevators, and much smaller shafts for mechanical and electrical services.

These percentages also vary with the relative requirements for mechanical and electrical services; they can be higher in a hospital or laboratory and are much lower in a hotel or apartment building. Core area is directly related to the type of heating and cooling system used: The percentages quoted in the preceding paragraph apply to buildings with all-air systems. Buildings with air-and-water and all-water systems require somewhat less shaft space.

A building with a fan room on each floor will need very little core area for ductwork, but the fan room is likely to occupy at least as much floor space as the vertical ductwork it eliminates.

The structural scheme of a building can also have a direct effect on core area. Of the total core area of a tall office building, about 12% is usually occupied by columns, bracing, walls, and partitions. This percentage is lower for lower buildings and can be very low in buildings whose core areas contain no columns or lateral bracing.

The most critical elements of the core, those that should be located first in at least a tentative way, are the columns and bracing, the exit stairways, and the elevators and elevator lobbies. Next should come the plumbing walls and the shafts for ductwork. For help in laying out the structural elements, see pages 33–46. Details of the location and configuration of exit stairways are given on pages 252–257. Pages 181 and 182 give advice on the number, size, and layout of elevator shafts and lobbies. Plumbing walls are illustrated on page 179, and ductwork shafts can be sized using the chart on pages 192–193.

The chimney is another element for which there may be little flexibility of location. Usually the chimney exits from a corner of the boiler room. It may be sloped at an angle not less than 60° to the horizontal to bring it to a more convenient position in the core. For help sizing chimneys, refer to page 160.

TOTAL SHAFT AREA

The total open area of all the mechanical and electrical shafts in a tall office building is normally equal to about 4% of the area served on each floor, and can be estimated at about half this amount for a low-rise building. This should be divided into at least two separate shafts to relieve the congestion that would otherwise occur where the vertical and horizontal distribution networks connect. It is especially effective to provide separate shafts for supply and return ducts because it is often possible to use a separate return shaft as a plenum, a shaft that is itself the duct. Separate supply and return shafts also minimize conflict in the bulky ductwork connections and crossovers. For maximum utility, the horizontal proportions of each shaft should lie in the range of 1:2 to 1:4. To allow sufficient space for connections to horizontal distribution networks at each floor, no shaft should adjoin stair towers or elevator shafts on more than one long side and one short side. All shafts must be enclosed with 1- to 2-hour noncombustible walls, except in buildings of Wood Light Frame construction, where shaft enclosures do not need to be fire rated.

VERTICAL DISTRIBUTION OF SERVICES FOR LARGE BUILDINGS

ELECTRICAL CLOSETS AND TELECOMMUNICATIONS CLOSETS

Electrical and telecommunications closets must be accessible from public areas of the floor, must each be stacked above one another, must include wiring shafts, and must be kept free of plumbing, steam, and other types of wiring. Typical sizes and configurations for electrical closets are illustrated in the accompanying diagrams. In an office building, major electrical closets should be located in such a way that no point on a floor lies more than 125 ft (40 m) away. If this is difficult to arrange, satellite closets served by cables from the major closets may be used to feed electricity to the more distant areas. In smaller buildings or buildings other than offices, satellite-size closets may serve in place of major closets.

At least one telecommunications distribution closet should be provided for every floor and for every 10,000 sq ft (930 m^2) of area served. For commercial office space, telecommunications closets should measure 10 × 12 ft (3.0 x 3.7 m) internally. For less data-intensive occupancies, closets as small as 4 x 7 ft (1.2 x 2.1 m) may be acceptable. Separate cooling zones should be provided to permit independent temperature control of these areas.

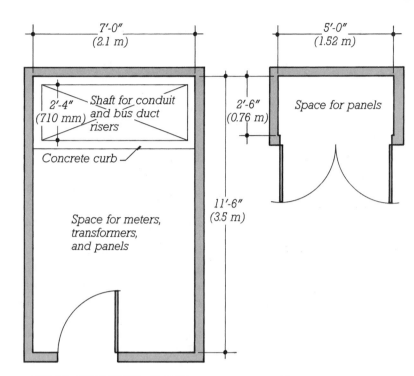

MAJOR ELECTRICAL CLOSET

SMALL OR SATELLITE ELECTRICAL CLOSET

FAN ROOMS

Local fan rooms, if their fresh air and exhaust air connections are provided by means of duct risers, should be placed against shafts. If local fan rooms need only hot and chilled water from central equipment, it is better to put them against outside walls, so that they may exchange air directly with the outdoors, and to serve them with water via horizontal piping from the core. (Alternatively, centrally-located local fan rooms can be connected to fresh air and exhaust louvers by horizontal ducts.) If fan rooms on an outside wall are stacked above one another, of course, it is usually possible to provide an immediately adjacent' shaft, separate from the main core, for the water riser piping. See pages 164–166 and 192–193 for information on planning fan rooms.

MAIL FACILITIES

Vertical gravity chutes for mail deposit are often provided in multistory buildings. The chute occupies an area of about 5 × 15 in. (125 × 375 mm) in plan and terminates in a receiving box in the base of the building.

Vertical mail conveyors are sometimes provided for delivery of mail in a large multistory office building. The mailroom at the base of the conveyor should be adjacent to the loading dock and can be sized at about 2/10 of 1% of the area it serves. The walls around the conveyor shaft itself will vary in plan from 4 ft × 4 ft 6 in. (1220 × 1370 mm) to 7 ft 3 in. × 8 ft 6 in. (2210 × 2590 mm) inside dimensions, depending on the system's capacity and manufacturer. The conveyor should discharge into a service mailroom of at least 6 × 7 ft (1830 × 2135 mm) on each floor. A 1- or 2-hour fire enclosure is required around the conveyor shaft.

PIPE RISERS FOR HEATING AND COOLING

The insulated pipes that conduct heated and chilled water to and from the spaces in a building require considerable space. In a tall apartment building or hotel, a clear shaft of 12 × 48 in. (300 × 1200 mm) is generally sufficient to serve two stacks of units. This may be sandwiched between units at the perimeter of the building or located adjacent to the central corridor, depending on where the heating and cooling equipment is located in the units.

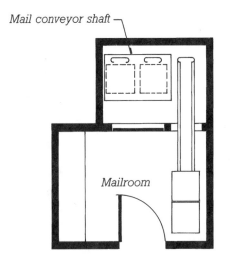

Mail conveyor shaft

Mailroom

VERTICAL DISTRIBUTION OF SERVICES FOR LARGE BUILDINGS

PLUMBING WALLS, JANITOR CLOSETS, AND TOILET ROOMS

Fixtures in bathrooms, toilet rooms, shower rooms, kitchens, laundries, and other areas with plumbing should back up to plumbing walls. A plumbing wall has an internal cavity large enough to house the supply, waste, and vent piping necessary to serve the fixtures. Plumbing walls should be stacked vertically from the bottom of the building to the top. It is possible to offset plumbing walls a few feet from one floor to the next, but the horizontal offsets are expensive and cause maintenance headaches. A typical plumbing wall arrangement, complete with janitor closet, is illustrated and dimensioned on the diagram to the right. The given widths are adequate for floor-mounted fixtures. If wall-hung fixtures are used, a 24 in. (600 mm) dimension is needed to accommodate the fixture carriers.

Fixture requirements for toilet rooms are established by plumbing codes and vary widely from one code to the next. Requirements for the model plumbing codes included in this book are reproduced on the following pages. The designer must also keep in mind the general requirement that toilet rooms be usable by disabled persons. For detailed layout dimensions of toilet rooms and accessible facilities, consult *Architectural Graphic Standards.*

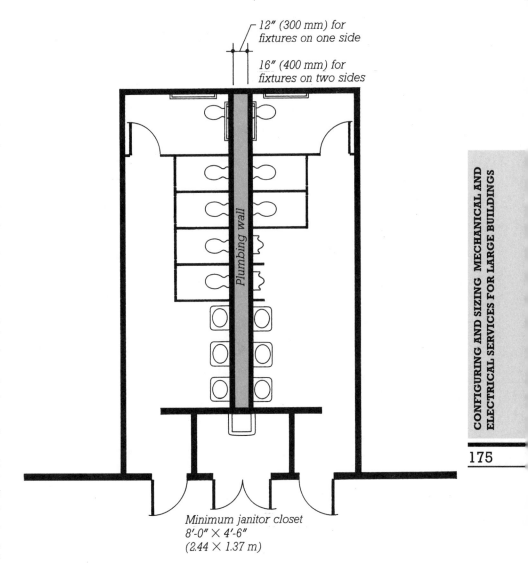

12" (300 mm) for fixtures on one side

16" (400 mm) for fixtures on two sides

Plumbing wall

Minimum janitor closet 8'-0" × 4'-6" (2.44 × 1.37 m)

Minimum Toilet Fixture Requirements in the International Building Code

Consult the table on the facing page to determine the minimum number of toilet fixtures required based on the type of occupancy and number of occupants served. See pages 7–10 for more information on determining the occupancy type for your building, and page 270 for determining occupant load. For occupancy types not listed in the table, select the most comparable type in terms of patterns of use and occupant density.

When determining fixture requirements, the following should also be considered:

■ Under most circumstances separate toilet facilities are required for each sex. Separate facilities are not required for private facilities, for areas where the total occupant load is 15 or less, or for employee facilities where 15 or fewer persons are employed.

■ Fixture requirements should be based on the assumption of equal numbers of male and female occupants, unless an unequal distribution of the sexes in the occupant population can be demonstrated.

■ For male toilet facilities, urinals may be substituted for not more than two-thirds of the required water closets.

■ In most circumstances, required toilet facilities must be located in the same building as the area served, be located not more than one floor above or below the occupied area, and be reachable along a path of travel distance not exceeding 500 ft (152 m).

■ In covered malls, the maximum path of travel to toilet facilities must not exceed 300 ft (91 m). Facilities may be located within individual stores or be centrally located. Where facilities are centrally located, the path of travel is measured from each store's main entrance to the facilities.

■ In most areas occupied by both employees and members of the public such as customers or tenants, the required facilities for each occupant group may be combined. In Institutional occupancies, employee and patient or inmate facilities must be separate, with the exception of Residential Care facilities, where they may be combined.

■ One-, Two- and Multifamily Residential occupancies must provide, in addition to the requirements of the table below, one kitchen sink per dwelling unit. One- and Two-Family occupancies must provide one automatic clothes washer connection per dwelling unit, and Multifamily occupancies must provide one such connection per 20 dwelling units.

■ Required toilet room facilities must be free of charge.

■ At least one service sink for maintenance personnel should be provided per floor or use area.

Accessible Toilet Facilities in the International Building Code

In buildings required to provide access to disabled persons, accessible routes must be provided to toilet and bathing facilities, and each facility must have at least one accessible fixture of each type. In toilet rooms with partitioned water closet compartments, at least one such compartment must be wheel-chair accessible. Where six or more compartments are provided, one additional compartment must be at least 36 in. (914 mm) in width, must have an outward-swinging door, and must be equipped with grab bars. In accessible buildings at least one-half of the required drinking fountains, but no fewer than one per floor, must be accessible.

In Group A Assembly and Group M Mercantile occupancies, unisex toilet rooms that provide private access to facilities for disabled individuals and their assistants are required wherever an aggregate of six or more male or female water closets are required. In recreational facilities providing separate-sex bathing facilities with more than one set of fixtures in each bathing room, at least one unisex bathing room is also required. Generally, unisex toilet or bathing rooms should have only one set of each fixture type, although in some circumstances separate-sex facilities with two water closets may be used to meet the unisex facility requirement. Unisex facilities must be located on accessible routes, not more than one story above or below the area of occupancy, and with a maximum path of travel distance of 500 ft (152 m). Unisex toilet and bathing facilities may be counted toward the total fixture requirements in a space.

In addition to noting the International Building Code requirements summarized here, be sure to determine what other codes or regulations pertaining to accessibility, such as the Americans with Disabilities Act, may apply to your project.

176

VERTICAL DISTRIBUTION OF SERVICES FOR LARGE BUILDINGS

Occupancy	Water Closets	Lavatories	Bathrooms/ Showers	Drinking Fountains
Assembly				
Coliseums, arenas with 3000 seats or more	Male: 1 per 120 Female: 1 per 60	Male: 1 per 200 Female: 1 per 150	None	1 per 1000
Coliseums, arenas with less than 3000 seats	Male: 1 per 75 Female: 1 per 40	1 per 150	None	
Stadiums with 3000 seats or more	Male: 1 per 150 Female: 1 per 75	Male: 1 per 200 Female: 1 per 150	None	
Stadiums, pools, etc. with less than 3000 seats	Male: 1 per 100 Female: 1 per 50	1 per 150	None	1 per 1000
Theaters, halls, museums, etc.	Male: 1 per 125 Female: 1 per 65	1 per 150	None	1 per 500
Churches	Male: 1 per 150 Female: 1 per 75	1 per 200	None	1 per 1000
Nightclubs	1 per 40	1 per 75	None	1 per 500
Restaurants	1 per 75	1 per 200	None	1 per 500
Business	1 per 50	1 per 80	None	1 per 100
Educational	1 per 50	1 per 50	None	1 per 100
Factory and industrial	1 per 100	1 per 100	Emergency showers and eyewash stations may be required	1 per 400
Passenger terminals and transportation facilities	1 per 500	1 per 750	None	1 per 1000
Institutional				
Residential care	1 per 10	1 per 10	1 per 8	1 per 100
Hospitals, ambulatory nursing homes	1 per room, or 1 per two adjacent rooms when provided with direct access from each room	1 per room, or 1 per two adjacent rooms when provided with direct access from each room	1 per 15	1 per 100
Day nurseries, sanitariums, nonambulatory nursing homes, etc.	1 per 15	1 per 15	1 per 15, but 1 only within day nurseries	1 per 100
Employees, other than residential care	1 per 25	1 per 35	none	1 per 100
Visitors to institutional facilities, other than residential care	1 per 75	1 per 100	none	1 per 500
Prisons	1 per cell	1 per cell	1 per 15	1 per 100
Asylums, reformatories, etc.	1 per 15	1 per 15	1 per 15	1 per 100
Mercantile	1 per 500	1 per 750	none	1 per 1000
Residential				
Hotels, motels	1 per guestroom	1 per guest room	1 per guest room	None
Lodges, dormitories	1 per 10	1 per 10	1 per 8	1 per 100
Multiple family, one- and two-family dwellings	1 per dwelling unit	1 per dwelling unit	1 per dwelling unit	None
Storage	1 per 100	1 per 100	Emergency showers and eyewash stations may be required	1 per 1000

Minimum Toilet Fixture Requirements in the National Building Code of Canada

Consult the table on the facing page to determine the minimum number of toilet fixtures required for projects located in Canada based on the type of occupancy and number of occupants served. See pages 11–13 for more information on determining the occupancy type for your building, and page 277 for determining occupant load.

In determining fixture requirements, the following should also be considered:

■ Under most circumstances, separate toilet facilities are required for each sex. Separate facilities are not required for Assembly, Residential, Business and Personal Services, Mercantile, and Industrial Occupancy Groups with an occupant load of 10 or less.

■ Fixture requirements should be based on the assumption of equal numbers of male and female occupants, unless an unequal distribution of the sexes in the occupant population can be demonstrated with reasonable accuracy.

■ For male toilet facilities, urinals may be substituted for not more than two-thirds of the required water closets. Where only two water closets are required, a urinal may be substituted for one closet.

■ For Business and Personal Service Occupancy Groups with a floor area of more than 600 m² (6460 sq ft), toilet facilities must be available to the public.

Accessible Toilet Facilities in the National Building Code of Canada

Most buildings must provide at least one accessible, barrier-free washroom. All washrooms on floors requiring barrier-free access must themselves be barrier-free, except that barrier-free washrooms are not required:

■ Within a residential occupancy suite

■ Where other barrier-free facilities are located on the same floor area and within a path of travel of 45 m (148 ft)

■ Within individual suites less than 500 m² (5380 sq ft) in area that are separated from the rest of the building and to which no barrier-free access is provided.

In Assembly occupancies with shower facilities, at least one shower stall must be barrier-free.

Special barrier-free, single-fixture, unisex washrooms may be provided as an alternative to the barrier-free washroom requirements above. When such special washrooms are provided, the occupant load used to calculate fixture requirements for the general public may be reduced by 10 persons in Assembly, Business and Personal Services, Mercantile, or Industrial occupancies, as well as in primary schools, day care facilities, places of worship, and undertaking premises.

178

VERTICAL DISTRIBUTION OF SERVICES FOR LARGE BUILDINGS

Occupancy	Number of Occupants of Each Sex	Number of Water Closets	Lavatories
Assembly	1–50	Male: 1 male; Female: 2	At least 1, and not less than 1 for every 2 water closets
	51–75	Male: 2; Female: 3	
	76–100	Male: 2; Female: 4	
	101–125	Male: 3; Female: 5	
	126–150	Male: 3; Female: 6	
	151–175	Male: 4; Female: 7	
	176–200	Male: 4; Female: 8	
	201–250	Male: 5; Female: 9	
	251–300	Male: 5; Female: 10	
	301–350	Male: 6; Female: 11	
	351–400	Male: 6; Female: 12	
	Over 400	Male: 7 plus 1 for each additional increment of 200 occupants; Female: 13 plus 1 for each additional increment of 100 occupants	
Primary schools and day care centers	Male: 1 per 30 Female: 1 per 25		Same as above
Places of worship and undertaking premises	Any number	1 per 50	Same as above
Care or detention occupancy	Any number	Based on the specific needs of the occupants on a case-by-case basis	Same as above
Residential	Any number	1 per 10	Same as above
Dwelling units	Any number	1 per unit	Same as above
Business and personal services	1-25	1	Same as above
	26-50	2	
	Over 50	3 plus 1 for each additional increment of 50 occupants	
Mercantile	Any number	Male: 1 per 300 Female: 1 per 150	Same as above
Industrial	1-10	1	Same as above
	11-25	2	
	26-50	3	
	51-75	4	
	76-100	5	
	Over 100	6 plus 1 for each additional increment of 30 occupants	

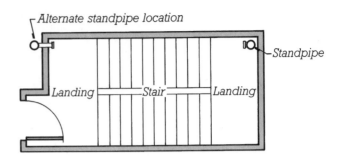

Alternate standpipe location

Standpipe

Landing — *Stair* — *Landing*

STANDPIPES

A standpipe is a large-diameter steel water pipe extending vertically through a building, with fire hose connections at every floor. There are two types of standpipes: A *wet standpipe* is continually filled with water and is fitted with hoses for emergency use by building occupants. A *dry standpipe* contains no water and is reserved for use by firefighters. In case of fire, the firefighters supply water to the dry standpipe by connecting pumper trucks to a Y-shaped Siamese connection on the front of the building at street level, and they carry their own hoses into the building to connect to the standpipe.

Standpipe requirements in the building codes are fairly complex. A safe initial assumption is that there is a dry standpipe in a corner of every exit stairway enclosure or in the vestibule of a smokeproof stair enclosure. Some fire departments prefer that the dry standpipes be located on the landings between floors, where each hose connection can serve two floors. It should also be assumed that wet standpipes and fire hose cabinets will be located in such a way that every point on a floor lies within reach of a 30-ft (9-m) stream from the end of a 100-ft (30-m) hose. A typical recessed wall cabinet for a wet standpipe hose and a fire extinguisher is 2 ft 9 in. (840 mm) wide,

9 in. (230 mm) deep, and 2 ft 9 in. (840 mm) high.

Under some codes, a wet standpipe may also serve as the riser to supply water to an automatic sprinkler system, but usually a separate sprinkler riser is required. The horizontal piping for the sprinkler system branches from the standpipe at each floor and, if it is concealed, runs just above the ceiling. An assembly of

valves and alarm fittings must be furnished at the point where the sprinkler system joins the domestic water system, usually in the same room with the domestic water pumps. Two Siamese fittings are required in readily accessible locations on the outside of the building to allow the fire department to attach hoses from pumper trucks to the dry standpipe and to the sprinkler riser.

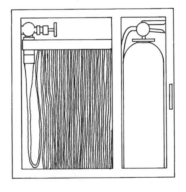

HOSE CABINET

SIAMESE FITTING

DESIGNING ELEVATORS AND ELEVATOR LOBBIES

Because of its many complexities, an elevator system is usually designed by an elevator consultant or the engineering department of an elevator manufacturer. The discussion that follows will help you in making a preliminary allocation of spaces for vertical transportation and in communicating with the final designer of the system.

Number and Size of Elevators

The tables to the right can be used to arrive at an approximate number of elevators and appropriate sizes for the cars. In very tall buildings, the number of shafts can be reduced somewhat with schemes of express and local elevators. Local elevators in high and low zones of the building can even run in the same shaft to save floor space. In very tall buildings, two-story elevators served by two-story lobbies can reduce the number of shafts by as much as one-third. Walking distance from the elevator lobby to any room should not exceed 150 ft (45 in).

Laying Out Banks of Elevators

Elevators serving the same zone of the building should be arranged in a single bank so that waiting persons can keep all the doors in sight at one time. A bank of three in a row is the largest that is desirable; four in a row is acceptable. Banks of elevators serving different zones of the building may open on opposite walls of the same elevator lobby or onto separate lobbies. The minimum width of an elevator lobby serving a single bank of elevators is 8 ft (2.45 m); and for a lobby with banks of elevators on both sides, the minimum width is 10 ft (3 m).

APPROXIMATE NUMBERS OF ELEVATOR SHAFTS

Use	Number of Shafts	Capacity of Elevator
Apartment Buildings	1 per 75 units, plus 1 service elevator for 300 units or more in a high-rise building	2000 lb to 2500 lb (900 kg to 1140 kg)
Hotels	1 per 75 rooms, plus 1 service elevator for up to 100 rooms and 1 service elevator for each additional 200 rooms	2500 lb to 3000 lb (1140 kg to 1360 kg)
Office Buildings	1 per 35,000 sq ft (3250 m²) of area served, plus 1 service elevator per 265,000 sq ft (24,600 m²) of area served	2500 lb to 3500 lb (1360 kg to 1590 kg)

ELEVATOR DIMENSIONS

Use	Capacity	Inside Car Dimensions	Inside Shaft Dimensions (width × depth)
Apartments, Hotels, Office Buildings, Stores	2000 lb (900 kg)	5'-8" × 4'-3" (1727 × 1295 mm)	6'-7" × 7'-4" (2006 × 2235 mm)
	2500 lb (1140 kg)	6'-8" × 4'-3" (2032 × 1295 mm)	8'-4" × 6'-8" (2540 × 2032 mm)
Office Buildings, Hotels, Stores	3000 lb (1360 kg)	6'-8" × 4'-9" (2032 × 1448 mm)	8'-4" × 7'-5" (2540 × 2261 mm)
Office Buildings, Stores	3500 lb (1590 kg)	6'-8" × 5'-5" (2032 × 1651 mm)	8'-4" × 8'-1" (2540 × 2464 mm)
Hospitals, Nursing Homes	6000 lb (2730 kg)	5'-9" × 10'-0" (1750 × 3050 mm)	8'-2" × 11'-9" (2490 × 3580 mm)
Freight, Service	4000 lb to 6000 lb (1820 kg to 2730 kg)	8'-4" × 10'-0" (2540 × 3050 mm)	10'-10" × 10'-8" (3300 × 3250 mm)

Elevator shafts are noisy and should not be located next to occupied space, especially in hotels and residential buildings.

Elevator cars ordinarily have doors on one side only. Cars with doors on opposing sides are available; this necessitates a shaft that is slightly wider than normal, to allow the counterweights to be placed next to the side of the car.

Freight and service elevators should open to separate service rooms or workrooms. Mailrooms, receiving rooms, and maintenance and housekeeping facilities should relate closely to service elevators.

See the following page for information on elevator types, penthouses, pits, and machine rooms.

ELEVATOR TYPES, PENTHOUSES, PITS, AND MACHINE ROOMS

The most widely used elevator type for most buildings, including very tall ones, is an electric traction elevator with its machine room in a penthouse at the top of the shaft. A penthouse machine room is approximately 9 ft (2.7 m) high, as wide as the shaft itself, and 16 to 18 ft (5 to 5.5 m) long, inside dimensions. It exactly covers the top of the shaft and extends beyond the shaft on the side above the elevator doors.

In buildings of modest height, the penthouse may be reduced in height and restricted in area to the area of the shaft itself by using an underslung traction elevator, which has its machine room at the bottom.

The penthouse may be minimized or eliminated entirely in buildings of up to seven floors in height by using a hydraulic elevator. The ceiling of the shaft may be as little as 12 ft (3.7 m) above the surface of the top floor. The hydraulic piston that lifts the car is either placed in a drilled well at the bottom of the shaft, or located in the shaft itself. A machine room of approximately 45 sq ft (4.2 m²) is required; it may be located anywhere in the building, although a location near the shaft on the lowest floor is preferred. For inside car dimensions of hydraulic elevators with capacities of up to 3500 lb (1600 kg), refer to the Elevator Dimensions table on the previous page. Due to differences in lifting machinery within the shaft, allow an inside width 6 in. (150 mm) greater than the dimensions shown in the table, and and inside depth 12 in. (300 mm) less than shown. For larger capacity hydraulic elevators, consult manufacturers' literature.

182

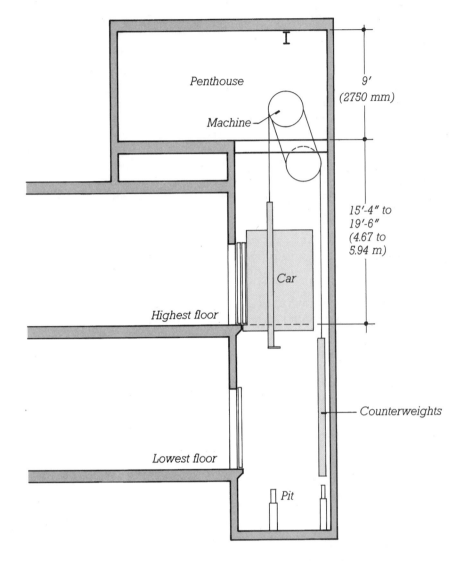

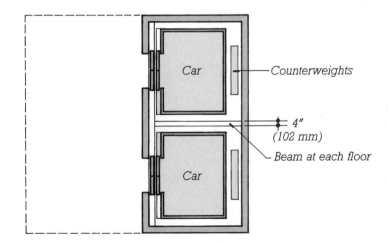

VERTICAL DISTRIBUTION OF SERVICES FOR LARGE BUILDINGS

With recent innovations in electric traction technology, a second option for buildings up to seven floors in height has recently become available. These systems utilize hoisting machines sufficiently reduced in size to allow their placement within the elevator shaft itself, thereby eliminating the need for any separate equipment space —either rooftop penthouse or adjacent machine room. At the time of this writing, such "machine-roomless" systems are available with cab capacities of up to 2000 to 2500 lb (1000 to 1140 kg). For preliminary sizing of the cab and shaft, refer to the Elevator Dimensions table on the previous page for elevators in this capacity range.

Every type of elevator shaft must terminate in a pit at the bottom. For electric traction elevators, the inside depth of the pit below the lowest floor varies from 5 ft to 11 ft 6 in. (1.52 to 3.51 m), depending on the speed and capacity of the elevator; the bigger and faster the elevator, the deeper the pit. Hydraulic elevator pits are 4 ft (1.22 m) deep.

ESCALATORS

Escalators are useful in situations where large numbers of people wish to circulate among a small number of floors on a more or less continual basis. An escalator cannot be counted as a means of egress. The structural and mechanical necessities of an escalator are contained in the integral box that lies beneath the moving stairway. Structural support is required only at the two ends of the unit, Some basic dimensional information on escalators is tabulated to the right.

	32" Escalator	48" Escalator
A	3'-9" (1145 mm)	5'-1" (1550 mm)
B	3'-7" (1090 mm)	4'-11" (1500 mm)

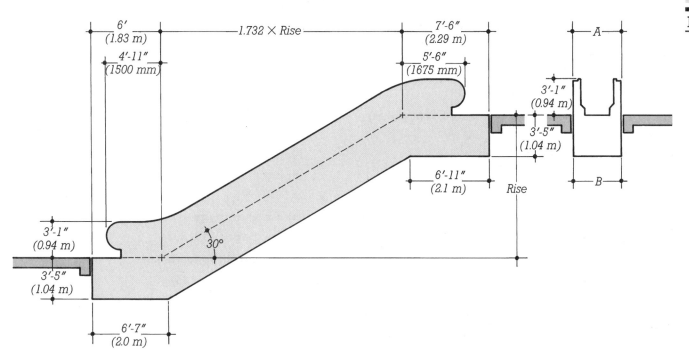

A CHECKLIST OF CORE COMPONENTS

The following is an alphabetical listing of components that are often incorporated into the cores of a building. For more information on any component, follow the accompanying page reference.

Chimneys (page 160)

Drinking fountains and water coolers (page 176)

Electrical closets (page 173)

Elevators (page 181)

    Dumbwaiters and vertical conveyors

    Elevator lobbies

    Freight elevators and freight rooms

    Passenger elevators

    Service elevators and service lobbies

Escalators (page 184)

Fan rooms (page 165)

Fire hose and fire extinguishers cabinets (page 180)

Janitor closets (page 175)

Kitchens

Mail facilities (page 174)

    Mail chutes

    Mail conveyors

    Mailrooms

Plumbing walls (including waste and vent pipes) (page 175)

Refuse facilities (page 168)

    Refuse chute

    Refuse room

Shafts (pages 170–175)

    Domestic water piping:

        Chilled drinking water supply and return piping

        Domestic cold water supply and return piping

        Domestic hot water supply and return piping

        Liquid soap supply piping to toilet rooms

        Supply riser to rooftop gravity tank

    Electrical and communications shafts:

        Electrical wires or bus bars

        First communications wiring: Alarms, smoke and heat detectors, firefighter communications

        Telephone, telex, local area networks, cable television, community antenna, etc.

    Heating and cooling shafts:

        Control wiring

        Ducts (page 192)

            Exhaust ducts from toilets, baths, janitor closets, shower rooms, locker rooms, storage rooms, kitchens, corridors, fume hoods, laboratory areas, workshop areas, industrial processes (page 164)

            Fire exhaust and pressurization ducts

            Outdoor air and exhaust air ducts to local fan rooms

            Supply ducts (page 192)

            Return ducts (page 192)

        Piping

            Air piping for controls

            Chilled water supply and return

            Condenser water supply and return between chilled water plant and cooling towers

            Fuel oil piping

            Gas piping

            Hot water and/or steam supply and return

    Piping, miscellaneous: Compressed air, vacuum, deionized water, distilled water, fuel gas, medical gases, scientific gases, industrial gases

    Piping, plumbing waste and vent (page 175)

    Piping, storm drainage risers from roofs and balconies

Sprinkler riser (page 180)

Stairways (pages 279–293)

Standpipes, fire (page 180)

Structure (pages 15–135)

    Beams and girders, including special support around shafts and under heavy equipment

    Bracing

    Columns

    Shear walls

Telecommunications closets (page 173)

Toilet rooms (pages 175–179)

The horizontal distribution system for mechanical and electrical services in a large building should be planned simultaneously with the structural frame and the interior finish systems, because the three are strongly interrelated. The floor-to-floor height of a building is determined in part by the vertical dimension needed at each story for horizontal runs of ductwork and piping. The selection of finish ceiling, partition, and floor systems is often based in part on their ability to contain the necessary electrical and mechanical services and to adjust to future changes in these services. All these strategies involve close cooperation among the architect and the structural and mechanical engineers.

CONNECTING HORIZONTAL AND VERTICAL DISTRIBUTION LINES

Horizontal mechanical and electrical lines must be fed by vertical lines through smooth, functional connections. Plumbing waste lines, which must be sloped to drain by gravity, have top priority in the planning of horizontal service lines; if they are confined to vertical

plumbing walls, they will not interfere with other services. Sprinkler heads, which have next highest priority in the layout of horizontal services, are served from the fire standpipe by horizontal piping that seldom exceeds 4 in. (100 mm) in outside diameter. The spacing of the heads is coordinated with the placement of walls and partitions; the maximum coverage per head is about 200 sq ft (18.6 m^2) in light-hazard buildings such as churches, schools, hospitals, offices, museums, apartments, hotels, theaters, and auditoriums. Coverage in industrial and storage buildings ranges from 130 to 90 sq ft (12.1 to 8.4 m^2) per head, depending on the substances handled in the building.

Air conditioning ducts, the next priority, branch out from a local fan room or from vertical ducts in supply and return shafts. Return ducts are often very short and confined to the interior areas of the building. Supply ducts extend from the main ducts through VAV or mixing boxes, then through low-velocity secondary ducts to air diffusers throughout the occupied area of the floor, with special emphasis on the perimeter, which may be on an independent, separately zoned set of ducts. Diffusers are generally required at the rate of 4 to 7 diffusers per 1000 sq ft (100 m^2). For some typical diffuser designs, see the illustration on page 189.

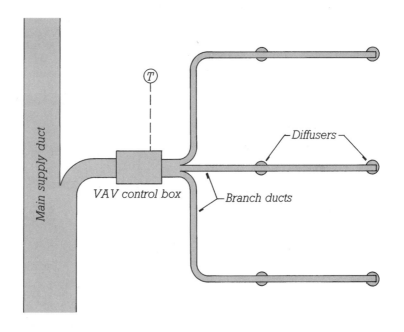

PLAN OF VAV DUCTING

GROUPED HORIZONTAL DISTRIBUTION

Sometimes the major runs of ductwork, piping, and wiring can be grouped in the ceiling area above the central corridor of each floor of a building, leaving the ceilings of the surrounding rooms essentially "clean." This works especially well in hotels, dormitories, and apartment buildings that rely on above-ceiling all-water or electric equipment in the area adjacent to the corridor for heating, cooling, and ventilating. A low corridor ceiling is readily accepted in exchange for high, unobstructed space in the occupied rooms, where the structure may be left exposed as the finish ceiling, saving cost and floor-to-floor height. If the building has a two-way flat plate or hollow-core precast slab floor structure, the overall thickness of the ceiling–floor structure can be reduced to as little as 8 in. (200 mm). Conduits containing wiring for the lighting fixtures may be cast into the floor slabs or exposed on the surface of the ceilings. Wiring to wall outlets is easily accommodated in permanently located partitions.

186

FLOORWIDE HORIZONTAL DISTRIBUTION

In broad expanses of floor space, particularly where all electrical and communications services must be available at any point in the area, an entire horizontal layer of space is reserved on each story for mechanical and electrical equipment. This layer may be beneath a raised access floor just above the structural floor. It may also lie within the structural floor, or just beneath the floor, above a suspended ceiling. Sometimes combinations of these locations are used.

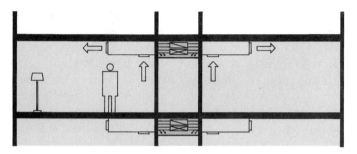

GROUPED HORIZONTAL DISTRIBUTION OVER A CENTRAL CORRIDOR

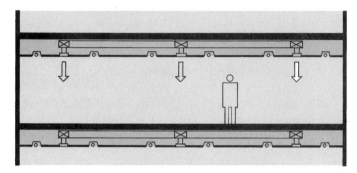

FLOORWIDE ABOVE-CEILING HORIZONTAL DISTRIBUTION

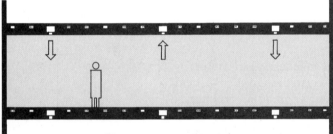

FLOORWIDE IN-FLOOR HORIZONTAL DISTRIBUTION

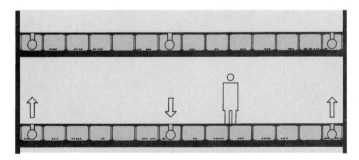

FLOORWIDE RAISED ACCESS FLOOR HORIZONTAL DISTRIBUTION

HORIZONTAL DISTRIBUTION OF SERVICES FOR LARGE BUILDINGS

Distribution above a Suspended Ceiling

Above a ceiling, wiring is run in conduits or cable trays attached to the structure above. Lighting fixtures are served directly from this horizontal wiring. Outlets on the floor below may be served by electrified partitions or power poles. Outlets on the floor above may be fed via poke-through fixtures that are cut through the structural floor. Poke-through fixtures can be added or removed at any time during the life of the building; their major disadvantage is that electrical work being done for the convenience of a tenant on one floor is done at the inconvenience of the tenant on the floor below.

Distribution within the Structural Floor

Electrical and communications wiring may be embedded in the floor slab in conventional conduits. For greater flexibility in buildings where patterns of use are likely to change over time, systems of cellular steel decking over steel framing, or cellular raceways cast into a topping over concrete slabs, may be selected. These provide a tree-like structure: The trunk is a wiring trench that runs from the electrical closet to the outside wall of the building, and the branches are the hollow cells that run in the perpendicular direction. Electrical and communications wires and outlets can be added, removed, or changed at any time during the life of the building. Cellular steel decking can affect the layout of the beams and girders in a steel-framed building: For optimum distribution of wiring, the cells in the decking generally run parallel to the wall of the core, and for structural reasons the cells must run perpendicular to the beams. This requires close coordination among the architect and the electrical and structural engineers.

Distribution above the Structural Floor

A raised access floor system allows maximum flexibility in running services because it can accommodate piping, ductwork, and wiring with equal ease. It is especially useful in industrial or office areas where large numbers of computers or computer terminals are used and where frequent wiring changes are likely. It is also valuable in retrofitting old buildings for modern services. Though floors can be raised to any desired height above the structural deck, heights of 4 to 8 in. (100 to 200 mm) are most common. Less costly, lower-profile systems, ranging from 2½ to 3 in. (65 to 75 mm) in height, are also available.

Undercarpet flat wiring may be used instead of a raised access floor in buildings with moderate needs for future wiring changes. Flat wiring does not increase the overall height of the building as raised access floors usually do, but it does not offer the unlimited capacity and complete freedom of wire location of the raised floors. Flat wiring is used in both new buildings and retrofit work.

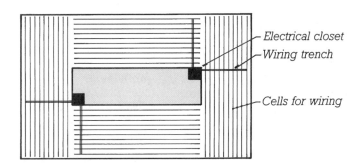

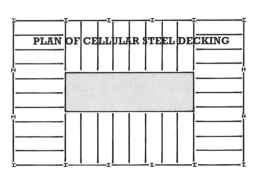

STEEL FRAMING PLAN FOR CELLULAR STEEL DECKING

DESIGNING THE CEILING/FLOOR PLENUM SPACE

An above-ceiling location is ordinarily best for ductwork, which is often too large and bulky to fit above or within the structural floor. The wiring and ductwork must share the above-ceiling plenum space with lighting fixtures and sprinkler piping. This requires careful planning. Generally the lowest stratum, about 8 in. (200 mm) thick, is reserved for the sprinkler piping and lighting fixtures. Lighting fixture selection plays an important role in determining the thickness of this stratum, because some types of lighting fixtures require more space than others. The ducts, which are usually 8 to 10 in. (200 to 250 mm) deep, run between this layer and the beams and girders. Adding about 2 in. (50 mm) for the thickness of a suspended ceiling, we see that a minimum height of about 18 in. (460 mm), and preferably 20 in. (500 mm), must be added to the thickness of the floor structure and fireproofing in a typical building to allow for mechanical and electrical services. A larger dimension is often called for, depending on the requirements of the combination of systems that is chosen.

As an example, let us assume that a steel-framed building has a maximum girder depth of 27 in. (690 mm) and a 4-in. (100-mm) floor slab, for a total floor structure height of 31 in. (790 mm). Adding 20 in. (510 mm) for ceiling and services, we arrive at an overall ceiling-to-floor height of 51 in. (1300 mm) that must

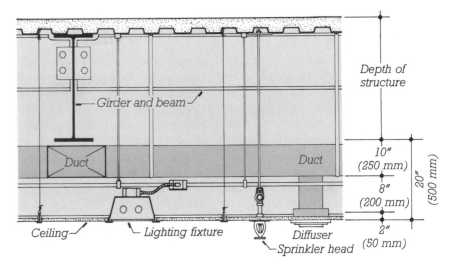

SECTION THROUGH CEILING/FLOOR ASSEMBLY

be added to the desired room height to give the floor-to-floor height of the building. If fireproofing must be added to the girders, this dimension will increase by a couple of inches (50 mm or so).

There is tremendous economic pressure to reduce this height to a practical minimum in a tall building. A few inches saved per floor adds up to an enormous saving in the cost of structure, core components, and cladding. Sometimes it is possible to arrange the framing so that ductwork never passes beneath a girder. If the ductwork must cross the girders, the designers should explore such options as shallower ducts, running the ducts through holes cut in the webs of the girders, or reducing the depth of the girders by using a heavier steel shape. In the average tall office building, the height of the ceiling-floor assembly is about 46 in. (1170 mm).

In some medical, research, and industrial buildings, the underfloor services are unusually complex, bulky, and subject to change. In these cases the layer above the ceiling and below the floor structure is expanded to a height that allows workers to walk freely in it, and the ceiling is strengthened into a structure that can support their weight. This arrangement, called an interstitial ceiling, allows workers to maintain and change the services without disrupting the occupied spaces above or below.

With all its service penetrations—lighting fixtures, air diffusers and grilles, sprinkler heads, smoke detectors, intercom speakers—a ceiling can take on a visually chaotic appearance. It is advisable to compose the relationships of these penetrations carefully on a reflected ceiling plan.

188

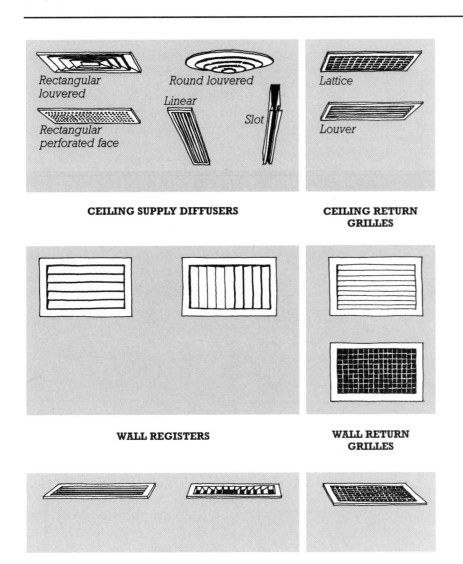

CEILING SUPPLY DIFFUSERS

Rectangular louvered
Round louvered
Linear
Slot
Rectangular perforated face

CEILING RETURN GRILLES

Lattice
Louver

WALL REGISTERS

WALL RETURN GRILLES

FLOOR REGISTERS

FLOOR RETURN GRILLE

TYPICAL GRILLE AND DIFFUSER DESIGNS

EXPOSED VERSUS CONCEALED SERVICES

In many buildings, the designer has a choice between exposing the mechanical and electrical services and concealing them above a suspended ceiling. Exposed services are the rule in warehouses and industrial buildings. In other types of buildings, exposed pipes and ducts can have an attractive, sculptural complexity. They are easy to reach for maintenance and revision. They make sense in many large, open buildings (athletic arenas, exhibition halls), as well as in certain other kinds of buildings in which partitions are not often changed and a frank, functional appearance is appropriate (schools, art galleries, pubs and restaurants, avant-garde stores). There are some disadvantages: Exposed services that must look good are more expensive to design and install, and usually the cost of painting them must be added to the bill. They also need to be cleaned from time to time. Although exposed services are readily accessible for changes, any changes must be made with care, and a painter has to follow after the mechanics who do the work. For these reasons, it is usually cheaper to install a suspended ceiling than to omit one.

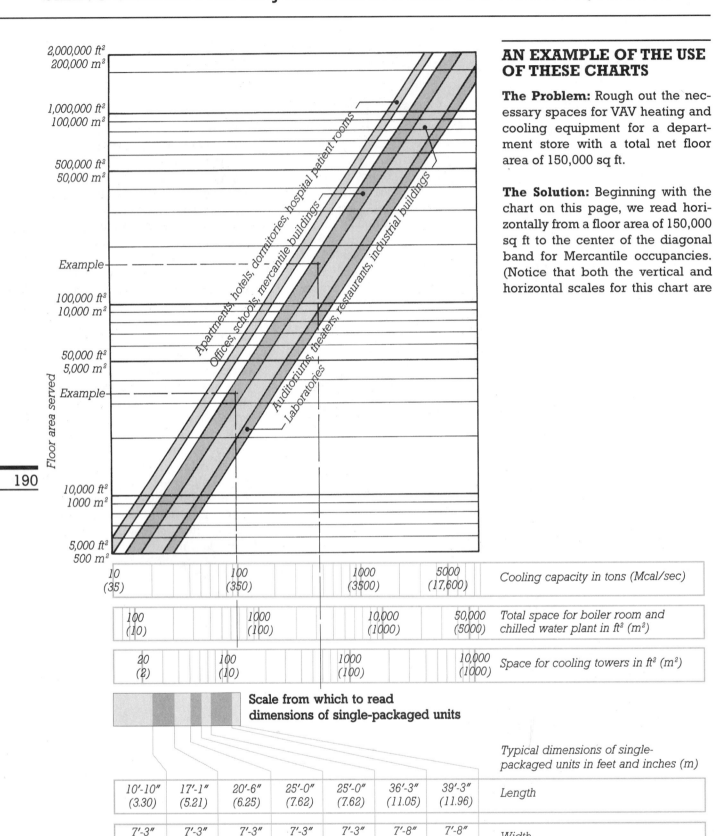

AN EXAMPLE OF THE USE OF THESE CHARTS

The Problem: Rough out the necessary spaces for VAV heating and cooling equipment for a department store with a total net floor area of 150,000 sq ft.

The Solution: Beginning with the chart on this page, we read horizontally from a floor area of 150,000 sq ft to the center of the diagonal band for Mercantile occupancies. (Notice that both the vertical and horizontal scales for this chart are

190

Cooling capacity in tons (Mcal/sec)

Total space for boiler room and chilled water plant in ft² (m²)

Space for cooling towers in ft² (m²)

Scale from which to read dimensions of single-packaged units

Typical dimensions of single-packaged units in feet and inches (m)

10'-10" (3.30)	17'-1" (5.21)	20'-6" (6.25)	25'-0" (7.62)	25'-0" (7.62)	36'-3" (11.05)	39'-3" (11.96)	Length
7'-3" (2.21)	7'-3" (2.21)	7'-3" (2.21)	7'-3" (2.21)	7'-3" (2.21)	7'-8" (2.34)	7'-8" (2.34)	Width
4'-11" (1.50)	4'-11" (1.50)	4'-11" (1.50)	4'-11" (1.50)	4'-11" (1.50)	7'-9" (2.36)	7'-9" (2.36)	Height

logarithmic; 150,000 lies much closer to 200,000 than to 100,000.) Reading downward, we find that the required cooling capacity for this building is approximately 450 tons, requiring a chilled water plant and boiler room that together will occupy an area of approximately 3200 sq ft. Cooling towers will occupy about 560 sq ft on the roof or alongside the building. The width of the diagonal band from which we have read gives us a range of 400 to 520 tons for the cooling requirement, so we know that these space requirements may grow somewhat smaller or larger as the system is designed in detail.

These values assume a central plant for heating and cooling. Could rooftop single-packaged units be used instead? We see at the bottom of the chart that no single-packaged unit is large enough to handle the entire load. Starting from the largest available packaged unit and reading upward, we intersect the diagonal band and read to the left to find that the unit could serve about 33,000 sq ft of this building. Five such units could be distributed about the roof to furnish heating and air conditioning for the entire building, each serving about 30,000 sq ft. Each would need a capacity of about 90 tons and would measure 39 ft 3 in. long, 7 ft 8 in. wide, and 7 ft 9 in. high. A larger number of smaller units could also be used.

For more detailed information on boiler rooms, see page 160. Chilled water plants and cooling towers are explained on page 161 and single packaged units on page 166.

Move to the following page to continue this example.

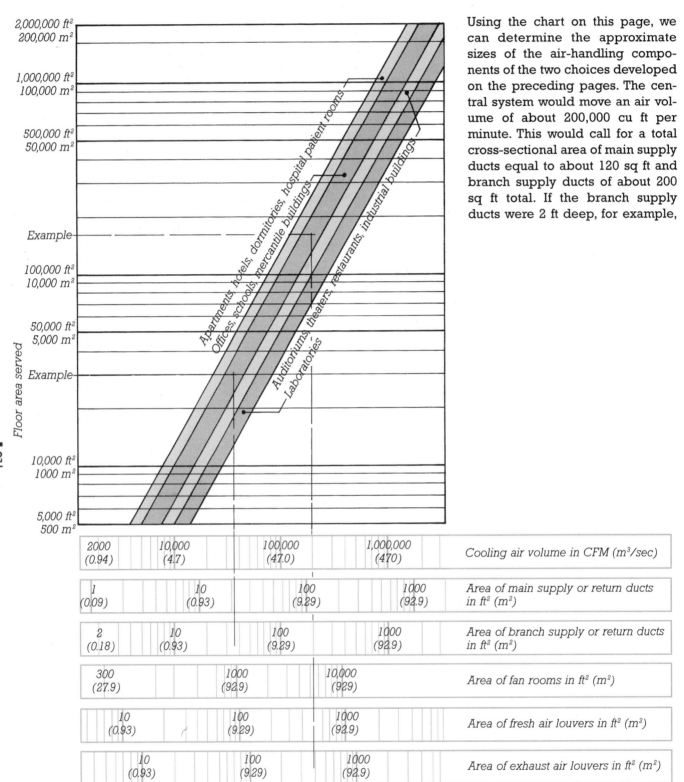

Using the chart on this page, we can determine the approximate sizes of the air-handling components of the two choices developed on the preceding pages. The central system would move an air volume of about 200,000 cu ft per minute. This would call for a total cross-sectional area of main supply ducts equal to about 120 sq ft and branch supply ducts of about 200 sq ft total. If the branch supply ducts were 2 ft deep, for example,

192

Floor area served

2,000,000 ft²
200,000 m²

1,000,000 ft²
100,000 m²

500,000 ft²
50,000 m²

Example

100,000 ft²
10,000 m²

50,000 ft²
5,000 m²

Example

10,000 ft²
1000 m²

5,000 ft²
500 m²

Apartments, hotels, dormitories, hospital patient rooms
Offices, schools, mercantile buildings
Auditoriums, theaters, restaurants, industrial buildings
Laboratories

2000 (0.94)	10,000 (4.7)	100,000 (47.0)	1,000,000 (470)	Cooling air volume in CFM (m³/sec)
1 (0.09)	10 (0.93)	100 (9.29)	1000 (92.9)	Area of main supply or return ducts in ft² (m²)
2 (0.18)	10 (0.93)	100 (9.29)	1000 (92.9)	Area of branch supply or return ducts in ft² (m²)
300 (27.9)	1000 (92.9)	10,000 (929)		Area of fan rooms in ft² (m²)
10 (0.93)	100 (9.29)	1000 (92.9)		Area of fresh air louvers in ft² (m²)
10 (0.93)	100 (9.29)	1000 (92.9)		Area of exhaust air louvers in ft² (m²)

their aggregate width would be about 100 ft. Similar areas of return ducting would also be needed. Reading from the last three scales, we further determine that fan rooms totaling about 5200 sq ft are needed, served by fresh air louvers adding up to about 500 sq ft in area and exhaust air louvers totaling nearly 400 sq ft. The location and distribution of this louver area on the outside surfaces of the building are of obvious architectural importance.

Each of the rooftop single-packaged units would need about 21 sq ft of main duct for supply air and the same for return, with a total area of 35 sq ft for branch ducts. Fans and louvers are incorporated into the units and do not need to be provided separately.

For further information on fan rooms and louvers, see page 165.

MECHANICAL AND ELECTRICAL SYSTEMS FOR SMALL BUILDINGS

This section will help you select a heating and cooling system for the preliminary design of a small building. It also summarizes typical plumbing and electrical systems for small buildings.

DESIGNING SPACES FOR MECHANICAL AND ELECTRICAL SERVICES FOR SMALL BUILDINGS

Small buildings are defined for purposes of this section as those that use residential-scale mechanical and electrical systems. This category includes small educational, commercial, retail, industrial, and institutional buildings as well as houses, rowhouses, and small apartment buildings.

Heating and cooling loads in small buildings are usually dominated by heat gains and losses through the skin of the building. In many small buildings, mechanical fresh air ventilation is not an issue because of the low density of occupancy and the ability of operable windows and normal air leakage through the skin of the building to provide adequate ventilation. Most of the distribution lines for the mechanical and electrical systems in small buildings can be concealed within the hollow cavities that are a normal part of the floor, wall, and ceiling structures. A base-ment, crawl space, or attic is often available as a location for the major mechanical equipment and larger horizontal distribution lines. There is an enormous variety of heating and cooling systems from which the designer may choose. This section summarizes the choices of heating and cooling systems and the typical plumbing and electrical systems. Approximate dimensions of the components of the various systems are also given.

DESIGN CRITERIA FOR THE SELECTION OF HEATING AND COOLING SYSTEMS FOR SMALL BUILDINGS

Decide first if the building needs a heating system only, or both heating and cooling:	Some systems are capable of heating only, such as: Hydronic heating (pages 206–207) Solar heating (pages 208, 216–217) Electric convectors and heaters (pages 211–212) Radiant panel heating (page 213) Wall furnace and direct-vent space heaters (page 214) Heating stoves (page 215) Some systems are capable of both heating and cooling the building, such as: Forced air (pages 203–205) Heat pump (pages 158, 204–205) Packaged terminal units or through-the-wall units (page 210) Single-packaged and split-packaged systems (pages 166–167)
If you wish to minimize the first cost of the system:	Choose systems that do not require the installation of extensive piping or ductwork, such as: Evaporative cooler (page 209) Packaged terminal units or through-the-wall units (page 210) Electric convectors or fan-forced heaters (pages 211–212) Wall furnace and direct-vent space heaters (page 214) Heating stoves (page 215)
If you wish to minimize operating costs in cold climates:	Choose systems that burn fossil fuels efficiently, systems that utilize solar heat, or systems that burn locally available, low-cost fuels, such as: Forced air (pages 203–205) Hydronic heating (pages 206–207) Active and passive solar (pages 208, 216–217) Heating stoves (page 215)
If you wish to minimize operating costs in moderate climates:	Choose systems that utilize ambient energy sources, such as: Heat pump systems (pages 158, 204–205) Solar heating systems (pages 208, 216–217) Heating stoves (page 215) Evaporative cooler (page 209)
If you wish to maximize control of air quality and air velocity for maximum comfort:	Choose a system that filters and moves the air mechanically, namely: Forced air (pages 203–205)
If you wish to maximize individual control over temperature:	Choose systems that offer separate thermostats in a number of rooms or zones, such as: Hydronic heating (pages 206–207) Packaged terminal units or through-the-wall units (page 210) Electric convectors or fan-forced heaters (pages 211–212)

DESIGN CRITERIA FOR THE SELECTION OF HEATING AND COOLING SYSTEMS FOR SMALL BUILDINGS

If you wish to minimize the noise created by the heating and cooling system:	Choose systems in which motors, pumps, and fans are distant from the occupied space, such as: Forced air (pages 203–205) Hydronic heating (pages 206–207) Electric convectors and radiant heating (pages 211–213) Passive solar heating (pages 216–217)
If you wish to minimize the visual obtrusiveness of the heating and cooling system:	Choose systems that place as little hardware as possible in the occupied spaces, such as: Forced air (pages 203–205) Radiant heating (page 213)
If you wish to maximize the inhabitants' enjoyment of the changing weather and seasons:	Choose systems that change prominently with the seasons, such as: Passive solar heating (pages 216–217) Heating stoves (page 215)
If you wish to minimize the amount of floorspace occupied by heating and cooling equipment:	Choose systems that do not occupy floorspace, such as: Evaporative cooler (page 209) Packaged terminal units or through-the-wall units (page 210) Electric fan-forced heaters (page 212) Electric radiant heating (page 213) Wall furnace and direct-vent space heaters (page 214) Passive solar heating (pages 216–217)
If you wish to minimize system maintenance:	Choose systems with few or no moving parts, such as: Forced air (pages 203–205) Hydronic heating (pages 206–207) Electric convectors (page 211) Electric radiant heating (page 213) Wall furnace and direct-vent space heaters (page 214) Passive solar heating (pages 216–217)
If you wish to avoid having a chimney in the building:	Choose systems that do not burn fuel in the building, such as: Heat pump furnace (pages 204–205) Single-packaged and split-packaged systems (pages 166–167) Packaged terminal units or through-the-wall units (page 210) All types of electric heat (pages 203–204, 211–213) With some fuel-burning systems, high-efficiency furnaces may be available that can be ventilated through a wall and do not require a chimney. Consult manufacturers' literature for more detailed information.
If you wish to maximize the speed of construction:	Choose systems that involve as few components and as few trades as possible, such as: Packaged terminal and through-the-wall units (page 210) All types of electric heat (pages 211–213)

HEATING AND COOLING SYSTEMS FOR SMALL BUILDINGS: SUMMARY CHART

GIVE SPECIAL CONSIDERATION TO THE SYSTEMS INDICATED IF YOU WISH TO:	Forced Air (page 203)	Heat Pump Furnace (page 204)	Hydronic Heating[†] (page 206)	Active Solar Heating[†] (page 208)	Evaporative Cooler[‡] (page 209)
Combine heating and cooling in one system	●	●			
Minimize first cost					●
Minimize operating cost in very cold climates	●		●	●	
Minimize operating costs in moderate climates		●		●	●
Maximize control of air velocity and air quality	●	●			
Maximize individual control over temperature			●		
Minimize system noise	●	●	●	●	
Minimize visual obtrusiveness	●	●			
Maximize enjoyment of the seasons					
Minimize floor space used for the mechanical system					●
Minimize system maintenance	●				
Avoid having a chimney		●			
Maximize the speed of construction					

[†]System for heating only
[‡]System for cooling only

HEATING AND COOLING SYSTEMS FOR SMALL BUILDINGS: SUMMARY CHART

Packaged Terminal Units or Through-the-Wall Units (page 210)	Electric Baseboard Convectors† (page 211)	Electric Fan-Forced Unit Heaters† (page 212)	Radiant Heating† (page 213)	Wall Furnace and Direct-Vent Space Heaters† (page 214)	Heating Stoves† (page 215)	Passive Solar Heating† (page 216)
●						
●	●	●		●	●	
					●	●
				●	●	●
●	●	●				
	●		●			●
			●			
					●	●
●	●	●	●	●		●
	●	●	●	●		●
●	●	●	●			
●	●	●		●		

CENTRAL SYSTEMS VERSUS LOCAL SYSTEMS

In a *central system,* heat is supplied to a building or extracted from it by equipment situated in a mechanical space—a furnace or a boiler in a basement, for example. Air or water is heated or cooled in this space and distributed to the inhabited areas of the building by ductwork or piping to maintain comfortable temperatures. In a *local system,* independent, self-contained pieces of heating and cooling equipment are situated throughout the building, one or more in each room. Central systems are generally quieter and more energy-efficient than local systems and offer better control of indoor air quality. Central equipment tends to last longer than local equipment and is easier to service. Local systems occupy less space in a building than central systems because they do not require a central mechanical space, ductwork, or piping. They are often more economical to buy and install. They can be advantageous in buildings that have many small spaces requiring individual temperature control.

Pages 203–208 describe central heating and cooling systems for small buildings, and pages 209–217 describe local systems.

FUELS

Heating equipment in small buildings may be fueled by oil, pipeline gas, liquid propane gas, kerosene, electricity, sunlight, or solid fuels—coal or wood. Cooling equipment is almost always powered by electricity. In functional respects electricity is the ideal fuel: It is clean, it is distributed through small wires, no chimney is needed, and electrical heating and cooling equipment is compact and often lower in first cost than equivalent fossil-fuel-burning equipment: In most geographic areas, however, electricity is a very costly fuel as compared to oil or gas. Gas and oil are usually the fuels of choice for small buildings. Sunlight, wood, and coal are generally less convenient energy sources than electricity, gas, and oil. They are appropriate in particular buildings where owner preferences and building occupancy patterns permit or encourage their use.

On-site storage requirements for the various fuels are summarized in the table below.

TYPICAL DIMENSIONS OF FUEL STORAGE COMPONENTS

Component	Width	Depth	Height
Coal storage, minimum, 1 ton (1 tonne)	4'-0" (1.2 m)	4'-0" (1.2 m)	4'-0" (1.2 m)
Firewood storage, minimum, ½ cord	4'-0" (1.2 m)	4'-0" (1.2 m)	4'-0" (1.2 m)
Liquid propane tanks, upright cylinders	16" (410 mm) diameter		60" (1525 mm)
Liquid propane tank, horizontal	41" (1040 mm) diameter, 16'-3" (5.0 m) long		

There are many sizes of propane tanks, of which these are two of the most common. Upright cylinders are located outdoors, usually against the wall of the building, often in pairs. They may not be closer than 36" (915 mm) to a door or a basement window. The horizontal tank must be at least 25' (7.6 m) from the building or a property line and may be buried if desired.

Oil or kerosene storage tank, 275 gal (1000 l)	27" (685 mm)	60" (1525 mm)	54" (1375 mm)

For greater capacity, multiple tanks may be installed inside the building, or a larger tank may be buried just outside the foundation.

FORCED AIR HEATING AND COOLING

Description

A furnace heats air with a gas flame, an oil flame, or electric resistance coils. The heated air is circulated through the inhabited space by a fan and a system of ductwork. With an upflow furnace, the horizontal ducts are located above the furnace at the ceiling of the floor on which the furnace is located. With a downflow furnace, the ducts are located beneath the furnace in the crawlspace or floor slab. A third type, the horizontal furnace, is designed to fit in a low attic or under-floor crawl space.

Cooling capability may be added to the furnace by installing evaporator coils in the main supply ductwork adjacent to the furnace. An outdoor compressor and condensing unit supplies cold refrigerant to the evaporator coils through small-diameter insulated tubing.

Typical Applications

Forced air heating and air conditioning is the most versatile and most widely used system for heating and cooling small buildings. Multiple furnaces may be installed to establish multiple zones of control and to heat and cool buildings of up to 10,000 sq ft (1000 m^2) and more.

Advantages

A forced air system can incorporate every type of humidification, dehumidification, air filtration, and cooling equipment. If properly designed, installed, and maintained, it is quiet and fuel efficient and distributes heat evenly.

(continued)

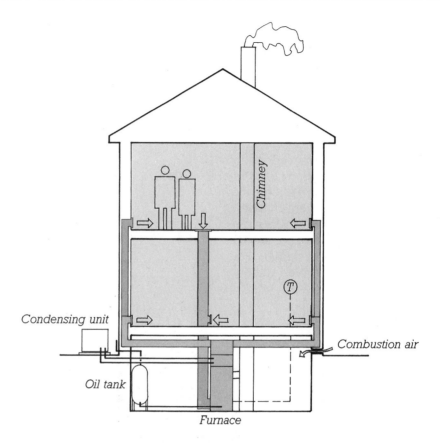

Condensing unit

Oil tank

Furnace

Combustion air

UPFLOW FURNACE

Disadvantages

Multiple zones of control are relatively difficult to create and can be wasteful of energy.

Major Components

Furnace, fuel storage, chimney, ductwork, and, if cooling capability is included, an outdoor condensing unit. Some high-efficiency gas furnaces may be vented through the wall and do not require a chimney. Typical dimensions for these components are summarized in the table on the facing page. For dimensions of fuel storage components, see page 202.

Variations

1. A heat pump furnace uses a reversible refrigeration cycle to create and circulate either heated or cooled air as required: An outdoor heat pump unit either extracts heat from the outdoor air and releases it through coils in the furnace, or extracts heat from the coils in the furnace and releases it to the outdoor air, depending on whether heating or cooling is required. A heat pump furnace is generally economical to operate in moderate climates, but when outdoor temperatures fall well below freezing, the heat pump cycle becomes inefficient and is turned off automatically.

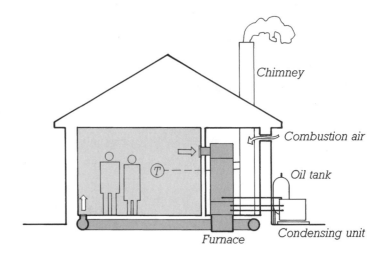

DOWNFLOW FURNACE ON SLAB

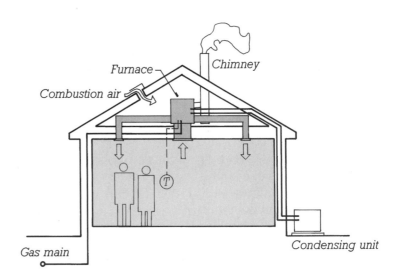

HORIZONTAL FURNACE IN ATTIC

FORCED AIR HEATING AND COOLING

Electric resistance coils are then activated to generate heat, which raises operating costs dramatically. For this reason, heat pumps are not usually used in severe climates unless they use water or earth as a heat source rather than air. Heat pump furnaces are available in vertical upflow, vertical downflow, and horizontal configurations, and are similar in dimension to other furnaces.

2. A multifuel furnace is designed to burn solid fuel (wood or coal) as well as a backup fuel (gas or oil). It is larger and more expensive than a single-fuel furnace.

3. A packaged system, either a single-packaged or a split-packaged system, is often used to heat and cool small commercial, industrial, and institutional buildings. For information on packaged systems, see pages 166–167.

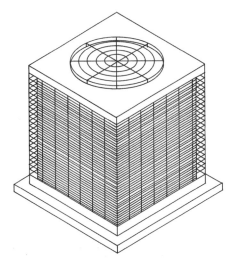

CONDENSING UNIT

TYPICAL DIMENSIONS OF COMPONENTS OF FORCED AIR HEATING SYSTEMS

Component	Width	Depth	Height
Chimney, masonry	20" (510 mm)	20" (510 mm)	*
Chimney, metal	10" (255 mm) diameter		*
Condensing unit, outdoor			
Small	24" (610mm)	24" (610mm)	24" (610mm)
Large	40" (1015 mm)	50" (1270 mm)	33" (840 mm)
Ducts, sheet metal			
Main horizontal supply and return ducts, each	24" (610 mm)		12" (305 mm)
Supply risers, typical (notice that these are made to fit between wall studs)	10" (255 mm) 12" (305 mm) 7" oval (175 mm oval)	3.25" (83 mm) 3.25" (83 mm)	
Return risers (these are usually fewer in number than the supply risers and require special wall framing provisions)	8" (200 mm)	14" (360 mm)	

For duct insulation, add 1" (25 mm) all around. Insulation is recommended on heating ducts and is mandatory on cooling ducts that run through non-air-conditioned space.

Fuel storage—see page 202

Furnaces, including adjacent primary ductwork			
Horizontal furnace	24" (610 mm)	84" (1170 mm)	28" (710 mm)
Upright furnace, upflow or downflow	24" (610 mm)	30" (760 mm)	84" (1170 mm)
Multifuel furnace, upright, upflow	48" (1220 mm)	60" (1525 mm)	84" (1170 mm)

A working space 3' (900 mm) square is required on the side of the furnace adjacent to the burner. Furnaces have varying requirements for installation clearances to combustible materials; some need only an inch or two.

---

*Under most codes a chimney must extend at least 3' (900 mm) above the highest point where it passes through the roof and at least 2' (600 mm) above any roof surface within a horizontal distance of 10' (3 m).

HYDRONIC (FORCED HOT WATER) HEATING

Description

A flame or electric resistance coil heats water in a boiler. Small pumps circulate the hot water through fin-tube convectors, which are horizontal pipes with closely spaced vertical fins, mounted in a simple metal enclosure with inlet louvers below and outlet louvers above. The heated fins, working by convection, draw cool room air into the enclosure from below, heat it, and discharge it out the top. Instead of fin-tube convectors, especially where space is tight, fan-coil units, either surface-mounted or wall-recessed, may be used. The fan in a fan-coil unit blows room air past a hot water coil to heat it.

Typical Applications

Hydronic heating is a premium-quality heating system for any type of building.

Advantages

Hydronic heating is quiet if properly installed and maintained. It gives excellent heat distribution and is easily zoned for room-by-room control by adding thermostatically controlled zone valves or zone pumps at the boiler. The boilers for small-building systems are very compact—some gas or electric boilers are so small they can be mounted on a wall.

Disadvantages

Cooling, air filtration, and humidification, if desired, must be accomplished with independent systems, which raises the overall system cost. The convectors occupy considerable wall perimeter and can interfere with furniture placement.

Major Components

Boiler, chimney, fuel storage, expansion tank, circulator pumps, zone valves, convector or fan-coil units. Some high-efficiency gas boilers may be vented through a wall and do not require a chimney.

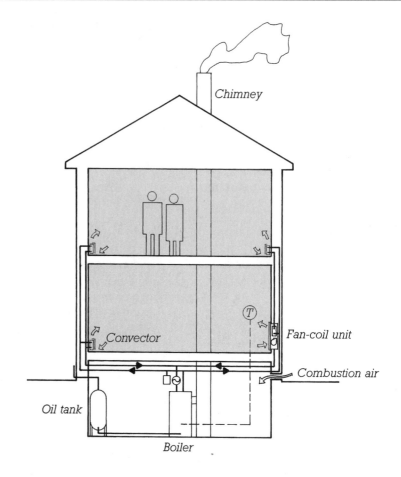

Chimney

Convector

Fan-coil unit

Combustion air

Oil tank

Boiler

HYDRONIC (FORCED HOT WATER) HEATING

Typical dimensions for these components are summarized in the table to the right. For dimensions of fuel storage components, see page 202.

Variations

1. A *multifuel boiler* is designed to burn both solid fuel (coal or wood) and a backup fuel (gas or oil). It is larger and more expensive than a single-fuel boiler.

2. Radiant heating panels in ceilings or floors may be warmed with hot water from a hydronic boiler (see pages 206–207).

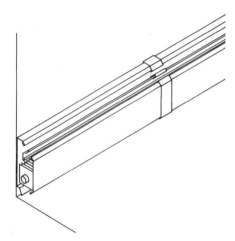

HYDRONIC CONVECTOR

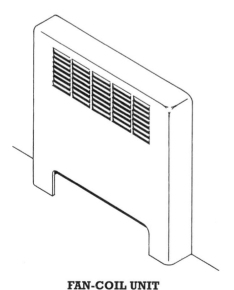

FAN-COIL UNIT

TYPICAL DIMENSIONS OF COMPONENTS OF A HYDRONIC HEATING SYSTEM

Component	Width	Depth	Height
Chimney, masonry	20" (510 mm)	20" (510 mm)	*
Chimney, metal	10" (250 mm) diameter		*
Boiler, hydronic, with expansion tank, valves, and pumps (add 10" or 250 mm on two adjacent sides for piping)			
Upright	25" (635 mm)	25" (635 mm)	84" (2135 mm)
Wall-mounted, gas or electric	30" (760 mm)	24" (610 mm)	84" (2135 mm)
Solid fuel or combination fuel	36" (900 mm)	60" (1530 mm)	84" (2135 mm)

A boiler requires a working space 3' (910 mm) square on the side adjacent to the burner. Required clearances to combustible surfaces vary depending on the design of the boiler; for some boilers they may be as little as an inch or two.

Component	Width	Depth	Height
Convector, baseboard	3" (75 mm)	7.5" (190 mm)	
Fan-coil units			
Recessed or surface-mounted	24" (610 mm)	4" (100 mm)	30" (760 mm)
Toespace heater	21" (535 mm)	18" (460 mm)	4" (100 mm)

*Under most codes a chimney must extend at least 3' (900 mm) above the highest point where it passes through the roof and at least 2' (600 mm) above any roof surface within a horizontal distance of 10' (3 m).

ACTIVE SOLAR SPACE HEATING

Description

Outdoor south-facing collector panels, usually mounted on the roof of the building, are heated by sunlight. A pump or fan circulates liquid or air to withdraw the heat from the panels and store it in a tank of liquid or a bin of rocks or phase-change salts. This storage is usually located in the basement or a mechanical equipment room. A fan circulates indoor air through a heat exchanger coil filled with the warm storage liquid, or through the rock bin, and distributes the heated air to the inhabited space of the building through a system of ductwork.

Typical Applications

Active solar heating is feasible in buildings that are exposed to sunlight throughout the day in climates with a high percentage of sunny weather during the winter.

Advantages

Solar heating has zero fuel cost and does not pollute the air.

Disadvantages

The initial cost of active solar heating systems tends to be so high that they are uneconomical at present fuel prices. The collector surfaces become a very prominent and often dominating part of the architecture of the building. A full backup heating system (such as forced air or hydronic heating) is required to heat the building during extended sunless periods. Cooling must be done by a separate system.

Major Components

Solar collector panels, heat storage tank or bin, ductwork for air collectors or piping for water collectors, heat exchanger, and building heating ductwork. Typical dimensions for these components are summarized in the table to the right. For dimensions of fuel storage components, see page 202.

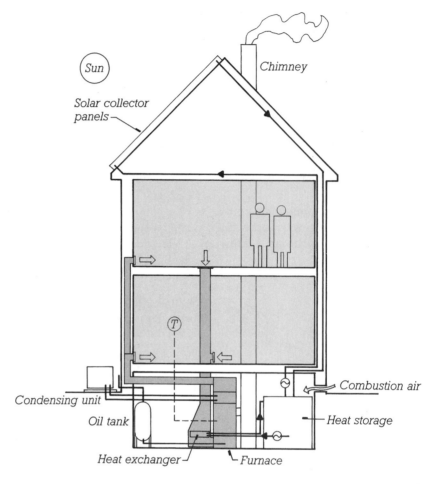

Variations

A heat pump may be added to the system to draw heat from the storage medium at relatively low temperatures and distribute it to the occupied spaces at higher temperatures. This provides a higher degree of comfort and increases the efficiency of the solar collectors.

TYPICAL DIMENSIONS OF ACTIVE SOLAR HEATING COMPONENTS

Component	Width	Depth	Height
For dimensions of the backup furnace, chimney, fuel storage, and ductwork, see pages 202 and 205.			
Collector panels, average residence	24' (7.3 m)	6" (150 mm)	20' (6 m)
Collector panels should face within 20° of true South and should be sloped at an angle to the ground equal to or up to 15° more than the latitude of the site.			
Heat exchanger with ductwork	30" (760 mm)	30" (760 mm)	30" (760 mm)
Heat storage			
Rock bed	minimum of 600 ft³ (17 m³)		
Water storage tank	8' (2.4 m) diameter		7' (2.1 m)

EVAPORATIVE COOLER

Description

A fan blows air through a wetted pad. Water evaporates from the pad into the air, cooling the air by extracting from it the latent heat of vaporization. The fan circulates the cooled air through the building. The metal cabinet in which the pad and fan are located is usually located on the roof or adjacent to the building.

Typical Applications

The cooling of buildings in which humidity control is not critical in hot, dry climates.

Advantages

Cooling costs are low.

Disadvantages

The humidity inside the building is difficult to control and may become excessive. The system is inefficient in humid climates. A separate system is required for heating the building.

Major Components

Evaporative cooling unit, ductwork. Typical dimensions for these components are summarized in the accompanying table.

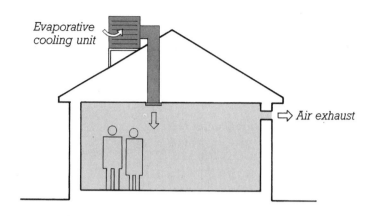

Evaporative cooling unit

Air exhaust

TYPICAL DIMENSIONS OF EVAPORATIVE COOLING SYSTEM COMPONENTS

Component	Width	Depth	Height
Evaporative cooler, average	36" (915 mm)	36" (915 mm)	36" (915 mm)
Duct	18" (460 mm)	18" (460 mm)	

Packaged terminal units and through-the-wall units are used extensively in small buildings as well as large. See page 158 for more detailed information on these systems.

Small split-packaged units are also available for use in small buildings.

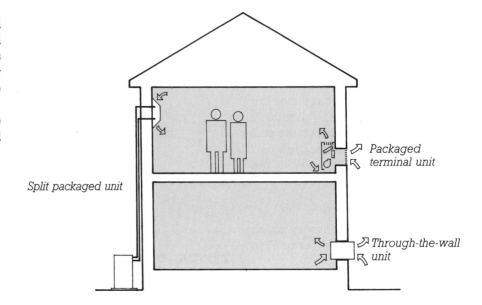

Split packaged unit

Packaged terminal unit

Through-the-wall unit

ELECTRIC BASEBOARD CONVECTORS

Description

Electric resistance wires in sheet metal enclosures are installed around the perimeter of the room at the junction of the floor and the wall. Room air circulates through slots in the enclosures by means of convection and is heated by the resistance wires.

Typical Applications

Heating systems in buildings of any type, especially where electric rates are low.

Advantages

Electric baseboard convectors are quiet and distribute heat evenly. Each room has individual temperature control. Installation costs are low. No chimney is required.

Disadvantages

The baseboard convectors occupy considerable wall perimeter and can interfere with furniture placement. There is no means of controlling humidity or air quality. Electricity is an expensive fuel in most areas. A separate system is required for cooling.

Major Components

Electric baseboard convector units. A typical convector is 3 in. (75 mm) deep and 7.5 in. (190 mm) high and extends for some feet along a wall.

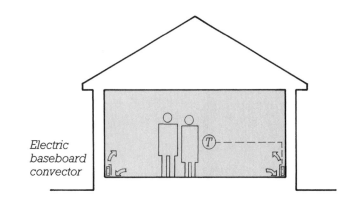

Electric baseboard convector

ELECTRIC FAN-FORCED UNIT HEATERS

Description

Fan-forced electric unit heaters are compact units inside which a fan draws in room air and heats it by passing it over electric resistance wires before blowing it back into the room.

Typical Applications

Any room or building that requires electric heating from small sources.

Advantages

They are economical to buy and install, and they do not interfere with furniture placement as much as baseboard convectors. Each room has individual temperature control. No chimney is required.

Disadvantages

Heat distribution in the room can be uneven, and the fans become noisy unless they are maintained regularly. There is no means of controlling humidity or air quality. Electricity is an expensive fuel in most areas. Separate systems are required for humidification and cooling.

Major Components

Electric fan-forced unit heaters. Typical dimensions for these components are summarized in the table to the right.

Variations

Fan-forced unit heaters are available for wall mounting in recessed or surface-mounted configurations. Toespace heaters are designed for use in the low, restricted space under kitchen cabinets or shelves. Recessed floor units lie beneath a simple floor register. Industrial unit heaters are mounted in rectangular metal cabinets that are designed to be suspended from the roof or ceiling structure.

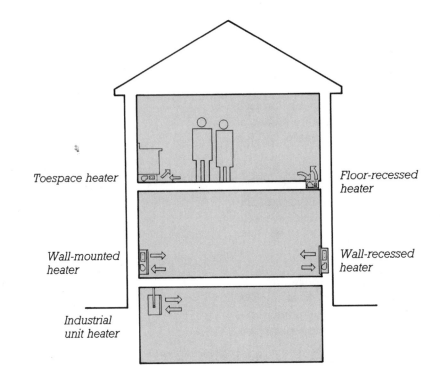

Toespace heater

Floor-recessed heater

Wall-mounted heater

Wall-recessed heater

Industrial unit heater

TYPICAL DIMENSIONS OF EVAPORATIVE COOLING SYSTEM COMPONENTS

Component	Width	Depth	Height
Floor-recessed heater	16" (400 mm)	8" (200 mm)	8" (200 mm)
Industrial unit heater	16" (400 mm)	12" (300 mm)	16" (400 mm)
Toespace heater	24" (610 mm)	12" (300 mm)	4" (100 mm)
Wall-recessed or wall surface-mounted heater	16" (400 mm)	4" (100 mm)	20" (510 mm)

ELECTRIC RADIANT HEATING

Description

Electric resistance heating wires are embedded in the ceiling or floor. The warm surface radiates heat directly to the body and also warms the air in the room.

Typical Applications

Residences, nursing homes.

Advantages

Heating is even and comfortable. No heating equipment is visible in the room.

Disadvantages

The system is slow to react to changing needs for heat. Tables and desktops beneath a radiant ceiling cast cold "shadows" on the legs and feet. Carpeting and furniture reduce the effectiveness of radiant floor panels. Cooling and humidity control must be provided by a separate system. Electricity is an expensive fuel in most areas.

Major Components

Resistance wires, resistance mats, or prefabricated, electrified ceiling panels.

Variations

Ceiling or floor radiant panels may be heated by hot water coils fed from a hydronic boiler.

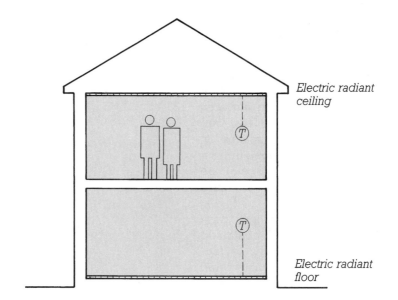

Electric radiant ceiling

Electric radiant floor

Description

A wall furnace is a tall, wall-recessed or surface-mounted heating unit in which air flows from the room and circulates by convection past metal heat exchange surfaces warmed by a gas flame. Most wall furnaces can heat the spaces on both sides of the wall. Sometimes a short run of ductwork can be added to circulate heat to a third room.

Direct-vent space heaters are a newer generation of self-contained heating units. Inside air is fan-forced over a sealed burner unit. The unit draws exterior air for combustion and may be fueled by kerosene, natural gas, or propane. In comparison to the wall furnace, direct-vent space heaters are smaller in size, have greater fuel-efficiency, provide improved heat distribution, and offer more choices of fuel source. These units are usually surface-mounted on the inside of an exterior wall, or vent pipes may be extended 10 to 15 ft (3 to 4.5 m) horizontally or vertically to permit more choice in heater location.

Typical Applications

Low-cost dwellings, offices, and motels in mild climates.

Advantages

Both systems are inexpensive to buy and install. Direct-vent space heaters are also highly fuel efficient.

Disadvantages

They require vent pipes to the outdoors, they distribute heat unevenly, and they are unattractive visually. Cooling and humidity control must be provided by separate systems.

Major Components

For wall furnaces, gas meter and service entrance or propane tank and regulator, gas piping, wall fur-

214

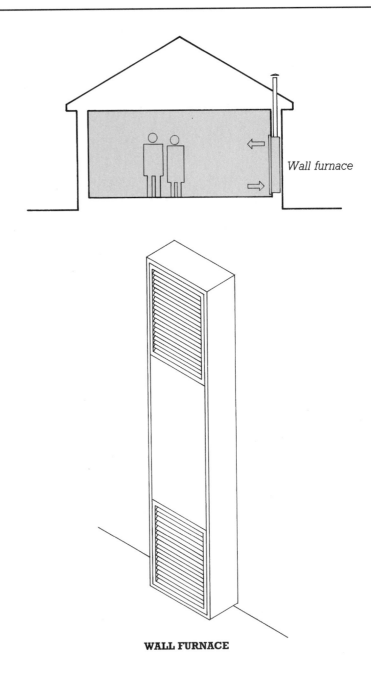

Wall furnace

WALL FURNACE

nace, vent pipes through the wall or to the roof. A typical wall furnace is 14 in. wide, 12 in. deep, and 84 in. high (360 × 305 × 2135 mm). The vent pipe to the roof is typically a 4-in. (100-mm) oval that may be concealed between the studs in a wall.

For direct-vent space heaters, the fuel supply may consist of gas service entrance and meter, propane tank and regulator, or kerosene tank. Kerosene may be

gravity-fed, or if the heater is above the level of the tank, a lift pump may be used. Heater unit dimensions range from 16–38 in. wide, 9–16 in. deep, and 21–28 in. high (405–965 mm × 230–450 mm × 535–710 mm). Dual concentric vent pipes that provide both fresh air intake and combustion exhaust may be extended through exterior wall or roof, and range in size from 2 to 3 in. (50 to 75 mm) in outside diameter.

HEATING STOVES

Description

Heating stoves are small appliances that sit conspicuously within each room they heat. They burn wood, coal, gas, oil, or kerosene, and transmit heat to the room and its occupants by a combination of convection and radiation.

Typical Applications

Residential, industrial, and commercial buildings, especially in areas where firewood or coal is inexpensive and readily available. Wood- and coal-burning stoves are frequently used as supplementary sources of heat in centrally-heated houses.

Advantages

Wood and coal are cheap fuels in many areas, and the experience of tending a stove and basking in its warmth can be aesthetically satisfying. Some stoves are visually attractive.

Disadvantages

Heating stoves use a surprisingly large amount of floor space and require chimneys. Most stoves are hot enough to burn the skin. They do not distribute heat evenly. Solid fuel stoves require constant tending and are difficult to control precisely. Solid fuel and ashes generate considerable dirt within the building. A stove becomes a fire hazard unless it and its chimney are conscientiously maintained and operated. Most solid-fuel stoves pollute the air through incomplete combustion.

Major Components

Chimney, stove and stovepipe, floor protection, wall protection, fuel storage, ash storage for solid-fuel stoves. Typical dimensions for these components are summarized in the table to the right. For dimensions of fuel storage components, see page 202.

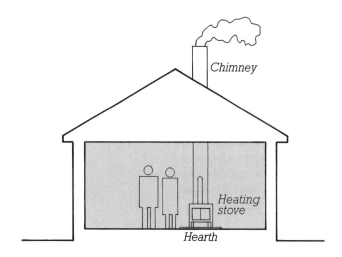

Chimney

Heating stove

Hearth

TYPICAL DIMENSIONS OF HEATING STOVES

Component	Width	Depth	Height
Ash storage	Covered metal bucket 14" (360 mm) in diameter		
Chimney, masonry			
One stove	20" (510 mm)	20" (510 mm)	*
Two stoves	20" (510 mm)	28" (710 mm)	*
Chimney, metal	10" (254 mm) diameter		
Fuel storage: see page 202			
Stove			
Gas-fired	38" (965 mm)	13" (330 mm)	40" (1015 mm)
Oil-fired	32" (815 mm)	30" (760 mm)	40" (1015 mm)
Wood-fired	Varies widely, up to the dimensions shown for gas-fired and oil-fired stoves		
Stovepipe, uninsulated, typical	7" (180 mm) diameter		
Stovepipe, insulated, typical	9" (230 mm) diameter		

Heating stoves typically require a clearance of 36" (914 mm) to combustible or plaster surfaces. They also require a noncombustible hearth that extends 12" (305 mm) to each side and to the back of the stove and 18" (460 mm) to the front. Some stoves are shielded to allow them to be as close as 12" to combustible surfaces to the back and sides. An uninsulated metal stovepipe may not come closer than 18" (460 mm) to the ceiling. Insulated pipes are usually designed for a 2" (51 mm) clearance to combustible materials.

*Under most codes a chimney must extend at least 3' (900 mm) above the highest point where it passes through the roof and at least 2' (600 mm) above any roof surface within a horizontal distance of 10' (3 m).

PASSIVE SOLAR HEATING

Description

The interior space of the building acts as a solar collector, receiving sunlight directly through large south-facing windows and storing excess heat in concrete, masonry, or containers of water or phase-change salts. During sunless periods, as the room temperature drops below the temperature of the heat storage materials, the stored heat is released into the interior air.

Typical Applications

Dwellings, schools, offices, industrial buildings.

Advantages

Passive solar heating has zero fuel cost, does not pollute the air, requires little or no maintenance, and can be aesthetically satisfying.

Disadvantages

Construction cost is high for passive solar heating schemes, and a full backup heating system must be provided to heat the building during long sunless periods. Relatively large swings in interior temperature must be expected. Most passive solar systems require the occupants of the building to perform daily control duties such as opening and closing insulating shutters or curtains. The architecture of solar heated buildings is strongly influenced by the need to orient and configure the building for optimum solar collection. Cooling and humidity control must be accomplished with separate systems.

Variations

1. In *direct gain passive heating,* sunlight enters south-facing windows and warms the interior directly. Roof overhangs or louvers are configured to block out high summer sun. Internal mass (masonry, concrete, large containers of water, or small containers of phase-change salts) must be provided,

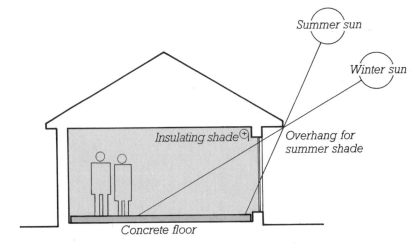

DIRECT GAIN PASSIVE SOLAR HEATING

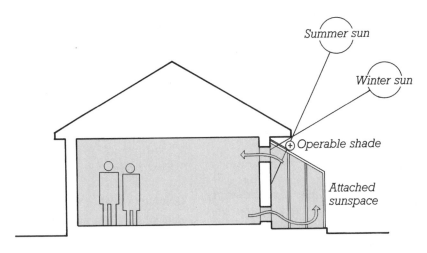

ATTACHED SUNSPACE PASSIVE SOLAR HEATING

preferably in direct sunlight, to absorb excess heat. Insulating closures are needed to cover the glass during sunless periods. This is a simple, enjoyable way of bringing heat into a building, one that puts the occupants into a very intimate relationship with the seasons and the weather. However, the direct sunlight causes visual glare, and it fades and deteriorates interior materials. Heat loss through the large glass areas during nights and cloudy days is considerable. Temperature control is often unsatisfactory.

2. In *attached sunspace passive solar heating,* an intermittently occupied greenhouse or glassy atrium attached to the building col-

lects solar heat by direct gain. Heated air is "borrowed" by the adjacent, fully inhabited spaces of the building by means of convection or small circulating fans. Undesirable glare and fading are largely or wholly confined to the sunspace. The sunspace can be closed off during sunless periods and allowed to grow cold. The extreme range of temperatures that occurs in the sunspace allows it to be inhabited only during limited periods and prevents plant growth unless additional temperature control mechanisms are provided.

3. *Fan-forced rock bed solar heating* is a hybrid of passive and active systems. Sunlight is received.

directly into the inhabited space of the building. When the interior air becomes heated above the comfort level, a thermostat actuates a fan that draws the overheated air through a large container of stones, where the excess heat is absorbed. During sunless periods, the fan is actuated again to warm the room air by passing it through the heated stones. Compared to direct gain solar heating, a fan-forced rock bed system gives better control of temperature and does not require the presence of massive materials within the inhabited spaces. The rock bed is large and expensive to construct. Glare and fading are a problem unless the system is coupled with an attached sunspace.

4. Trombe wall passive solar heating features a massive wall made of masonry, concrete, or containers of water. This wall is located immediately inside the windows that receive sunlight. The interior of the building is warmed by the heat that is conducted through the Trombe wall, by allowing room air to convect between the wall and the glass, or both. As compared to direct gain solar heating, a Trombe wall system blocks most or all direct sunlight from the inhabited space, preventing glare and fading. The wall occupies considerable space, however, and obstructs desirable visual contact between the inhabitants and the sun. The room temperature is difficult to control. An insulating closure is needed to reduce heat losses through the glass during sunless periods.

Typical dimensions of passive solar components are summarized in the table to the right. A backup heating system must also be provided; the backup system may be selected from the other heating systems described in this section.

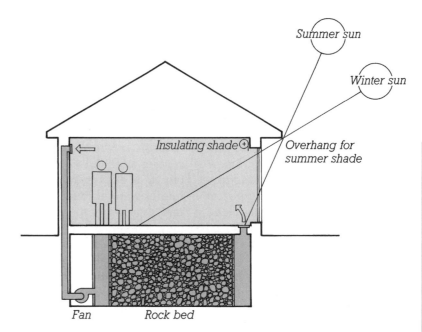

FAN-FORCED ROCK BED PASSIVE SOLAR HEATING

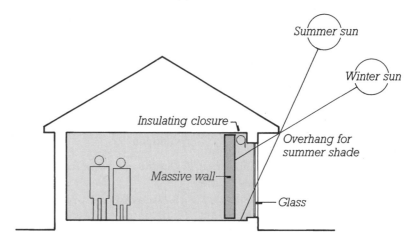

TROMBE WALL PASSIVE SOLAR HEATING

TYPICAL DIMENSIONS OF PASSIVE SOLAR HEATING COMPONENTS

Component

South-facing windows for passive solar heating for an average house should total at least 150 sq ft (14 m²) in area.

If the floor is used for thermal storage, it should be made of masonry or concrete at least 4" (100 mm) thick.

An attached sunspace should have a minimum floor area of 10' × 12' (3 × 3.7 m). A rock bed should have a minimum volume of 600 ft³ (17 m³).

A Trombe wall is typically 12" (300 mm) thick and as tall as the adjacent windows. There is usually a space of a foot or two between the glass and the wall.

WATER SUPPLY

Water from a municipal main reaches the building via an underground service pipe and a water meter. In warm climates, the meter may be outside the building, but in cold climates, it must be installed in a heated space, usually the basement or the mechanical equipment room. In many areas a tiny electronic readout, connected by wires to the inside water meter, is mounted on the outside of the building so that the meter reader does not need to enter the building.

From the water meter, domestic cold water flows directly to the fixtures by means of small diameter copper or plastic pipes. If the water is "hard" (contains a heavy concentration of calcium ions), a water softener may be installed to remove these ions from the water that goes to the domestic water heater. The water heater uses a gas flame, an oil flame, solar-heated liquid, or electric resistance heating to warm the water to a preset temperature at which it is held in an insulated tank for subsequent use. A tree of hot water piping parallels the cold water piping as it branches to the various fixtures in the building. Supply piping should be kept out of exterior walls of buildings in cold climates to prevent wintertime freezeups.

If water is obtained from a private well, it is lifted from the well and pressurized by a pump. If the well is deep, the pump is usually placed at the bottom of the well. If the well is shallow (less than 20 to 25 ft, or 6 to 8 meters), the pump may be located inside the building. In either case, the pump pushes the water into a pressure tank, from which it flows on demand into the hot and cold water piping. The pressure tank may be located inside the well, or in the basement or mechanical equipment room of the building.

WASTE PIPING AND SEWAGE DISPOSAL

Sewage flows from each fixture through a trap into waste pipes that drain by gravity. To assure that the traps do not siphon dry and to maintain constant atmospheric pressure in the waste piping, a vent pipe is attached to the waste system near each trap. The vent pipes rise upward through the building until they penetrate the roof, where they are left open to the air. The vent pipes may be gathered together into a single pipe in the attic of the building to minimize the number of roof penetrations. A horizontal run of vent can be used to move a plumbing vent to a less prominent rooftop location.

The waste piping descends through the building, gathering waste from all the fixtures, until it reaches the ground, the crawl space, or the basement. If it lies above the sewer or the private dis-

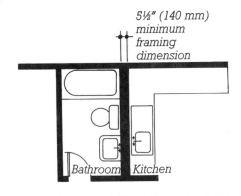

5½" (140 mm) minimum framing dimension

Bathroom   Kitchen

posal system at this point, it turns to an almost horizontal orientation, sloping toward its outlet (the sewer main or the septic tank) at a pitch of at least 1 in 100. If it lies below the elevation of its outlet at this point, an automatically operated underground ejector pump must be installed to lift the sewage and empty it into the outlet.

Waste and vent piping is larger in diameter than supply piping and requires careful planning to fit

TYPICAL DIMENSIONS OF PLUMBING COMPONENTS

Component	Width	Depth	Height
Gas meter and piping	18" (460 mm)	12" (305 mm)	24" (610 mm)

Sewage disposal, private

The size and configuration of private sewage disposal systems vary widely depending on soil conditions, topography, local laws, and the required capacity of the system. As a starting point, allow an area of level or nearly level ground 40' × 80' (12 × 25 m), with its short side against the building. No part of this area may be closer than 100' (30 m) to a well, pond, lake, stream, or river.

Component	Width	Depth	Height
Water heater			
Gas-fired	20" (510 mm) diameter		60" (1525 mm)
Electric	24" (610 mm) diameter		53" (1350 mm)
Water meter and piping	20" (510 mm)	24" (305 mm)	10" (255 mm)
Water pressure tank for a pump that is located in a well	20" (510 mm) diameter		64" (1625 mm)
Water pump and pressure tank for a shallow well	36" (915 mm)	20" (510 mm)	64" (1625 mm)
Water softener	18" (460 mm) diameter		42" (1070 mm)

PLUMBING SYSTEMS FOR SMALL BUILDINGS

gracefully and efficiently into a building. Bathrooms and toilet rooms should be stacked to avoid horizontal displacements of the waste and vent stacks. For maximum economy, fixtures should be aligned along thickened plumbing walls, and rooms containing fixtures should be clustered back-to-back around the plumbing walls. The major horizontal runs of waste piping should be located in a crawl space, beneath a slab, or just inside the perimeter of a basement. Some typical wood framing details for plumbing walls are shown in the diagram to the right.

Private sewage disposal systems vary considerably in configuration and size, depending chiefly on soil conditions and local health regulations. The most common type includes a septic tank, usually 1000 to 1500 gal (4000 to 6000 l) in capacity, in which the sewage is digested by anaerobic action. Effluent from the septic tank flows by gravity to a disposal field of open-jointed pipe laid below ground in a bed of crushed stone. In nearly all areas of North America, private sewage disposal systems may be designed only by a registered sanitary engineer. The engineer's design is based on soil tests that in some municipalities may be performed only during those limited periods of the year when the soil is saturated, and a building permit will not be issued until a permit has been granted for the construction of the disposal system. This often delays the start of a construction project for many months.

Typical dimensions of plumbing components are summarized in the table on the facing page.

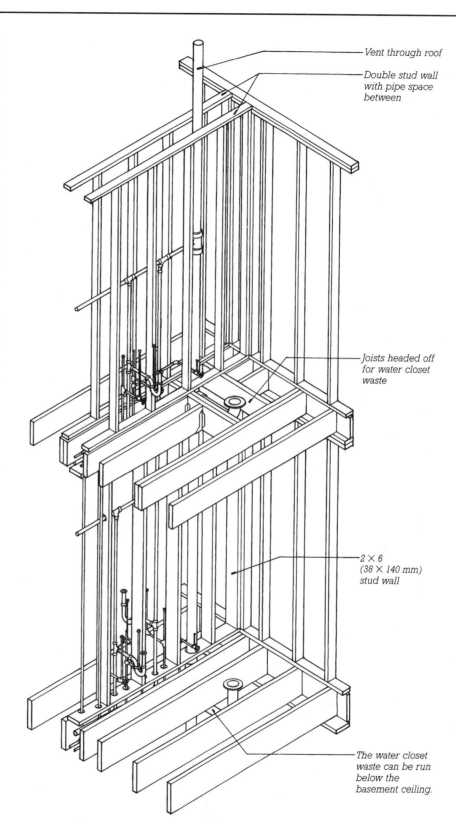

Vent through roof

Double stud wall with pipe space between

Joists headed off for water closet waste

2×6 (38×140 mm) stud wall

The water closet waste can be run below the basement ceiling.

FRAMING DETAILS FOR PLUMBING WALLS

GAS SERVICE

Natural gas is distributed to buildings through mains located beneath the street. Each building is served by an underground pipe that surfaces at a gas meter and pressure regulator next to or just inside the building. From this service entrance, the gas is piped through the building to the various appliances — furnaces, boilers, water heaters, clothes dryers, fireplaces, barbecues, kitchen ranges, and industrial equipment.

Where there are no gas mains, liquid propane gas can be delivered by tanker truck to pressurized tanks outside the building. The gas flows from the tanks through a pressure regulator and evaporator into the building's gas piping system.

Gas piping is small in diameter and is made up of threaded black iron pipe and fittings. It does not usually require special consideration in the design of the building, but space does need to be provided, usually at the basement ceiling or in the crawlspace or slab, for long horizontal runs of gas piping. For dimensions of gas meters in a small building, see the table on page 218. For dimensions of liquid propane storage tanks, see the table on page 202.

SPRINKLER SYSTEMS IN SMALL BUILDINGS

In most small buildings, sprinkler protection, when it is required, can be provided at a maximum rate of one sprinkler head per 144 sq ft (13.4 m^2) of floor area. The average coverage per sprinkler head will be somewhat less than this because of the problems of fitting sprinkler layouts to rooms of varying sizes and shapes. The horizontal piping to the sprinklers is small in diameter and must run below the roof insulation in cold climates, either above a suspended ceiling or just on top of the ceiling material and between the joists. Vertical risers must be installed on the warm side of the wall insulation or in interior partitions. A small assembly of valves and alarm fittings must be furnished at the point where the sprinkler system joins the domestic water system, and a Siamese fitting is required for many installations. If the available water supply is inadequate to feed the sprinkler system, a backup water supply has to be furnished in the form of a gravity tank, an air-pressurized tank, or a reservoir and pump, any of which is custom designed for the given situation.

ELECTRICAL AND COMMUNICATIONS WIRING FOR SMALL BUILDINGS

Electrical, telephone, and cable television services reach the building via either overhead or underground wires, depending on the practices of the local utilities. Overhead wires at the street may be converted to an underground service to the building by running the service wires down the face of the pole to the required depth and then laterally to the building.

An electric meter is mounted at eye level in an accessible location on the outside surface of the building. Wires from an overhead service arrive at the building high above the meter and descend to it in a large cable or a metal conduit mounted on the exterior wall surface. Wires from an underground service are brought up to the meter in a conduit. A cable or conduit from the meter enters the building at the basement or main floor level and connects to the main electric panel, which should be as close to the meter as possible.

From the main panel, wiring fans out to branch panels and individual circuits. Exposed wiring or wiring in masonry or concrete must be placed in metal or plastic conduits. In frame buildings, most wiring is done with flexible plastic-sheathed cable that is routed through the cavities of the frame. In a very small building, all the branch circuits connect directly to the main panel. In a larger building, especially one with multiple tenant spaces, most circuits connect to branch panels scattered at convenient points around the building. The branch panels, in turn, are connected by cables or conduits to the main panel.

Panel locations need to be worked out fairly early in the building design process. In small framed buildings, the designer seldom needs to be concerned about providing space for the wires and cables, unless the construction system features exposed framing members and decking. In this case, conduit routes for the wiring must be carefully planned to avoid visual chaos.

Wiring systems for telephone service, cable television, computer local area networks, centralized entertainment systems, security systems, fire alarms, intercoms, antennas, and so on generally have minimal impact on the planning of a small building in the early stages of design. At their simplest, such systems may not require any dedicated space, or may require only small, wall-mounted panels that can share space in general purpose closets, basements, or mechanical equipment rooms. As systems increase in complexity, dedicated wiring closets may be necessary. Such closets should be centrally located to best accommodate the star topology of most such systems and to minimize the length of individual cable runs. For example, a central stair may offer closet space at its lowest level as well as easy cable access up through the center of the building— at each floor or ceiling level cables can then branch out to reach their final destinations. Closets must be located so that cable lengths do not exceed their maximum limits for reliable performance. For example, with the most common type of local area network cabling, referred to as unshielded twisted pair or Category 5 cabling, individual cables should not exceed approximately 285 ft (85 m) in length. To avoid electrical interference from other systems, communications closets should be separated from electrical service entrance cables, service panels, lightning protection, and mechanical equipment by at least 6 ft (1.8 m).

Typical dimensions of components of electrical systems in small buildings are summarized in the table below.

TYPICAL DIMENSIONS OF COMPONENTS OF ELECTRICAL SYSTEMS

Component	Width	Depth	Height
Electric meter	12" (305 mm)	9" (230 mm)	15" (380 mm)
Main panel	14" (360 mm)	4" (100 mm)	27" (685 mm)
Branch panel	14" (360 mm)	4" (100 mm)	20" (685 mm)

▪▪▪▪
DESIGNING
WITH
DAYLIGHT

■■■■
DESIGN
CRITERIA
FOR
DAYLIGHTING
SYSTEMS

This section will help you evaluate the suitability of daylight illumination to your project, and if you choose to proceed with daylighting design, to select appropriate daylighting strategies.

DESIGN WITH DAYLIGHT

Daylighting is the use of natural light to illuminate the interior of a building. Daylight can provide high-quality, color-balanced lighting. It can reduce a building's energy consumption, contribute to the conservation of natural resources and the protection of the environment, improve the aesthetic quality of the workplace, provide a psychological connection to nature and the outdoors, and increase business productivity. There are many factors that influence the potential for daylighting design on any given project. Location, climate, building form, program, and the perceived value of daylighting by both the building's owners and its occupants can all play a role. When buildings are designed for daylight illumination, the architectural impact is significant. Massing, orientation, structural configuration, layout of interior elements and spaces, and choice of materials are all influenced by daylighting considerations. For these reasons, daylighting should be addressed at the earliest stages of design, when the opportunities for successfully incorporating effective strategies into a project are greatest. The information in the following pages will help you evaluate the potential of daylighting design for your project, and provides preliminary guidelines for developing a building that effectively utilizes natural daylight for illumination.

A quality luminous environment requires adequate levels of illumination; it requires light that is well distributed so as to prevent excessive contrast, brightness, and glare; and it requires light that is reliably available. Sources of daylight include both the sun and the surrounding, clear or clouded, luminous sky. Direct sunlight is too intense to be allowed to fall directly on tasks or within the visual field. It must be diffused, reflected, or moderated in some way. Furthermore, direct sunlight is not necessarily the most reliable source of daylight. The sun's position in the sky changes constantly, causing the quality of its light to vary with orientation, time of day, and season. At any time, the sun may be obscured by cloud cover, geographic features, or nearby man-made structures. For these reasons, the simplest way to incorporate daylighting into most projects is to rely on indirect sky light as the primary source of illumination, and where sunlight is present, to ensure that it does not directly intrude into the task area. This is the daylighting approach emphasized in the following pages.

Designs utilizing direct sunlight as the primary source of illumination are also feasible, particularly in areas with prevailing clear skies. The information provided here is relevant to such projects as well. However, the behavior of such systems is more complex, and their design will require more sophisticated analysis and modeling techniques than provided here.

SKY COVER

The map on this page indicates average clear and covered (cloudy) sky conditions within the continental United States. Conditions are characterized as *predominantly clear, moderate,* or *heavily covered,* corresponding to an average annual sky cover of less than 50%, from 50% to 70%, or greater than 70%, respectively. Only in areas indicated as predominantly clear—mainly the Southwest and parts of Florida—are clear skies prevalent on average more than half of all daylight hours. In the remaining areas—most of the continental United States—covered or partially covered sky conditions predominate more than half the time. Though not shown on this map, the heavily populated regions of Canada are also within moderate or heavily covered areas as well.

In predominantly clear areas, direct sun is most prevalent and daylight conditions are most constant. In these areas, the levels of available daylight are consistently highest. Consequently, in using the sizing charts shown toward the end of this chapter for projects falling within predominantly clear areas, you should read low in the recommended lighting level ranges because of the higher available light levels. In areas characterized as moderate, sky conditions are more variable. In using the sizing charts for projects falling within moderate sky cover areas, you should read near the middle of the recommended lighting level ranges. In heavily covered areas, cloudy skies predominate, and average daylight availability is lowest. When using the sizing charts for these projects, you should read near the top of the recommended lighting level ranges. Because local sky conditions can vary from regional averages, this information should be supplemented with local data whenever possible.

Regardless of sky cover conditions, control of direct sunlight is always an important consideration. To prevent unacceptable levels of glare and contrast, sunlight should always be prevented from falling directly within the visual field of task areas.

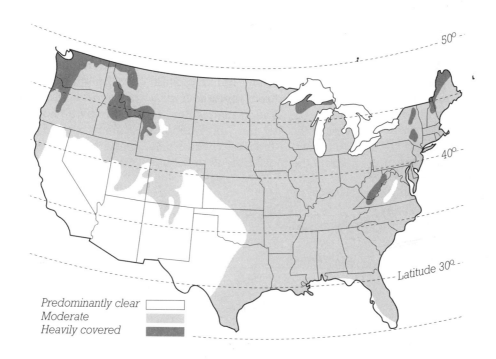

Predominantly clear
Moderate
Heavily covered

SKY COVER CONDITIONS

DESIGN CRITERIA FOR DAYLIGHTING SYSTEMS

227

THE PATH OF THE SUN

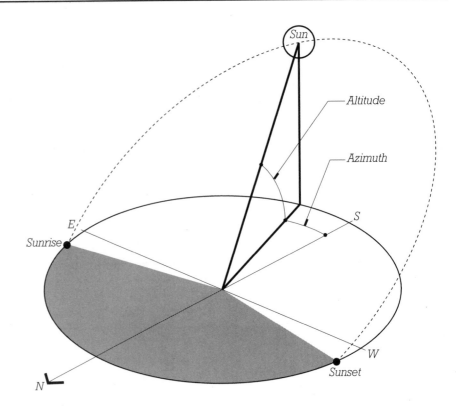

The sun moves over and around a building during the course of each day. Successful daylighting design requires that the building occupants receive acceptable levels of consistent, quality illumination throughout this cycle. The chart below provides information about the path of the sun for various latitudes and different times of the year, information that is important to understanding the impact of the sun on a building. To find the approximate latitude for a project located in the continental United States, use the latitude indications on the Sky Cover Conditions map on the previous page. For other locations, consult comparable sources of information. For example, Savannah, Georgia, lies approximately at 32° North latitude. At the summer solstice, June 21, the sun rises at an azimuth of 115° (measured from the South axis), and at solar noon, reaches an altitude of 81° (measured from the horizon). The length of the day from sunrise to sunset is approximately 14 hours.

The path of the sun also varies over the course of the year, the magnitude of this variation increasing with greater distance from the equator. For example, at 24° North latitude, the length of the day varies 4 hours over the span of a year. At 52° North, the difference is 8 hours. At 24° North, the altitude of the winter solstice noon sun reaches 42°. At 52° North, the same sun swings through a much lower arc, reaching only 15° above the horizon. At 24° North, the position of the rising or setting sun moves 47° across the horizon over the course of the year. At 52° North, the movement is 2½ times as great.

Use the information in this table to chart the approximate path of the sun around the building. As you continue on the following pages, this information will help you to determine a favorable building orientation and opening

configuration in order to maximize daylight access and limit exposure to unwanted direct sunlight. In particular, pay special attention to times of the day and year when the sun is low in the sky. These times present the most difficult problems

for sunlight control, and attention to building orientation, configuration of daylight openings, and the anticipated hours of building occupancy should all be considered relative to these low-angle sun conditions.

Latitude	Hours of Daylight (sunrise to sunset)	Altitude of Noon Sun	Azimuth of Rising or Setting Sun
24° North			
Summer Solstice	14 hours	90°	115°
Winter Solstice	10 hours	42°	68°
32° North			
Summer Solstice	14 hours	81°	115°
Winter Solstice	10 hours	36°	62°
40° North			
Summer Solstice	14 hours	74°	120°
Winter Solstice	9 hours	28°	60°
48° North			
Summer Solstice	15 hours	66°	125°
Winter Solstice	8 hours	20°	55°
52° North			
Summer Solstice	16 hours	62°	130°
Winter Solstice	8 hours	16°	50°

SKY DOME OBSTRUCTION

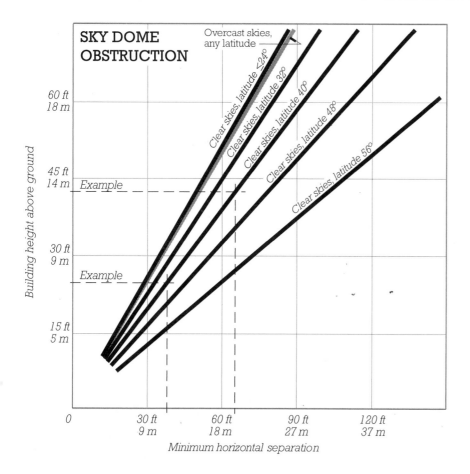

SKY DOME
OBSTRUCTION

Overcast skies, any latitude
Clear skies, latitude <24°
Clear skies, latitude 32°
Clear skies, latitude 40°
Clear skies, latitude 48°
Clear skies, latitude 56°

Building height above ground

60 ft / 18 m
45 ft / 14 m — Example
30 ft / 9 m
Example
15 ft / 5 m

0 — 30 ft / 9 m — 60 ft / 18 m — 90 ft / 27 m — 120 ft / 37 m

Minimum horizontal separation

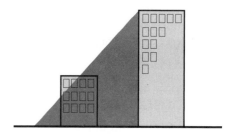

This chart is for determining daylight obstruction between buildings.

■ To ensure full access to daylight for your building, read the chart using the height of adjacent buildings or structures. Locate your building so that it is at least as far from each of these structures as indicated on the chart.

■ To ensure that your building does not obstruct access to daylight for adjacent structures, read the chart using the height of your building and locate your building at least as far away from the adjacent structures as indicated.

■ For buildings in predominantly covered sky conditions at any latitude, read the chart along the sloped line for overcast skies. For buildings located in predominantly clear sky areas, read the chart along the sloped line for the latitude of the project, or interpolate between lines for other latitudes. For buildings located in moderate sky cover areas, read along the line for overcast skies to find optimum building separation under worst case conditions, or read along the appropriate line for clear skies to determine building separation under more favorable clear sky conditions. To determine sky conditions and the latitude of a project located in the continental United States, consult the Clear Sky Cover Conditions map on page 227. For other project locations, use comparable sources of information.

Daylighting design requires a building to have line-of-sight access to sufficient sky area for adequate daylight exposure. The chart above can be used in two ways: first, to determine the extent to which surrounding structures may obstruct your building's access to daylight, and second, to determine the extent to which your building obstructs surrounding structures' access to daylight.

For example, assume a project location at 40° North latitude, with clear sky conditions, a neighboring building 24 ft (7 m) tall, and a planned height of 42 ft (13 m) for your building. To ensure that your building has full access to daylight, read the chart using the adjacent building's height of 24 ft (7 m) to determine that there should at least 37 ft (11 m) between the two structures. To ensure that the adjacent building's daylight is not obstructed by your project, read the chart using your building's height of 42 ft (13 m) to determine that there should be at least 65 ft (20 m) between the two structures. To protect access to daylight for both buildings, use the larger of the two answers, in this case, 65 ft (20 m).

BUILDING SITING AND SHAPE

Daylighting design is intimately related to building form. This section provides guidelines for the siting, massing, and internal configuration of a building so as to provide the greatest opportunities for successful daylighting.

BUILDING SIZE

Strategies for daylighting differ with building size. For small buildings, the ratio of exterior skin area to the enclosed volume is relatively large. This means that residences and small-scale nonresidential buildings generally have ample opportunities to locate occupied areas in close proximity to daylight sources such as windows and rooftop openings. In small buildings, the main challenge for the designer is to control the quality of the daylight, distributing it effectively and avoiding excessive contrast or brightness. On the other hand, in large buildings, the ratio of exterior envelope area to enclosed space is less, and providing adequate levels of daylight to interior areas becomes a design challenge with significant formal implications. Both the shape of the building and its interior configuration are critical to a successful daylighting scheme.

ORIENTATION

Daylight openings should be oriented so as to allow the control of direct sunlight while providing access to sources of daylight that are consistent in quality and provide high levels of illumination. In the Northern Hemisphere, these conditions are best met in a south orientation, where for the largest part of the day, the sun remains high in the sky and the surrounding sky provides high levels of manageable daylight. Northern exposure is also favorable, providing consistent daylight, though at illumination levels lower than from a southern exposure. The most difficult orientations for daylight openings are toward those portions of the sky in which the sun is low in its daily path, generally toward the east and west, though precise orientation varies with location and time of year. These exposures should be avoided, or if used, studied carefully, as the quality of the daylight is highly variable and the control of direct sunlight problematic. Thus, buildings elongated in the east–west direction, and plan configurations that otherwise maximize exposure to the north and south sky while shielding exposure to the east and west, will generally provide the most favorable daylighting opportunities. In some cases, strategically located adjacent structures may also play a positive role in shielding a building from unfavorable exposure to the sun when it is low in the sky.

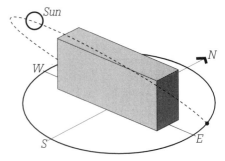

BUILDING ORIENTATION

BUILDING SITING AND SHAPE

BUILDING SHAPE

In large multistory buildings, daylighting is most often provided through windows in exterior walls. Daylighting such as this is termed *sidelighting,* and its effectiveness is limited by the depth to which it can penetrate horizontally into the building interior. For example, in a typical office building daylighting can provide full illumination to task areas no farther than 12 to 15 ft (3.5 to 4.5 m) from exterior wall openings and can provide partial illumination to areas no farther than 24 to 30 ft (7.5 to 9 m) from the exterior. Thus, to maximize effective daylighting in a commercial office building, work areas should be located, to the greatest extent possible, no more than 30 ft (9 m) from exterior walls with daylight access. Consider, for example, a double-loaded corridor plan. Total building depth in the north–south direction should not exceed approximately 70 ft (21 m), allowing 30 ft (9 m) for work areas on either side of a 10 ft (3 m) wide central corridor. In general, narrow or elongated plans, L- or U-shaped plans, and courtyard or atrium buildings provide greater access to daylight than more compact arrangements.

Where occupied areas occur directly below roofs, daylighting may also be provided through overhead skylights or other types of roof openings, devices collectively referred to as *toplighting.* Large single-story buildings, such as industrial factory buildings, are well suited to toplighting configurations, as are the topmost floors of many multistory buildings. Opportunities for toplighting can be increased with building sections that step or are otherwise configured to create increased roof area. Considering sidelighting and toplighting together, daylighting design generally benefits from elongated or articulated building massing that increases the building perimeter and thereby increases opportunities for daylight access to the interior.

BUILDING DESIGN DEVELOPMENT

As a design progresses and building configuration continues to develop, the impact of daylighting should be investigated in more detail and with more attention to specific local conditions. For example, a building not oriented on the cardinal points of the compass may interact with early morning and late afternoon sun in ways that require more detailed investigation. Local topography and climatic conditions may affect access to daylight at various times of the day or year. Adjacent structures may reflect light or obscure the sky in ways that positively or negatively affect a project. Patterns of use within a building may also favor certain orientations or times of day. For example, an elementary school building in which classrooms are unoccupied after three o'clock in the afternoon may be more tolerant of western exposure than a commercial office space habitually occupied until later in the day. As the project design develops, more detailed analysis, daylighting modeling, and the advice of daylighting experts should all be used.

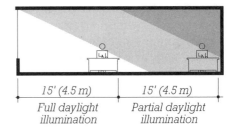

Full daylight illumination   *Partial daylight illumination*

15' (4.5 m)   15' (4.5 m)

SIDELIGHTING

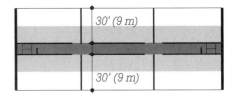

30' (9 m)

30' (9 m)

DOUBLE-LOADED CORRIDOR

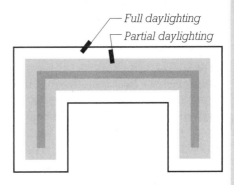

Full daylighting

Partial daylighting

ELONGATED BUILDING PLANS

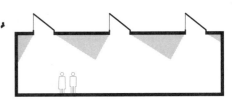

TOPLIGHTING

BUILDING INTERIOR CONFIGURATION

Not all activities within a building necessarily benefit equally from daylighting, and an analysis of the daylighting needs of the various components of the program can help guide decisions regarding where each component may be located. For example, vertical circulation, bathrooms, and storage gain little if any benefit from daylighting and can be located in portions of the floor plate that daylight cannot reach. Or such functions can be grouped on the east and west ends of a building, acting as shields against these problematic exposures.

A critical factor in daylighting design is the treatment of ceiling height, especially close to the exterior. Considering the section diagram on this page, the exterior wall can be divided into three distinct zones. The portion of the wall below 30 in. (760 mm), roughly the level of a typical work surface, makes no significant contribution to daylighting. Openings in the middle portion of the wall, up to approximately 7 ft (2.1 m), provide daylighting in areas closest to the opening and offer exterior views. To maximize the effectiveness of daylight illumination deeper in the space, the window opening must extend above 7 ft (2.1 m), necessitating a ceiling as high as possible and the avoidance of spandrel beams or other elements close to the perimeter that can obscure this portion of the wall opening. This criterion places significant constraints on the planning of structural and mechanical building systems, such as the location of deep beams or HVAC ductwork, and must be considered in the earliest stages of design if it is to be achieved. (For

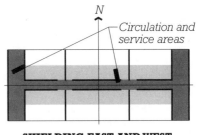

SHIELDING EAST AND WEST EXPOSURES

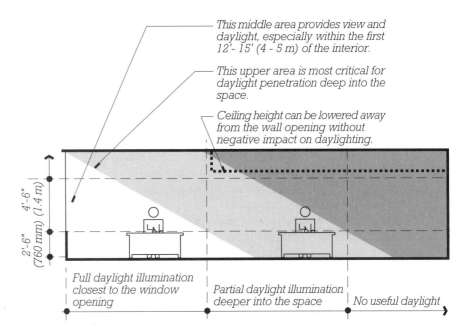

This middle area provides view and daylight, especially within the first 12'- 15' (4 - 5 m) of the interior.

This upper area is most critical for daylight penetration deep into the space.

Ceiling height can be lowered away from the wall opening without negative impact on daylighting.

Full daylight illumination closest to the window opening

Partial daylight illumination deeper into the space

No useful daylight

DAYLIGHT ZONES AND THE WINDOW WALL (*Thanks to Joel Loveland, University of Washington Department of Architecture and Seattle Lighting Design Lab for the concept of this diagram*).

more detailed information about window opening height and daylight horizontal penetration, see pages 237–239.)

For a task area to benefit significantly from daylight illumination, a source of daylight, such as a window, skylight, or a surface off which daylight is reflected, must be directly in line of sight with that task area.

Partitions, structural elements, mechanical and electrical system components, furnishings, and other elements that extend above the lower third of the space should be arranged to minimize their potential to obstruct daylight sources. See page 238 for more information about configuring interior elements for optimal daylighting.

DAYLIGHTING AND ENERGY CONSERVATION

SMALL BUILDINGS

Small building energy consumption tends to be driven primarily by heating and cooling loads associated with thermal exchange through the building's exterior skin. Thus, in cold climates energy consumption is dominated by the need to replace heat lost through the walls and roof during the cold months. In warmer regions energy consumption is driven by the removal of heat gained through the exterior envelope during the warm months. Daylighting design can contribute to the reduction of energy consumption in both these circumstances.

In cold climates, south-facing sidelighting can provide daylight illumination as well as solar heat gain for energy savings. Where sunlight is admitted into the structure as a source of heat, internal shading, diffusing, or reflecting devices should be used to protect visual task areas from direct sun and conditions of excessive brightness or contrast. To control heat gain during warmer months, external overhangs or other shading devices can be used to exclude direct sun entirely from the interior. For more information on solar heating strategies for small buildings, see pages 216–217.

Daylight illumination can also contribute to reduced cooling loads in warm climates. Indirect light from the north sky or from well-shaded southern exposures is an excellent source of illumination with low heat content. Direct sunlight can be reflected off exterior surfaces before it is admitted into a structure, thereby leaving a significant portion of its heat content outside the building. And, as explained in more detail in the next section, even direct sunlight can be an energy-efficient source of illumination when it is properly controlled and efficiently distributed within the interior.

LARGE BUILDINGS

In large buildings energy consumption is most often dominated by internally generated heat loads, rather than by exterior climate conditions or characteristics of the building skin. The removal of heat generated by occupants, lighting, and equipment is quite often the most significant factor in the overall energy performance of a large building.

In conditions such as these, daylighting can contribute significantly to energy savings. Natural daylight illumination is "free." Wherever daylighting can replace an electric light source, electric energy consumption is reduced directly. In addition, because well-designed daylight illumination generates less heat than common sources of artificial illumination, daylighting can lessen a building's internal heat load, further reducing energy consumption. The following chart tabulates the *efficacy* of daylight and several forms of electric lighting—that is, the amount of useful light in relation to the heat produced (measured in lumens per watt). The higher the efficacy, the more energy-efficient the light source. Note that daylighting compares favorably to all common types of electric lighting:

For daylight to achieve its potential for high efficacy, it must be well utilized within the building. Direct sunlight that causes excessive heat gain, or daylighting that in any way creates an unsatisfactory visual environment, will not reduce the use of electric light or save energy. However, when well designed and implemented, natural daylighting offers significant opportunities for savings in large building energy consumption.

Light Source Efficacy, measured in lumens/watt*	
Natural daylighting	90–150 lm/W
Incandescent electric lighting	15–25 lm/W
Fluorescent electric lighting	55–90 lm/W
Metal halide electric lighting	80–100 lm/W

*Higher values represent higher efficiency.

■■■■
CONFIGURING AND SIZING DAYLIGHTING SYSTEMS

This section will help you lay out the components of a daylighting system and estimate the size of daylight openings to provide the required levels of interior illumination for a project.

RECOMMENDED ILLUMINANCE LEVELS

Different tasks require different levels of illumination. The nature of a task, the need for accuracy and efficiency, and the visual acuity of the occupants are all contributing factors. For example, navigating the lobby of a commercial office building requires minimal attention to detail and is not a task with unusual demands for speed or accuracy. Consequently, relatively low ambient lighting levels are acceptable. On the other hand, an accountant who spends much of her day reading and transcribing densely formatted, low-contrast financial statements and ledgers, and whose efficiency and accuracy of work are critical, requires significantly higher levels of task illumination. Follow the steps below to determine recommended lighting levels for a project and to estimate the size and quantity of daylight sources for your building.

Step 1: Choose a Lighting Level Category

From the chart above, make a preliminary choice of lighting level by selecting the category that most closely matches the activity that takes place in the given space.

Step 2: Adjust Your Choice

Each lighting level category represents a range of illumination levels suitable for the tasks described. On the charts on the following pages, each category is shown as a band, representing the range of values. When reading from charts, you may read higher or lower in the appropriate band, depending on the following factors:

Higher light levels are recommended in areas with occupants primarily of age 55 years or older, in areas with predominantly dark, nonreflective surroundings or task backgrounds, and in areas where

General Space Illumination

Category A—Public spaces, dark spaces	Nighttime corridors and lobbies, waiting rooms, bedrooms
Category B—Simple orientation	Dance halls, dining halls, transportation terminal concourses, residential living spaces
Category C—Occasional visual tasks	Daytime corridors and lobbies, reception areas, auditoriums, banks, worship spaces

Task Illumination

Category D—Visual tasks of high contrast or large size	Conference rooms, office work with high contrast tasks, factory simple assembly, residential kitchens
Category E—Visual tasks of medium contrast or small size	Drafting of high-contrast work, classrooms, offices, clerical tasks, factory work of low contrast or moderately difficult assembly
Category F—Visual tasks of low contrast or very small size	Drafting of low-contrast work, laboratories, factory work with difficult assembly

tasks are carried out that require an unusually high degree of speed and accuracy. If two or more of these factors apply, read *high* in the lighting level category bands in the following charts. Conversely, lower light levels are recommended in areas with occupants primarily under the age of 40, in areas with light-colored, highly reflective surroundings or task backgrounds, and in areas where tasks are carried out that do not demand unusual speed or accuracy. If two or more of these factors apply, read *low* in the lighting level category bands in the following charts.

AMBIENT SPACE AND TASK ILLUMINATION

The table above lists recommended lighting levels for both general space illumination and task illumi-

nation, with task illumination requiring higher light levels because of the greater visual demands associated with these activities. For projects for which full reliance on daylighting is not achievable or desired, a strategy that may be considered is to provide ambient space illumination with daylighting and supplement this with electric lighting for task illumination. Thus, for example, where a typical office space may require Category E task illumination levels at the worker's desk, Category C illumination levels should be adequate for movement around these areas. In this case, daylighting design can be based on Category C illumination levels and task lighting at the desk can be provided from electric sources.

SIDELIGHTING

With the exception of large single-story structures, sidelighting through windows and clerestories is the predominant means of providing daylight illumination in buildings.

The intensity of sidelighting is highest near the opening and diminishes with increasing distance from the opening. The depth to which sidelighting can provide illumination within a building is largely dependent on the height of the opening. Under typical conditions, sidelighting can provide effective illumination for depths up to approximately 2½ times the height of the opening above the plane of the work surface. For example, in an office with 9 ft (2.7 m) high windows and 30 in. (760 mm) high desks, the top of the window is 6½ ft (2.0 m) above the work plane, and daylight should be able to provide full illumination up to a depth of approximately 16 ft (5 m) (6.5 ft × 2.5 = 16.25 ft). For more detailed information on the depth of sidelighting penetration for various illumination levels and opening heights, see page 239.

In designing with sidelighting, attention must be given to maximizing its reach deep into the structure, as well as minimizing excessive brightness close to the wall openings. A variety of techniques are possible. *Light shelves* create more evenly distributed illumination levels throughout a space. Though light shelves may reflect some light deeper into the interior, their primary benefit comes from reducing brightness levels close to the window. By reducing the highest illumination levels, more uniform lighting is achieved overall, giving the impression of an improved lighting environment. Light shelves can also prevent direct sunlight from falling directly within the work area.

Exterior overhangs may be solid or louvered. Extending a solid overhang beyond the building wall is essentially the same as increasing the depth of the room, and illumination is reduced comparably. If light levels are adequate, this can be an effective way to block direct sun as well as reduce excessive brightness close to the window. Louvered overhangs, if designed with attention to prevailing sun angles, can block direct sunlight selectively while admitting indirect light.

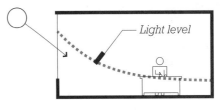

SIDELIGHTING

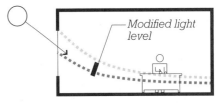

REDUCED WINDOW HEAD HEIGHT

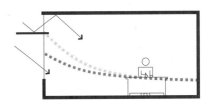

LIGHT SHELF

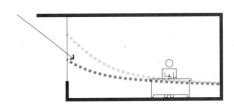

EXTERIOR OVERHANG

CONFIGURING AND SIZING DAYLIGHTING SYSTEMS

237

Reflective sills can increase the depth to which light penetrates within the space. However, care must be taken to avoid creating excessive glare for occupants close to the opening.

Secondary sources of daylight that are located at some distance from a primary wall opening, such as rear windows or skylights, can be used to increase light levels deep within a space, thereby creating more uniform lighting, as well as reducing strong shadowing and contrast.

Obstructions to daylight within the space should be prevented. Wherever possible, elements that can block daylight, particularly those high up in the space, should be located as far from wall openings as possible. Where a plan includes both open plan areas and enclosed space, the open plan areas should be placed closest to the wall openings and the enclosed spaces should be located so as to minimize the obstruction of daylight. Where enclosed spaces must be located close to wall openings, consider transparent or translucent enclosing materials to allow daylight to penetrate beyond these areas. Opaque elements, such as partitions or ceiling beams, can assist in daylight distribution when oriented perpendicular to wall openings. Particularly when such elements are light-colored and located close to such openings, they can both reflect daylight more deeply into the space and reduce contrast levels close to the opening.

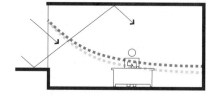

REFLECTIVE SILL

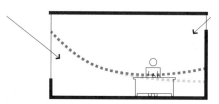

SECONDARY DAYLIGHT SOURCE

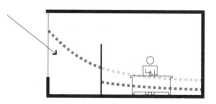

DAYLIGHT OBSTRUCTIONS

SIZING SIDELIGHTING

Use the charts on the opposite page to estimate the required size of wall openings for natural daylighting. Both charts assume that window bottoms are no higher than 30 in. (760 mm) above the floor, window glazing is clear, and walls and ceilings are white or light-colored. If these conditions are not met, daylighting effectiveness may be reduced.

For example, reading the top chart, a window extending 9 ft (2.7 m) above the floor will provide full daylighting for normal office tasks up to a horizontal distance of approximately 16 ft (4.9 m) from the window. Daylighting supplemented with electric lighting can be provided up to 29 ft (8.8 m) away.

For example, reading the bottom chart, a 6000 sq ft (560 m^2) business office area is to be illuminated with daylight from adjacent windows. Using the chart on page 236, we select Category E, visual tasks of medium contrast and size, as the appropriate lighting level. Reading the chart to the left, we determine that 6000 sq ft (560 m^2) of floor area requires between 1000 and 2000 sq ft (93 and 186 m^2) of window area for full daylighting.

SIDELIGHTING

WINDOW HEIGHT

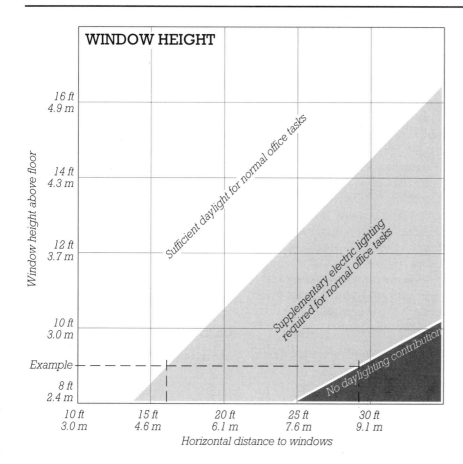

Window height above floor

16 ft / 4.9 m
14 ft / 4.3 m
12 ft / 3.7 m
10 ft / 3.0 m
Example
8 ft / 2.4 m

Sufficient daylight for normal office tasks

Supplementary electric lighting required for normal office tasks

No daylighting contribution

10 ft / 3.0 m   15 ft / 4.6 m   20 ft / 6.1 m   25 ft / 7.6 m   30 ft / 9.1 m

Horizontal distance to windows

WINDOW AREA

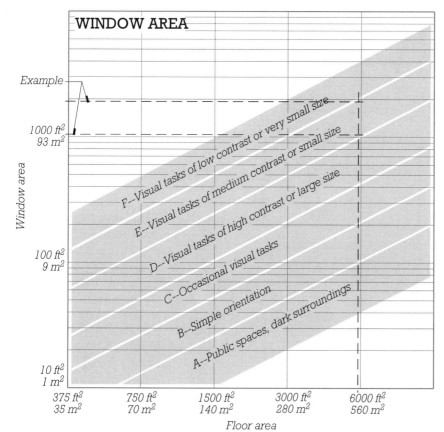

Window area

Example

1000 ft² / 93 m²

100 ft² / 9 m²

10 ft² / 1 m²

F--Visual tasks of low contrast or very small size
E--Visual tasks of medium contrast or small size
D--Visual tasks of high contrast or large size
C--Occasional visual tasks
B--Simple orientation
A--Public spaces, dark surroundings

375 ft² / 35 m²   750 ft² / 70 m²   1500 ft² / 140 m²   3000 ft² / 280 m²   6000 ft² / 560 m²

Floor area

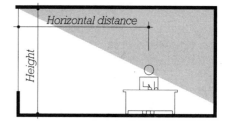

Horizontal distance

Height

Use the top chart to determine the minimum wall opening height for adequate horizontal daylight penetration for normal office tasks.

■ To ensure even light distribution throughout a space, window openings should be at least half as wide as the length of the wall in which they are located. For more detailed help in estimating required window area, see the chart below.

■ Use the bottom chart to determine the total wall opening area necessary for full daylighting of various tasks occupying a given floor area. To determine the most appropriate illumination category for the space under consideration, see page 236. For floor areas larger than those tabulated on the chart, read the chart using a smaller area and then multiply the result proportionally.

■ For buildings in predominantly clear sky areas, read low in the ranges indicated on the chart. For buildings in heavily covered sky areas, read high in the indicated ranges. See page 227 to determine sky cover conditions for your project's location.

CONFIGURING AND SIZING DAYLIGHTING SYSTEMS

239

TOPLIGHTING

Toplighting is most effectively employed in large single-story structures and in the topmost floors of multistory buildings.

Toplighting can be provided either by *skylights,* with horizontal or low-sloped glazing, or *roof monitors,* with vertical or steeply sloped glazing. Because of variation in the brightness of the sky from horizon to directly overhead, illumination levels from skylights are roughly three times greater than those associated with windows of the same opening area. Illumination is highest directly below a skylight opening and diminishes with increasing horizontal distance. With roof monitors, which admit daylight from the side, highest illumination levels tend to be offset to the side opposite the monitor glazing. The intensity of illumination from roof monitors varies with their orientation. In the Northern Hemisphere, south-facing monitors provide illumination levels approximately equal to skylights of the same glazing area. Monitors facing other directions provide approximately one-half the illumination of a skylight of the same area.

Spaced toplighting with multiple sources can minimize extremes in illumination levels. Sources of toplighting should be spaced no more than one to two times the height of the openings above the floor in order to provide acceptably uniform levels of illumination within the space.

In predominantly overcast areas, toplighting with clear glazing and no other means of sunlight control may be acceptable. In most areas, toplighting should be oriented away from the sun, or control devices should be used to prevent sunlight from passing unimpeded to the task area. *Interior reflectors,* exterior louvers, translucent light-diffusing materials, and deep openings with reflective sides can all be effective in this regard. When

these devices are placed on the interior, they may also be helpful in distributing daylight farther from the opening and creating more even illumination within the space. Devices located exterior to the opening can exclude solar heat from the interior and may be helpful in areas where high heat gain is particularly a concern.

Combined sidelighting and toplighting can be used to distribute daylighting deeper into the interior than is possible with sidelighting alone. To avoid excessive variation in illumination levels, spacing of daylight sources should not exceed the recommendations in the adjacent diagram.

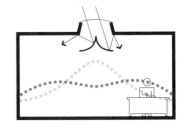

INTERIOR REFLECTORS

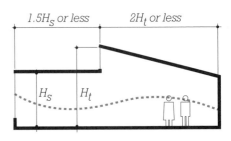

COMBINED SIDELIGHTING AND TOPLIGHTING

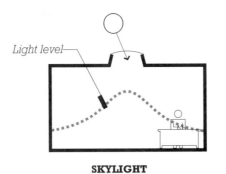

SKYLIGHT

Modified light level

ROOF MONITOR

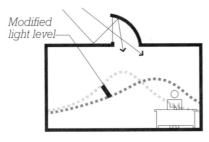

1H - 2H

H

SPACED TOPLIGHTING

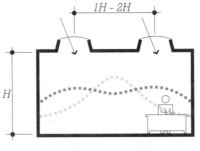

SIZING TOPLIGHTING

Use the charts on the facing page to estimate the required area of roof openings for natural daylighting.

For example, reading the top chart, with a floor-to-ceiling height of 15 ft (4.5 m), small skylights should be spaced horizontally no more than 15 ft (4.5 m) center-to-center, roof monitors should be spaced no more than 22 ft (7 m), and large skylights no more than 30 ft (9 m).

For example, reading the bottom chart, a 1000-sq-ft (93-m2) hotel lobby area is to be illuminated with north-facing roof monitors. Using the chart on page 236, we select Category C, simple orientation, as the appropriate lighting level. Reading the chart to the left, we determine that 1000 sq ft (93 m2) of floor area requires between 10 and 20 sq ft (0.9 and 1.9 m2) of skylight area for full daylighting. Doubling the result for a north-facing monitor, our final answer is 20 to 40 sq ft (1.9 to 3.7 m2) of glass area.

240

TOPLIGHTING

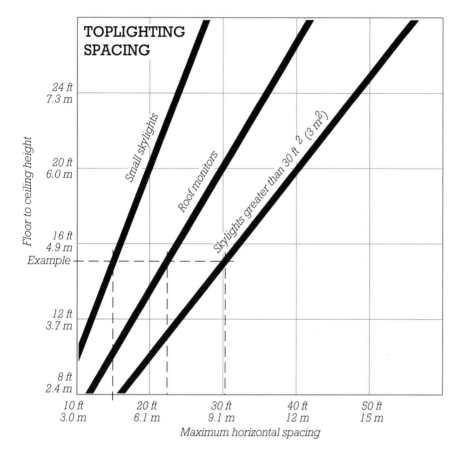

TOPLIGHTING SPACING

Floor to ceiling height

- 24 ft / 7.3 m
- 20 ft / 6.0 m
- 16 ft / 4.9 m
- Example
- 12 ft / 3.7 m
- 8 ft / 2.4 m

Small skylights
Roof monitors
Skylights greater than 30 ft² (3 m²)

Maximum horizontal spacing

- 10 ft / 3.0 m
- 20 ft / 6.1 m
- 30 ft / 9.1 m
- 40 ft / 12 m
- 50 ft / 15 m

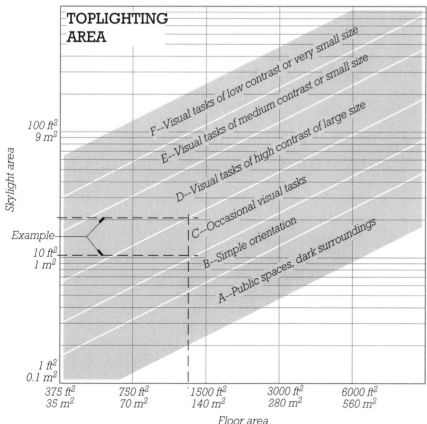

TOPLIGHTING AREA

Skylight area

- 100 ft² / 9 m²
- Example
- 10 ft² / 1 m²
- 1 ft² / 0.1 m²

F--Visual tasks of low contrast or very small size
E--Visual tasks of medium contrast or small size
D--Visual tasks of high contrast of large size
C--Occasional visual tasks
B--Simple orientation
A--Public spaces, dark surroundings

Floor area

- 375 ft² / 35 m²
- 750 ft² / 70 m²
- 1500 ft² / 140 m²
- 3000 ft² / 280 m²
- 6000 ft² / 560 m²

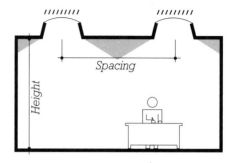

Spacing

Height

Use the top chart to determine maximum horizontal spacing for skylights and roof monitors so as to maintain acceptably even lighting levels throughout a space.

Use the bottom chart to determine the skylight or roof monitor opening area necessary for daylighting various tasks over a given floor area. To determine the most appropriate illumination category for the space under consideration, see the table on page 236. For floor areas larger than those tabulated on the chart, read the chart using a smaller area and then multiply the result proportionally.

■ For skylights and south-facing roof monitors, read directly from the chart. For roof monitors facing other than south, use twice the indicated area.

■ For buildings in predominantly clear sky areas, read low in the ranges indicated on the chart. For buildings in heavily covered sky areas, read high in the indicated ranges. See page 227 to determine sky cover conditions for the project's location.

■■■■■
DESIGNING
FOR
EGRESS

> *This section will assist you in laying out doors, corridors, stairways, and exit discharges for a preliminary building design in accordance with the egress requirements of the model building codes.*

COMPONENTS OF THE EGRESS SYSTEM

The function of a building egress system is to conduct the occupants of the building to a safe place in case of a fire or other emergency. In most instances that safe place is a public way or other large open space at ground level. For the occupants of the upper floors of a tall building, or for people who are incapacitated or physically restrained, the safe place may be a fire-protected area of refuge within the building itself.

Although the model building codes differ in their approaches to sizing the components of an egress system, their requirements for the configuration of egress systems are similar and are summarized together in this section.

A building egress system has three components:

1. *The exit access* conducts occupants to an exit. The most common type of exit access is an exit access corridor, but it may also be an aisle, a path across a room, or a short stair or ramp.

2. *The exit* is an enclosed, protected way of travel leading from the exit access to the exit discharge. From a ground floor room or exit access corridor, it may be simply a door opening to the outdoors, or an enclosed, protected exit passageway leading to such a door. From a room or an exit access corridor on a story above or below grade, it is usually an enclosed exit stairway, or sometimes an enclosed exit ramp.

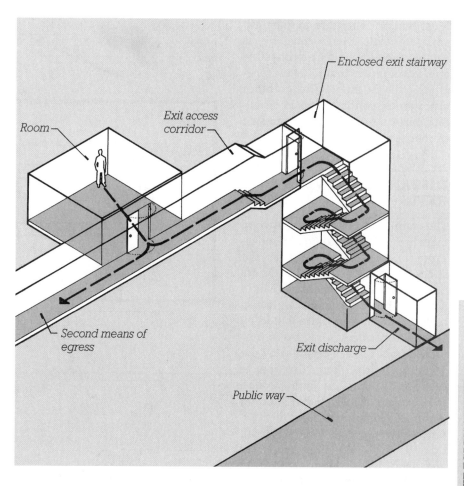

Room — Exit access corridor — Enclosed exit stairway

Second means of egress

Exit discharge

Public way

3. *The exit discharge* is a means of moving from an exit to a public way. It may be as simple as a door opening from an enclosed exit stairway to the street, but it can also be a protected exit corridor to an exterior door, or a path across a ground floor vestibule or lobby.

These three components of an egress system are discussed in greater detail on the pages that fol-

low. Also included are simplified standards for the preliminary design of these components, condensed from the model building codes treated in this book.

The standards summarized here apply to new buildings. For existing buildings, certain of the standards are more permissive; consult the appropriate building code for details.

Most buildings require at least two separate exits. These must be as remote from each other as possible and arranged to minimize the possibility that a single fire or other emergency condition could simultaneously render both exits unsafe or inaccessible.

DISTANCE BETWEEN EXITS

The minimum distance between exits is one-half the diagonal measurement of the building or the space served by the exits. On an open floor, this is measured as a straight-line distance between exits. Where the exits are joined by an exit access corridor that is protected from fire as specified by the building code, this distance is measured along the path through the corridor. (The National Building Code of Canada permits the distance between exits to be not more than 9 m (30 ft) when exits are accessed by a corridor serving more than one suite or space.)

With only minor exceptions, an exit access path may not pass through kitchens, rest rooms, storerooms, workrooms, bedrooms, hazardous areas, or rooms subject to being locked.

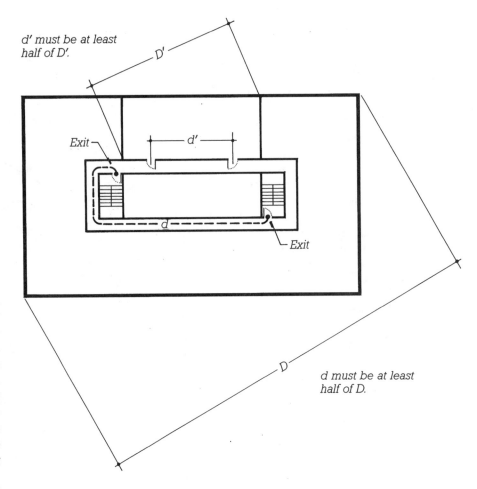

d′ must be at least half of D′.

d must be at least half of D.

THE EXIT ACCESS

EXTERIOR CORRIDORS

Exit access corridors may be open balconies on the exterior of a building. Such access ways should be designed to prevent the accumulation of standing water, and in cold climates, should be protected from the accumulation of snow by overhangs or roofs above.

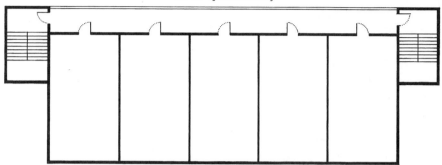

Exit access corridor on an open balcony

DEAD-END CORRIDORS

Dead-end pockets in exit access corridors are undesirable, but they are tolerated for most building occupancies within the length restrictions listed for each model code on pages 266–267 and 274–275.

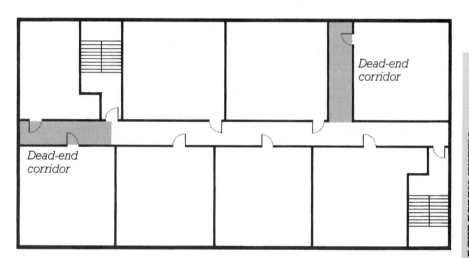

Dead-end corridor

Dead-end corridor

MAXIMUM TRAVEL DISTANCE

The maximum permitted travel distance to the nearest exit is specified by code and Occupancy on pages 266 and 274. Travel distance is always measured along the actual path an occupant must take to reach the exit. The International Building Code measures travel distance from the most remote point on a floor to the nearest exit. The National Building Code of Canada also measures travel distance this way, except that travel distance from rooms or suites separated from the rest of the floor and opening onto a corridor or exterior passageway may be measured from the door of the room. In addition, some model codes not addressed in this book measure travel distance starting at the doorway where a room opens into a corridor, so when working with different codes, be sure to apply the correct definition to your project design.

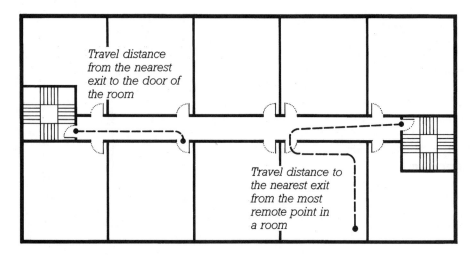

Travel distance from the nearest exit to the door of the room

Travel distance to the nearest exit from the most remote point in a room

The International Building Code also restricts the maximum length of the *common path of egress travel.* The common path of egress travel is the length of travel starting from anywhere in a building and continuing to a point at which two independent means of egress become available to the occupant. Thus, for example, in a room with just one doorway to a corridor, the corridor providing egress in two directions, the length of common path of egress travel would be the travel distance within the room to the doorway. Common path of egress travel limitations for the International Building Code are summarized on page 266.

THE EXIT ACCESS

DOORS

The International Building Code requires all doors serving an occupant load of more than 50 to swing in the direction of egress travel. The National Building Code of Canada requires all doors serving exits, and all exit access door serving an occupant load greater than 60, to swing in the direction of egress travel. Doors within dwelling units and exit doors from individual dwelings are not required to swing in the direction of egress travel. All doors serving exit access and exits in high-hazard occupancies should swing in the direction of egress travel regardless of occupant load.

Ideally, doors should be arranged so that their swing does not obstruct the required width of an aisle, corridor, stair landing, or stair. Building codes typically permit some obstruction, however: Up to one-half of the required width can be obstructed during the swing of the door, and when the door is fully open, it may project as much as 7 in. (178 mm) into the required width.

Even when locked, doors along an exit path must be easily openable in the direction of egress travel.

Exit access corridors must be enclosed in fire-resistant walls and

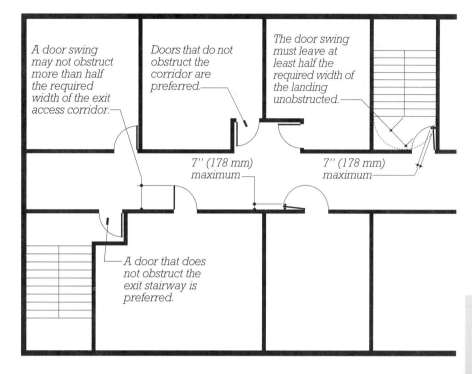

A door swing may not obstruct more than half the required width of the exit access corridor.

Doors that do not obstruct the corridor are preferred.

The door swing must leave at least half the required width of the landing unobstructed.

7" (178 mm) maximum

7" (178 mm) maximum

A door that does not obstruct the exit stairway is preferred.

accessed via fire-resistant doors. One-hour walls with 20-minute doors are required, except in some very small buildings and in certain buildings with automatic sprinkler systems.

The widths of exit access doors, aisles, and corridors must be determined according to the building occupancy and the number of occupants they serve. The tables on pages 270–271, 277 give

the quantities needed to make these determinations.

The model building codes also contain detailed provisions relating to illumination and emergency illumination of exit access facilities, marking of exit paths, combustibility of finish materials in exit access corridors, alarm systems, door hardware, and other safety concerns. Consult the appropriate building code for details.

THE EXIT

DIRECT EXIT

The simplest exit is a door opening directly from an interior room to a public way, as it might from an exhibition hall, theater, gymnasium, or classroom.

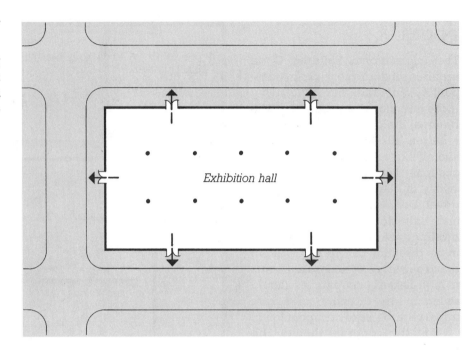

EXIT STAIRWAYS

The International Building Code requires stairway enclosures serving four stories or more to be built of 2-hour construction, with 1½-hour self-closing doors. Enclosures serving fewer than four stories may be of 1-hour construction with 1-hour self-closing doors.

The National Building Code of Canada requires the construction of an exit enclosure to match the construction of the floor above that on which the enclosure is located (or below, if there is no floor above), but to be not more than a 2-hour and not less than a ¾-hour enclosure. Doors must be self-closing, and in 2-hour enclosures must be 1½-hour rated; in 1½-hour enclosures, 1-hour rated; and in 1-hour or ¾-hour enclosures, ¾-hour rated.

The International Building Code requires doors in exit enclosures serving an occupant load of more than 50 to swing in the direction of egress travel. The National Building Code of Canada requires all doors in exit enclo-

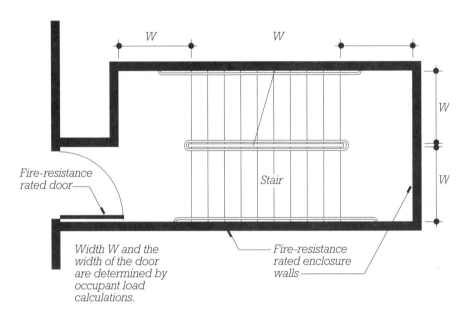

Width W and the width of the door are determined by occupant load calculations.

sures to swing in the direction of egress travel.

Stairway and landing widths are determined in accordance with the occupant load they serve. Dimensions and typical designs for stairways and stair enclosures are detailed on pages 279–293.

In general, escalators and elevators may not serve as required exits.

However, both the International Building Code and the National Building Code of Canada permit elevators in a smokeproof shaft to serve as a means of egress for disabled persons. For more information, see Accessible Means of Egress on page 254.

THE EXIT

SMOKEPROOF ENCLOSURES

The model building codes generally require exit stair enclosures in tall buildings to be designed as smokeproof enclosures to provide a higher degree of protection against the movement of smoke into the stairway during a fire emergency. The International Building Code requires smokeproof stair enclosures in buildings with occupied floors greater than 75 ft (23 m) above the lowest level of fire department vehicle access, excepting airport traffic control towers, open parking garages, Occupancy A-5 open-air arenas, as well as certain limited industrial and high-hazard occupancy conditions. Smokeproof stair enclosures are also required in the International Building Code in most buildings with underground occupancies more than 30 ft (9 m) below the lowest level of exit discharge. The National Building Code of Canada has similar requirements for most stairways in the following building types:

• Occupancy A Assembly, D Business or Personal Services, E Mercantile, or F Industrial buildings with occupied floors more than 36 m (188 ft) above grade

• Occupancy A Assembly, D Business or Personal Services, E Mercantile, or F Industrial buildings with occupied floors more than 18 m (59 ft) above grade in which the cumulative occupant load, on or above any story above the first-floor level divided by 1.8 times the width in meters of all exits at that level, exceeds 300.

• Occupancy B Care or Detention or C Residential buildings with occupied floors more than 18 m (59 ft) above grade

• Occupancy B-2 (Care or Detention, Unrestrained) buildings with occupied floors four or more stories above grade

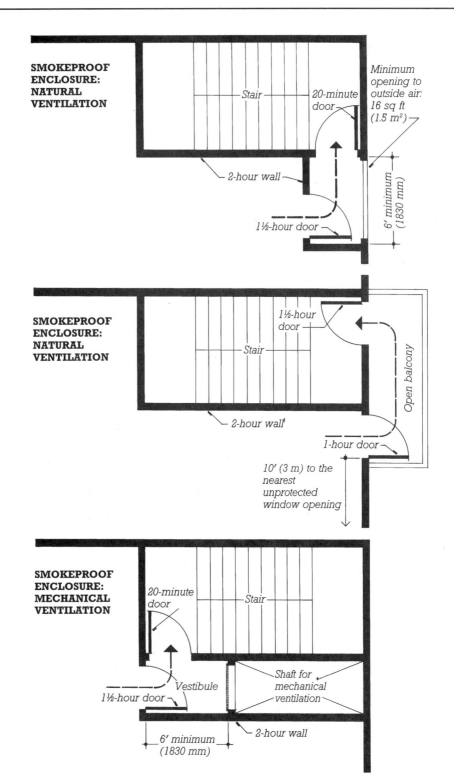

Specific design requirements for smokeproof enclosures are detailed, and vary with the particular code and building circumstances. The diagrams above summarize the most common requirements. See the applicable code for more information.

There are two ways to make a smokeproof enclosure, as illustrated above: natural ventilation and mechanical ventilation. In fully sprinklered buildings, a smoke-proof enclosure may also be created by means of mechanical pressurization without the need for the vestibule that is shown in the bottom drawing on this page. A mechanical ventilating system must be backed up with a standby power supply so that it will continue operating if the main source of power is interrupted during a fire.

A stairway in a smokeproof enclosure must discharge directly into a public way, an outdoor space having direct access to a public way, or an enclosed exit passageway with no other openings—it may not discharge through a vestibule or lobby at the exit discharge level.

OUTSIDE STAIRWAYS AND FIRE ESCAPES

Outside stairways may be used as exits. An outside stairway must be constructed with solid treads (as distinct from the open metal gratings used for treads of outside fire escapes). It must be built to the same fire-resistive requirements as an interior stair, including separation from the interior of the building by walls and openings with fire-resistance ratings as specified for interior stairs. Outside stairways must be protected against the accumulation of standing water, and must be roofed in snowy climates to prevent accumulation of snow.

A traditional metal fire escape is not permitted as an exit except as a second exit on existing buildings where it is impractical to construct a stair to current standards. Escape slides, rope ladders, escalators, and elevators cannot be counted as required exits. Fixed ladders are permitted as required exits only in certain situations in mechanical rooms and industrial occupancies where a very limited number of able-bodied workers are served by the ladder, and then the ladder may

254

serve only as a second means of egress from the space.

ACCESSIBLE MEANS OF EGRESS

In the United States, the Americans with Disabilities Act (ADA) entitles disabled people to full access to nearly all buildings: government buildings, schools, houses of worship, retail establishments, places of business, transportation facilities, health care facilities, bars, restaurants, hotels, dwelling units, places of entertainment and culture, recreational facilities, and places of work. Each building must provide continuous, unobstructed routes by which physically disabled persons can park their vehicles or leave public transportation, move to the building, enter, reach virtually any point in the building, and have access to such interior amenities as workplaces, retail counters, ticket windows, drinking fountains, toilet and washroom fixtures, and public telephones. Accessibility requirements in the United States are further defined by various additional federal acts, the building codes, and state and local ordinances. The following summarizes the ADA and International Building Code requirements for accessible egress but does not address all accessibility requirements, building types, or circumstances. Consult your code and other regulations applicable to your project for more information.

Means of egress from a building for disabled persons are required in the same number as normal means of egress. For most buildings, this means that disabled people must be furnished at least two continuous and unobstructed routes from any point in the building to a public way. Depending on particular circumstances, these routes may consist of (level) accessible means of egress, accessible ramps, horizontal exits,

or appropriately designed stairways or elevators. In buildings with accessible floors four or more stories above or below a level of exit discharge, at least one accessible means of egress must consist of either an elevator with a secure power supply in a smokeproof shaft or, in a fully sprinklered building, a horizontal exit. (For more information about horizontal exits, see page 256.)

Most buildings with accessible floors also rely on enclosed stairways as part of the required egress for disabled occupants. Such stairways must meet the following requirements:

The stairway must be at least 48 in. (1219 mm) in clear dimension between handrails, meaning that the overall width of the stair must be approximately 56 in. (1400 mm), to offer sufficient space for two rescuers to carry a wheelchair and its occupant. Unless the building is equipped throughout with an approved, supervised sprinkler system, an area of refuge, also called an area of rescue assistance, must be provided adjacent to the stairway on each accessible level of the building.

An area of refuge is a place where people who are unable to use stairs may safely await assistance during an emergency evacuation. The area of refuge must have direct access to the stairway. It must be clearly identified with visual and tactile signage, within an enclosure, protected from smoke and fire, provided with instructions for use, and provided with two-way electronic communications with the primary entry point of the building. A wheelchair space 30 in. by 48 in. (760 mm by 1220 mm) must be provided for each 200 occupants or portion thereof on each floor, with a minimum provision of two such spaces for each area of refuge.

There are many ways to create an area of refuge. It may be on a

THE EXIT

landing of a stairway in a smoke-proof enclosure. It may be on an outdoor balcony leading to a stairway in a smokeproof enclosure. It may be adjacent to a stairway in a corridor enclosed with one-hour fire resistive walls, or in a vestibule with the same degree of fire protection. It may be in an elevator lobby if the lobby and the adjacent shafts are pressurized as smokeproof enclosures. And an area of refuge may be created by a horizontal exit, as detailed on the following page. In each of these cases, the wheelchair spaces may not encroach on the required width of the egress path.

The National Building Code of Canada generally requires all buildings, except the following, to meet barrier-free design requirements:

- Houses
- Industrial, High-Hazard occupancy buildings
- Buildings not intended for daily or full-time occupancy (e.g., pump houses, telephone exchanges, etc.)

Barrier-free access may be provided by level, unobstructed pathways or by ramps, elevators, and other devices. Every accessible floor area above or below the ground-level floor that is not fully sprinklered must be served by an elevator meeting requirements for firefighter use. Elevator entrances must be protected from fire at each floor by vestibules or corridors with fire-rated separations from surrounding floor areas. If the building is four or more stories in height, the elevator must be provided with smoke protection as well. Alternatively, such floors may be divided into at least two separate zones by fire separation walls, providing protected areas for disabled occupants while they await rescue assistance. In residential occupancies, exterior balconies are also permitted to serve as such protected areas.

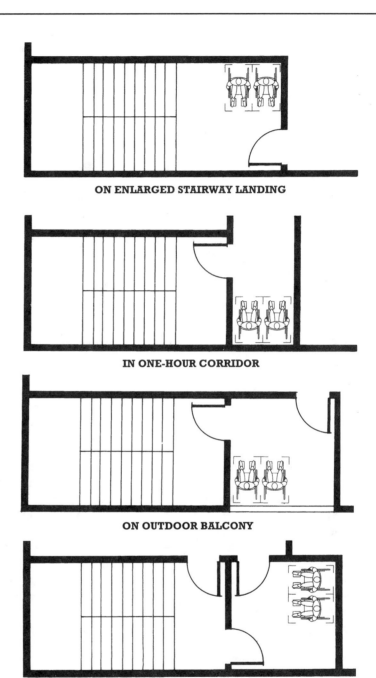

ON ENLARGED STAIRWAY LANDING

IN ONE-HOUR CORRIDOR

ON OUTDOOR BALCONY

IN STAIRWAY VESTIBULE

THE EXIT

HORIZONTAL EXITS

A horizontal exit is a way of passage through a fire-resistant wall to an area of refuge on the same level in the same building or in an adjacent building. A horizontal exit may be designed to function for travel in one direction only, as in the case of a building that has one exit stairway and a horizontal exit to an adjoining building that has two or more exit stairways. In this case the corridors and lobbies of the adjoining building serve as the area of refuge. A horizontal exit may also be designed to function for travel in both directions, as shown on the drawing to the right. Here the corridor on the left side of the building serves as an area of refuge for the occupants of the right side of the building, and vice versa.

The fire-resistant wall must be of 2-hour construction. Wall penetrations for pipes or conduits must be tightly sealed. The exit doors must be rated at 1½ hours, must fit tightly, and must be self-closing.

The doors should swing in the direction of exit. If the area on each side of the wall serves reciprocally as an area of refuge for the area on the other side, the doors should be furnished in oppositely swinging pairs so that at least one door will swing in the direction of exit travel for a person approaching from either side. In sizing the doors for occupant load, only doors swinging in the direction of egress may be counted.

Horizontal exits are advantageous in tall buildings, because they allow a person to escape the danger of a fire much more quickly than a stairway to the ground. They

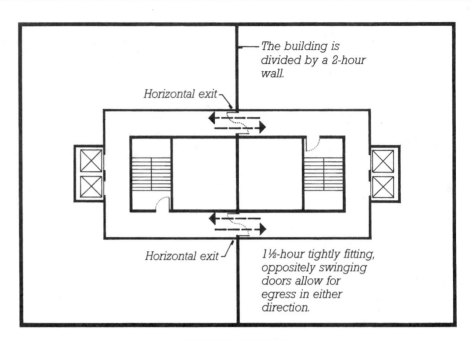

The building is divided by a 2-hour wall.

Horizontal exit

Horizontal exit

1½-hour tightly fitting, oppositely swinging doors allow for egress in either direction.

HORIZONTAL EXITS

are also useful in hospitals, because they allow patients to be moved to safety while still in their beds. In general, horizontal exits may provide up to half of the required exit capacity of a story or a building. The area of refuge on either side of a horizontal exit must be large enough to accommodate all the occupants from both sides of the exit. The area of refuge must also meet all exit requirements and have sufficient exit capacity for its original occupants, but it need not be designed with exit capacity for added occupants.

In the International Building Code, the area of refuge occupant capacity is calculated for most occupancies at the rate of 3 sq ft (0.28 m²) per person. In Institutional, Restrained I-3 occupancies, 6 sq ft (0.56 m²) per person is required. In Institutional, Medical I-2 occupancies, 15 sq ft (1.4 m²) per ambulatory occupant is required, and 30 sq ft (2.8 m²) per nonambulatory occupant. The International Building Code allows horizontal exits in Institutional, Medical Care Group I-2 occupancies to provide up to two-thirds of the required exit capacity of a floor or a building, and in Institutional, Restrained Group I-3 occupancies to provide up to 100% of the required exit capacity. In addition, at least one of the exits from the area of refuge must lead directly to the exterior or into an exit enclosure.

The National Building Code of Canada requires area of refuge occupant capacity to be calculated at the rate of 0.5 m² (5.4 sq ft) per person, with the exception of 1.5 m² (16 sq ft) per wheelchair occupant and 2.5 m² (27 sq ft) per bedridden occupant.

EXIT PASSAGEWAYS

An exit passageway is a horizontal means of exit travel that is protected from fire in the same manner as an enclosed interior exit stair. An exit passageway has several uses: It may be used to preserve the continuity of enclosure for an exit stair whose location shifts laterally as it descends through the building. It may be used to eliminate excessive travel distance to an exit. And it may be used as part of an exit discharge, to connect an enclosed stair to an exterior door.

The widths of passages, doors, landings, and stairs used as exits must be determined in accordance with values given by the various codes, as shown on pages 270–271 and 277. For detailed design requirements concerning illumination, emergency illumination, marking, finish materials, and hardware of exits, consult the appropriate building code.

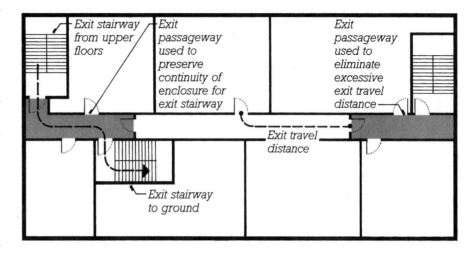

THE EXIT DISCHARGE

An exit discharge at its simplest is a door opening from an exit stairway, a corridor, or the interior space of a building, directly onto a public way or an outdoor space leading to a public way. (An exit may not discharge into a courtyard from which there is no access to a public way.)

Where an exit stairway is not located at the outside wall of a building, an exit passageway may lead from the base of the stair to the discharge door. This passageway may not have any openings other than required exit doorways.

Both the International Building Code and the National Building Code of Canada, under some circumstances, permit exits to discharge through a lobby area. The International Building Code requires that the way to the exterior through the lobby be readily visible and identifiable from the point of discharge from the exit, that the entire story at the lobby level be sprinklered, and that the fire-resistance rating of the floor construction at the lobby level be at least equal to the required rating of an exit enclosure. The National Building Code of Canada limits the path of travel through the lobby to 15 m (49 ft), forbids direct access from residential or industrial occupancies to the lobby, and requires the lobby and all areas not separated from it by a fire separation to be sprinklered.

The International Building Code also permits exits to discharge through an enclosed vestibule, whose maximum dimensions are shown to the right. The vestibule must have self-closing doors and may serve only as a means of egress. The vestibule must be separated from the other spaces of the building by at least the equivalent of wired glass in steel frames (a ¾-hour partition), and the fire-resistance rating of the vestibule floor construction must

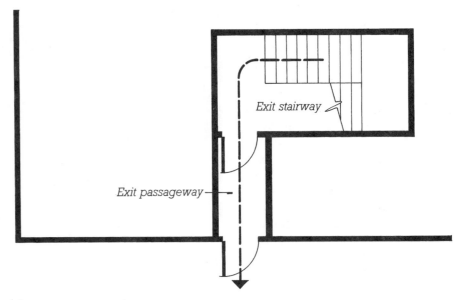

EXIT DISCHARGE THROUGH AN EXIT PASSAGEWAY

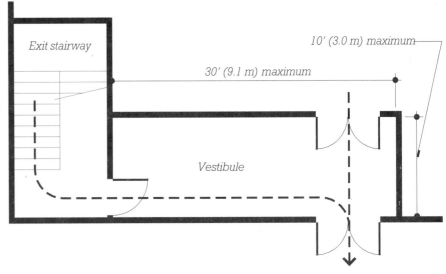

EXIT DISCHARGE THROUGH A VESTIBULE

be at least equal to the required rating of the exit enclosure.

Revolving doors are also permitted as exit discharge components, provided they are constructed so as to allow free passage in a panic situation by collapsing under pressure into a book-fold position. The International Building Code limits revolving doors to a capacity of 50 persons per door and, in total, to no more than half the required exit capacity of a building. There must be a swinging

door in the same wall and within 10 ft (3 m) of the revolving door, and revolving doors may not be located within 10 ft (3 m) of the foot or top of a stair or escalator. The National Building code of Canada limits the exit capacity of each revolving door to 45 persons and permits revolving doors to serve as egress for ground-floor occupants only. Swinging doors must be located adjacent to revolving doors, and revolving doors must not be located at the foot of a stairway.

EGRESS FROM AUDITORIUMS, CONCERT HALLS, AND THEATERS

Assembly rooms, with their intense concentration of occupants, require special egress provisions. In the past, the various building codes have recognized two distinct types of seating arrangements: *conventional seating* and *continental seating.* In conventional seating, the length of seating rows is more limited, and a network of broad aisles is laid out to conduct the audience to a relatively small number of exits. In continental seating, longer rows of seating are permitted. Rows must be spaced farther apart, and more exit doors must be provided. See the illustrations on this page diagramming these two approaches to assembly seating. The most recent editions of the International Building Code and the National Building Code of Canada still permit both approaches to assembly seating but now present a single, consolidated set of egress requirements applicable to both approaches. Specific requirements for the two model codes are tabulated on the following pages.

INTERNATIONAL BUILDING CODE ASSEMBLY EGRESS REQUIREMENTS

For Assembly occupancies serving more than 300 occupants, the International Building Code requires that the main exit of the

building provide capacity for at least half the total building occupant load. Each individual level having an occupant load greater than 300 must provide access both to the main exit, and to alternative exits

with an aggregate capacity equal to at least one-half the required exit capacity for that level. For buildings without a main exit, or with multiple main exits, exits should be distributed around the building.

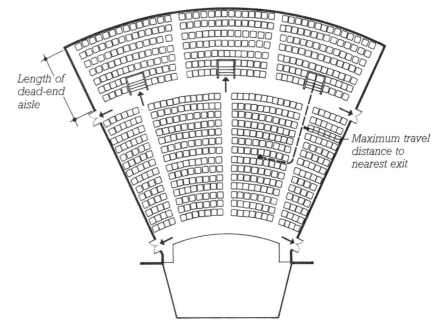

CONVENTIONAL ASSEMBLY SEATING

Length of dead-end aisle

Maximum travel distance to nearest exit

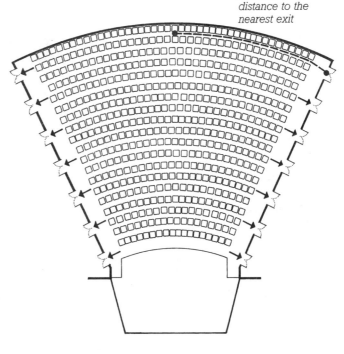

Back-to-back row spacing

Clear row spacing with self-rising seat

Clear row spacing

Maximum travel distance to the nearest exit

CONTINENTAL ASSEMBLY SEATING

	Seating		Aisles[1]			
	Maximum Row Length	**Row Spacing**	**Minimum Aisle Width**	**Longest Dead-End Aisle**	**Cross-Aisle Width**	**Maximum Slope of Aisle**
International Building Code[2]	For a row with egress at both ends: 100 seats; for a row with egress at one end only: 30' (9 m) to an aisle that offers a choice of two paths of egress (one choice may be across an additional row of not more than 24 seats).	For a row with egress at both ends: 12" (305 mm) clear plus 0.3" (7.6 mm) for every seat above 14. For a row with egress at one end only: 12" (305 mm) plus 0.6" (15.2 mm) for every seat above 7. Maximum required clear spacing is 22" (559 mm).	36" (914 mm) for aisles serving seating on one side or not more than 50 seats on two sides. 42" (1067 mm) for aisles serving more than 50 seats on two sides.	20' (6 m) unless seats served by dead-end aisle are within no more than 24 seats of another aisle with row spacing 12" (305 mm) plus 0.6" (15.2 mm) for every seat above 7.	Same as for aisles, sized for the combined capacity of the converging aisles.	1:8
National Building Code of Canada: Conventional Seating	Not more than 7 seats with backs, or 20 seats without backs, between any seat and the nearest aisle.	400 mm (15.75") clear	1100 mm (43.3") for seating on both sides, 900 mm (35.4") for seating on one side, 750 mm (29.5") for any aisle serving not more than 60 seats. All of the above increase 25 mm (1") for each meter (39.4") of length from the farthest point to the cross aisle or exit.	6 m (19'8")	Equal to width of widest aisle served, plus 50% of remaining aisles served.	1:8
National Building Code of Canada: Continental Seating	100 seats, with exit doorways provided at each end of row, each doorway serving not more than 3 rows	Same as above	Same as above	Same as above	Same as above	Same as above

[1]Aisles providing egress in one direction only may vary in width; aisles serving egress in two directions must be uniform in width.

[2]With special smoke control provisions, the International Building Code permits reductions in egress widths in some circumstances, particularly in larger occupancies. Consult the code for details.

EGRESS REQUIREMENTS FOR ASSEMBLY SEATING

Stairs				Exits	
Stairs in Aisle	**Minimum Stair Width**	**Required Stair Width**	**Handrails**	**Maximum Travel to Exit: Unsprinklered**	**Maximum Travel to Exit: Sprinklered**
Tread depth 11" (279 mm) minimum. Riser height 8" (203 mm) maximum and 4" (102 mm) minimum. Risers up to 9" (229 mm) are permitted where necessitated by slope of adjacent seating.	36" (914 mm) for stairs serving seating on one side or not more than 50 seats on two sides. 48" (1219 mm) for stairs serving more than 50 seats on two sides. See also the next table column.	Add to the minimum stair width from the previous column: 0.3" (7.6 mm) per person for risers 7" (178 mm) or less, plus 0.005" (0.13 mm) per person for each additional 0.1" (2.5 mm) of riser height greater than 7".	Handrails are required at stairs and at aisles with a slope exceeding 1:15. Aisles or stairs subdivided by handrails must have a minimum width of 23" (574 mm) between the handrail and adjacent seating.	200' (61 m)	250' (76 m)
Tread depth 230 mm (9.1") minimum. Riser height 110 mm (4.3") minimum, 200 mm (7.9") maximum, with 6 mm (.25") maximum variation between adjacent risers if the tread depth is at least 430 mm (16.9").	See page 275.	See page 277.	No special requirements.	45 m (148')	45 m (148')
Same as above	Same as above	Same as above	Same as above	Same as above	Same as above

WHEELCHAIR SEATING CAPACITY

In Assembly spaces, accommodations for a minimum quantity of wheelchair seating must be provided according to the following tables.

Required	Total Capacity	Wheelchair Places
International Building Code	4–25	1
	26–50	2
	51–100	3
	101–300	5
	301–500	6
	Over 500	6, plus 1 additional for each 200 seats or portion thereof
National Building Code of Canada	2–100	2
	101–200	3
	201–300	4
	301–400	5
	401–500	6
	501–900	7
	901–1300	8
	1301–1700	9
	Over 1700	9, plus 1 additional for each 400 seats or portion thereof

SIZE AND ARRANGEMENT OF WHEELCHAIR SEATING PLACES

The International Building Code requires wheelchair spaces to be at least 33 in. (838 mm) wide, and if entered from the front or rear, at least 48 in. (1220 mm) deep, or if entered from the side, at least 60 in. (1525 mm) deep. At least one fixed seat for a companion must be provided beside each wheelchair space. Wheelchair seating must also be dispersed into a minimum number of *clusters,* according to the following table. Clusters should be located so as to provide a choice of admission prices and lines of sight comparable to those available to the general public, and should be separated from each other by at least five rows or ten seats. The number of clusters may be reduced by half where sight lines require more than one step between rows.

The National Building Code of Canada requires wheelchair spaces to be at least 900 mm (35.4 in.) wide, and if entered from the front or rear, at least 1220 mm (48 in.) deep, or if entered from the side, at least 1525 mm (60 in.) deep. Wheelchair spaces should be arranged so that at least two such spaces are located side by side; they should not infringe on any other egress path or width requirements, and they should be distributed so as to provide a choice of viewing location and a clear view of the event taking place.

	Total Capacity	Minimum Number of Wheelchair Space Clusters
International Building Code	Up to 300	1
	301–600	2
	601–900	3
	901–1500	4
	1501–2100	5
	2101–3000	6
	Over 3000	6, plus 1 additional for each 1000 seats or portion thereof

■■■■■
SIZING
THE
EGRESS
SYSTEM

This section presents simplified data for use in sizing egress components under the model building codes.

MISCELLANEOUS EGRESS REQUIREMENTS

Minimum Number of Exits

Normally, each floor of a building must have at least two exits, and not less than the minimum listed in the following table.

Occupant Load	Minimum Number of Exits
500 or fewer persons	2
501 to 1000 persons	3
More than 1000 persons	4

Buildings of limited height and occupancy may, under some circumstances, have only one exit:

- Single-story buildings of Occupancies A, B, E, F, M, and U having not more than 50 occupants and a maximum travel distance of 75 ft (23 m)

- Single-story buildings of Occupancies H-2 and H-3 having not more than 3 occupants and a maximum travel distance of 25 ft (8 m)

- Single-story buildings of Occupancies H-4, H-5, I, and R having not more than 10 occupants and a maximum travel distance of 75 ft (23 m)

- Single-story buildings of Occupancy S having not more than 30 occupants and a maximum travel distance of 75 ft (23 m)

- Buildings of Occupancies B, F, M, and S having not more than 2 stories and 30 occupants, and a maximum travel distance of 75 ft (23 m)

- Buildings of Occupancy R-2 having not more than 2 stories and 4 dwelling units per floor, and a maximum travel distance of 50 ft (15 m)

- Buildings of Occupancy R-3

Emergency Exterior Door or Window Egress

In Occupancies R and I-1, basements and each sleeping room below the fourth story must have an exterior door or window for emergency escape and rescue. Escape windows must have a sill height of not more than 44 in. (1118 mm), minimum clear opening dimensions of 24 in. (610 mm) high by 20 in. (508 mm) wide, and a minimum clear opening area of at least 5.7 sq ft (0.53 m^2). Emergency escape windows and doors are permitted to open onto interior atrium balconies, provided that a second exit access that does not pass through the atrium is also available. Emergency escape windows or doors are not required for:

- Occupancy R-3 bedrooms and basements in fully sprinklered buildings

- Occupancy R-3 bedrooms, where the door from the bedroom opens to a fire-rated corridor with access to two remote exits in opposite directions

- Basements with a ceiling height of less than 80 in (2030 mm)

- Buildings over 75 ft (23 m) tall conforming to the code requirements for high-rise buildings

Egress Width Calculations

Exit stair and exit discharge widths are based on the occupant load of the largest single floor served—occupant loads do not normally accumulate from one floor to the next. Where egress from floors above and below converge at an intermediate level, egress widths from the point of convergence are based on the sum of the converging occupant loads. Where mezzanines discharge through a floor below, egress components serving that floor are sized for the combined occupant load of the floor and the mezzanine.

High-Rise and Underground Buildings

Special requirements apply to buildings with occupied floors more than 75 ft (23 m) above grade or more than 30 ft (9 m) below grade. Most such buildings must be fully sprinklered, and exits must be designed as smokeproof enclosures. See page 253 for more information about the design of smokeproof enclosures. These requirements do not apply to:

- Open parking garages above grade and fully sprinklered garages below grade

- Airport traffic control towers, Occupancy A-5 outdoor sports arenas, and some unusually tall, low-hazard industrial occupancy buildings

- H-1, H-2, and H-3 high-hazard occupancies conforming to the special code requirements for these uses

- Underground fixed-guideway transit systems or below-grade stadiums

- Below-grade one- and two-family dwellings in fully sprinklered buildings

- Buildings in which only the lowest story is more than 30 ft (9 m) below grade, and that story is no more than 1500 sq ft (139 m^2) in area, with an occupant load of less than 10.

Buildings with occupied floors more than 30 ft (9 m) below grade must have smoke control and exhaust systems. Buildings with floors more than 60 ft (18 m) below grade must have each floor, up to the highest level of exit discharge, divided into at least two compartments with a 1-hour separation between. Where elevators are provided, each compartment must have direct access to an elevator; where one elevator serves multiple compartments, a lobby with a 1-hour separation from each compartment must be provided.

INTERNATIONAL BUILDING CODE

Accessibility for Disabled People

All buildings are required to be accessible, except Occupancy R-3 detached one- and two-family dwellings; Occupancy R-1 owner-occupied residential buildings containing not more than five rooms for rent or hire; Occupancy U utility buildings; equipment spaces, nonoccupiable service spaces, raised areas used primarily for security, life- or fire-safety; and certain single-occupancy structures accessed through tunnels or elevated walkways, such as toll booths.

Where a building is required to be accessible, at least one-half of its entrances must be accessible, at least one entrance to each separate tenant space must be accessible, and accessible routes must be provided connecting the public way and each portion of the building. If only one accessible route is provided within a building, it may not pass through kitchens, storage rooms, rest rooms, closets, or similar spaces, except that in dwelling units, a single accessible route may pass through a kitchen or storage room. In multilevel buildings, an accessible route must connect each level of the building, including mezzanines, except:

• Floors above and below accessible levels, not more than 3000 ft^2 (280 m^2) in area, unless such floors contain offices of health care providers, passenger transporation facilities and airports, or Group M Mercantile multiple tenant facilities

• Levels in Occupancy Groups A Assembly, I Institutional, R Residential, and S Storage, where the levels themselves are not required to be accessible

For more information regarding accessible means of egress, see page 254. For more information regarding wheelchair space requirements for Assembly seating areas, see page 262.

Toilet and bathing facilities in accessible buildings are required to be accessible. In Group A Assembly and Group M Mercantile occupancies, single-occupant unisex toilet and bathing rooms, intended for those with disabilities who may need assistance in the facility, must also be provided wherever a total of six or more male and female water closets is otherwise required. For more information regarding accessible toilet facilities, see pages 176, 178.

Where residential occupancies are required to be accessible, accessible sleeping accommodations or dwelling units must be provided according to the table below.

Most buildings constructed in the United States other than private residences may be subject to a variety of additional accessibility regulations such as the Americans with Disabilities Act, the Fair Housing Amendments Act, the Architectural Barriers Act, state access codes, local ordinances, and other regulations not covered in this book. Be sure to verify all requirements for your project.

The reference tables appearing on pages 265–271 are for preliminary design purposes only. They represent the authors' interpretation and simplification of certain major provisions of The International Building Code 2000. No official interpretation has been sought from or granted by International Code Council, Inc. For design development work and final preparation of building plans, you must consult the building code adopted by the building regulatory authorities in your project's location.

Occupancy	Minimum Number of Accessible Sleeping Accommodations or Dwelling Units
Occupancy R-2 multifamily residences containing 20 or more dwelling units	20%, but never less than 1
Occupancy I-1 supervised residential facilities	4%, but never less than 1
Occupancy I-2 medical facilities	50%, but never less than 1
Occupancy I-3 restrained residential facilities	5%, but never less than 1
Occupancy R-1 transient residential:	
With no more than 25 sleeping accommodations	1
With from 26 to 50 sleeping accommodations	2
With from 51 to 75 sleeping accommodations	3
With from 76 to 100 sleeping accommodations	4
With from 101 to 200 sleeping accommodations	Approximately 4%; see the code for details
With more than 200 sleeping accommodations	Approximately 3%; see the code for details

Occupancy (see index on pages 7–10 for specific uses)	Maximum Travel Distance from Most Remote Point to Nearest Exit Enclosure		Maximum Travel Distance to Two Independent Egress Paths	Largest Room That May Have Only One Door[1]
	Unsprinklered	Sprinklered		
A: Assembly (all types)	200 ft (61 m); for open-air seating, 400 ft (122 m) for combustible construction, or unlimited for noncombustible construction	250 ft (76 m)	75 ft (23 m)	50 occupants
B: Business	200 ft (61 m)	300 ft (91 m)	75 ft (23 m) unsprinklered, 100 ft (30 m) sprinklered, 100 ft (30 m) unsprinklered for tenant spaces with occupancy of 30 or less	50 occupants
E: Educational	200 ft (61 m)	250 ft (76 m)	75 ft (23 m)	50 occupants
F-1: Factory Industrial, Moderate-Hazard	200 ft (61 m)	250 ft (76 m); 400 ft (122 m) for single-story buildings equipped with automatic heat and smoke roof ventilation systems	75 ft (23 m) unsprinklered, or 100 ft (30 m) if sprinklered	50 occupants
F-2: Factory Industrial, Low-Hazard	300 ft (91 m)	400 ft (122 m)	75 ft (23 m) unsprinklered, or 100 ft (30 m) if sprinklered	50 occupants
H: Hazardous	Not Permitted	75 ft (23 m) - 200 ft (61 m), consult the code	25 ft (8 m) for Occupancies H-1, H-2, and H-3; 75 ft (23 m) for H-4, H-5	3 occupants for Occupancies H-1, H-2, H-3, and 10 occupants for H-4 and H-5
I-1: Institutional, Supervised Residential Facilities	200 ft (61 m)	250 ft (76 m)	75 ft (23 m)	10 occupants
I-2: Institutional, Medical Facilities	150 ft (46 m); travel distance is limited to 50 ft (15 m) within a room and 100 ft (30 m) within a suite.	200 ft (61 m)	75 ft (23 m)	Sleeping rooms or suites 1000 ft^2 (93 m^2) in area or non-sleeping rooms or suites 2500 ft^2 (232 m^2)
I-3: Institutional, Restrained Residential Facilities	150 ft (46 m)	200 ft (61 m)	100 ft (30 m)	10 occupants
I-4: Institutional, Child Care	150 ft (46 m)	200 ft (61 m)	75 ft (23 m)	10 occupants
M: Mercantile	200 ft (61 m)	250 ft (76 m)	75 ft (23 m)	50 occupants
M: Mercantile, Covered Mall	Not Permitted	200 ft from any point to an exit	75 ft (23 m)	50 occupants
R-1: Residential, Hotels and Transient	200 ft (61 m)	250 ft (76 m)	75 ft (23 m)	10 occupants
R-2: Residential, Mulifamily	200 ft (61 m)	250 ft (76 m)	75 ft (23 m)	10 occupants
R-3: Residential, One- and Two-Family	200 ft (61 m)	250 ft (76 m)	75 ft (23 m)	10 occupants
Detached one- and two-family dwellings and townhouses	not applicable	not applicable	not applicable	not applicable
R-4: Residential, Assisted Living	200 ft (61 m)	250 ft (76 m)	75 ft (23 m)	10 occupants
S-1: Storage, Moderate-Hazard	200 ft (61 m); 400 ft (122 m) for single-story buildings equipped with automatic heat and smoke roof ventilation systems.	250 ft (76 m)	75 ft (23 m) unsprinklered, 100 ft (30 m) sprinklered, 100 ft unsprinklered for tenant spaces with occupancy of 30 or less	30 occupants
S-2: Storage, Low-Hazard, Parking Garages	300 ft (91 m)	400 ft (122 m)	same as above	30 occupants
U: Utility, Private Garages	300 ft (91 m)	400 ft (122 m)	same as above	50 occupants

[1]Rooms with only one exit access door must not exceed the maximum travel distance to two independent egress path limitations shown in the previous column of this table.
[2]Dead-end corridors less than 2.5 times as long as their least width may be of unlimited length.

Maximum Length of Dead-End Corridor[2]	Minimum Clear Corridor Width[3]	Minimum Net Clear Egress Door Width[4]	Minimum Stair Width[5]	Additional Requirements
20 ft (6 m)	44 in. (1118 mm) for more than 50 occupants, 36 in. (914 mm) for 50 or fewer occupants	32 in. (813 mm)	44 in. (1118 mm) for more than 50 occupants and 36 in. (914 mm) for 50 or fewer occupants. See pages 260–261 for widths of steps within assembly aisles.	For assembly seating row spacing, aisles, and exits, see also pages 259–261.
20 ft (6 m), or 50 ft (15 m) if sprinklered	same as above	32 in. (813 mm)	44 in. (1118 mm) for more than 50 occupants and 36 in. (914 mm) for 50 or fewer occupants.	
20 ft (6 m)	Same, except 72 in. (1829 mm) for 100 or more occupants	32 in. (813 mm)	same as above	
20 ft (6 m), or 50 ft (15 m) if sprinklered	44 in. (1118 mm) for more than 50 occupants, 36 in. (914 mm) for 50 or fewer occupants	32 in. (813 mm)	same as above	
20 ft (6 m), or 50 ft (15 m) if sprinklered	same as above	32 in. (813 mm)	same as above	
4 ft (1.2 m)—20 ft (6 m); consult the code	same as above	32 in. (813 mm)	same as above	Consult the code for additional requirements.
20 ft (6 m)	same as above, 72 in. (1829 mm) where occupants are incapacitated	32 in. (813 mm)	same as above	Exterior door or window egress is required—see page 264.
20 ft (6 m)	same as I-1, 96 in. (2438 mm) where beds must be moved	32 in. (813 mm), 41.5 in. (1054 mm) where beds must be moved	same as above	Each floor must be subdivided by at least one smokeproof wall with horizontal exits.
20 ft (6 m), under some conditions 50 ft (15 m); consult the code	44 in. (1118 mm) for more than 50 occupants, 36 in. (914 mm) for 50 or fewer occupants	32 in. (813 mm), 28 in. (711 mm) for resident sleeping rooms	same as above	Each floor must be subdivided by at least one smokeproof wall with horizontal exits.
20 ft (6 m)	Same as above	32 in. (813 mm)	same as above	
20 ft (6 m)	Same as above	32 in. (813 mm)	same as above	
20 ft (6 m), no limit for mall spaces not longer than twice their width	20 ft (6 m) for the mall space, 66 in. (1676 mm) for corridors	32 in. (813 mm)	66 in. (1676 mm)	
20 ft (6 m)	44 in. (1118 mm) for more than 50 occupants, 36 in. (914 mm) for 50 or fewer occupants, 36 in. (914 mm) within dwelling units	32 in. (813 mm)	44 in. (1118 mm) for more than 50 occupants and 36 in. (914 mm) for 50 or fewer occupants.	Exterior door or window egress is required—see page 264.
20 ft (6 m)	same as above	32 in. (813 mm) for doors part of required egress	same as above	Exterior door or window egress is required--see page 264.
20 ft (6 m)	same as above	32 in. (813 mm) for doors part of required egress	same as above, 36 in. (914 mm) within a dwelling unit	Exterior door or window egress is required--see page 264.
not applicable	36 in. (914 mm)	Nominal 36 in. (914 mm) doors required at exits	36 in. (914 mm)	Exterior door or window egress is required--see page 264.
20 ft (6 m)	same as above	32 in. (813 mm)	36 in. (914 mm)	Exterior door or window egress is required--see page 264.
20 ft (6 m)	44 in. (1118 mm) for more than 50 occupants, 36 in. (914 mm) for 50 or fewer occupants	32 in. (813 mm)	44 in. (1118 mm) for more than 50 occupants and 36 in. (914 mm) for 50 or fewer occupants.	
20 ft (6 m)	same as above	32 in. (813 mm)	same as above, 36 in. (914 mm) for attendant-only areas in open parking garages	Open parking garage exit stairways may be open.
20 ft (6 m)	same as above	32 in. (813 mm)	same as above	

[3]Minimum corridor width for access to electrical, mechanical, or plumbing systems is 24 in. (610 mm).
[4]Maximum permitted nominal width for egress doors is 48 in. (1220 mm).
[5]For minimum stair widths for accessible egress stairways, see page 254.

EGRESS WIDTHS: INTERNATIONAL BUILDING CODE

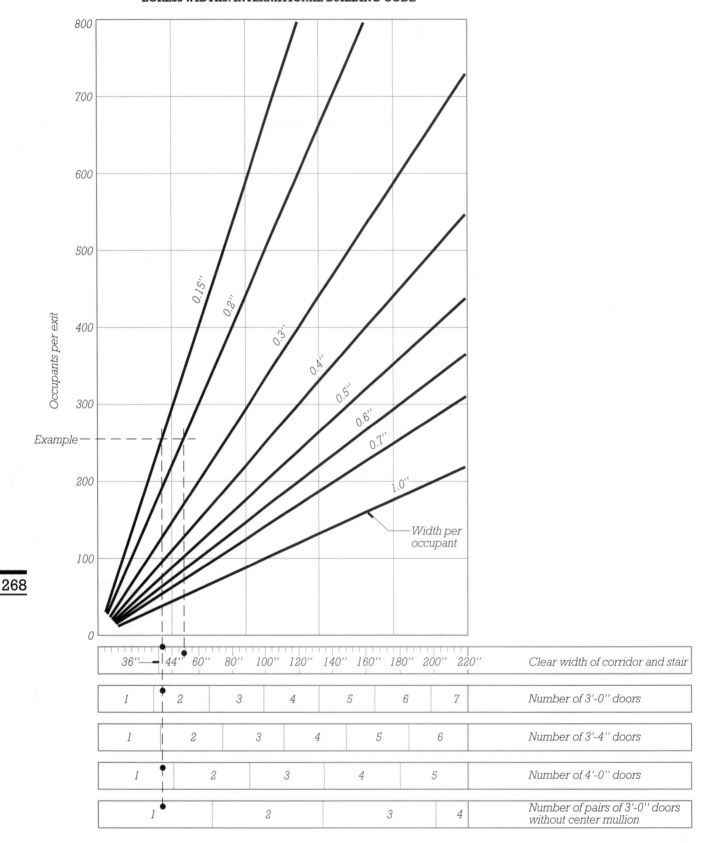

DETERMINING WIDTHS OF EGRESS COMPONENTS

An Example of the Use of this Chart

The Problem: Design an exit for a department store basement, sprinklered, dimensions 105 × 292.55 ft.

The Solution: From the index on page 9, we find that a department store belongs to Occupancy Group M, Mercantile. Multiplying the two dimensions of the building, we arrive at a gross floor area of 30,720 sq ft. From the table on pages 270–271, we see that for purposes of designing the exits we must allocate 30 sq ft per occupant, to arrive at an occupant load of 1024 for this floor. Assume that our design provides four exits, which is also the minimum number required by the table on page 264. Dividing 1024 occupants by 4 exits gives an occupant load per exit of 256.

From the same table (pages 270–271), we find that for Occupancy Group M, we must provide 0.15 in. of width must per occupant in corridors and doorways and 0.2 in. per occupant in stairways. Moving to the chart on the facing page, we read horizontally from 256 occupants to the 0.15-in. line and then downward to find that a width of 38 in. is required for the corridor. We must round this up to the 44-in. minimum width indicated on page 267. Extending this line farther downward, we select either two 3-ft doors, a single 4-ft door, or a pair of 3-ft doors without center mullion.

Reading horizontally from 256 occupants to the 0.2-in. line, then downward, we arrive at a required stair width of 52 in. (For stair design charts, see pages 283–293.)

QUANTITIES FOR DETERMINING WIDTHS OF EGRESS COMPONENTS

Use	Occupant Load: Floor Area per Occupant
Accessory storage areas	300 ft² (28 m²) gross
Agricultural buildings	300 ft² (28 m²) gross
Aircraft hangars	500 ft² (46 m²) gross
Airport terminal baggage claim	20 ft² (1.86 m²) gross
Airport terminal baggage handling	300 ft² (28 m²) gross
Airport terminal concourses	100 ft² (9.3 m²) gross
Airport terminal waiting areas	15 ft² (1.4 m²) gross
Assembly occupancy, gaming floors	11 ft² (1.0 m²) gross
Assembly occupancy with concentrated seating (chairs only, not fixed)	7 ft² (0.65 m²) net
Assembly occupancy with standing space	Standing space: 5 ft² (0.46 m²) net
Assembly occupancy with unconcentrated seating (tables, chairs, stages, platforms)	15 ft² (1.4 m²) net; for booth seating, assume 24" (610 mm) width per occupant
Assembly occupancy, fixed seating	Use the actual number of seats; for seating without dividing arms, assume 18" (457 mm) width per occupant
Bowling centers	7 ft² (0.65 m²) net plus 5 occupants per lane
Business areas	100 ft² (9.3 m²) gross
Courtrooms, other than fixed seating	40 ft² (3.7 m²) net
Educational occupancy, classroom areas	20 ft² (1.86 m²) net
Educational occupancy, shops and vocational areas	50 ft² (4.65 m²) net
Exercise areas	50 ft² (4.65 m²) gross
Factories, industrial areas	100 ft² (9.3 m²) gross
Hazardous occupancies H-1, H-2, H-3, H-4	Consult the code
Hazardous occupancy H-5	Consult the code
Institutional occupancies I-1, I-3, I-4 sleeping areas	120 ft² (11.2 m²) gross
Institutional occupancy I-2 inpatient treatment areas	240 ft² (22.3 m²) gross
Institutional occupancy I-2 outpatient areas	100 ft² (9.3 m²) gross
Institutional occupancy I-2 sleeping areas	120 ft² (11.2 m²) gross
Kitchens, commercial	200 ft² (19 m²) gross
Library reading rooms	50 ft² (4.6 m²) net
Library stack areas	100 ft² (9.3 m²) gross
Locker rooms	50 ft² (4.65 m²) gross
Mechanical equipment rooms	300 ft² (28 m²) gross
Mercantile occupancy areas other than listed below	60 ft² (5.6 m²) gross
Mercantile occupancy, basement and grade floor areas	30 ft² (2.8 m²) gross
Mercantile occupancy, enclosed shopping malls	Consult the code
Mercantile occupancy, storage, stock, and shipping areas	300 ft² (28 m²) gross
Parking garages	200 ft² (19 m²) gross
Residential occupancy, dormitories	50 ft² (4.6 m²) gross
Residential occupancy, general	200 ft² (19 m²) gross
Skating rinks, swimming pools	Rink and pool: 50 ft² (4.65 m²) gross
Skating rinks, swimming pools	Decks: 15 ft² (1.4 m²) gross
Storage, general	300 ft² (28 m²) gross
Warehouses	500 ft² (46 m²) gross

Width per Occupant			
For Doors, Corridors, and Ramps		For Stairs	
Unsprinklered	Sprinklered	Unsprinklered	Sprinklered
0.2" (5 mm)	0.15" (4 mm)	0.3" (8 mm)	0.2" (5 mm)
0.2" (5 mm)	0.15" (4 mm)	0.3" (8 mm)	0.2" (5 mm)
0.2" (5 mm)	0.15" (4 mm)	0.3" (8 mm)	0.2" (5 mm)
0.2" (5 mm)	0.15" (4 mm)	0.3" (8 mm)	0.2" (5 mm)
0.2" (5 mm)	0.15" (4 mm)	0.3" (8 mm)	0.2" (5 mm)
0.2" (5 mm)	0.15" (4 mm)	0.3" (8 mm)	0.2" (5 mm)
0.2" (5 mm)	0.15" (4 mm)	0.3" (8 mm)	0.2" (5 mm)
0.2" (5 mm)	0.15" (4 mm)	0.3" (8 mm)	0.2" (5 mm)
0.2" (5 mm)	0.15" (4 mm)	0.3" (8 mm)	0.2" (5 mm)
0.2" (5 mm)	0.15" (4 mm)	0.3" (8 mm)	0.2" (5 mm)
0.2" (5 mm)	0.15" (4 mm)	0.3" (8 mm)	0.2" (5 mm)
0.2" (5 mm)	0.15" (4 mm)	0.3" (8 mm)	0.2" (5 mm)
0.2" (5 mm)	0.15" (4 mm)	0.3" (8 mm)	0.2" (5 mm)
0.2" (5 mm)	0.15" (4 mm)	0.3" (8 mm)	0.2" (5 mm)
0.2" (5 mm)	0.15" (4 mm)	0.3" (8 mm)	0.2" (5 mm)
0.2" (5 mm)	0.15" (4 mm)	0.3" (8 mm)	0.2" (5 mm)
0.2" (5 mm)	0.15" (4 mm)	0.3" (8 mm)	0.2" (5 mm)
0.2" (5 mm)	0.15" (4 mm)	0.3" (8 mm)	0.2" (5 mm)
0.2" (5 mm)	0.15" (4 mm)	0.3" (8 mm)	0.2" (5 mm)
Not permitted	0.2" (5 mm)	Not permitted	0.3" (8 mm)
Not permitted	0.15" (4 mm)	Not permitted	0.2" (5 mm)
0.2" (5 mm)	0.15" (4 mm)	0.3" (8 mm)	0.2" (5 mm)
0.2" (5 mm)	0.2" (5 mm)	0.4" (10 mm)	0.3" (8 mm)
0.2" (5 mm)	0.2" (5 mm)	0.4" (10 mm)	0.3" (8 mm)
0.2" (5 mm)	0.2" (5 mm)	0.4" (10 mm)	0.3" (8 mm)
0.2" (5 mm)	0.15" (4 mm)	0.3" (8 mm)	0.2" (5 mm)
0.2" (5 mm)	0.15" (4 mm)	0.3" (8 mm)	0.2" (5 mm)
0.2" (5 mm)	0.15" (4 mm)	0.3" (8 mm)	0.2" (5 mm)
0.2" (5 mm)	0.15" (4 mm)	0.3" (8 mm)	0.2" (5 mm)
0.2" (5 mm)	0.15" (4 mm)	0.3" (8 mm)	0.2" (5 mm)
0.2" (5 mm)	0.15" (4 mm)	0.3" (8 mm)	0.2" (5 mm)
0.2" (5 mm)	0.15" (4 mm)	0.3" (8 mm)	0.2" (5 mm)
Not permitted	0.15" (4 mm)	Not permitted	0.2" (5 mm)
0.2" (5 mm)	0.15" (4 mm)	0.3" (8 mm)	0.2" (5 mm)
0.2" (5 mm)	0.15" (4 mm)	0.3" (8 mm)	0.2" (5 mm)
0.2" (5 mm)	0.15" (4 mm)	0.3" (8 mm)	0.2" (5 mm)
0.2" (5 mm)	0.15" (4 mm)	0.3" (8 mm)	0.2" (5 mm)
0.2" (5 mm)	0.15" (4 mm)	0.3" (8 mm)	0.2" (5 mm)
0.2" (5 mm)	0.15" (4 mm)	0.3" (8 mm)	0.2" (5 mm)
0.2" (5 mm)	0.15" (4 mm)	0.3" (8 mm)	0.2" (5 mm)
0.2" (5 mm)	0.15" (4 mm)	0.3" (8 mm)	0.2" (5 mm)

MISCELLANEOUS EGRESS REQUIREMENTS

Minimum Number of Exits

Normally, each floor of a building must have at least two exits. In buildings not exceeding 2 stories in height, a floor may have only one exit if it does not serve an occupant load of more than 60 persons, and does not exceed the maximum floor area and travel distance in the table below. In addition, single exits from floors classified as either Group B Care and Detention, or Group C Residential other than dwelling units, must be exterior doorways not more than 1.5 m (5 ft) above the adjacent ground level.

Egress Width Calculations

Where floors are located one above another, exit stair and exit discharge widths are based on the occupant load of the largest single floor served—occupant loads do not normally accumulate from one floor to the next. Where egress from floors above and below converge at an intermediate level, egress width from the point of convergence is based on the sum of the converging occupant loads. The width of stairs serving converging egress from

mezzanines, theater balconies, or other superimposed floor areas not separated by rated fire assemblies, is sized for the cumulative occupant load, or additional holding capacity must be provided to temporarily accommodate the excess occupant load—see the code for details.

Firefighter Access

On unsprinklered floors less than 25 m (82 ft) above grade, firefighter access must be provided by at least one unobstructed window or access panel, minimum dimensions 1100 mm (43 in) high by 550 mm (22 in) wide with a sill height not greater than 900 mm (35 in), for each 15 m (49 ft) of wall required to face the street. Access panels above the first floor must allow operation from both the inside and outside, or must be glazed with plain glass. Unsprinklered basements greater than 25 m (82 ft) in either horizontal dimension must provide firefighter access in the form of an exit stair connected directly to the outdoors, or a window or access panel as described above. In buildings more than three stories in height with a roof slope less than 1:4, rooftop access must be provided from the floor immediately below either by a stairway or by a fixed ladder and roof hatch.

High Buildings

The National Building Code of Canada defines high buildings as any of the following:

- Buildings containing Occupancy Groups A Assembly, D Business and Personal Services, E Mercantile, or F Industrial, with a story greater than 36 m (118 ft) above grade

- Buildings containing Occupancy Groups A Assembly, D Business and Personal Services, E Mercantile, or F Industrial, with a story greater than 18 m (59 ft) above grade where the total occupant load on any story above the first story, divided by 1.8, exceeds 300 times the width in meters of all exit stairs serving that story

- Buildings with Group B Care or Detention occupancy on a story greater than 18 m (59 ft) above grade

- Buildings with Group B-2, Care or Detention occupancy, with occupants having cognitive or physical limitations, on the fourth or higher story

- Buildings with Group C Residential occupancy on a story greater than 18 m (59 ft) above grade

In high buildings, at least one elevator must be provided for fire-

SINGLE EXIT OCCUPANCIES	Unsprinklered		Sprinklered	
Occupancy	Maximum Floor Area	Maximum Travel Distance	Maximum Floor Area	Travel Distance
A Assembly	150 m² (1615 ft²)	15 m (49 ft)	200 m² (2150 ft²)	25 m (82 ft)
B Care or Detention	75 m² (805 ft²)	10 m (33 ft)	100 m² (1075 ft²)	25 m (82 ft)
C Residential	100 m² (1075 ft²)	15 m (49 ft)	150 m² (1615 ft²)	25 m (82 ft)
D Business and Personal Services	200 m² (2150 ft²)	25 m (82 ft)	300 m² (3330 ft²)	25 m (82 ft)
E Mercantile	150 m² (1615 ft²)	15 m (49 ft)	200 m² (2150 ft²)	25 m (82 ft)
F-2 Industrial	150 m² (1615 ft²)	10 m (33 ft)	200 m² (2150 ft²)	25 m (82 ft)
F-3 Industrial	200 m² (2150 ft²)	15 m (49 ft)	300 m² (3330 ft²)	25 m (82 ft)
Interstitial Floor Service Spaces	200 m² (2150 ft²)	25 m (82 ft)	200 m² (2150 ft²)	25 m (82 ft)
Rooftop Enclosures	200 m² (2150 ft²)	Not applicable	200 m² (2150 ft²)	Not applicable
Occupied Rooftop Areas	2 exits required if occupant load is greater than 60			

fighter access. This elevator must be located within 15 m (49 ft) of firefighter access to the building, have a useable platform area of not less than 2.2 m^2 (24 ft^2), and be protected by an unoccupied ¾-hour vestibule or an unoccupied 1-hour corridor enclosure at each floor. Elevator access must be provided to all floors above grade, by a single elevator, or with not more than one change of elevators.

Special smoke control provisions are also required in high buildings, some of which are summarized here. For more information, consult the code. All floor areas within a high building must be provided with means of ventilating smoke from the interior, consisting of windows or ventilating wall panels, smoke shafts, or mechanical smoke exhaust systems. In addition, exit stairs serving stories below the exit level must be ventilated at the top of the shaft, be provided with mechanical ventilation designed to introduce fresh air at the bottom of the shaft, and be separated from stairs serving stories above the exit level by either a separate shaft or a fire separation wall within the shared shaft. Stairs serving stories above the exit level must be naturally ventilated at or near the bottom of the stair shaft, or must be mechanically pressurized. Where naturally ventilated, vent openings must be at least 1.8 m^2 (19 ft^2) in area and not less 0.05 m^2 (0.5 ft^2) in area for each door opening from the stair shaft. Elevator hoistways must not penetrate floors both above and below the exit level, or, at each floor below the exit level, the hoistway must be separated from adjacent floor areas by a protected vestibule. Where a high building is connected to an adjacent building, the two buildings must be separated not only by a firewall with protected openings, but also by a vestibule with large, naturally ventilated openings or

with mechanical pressurization so as to restrict the passage of smoke between the two buildings.

Accessibility for Disabled People

All buildings are required to be accessible except single-family residences (including detached and semidetached houses, triplexes, town houses, row houses, and boarding houses), Group F-1 High-Hazard Industrial occupancies, and buildings not intended to be occupied daily or full-time, such as automatic telephone exchanges, pump houses, and substations. In some cases, accessibility may not be required in all parts of lower-hazard Group F-2 or F-3 industrial occupancies where such areas contain greater than normal risks to occupants due to the storage of hazardous materials or the operation of hazardous processes.

The principal entrance to a building and not less than one-half of all its entrances must be accessible. Where accessibility is required, barrier-free paths of travel, not less than 920 mm (36 in) in width, must be provided throughout such areas, including entrance stories, and any other normally occupied floor areas served by passenger elevators or other accessible means. Where escalators provide public access to multiple levels, alternative accessible means of access must also be provided. Accessible paths of travel to the following locations are not required:

- Building service facilities, crawl spaces, attic or roof spaces

- Mezzanines not served by passenger elevators or other accessible means

- Portions of fixed-seating floor areas within assembly occupancies not part of the path of travel to designated wheelchair spaces

- Portions of residential occupancy suites not at the entrance level

- Portions of floor areas not at the same level as the entrance level, provided similar accessible amenities are provided at the entrance level

See also page 254 for requirements for wheelchair places in assembly occupancies.

All buildings required to be accessible must provide barrier-free access to accessible washrooms. All washrooms on accessible floors must be accessible, except washrooms located within residential suites or occupancies, washrooms located within a travel distance of 45 m (148 ft) of alternative accessible washrooms on the same floor, or washrooms within individual suites not exceeding 500 m^2 (5380 ft^2) in area when such suites are completely separate from the remainder of the building in which they are located.

Where barrier-free access is provided to unsprinklered floors above or below the first story, a smoke- and fire-protected elevator must be provided, each such floor must be divided with a fire-separation wall and horizontal exits into at least two zones, and the building must have an exterior exit at grade level or with a ramp leading to grade. In addition, any residences on upper floors must be furnished with accessible balconies with adequate areas to accommodate anticipated nonambulatory occupants.

The reference tables appearing on pages 274–277 are for preliminary design purposes only. They represent the authors' interpretation and simplification of certain major provisions of the National Building Code of Canada 1995. No official interpretation has been sought from or granted by International Code Council, Inc. For design development work and final preparation of building plans, you must consult the building code adopted by the building regulatory authorities in your project location.

Occupancy (see index on page 11–13 for specific uses)	Maximum Travel Distance from Most Remote Point to Nearest Exit Enclosure[1]		Largest Room or Suite That May Have Only One Door	
	Unsprinklered	Sprinklered	Unsprinklered	Sprinklered
A-1: Assembly, Performing Arts	30 m (98 ft)	45 m (148 ft)	Maximum occupancy of 60 persons, 150 m^2 (1615 ft^2) maximum area, and 5 m (49 ft) travel distance within the space	Maximum occupancy of 60 persons, 200 m^2 (2153 ft^2) maximum area, and 25 m (82 ft) travel distance within the space
A-2: Assembly, General	30 m (98 ft)	45 m (148 ft)	Same as above	Same as above
A-3: Assembly, Arenas	30 m (98 ft)	45 m (148 ft)	Same as above	Same as above
A-4: Assembly, Outdoors	45 m (148 ft) to the ground, an exit, an opening to a passage-way leading from the seating area, or a portal, vomitory or other opening in the seating deck structure.	Not Applicable	Same as above	Same as above
B-1: Care or Detention, Restrained	30 m (98 ft)	45 m (148 ft)	Maximum occupancy of 60 persons, and no area or travel distance limit	Maximum occupancy of 60 persons, 100 m^2 (1076 ft^2) maximum area, and 25 m (82 ft) travel distance with in the space
B-2: Care or Detention, Cognitively or Physically Limited	30 m (98 ft)	45 m (148 ft)	Same as above	Sleeping rooms same as above, other spaces 200 m^2 (2153 ft^2) maximum area
C: Residential	30 m (98 ft)	45 m (148 ft)	Maximum occupancy of 60 persons, 100 m^2 (1076 ft^2) maximum area, and 15 m (49 ft) travel distance within the space	Maximum occupancy of 60 persons, 150 m^2 (1615 ft^2) maximum area, and 25 m (82 ft) travel distance within the space.
D: Business or Personal Services	40 m (131 ft)	40 m (131 ft)	Maximum occupancy of 60 persons, 200 m^2 (2153 ft^2) maximum area, and 25 m (82 ft) travel distance within the space	Maximum occupancy of 60 persons, 300 m^2 (3229 ft^2) maximum area, and 25 m (82 ft) travel distance within the space
E: Mercantile	30 m (98 ft)	45 m (148 ft)	Maximum occupancy of 60 persons, 150 m^2 (1615 ft^2) maximum area, and 15 m (49 ft) travel distance within the space	Maximum occupancy of 60 persons, 200 m^2 (2153 ft^2) maximum area, and 25 m (82 ft) travel distance within the space
F-1: Industrial, High-Hazard	25 m (82 ft)	25 m (82 ft)	Maximum occupancy of 60 persons, and 15 m^2 (161 ft^2) maximum area	Maximum occupancy of 60 persons, and 15 m^2 (161 ft^2)
F-2: Industrial, Medium-Hazard	30 m (98 ft)	45 m (148 ft)	Maximum occupancy of 60 persons, 150 m^2 (1615 ft^2) maximum area, and 10 m (33 ft) travel distance within the space	Maximum occupancy of 60 persons, and 200 m^2 (2153 ft^2) maximum area, and 25 m (82 ft) travel distance within the space
F-3: Industrial, Low-Hazard	30 m (98 ft)	45 m (148 ft)	Maximum occupancy of 60 persons, 150 m^2 (1615 ft^2) maximum area, and 15 m (49 ft) travel distance within the space	Maximum occupancy of 60 persons, and 300 m^2 (3229 ft^2) maximum area, and 25 m (82 ft) travel distance within the space
F-3: Open-Air Garages	60 m (197 ft)	60 m (197 ft)	Not Applicable	Not Applicable

274

Maximum Length of Dead-End Corridor	Minimum Clear Corridor Width	Minimum Net Clear Egress Door Width	Minimum Stair Width	Additional Requirements
6 m (20 ft)	1100 mm (43 in)	800 mm (31 in)	1100 mm (43 in) for a stair serving more than three stories above grade or more than one story below grade, 900 mm (35 in) otherwise	See detailed requirements for row spacings, aisles, and exits on pages 260–261.
6 m (20 ft)	1100 mm (43 in)	800 mm (31 in) opening into or within a corridor, 790 mm (31 in) at exits	Same as above	See detailed requirements for row spacings, aisles, and exits on pages 260–261.
6 m (20 ft)	1100 mm (43 in)	Same as above	Same as above	See detailed requirements for row spacings, aisles, and exits on pages 260–261.
6 m (20 ft)	1100 mm (43 in)	Same as above	Same as above	A tier or balcony with occupant load of 1001 to 4000 persons requires at least three exits, an occupant load of more than 4000 requires at least four exits. See the code for aisle and bleacher requirements.
6 m (20 ft), for corridors serving the public or patients' sleeping rooms permitted only if these areas have a second separate means of egress	1100 mm (43 in), 2400 mm (94 in) for patients in bed	Same as above, except 1050 mm (41 in) for patients in bed	Same as above, except 1650 mm (65 in) for patients in bed	
Same as above	Same as above	Same as above	Same as above	
6 m (20 ft)	1100 mm (43 in)	800 mm (31 in) opening into or within a corridor, 790 mm (31 in) at exits	1100 mm (43 in) for a stair serving more than three stories above grade or more than one story below grade, 900 mm (35 in) otherwise	At least one stairway between each two floors within a dwelling unit must have a minimum width of 860 mm (34 in).
6 m (20 ft)	1100 mm (43 in)	Same as above	Same as above	
6 m (20 ft)	1100 mm (43 in)	Same as above	Same as above	
6 m (20 ft)	1100 mm (43 in)	Same as above	Same as above	[1]If a room is enclosed with at least a ¾-hour fire separation in nonsprinklered buildings or a nonrated separation in sprinklered buildings, and opens into a corridor or exterior passageway, travel distance may be measured from the door of the room. In fully sprinklered buildings, floor areas served by a public corridor not less than 9 m (30 ft) wide and 4 m (13 ft) tall may have a maximum travel distance of up to 105 m (344 ft).
6 m (20 ft)	1100 mm (43 in)	Same as above	Same as above	
6 m (20 ft)	1100 mm (43 in)	Same as above	Same as above	
6 m (20 ft)	1100 mm (43 in)	Same as above	Same as above	

SIZING THE EGRESS SYSTEM

275

EGRESS WIDTHS: NATIONAL BUILDING CODE OF CANADA

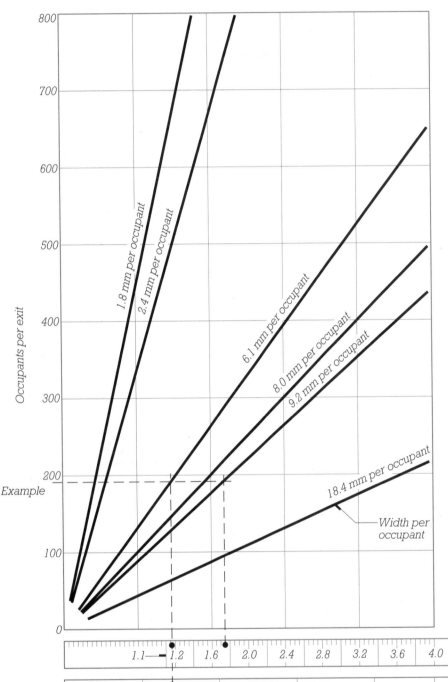

DETERMINING WIDTHS OF EGRESS COMPONENTS

An Example of the Use of this Chart

The Problem: Design an exit for a department store basement, sprinklered, dimensions 33 × 85.2 m.

The Solution: From the index on page 12, we find that a department store belongs to Occupancy Group E Mercantile. Multiplying the two dimensions of the building, we arrive at a gross floor area of 2812 m². From the table on the facing page we see that for purposes of designing the exits we must allocate 3.7 m² per occupant, to arrive at an occupant load of 760 for this floor. Assume that our design provides four exits. Dividing 760 occupants by 4 exits gives an occupant load per exit of 190.

From the table on the facing page we find that for Occupancy E, 6.1 mm of egress width per occupant is required for doors, corridors, and passageways. Moving to the chart on this page, we read horizontally from 190 occupants to the 6.1 mm line, then downward, to find that a corridor width of 1160 mm is required. Extending this line farther downward, we select either two 915-mm doors, or one pair of 915-mm doors without a center mullion. To find the required width for our egress stair, we read downward from the 9.2 mm line, finding that a width of 1750 mm is required for the steepest possible stair. (For stair design tables, see pages 283–293.)

QUANTITIES FOR DETERMINING WIDTHS OF EGRESS COMPONENTS			**Width per Occupant**		
Occupancy	Use	Occupant Load: Floor Area per Occupant	For Doors, Corridors, and Ramps Not More Than 1:8 slope	For Stairs with Rise Not More Than 180 mm (7") and Run Not Less Than 280 mm (11")	For Stairs with Rise More Than 180 mm (7") or Run Less Than 280 mm (11"), and Ramps with Slope More Than 1:8
A Assembly	Space with fixed seats	Actual number of fixed seats	6.1 mm (0.24")	8 mm (0.31")	9.2 mm (0.36")
	Space with nonfixed seats, performance stages	0.75 m² (8.1 ft²)	6.1 mm (0.24")	8 mm (0.31")	9.2 mm (0.36")
	Space with nonfixed seats and tables	0.95 m² (10 ft²)	6.1 mm (0.24")	8 mm (0.31")	9.2 mm (0.36")
	Standing space	0.40 m² (4.3 ft²)	6.1 mm (0.24")	8 mm (0.31")	9.2 mm (0.36")
	Bowling alleys, pool and billiard rooms, school shops and vocational rooms	9.30 m² (100 ft²)	6.1 mm (0.24")	8 mm (0.31")	9.2 mm (0.36")
	Classrooms, reading or writing rooms, lounges	1.85 m² (20 ft²)	6.1 mm (0.24")	8 mm (0.31")	9.2 mm (0.36")
	Dining, beverage, and cafeteria space	1.20 m² (13 ft²)	6.1 mm (0.24")	8 mm (0.31")	9.2 mm (0.36")
	Laboratories in schools	4.60 m² (50 ft²)	6.1 mm (0.24")	8 mm (0.31")	9.2 mm (0.36")
	Stadiums and grandstands	0.60 m² (6.5 ft²)	1.8 mm (0.07") per person for aisles, stairs other than exit stairs, and ramps and passageways in vomitories and exits, and 2.4 mm (0.09") per person in exit stairs	18.4 mm (0.72")	18.4 mm (0.72")
B Care or Detention	Treatment and sleeping room areas	10.00 m² (107 ft²)	18.4 mm (0.72")	18.4 mm (0.72")	18.4 mm (0.72")
	Detention quarters	11.60 m² (125 ft²)	18.4 mm (0.72")	8 mm (0.31")	9.2 mm (0.36")
C Residential	Dwelling units	2 persons per sleeping room	6.1 mm (0.24")	8 mm (0.31")	9.2 mm (0.36")
	Dormitories	4.60 m² (50 ft²)	6.1 mm (0.24")	8 mm (0.31")	9.2 mm (0.36")
D Business and Personal Services	Personal services shops	4.60 m² (50 ft²)	6.1 mm (0.24")	8 mm (0.31")	9.2 mm (0.36")
E Mercantile	Offices	9.30 m² (100 ft²)	6.1 mm (0.24")	8 mm (0.31")	9.2 mm (0.36")
	Basements and first stories	3.70 m² (40 ft²)	6.1 mm (0.24")	8 mm (0.31")	9.2 mm (0.36")
	Second stories having a principal entrance from a pedestrian thoroughfare or a parking area	3.70 m² (40 ft²)	6.1 mm (0.24")	8 mm (0.31")	9.2 mm (0.36")
F Industrial	Other stories	5.60 m² (60 ft²)	6.1 mm (0.24")	8 mm (0.31")	9.2 mm (0.36")
	Manufacturing or processing rooms	4.60 m² (50 ft²)	6.1 mm (0.24")	8 mm (0.31")	9.2 mm (0.36")
	Storage garages, aircraft hangars	46.00 m² (495 ft²)	6.1 mm (0.24")	8 mm (0.31")	9.2 mm (0.36")
Other Uses	Storage spaces (warehouses)	28.00 m² (300 ft²)	6.1 mm (0.24")	8 mm (0.31")	9.2 mm (0.36")
	Cleaning and repair goods	4.60 m² (50 ft²)	6.1 mm (0.24")	8 mm (0.31")	9.2 mm (0.36")
	Kitchens	9.30 m² (100 ft²)	6.1 mm (0.24")	8 mm (0.31")	9.2 mm (0.36")
	Public corridors intended for occupancies in addition to pedestrian travel	3.70 m² (40 ft²)	6.1 mm (0.24")	8 mm (0.31")	9.2 mm (0.36")

SIZING THE EGRESS SYSTEM

277

■■■■■
STAIRWAY
AND
RAMP
DESIGN

This section will help you design stairways and ramps in accordance with the model building codes.

STAIRWAY AND RAMP PROPORTIONS

	Stairs Other Than Residential					Residential Stairs[1]	
	Maximum Riser Height (R)	Minimum Riser Height (R)	Minimum Tread Depth (T)	Maximum Rise Between Landings	Minimum Number of Risers per Flight	Maximum Riser Height	Minimum Tread Depth
International Building Code	7" (178 mm)	4" (102 mm)	11" (279 mm)	12' (3658 mm)	no requirement	7.75" (197 mm)	10" (254 mm)
National Building Code of Canada	180 mm (7.1"); Small buildings 200 mm (7.9")[2]	125 mm (4.9")	280 mm (11.0") Small buildings 250 mm (9.8")[2]	3.7 m (12'-2"), except 2.4 m (7'–10") in a Group B Division 2 Occupancy	3, except within a dwelling unit, or Group A Division 2 Occupancy used for the serving of food and beverages when the stair is not less than 900 mm (35.4") wide	200 mm (7.9")	235 mm (9.25")

[1]In the International Building Code, Residential Stairs includes stairs in Occupancy Group R-3, in dwelling units within Group R-2, and in Group U occupancies when accessory to Group R-3. In the National Building Code of Canada, Residential Stairs includes stairs within dwelling units and exterior stairs serving a single dwelling unit.
[2]Includes buildings 3 stories or less in height, not exceeding 600 m² (6460 ft²) in area, and classified as Occupancies C, D, E, F-2, or F-3.

	Maximum Ramp Slope for Required Exits	Minimum Ramp Width	Landing Requirements
International Building Code	1:12 for ramps part of an accessible path of travel; 1:8 for other ramps	36" (914 mm) clear width between sides of ramp or handrails, if any	Landings are required at points of turning, ramp entrances and exits, and doors opening onto ramps. The maximum rise between landings is 30". Landings must be at least as wide as the ramp, with a minimum length of 60" (1525 mm), except in Group R-2 and R-3 individual dwelling units, where the minimum length is 36" (914 mm).
National Building Code of Canada	1:12 for barrier-free ramps; 1:10 for Assembly, Care or Detention, or Residential occupancy; 1:6 for Mercantile or Industrial occupancy; 1:8 for other interior ramps; 1:10 for exterior ramps	870 mm (34.25") between handrails for barrier-free ramps	Where a doorway or stairway opens onto the side of a ramp, a landing extending a minimum of 300 mm (11.8") beyond either side of the opening is required. Where a doorway or stairway opens onto the end of a ramp, a landing extending along the ramp for at least 900 mm (35.4") is required. In addition, barrier-free ramps require landings with a minimum size of 1500 mm × 1500 mm (59" × 59") at the top and bottom of the ramp, and landings at least 1200 mm (47.25") long and at least as wide as the ramp at abrupt changes in direction and at least every 9 m (29'-6") along the length of the ramp.

CURVED AND SPIRAL STAIRS

	MAY A CURVED STAIR SERVE AS A REQUIRED EXIT?	**Dimensional Restrictions**
International Building Code, except Residential Occupancies as noted below	Yes	The smaller radius of the stair must be at least twice the width of the stairway. Risers may not exceed 7" (178 mm) in height, and treads may not be less than 11" (279 mm) deep at a distance of 12" (305 mm) from the narrow end of the tread. Minimum tread depth at the narrow end is 10" (254 mm).
International Building Code Residential Occupancies R-3 and within Occupancy R-2 dwelling units	Yes	Risers may not exceed 7.75" (197 mm) in height, and treads may not be less than 10" (254 mm) deep at a distance of 12" (305 mm) from the narrow end of the tread. Minimum tread depth at the narrow end is 6" (152 mm).
National Building Code of Canada	Yes	The smaller radius of the stair must be at least twice the width of the stairway. Treads and risers must conform to the dimensions shown on page 280, measured 230 mm (9.1") from the narrow end of the tread. Minimum tread depth at the narrow end is 240 mm (9.4"), not including nosings. Curved stairs not serving as an exit may have a minimum average run of 200 mm (7.9") and a minimum run of 150 mm (5.9") at the narrow end.

	MAY A SPIRAL STAIR SERVE AS A REQUIRED EXIT?	**Dimensional Restrictions**
International Building Code	A spiral stair may serve as a required exit only within a dwelling unit, or from a space not more than 250 ft² (23.25 m²) in area and serving not more than five occupants.	The tread may not measure less than 7.5" (191 mm) at a distance of 12" (305 mm) from the narrow end of the tread. The riser height may not exceed 9.5" (241 mm). The clear width of the stair must be at least 26" (660 mm), and the minimum headroom must be 78" (1981 mm).
National Building Code of Canada	No	For spiral stairs not required as an exit, the tread may not measure less than 150 mm (5.9") in depth at any point, and must average at least 200 mm (7.9") in depth. Riser height must be no greater than 180 mm (7.1") and no less than 125 mm (4.9").

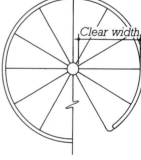

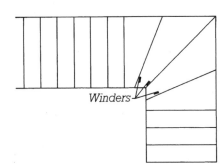

Winders

	MAY WINDERS BE USED IN A REQUIRED EXIT STAIRWAY?	Dimensional Restrictions
International Building Code	Winders may be used in a required exit stairway only within a dwelling unit.	The tread may not measure less than 11" (279 mm) at a distance of 12" (305 mm) from the narrow end. The narrow end of the tread may not be less than 6" (152 mm) in depth.
National Building Code of Canada	Only stairs within dwelling units may have winders.	Winders may converge to a point. Only one set of winders per floor is permitted. Individual treads must turn through an angle of at least 30° and the total angle of winders must not exceed 90°.

EXIT STAIRWAY DESIGN TABLES

The tables that follow allow you to make a very rapid preliminary design for an exit stairway. After selecting the desired stairway configuration, consult an accompanying table to find the required interior dimensions and the tread and riser proportions of a stairway that corresponds to the stair width and floor-to-floor height for which you are designing.

The stairway lengths for the English-unit tables are based on a maximum 7-in. (178-mm) riser and and 11-in. (279-mm) tread, conforming to the requirements of the International Building Code. Stairway lengths for the metric tables are based on a maximum 180-mm (7.1-in.) riser and a 280-mm (11-in.) tread, conforming to the requirements of the National Building Code of Canada for buildings not classified as small or residential. See page 280 for more information on stairway proportions.

The "Overall Inside Length of Stair Enclosure" figures represent an absolute minimum configuration. Handrail extension requirements will often dictate either that the door be recessed into an alcove that falls outside this length or that the length of the stair enclosure be increased, in order to satisfy the limitations on obstruction of the width of the landing by the open door. The minimum overall inside width for a stair enclosure is twice the required width of the stair itself, but construction of the stair may be facilitated by increasing this dimension by several inches. Under both the International Building Code and the National Building Code of Canada, the required stairway width is measured from the inside of the stairway or guards, and handrails may project into the required width of the stair for the purposes of computing its occupancy.

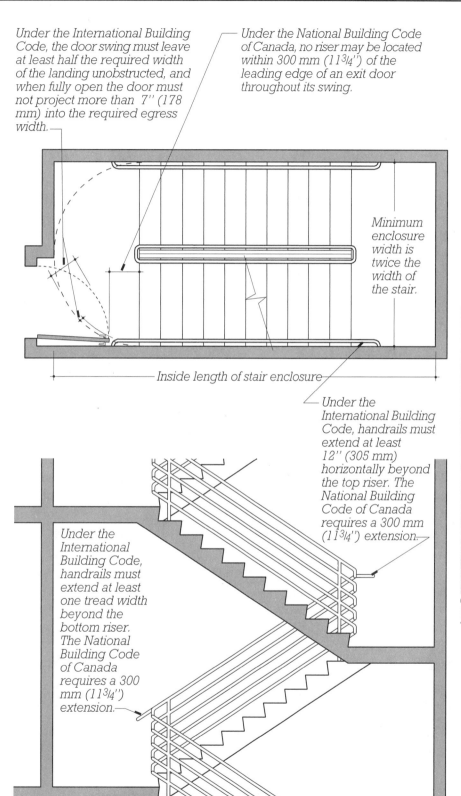

Under the International Building Code, the door swing must leave at least half the required width of the landing unobstructed, and when fully open the door must not project more than 7" (178 mm) into the required egress width.

Under the National Building Code of Canada, no riser may be located within 300 mm (11³⁄₄") of the leading edge of an exit door throughout its swing.

Minimum enclosure width is twice the width of the stair.

Inside length of stair enclosure

Under the International Building Code, handrails must extend at least 12" (305 mm) horizontally beyond the top riser. The National Building Code of Canada requires a 300 mm (11³⁄₄") extension.

Under the International Building Code, handrails must extend at least one tread width beyond the bottom riser. The National Building Code of Canada requires a 300 mm (11³⁄₄") extension.

EXIT STAIRWAY DESIGN TABLES

ONE-FLIGHT STAIR: ENGLISH UNITS

Floor-to-Floor Height (ft-in.)	Number of Risers	Riser Height (in.)	Tread Depth (in.)	Overall Inside Length of Stair Enclosure (ft-in.)				
				36" Width	44" Width	56" Width	66" Width	88" Width
1-8	3	6.67	11	7-10	9-2	11-2	12-10	16-6
2-0	4	6.00	11	8-9	10-1	12-1	13-9	17-5
2-4	4	7.00	11	8-9	10-1	12-1	13-9	17-5
2-8	5	6.40	11	9-8	11-0	13-0	14-8	18-4
3-0	6	6.00	11	10-7	11-11	13-11	15-7	19-3
3-4	6	6.67	11	10-7	11-11	13-11	15-7	19-3
3-8	7	6.29	11	11-6	12-10	14-10	16-6	20-2
4-0	7	6.86	11	11-6	12-10	14-10	16-6	20-2
4-4	8	6.50	11	12-5	13-9	15-9	17-5	21-1
4-8	8	7.00	11	12-5	13-9	15-9	17-5	21-1
5-0	9	6.67	11	13-4	14-8	16-8	18-4	22-0
5-4	10	6.40	11	14-3	15-7	17-7	19-3	22-11
5-8	10	6.80	11	14-3	15-7	17-7	19-3	22-11
6-0	11	6.55	11	15-2	16-6	18-6	20-2	23-10
6-4	11	6.91	11	15-2	16-6	18-6	20-2	23-10
6-8	12	6.67	11	16-1	17-5	19-5	21-1	24-9
7-0	12	7.00	11	16-1	17-5	19-5	21-1	24-9
7-4	13	6.77	11	17-0	18-4	20-4	22-0	25-8
7-8	14	6.57	11	17-11	19-3	21-3	22-0	26-7
8-0	14	6.86	11	17-11	19-3	21-3	22-11	26-7
8-4	15	6.67	11	18-10	20-2	22-2	23-10	27-6
8-8	15	6.93	11	18-10	20-2	22-2	23-10	27-6
9-0	16	6.75	11	19-9	21-1	23-1	24-9	28-5
9-4	16	7.00	11	19-9	21-1	23-1	24-9	28-5
9-8	17	6.82	11	20-8	22-0	24-0	25-8	29-4
10-0	18	6.67	11	21-7	22-11	24-11	26-7	30-3
10-4	18	6.89	11	21-7	22-11	24-11	26-7	30-3
10-8	19	6.74	11	22-6	23-10	25-10	27-6	31-2
11-0	19	6.95	11	22-6	23-10	25-10	27-6	31-2
11-4	20	6.80	11	23-5	24-9	26-9	28-5	32-1
11-8	20	7.00	11	23-5	24-9	26-9	28-5	32-1
12-0	21	6.86	11	24-4	25-8	27-8	29-4	33-0

Stairway widths may be determined rapidly by using the tables and graphs on pages 268–271 and 276–277.

EXIT STAIRWAY DESIGN TABLES

ONE-FLIGHT STAIR: METRIC UNITS (280-MM TREAD, 180-MM RISER)

Floor-to-Floor Height (m)	Number of Risers	Riser Height (mm)	Tread Depth (mm)	Overall Inside Length of Stair Enclosure (m)				
				900-mm Width	1100-mm Width	1400-mm Width	1650-mm Width	2200-mm Width
0.5	3	167	280	2.36	2.76	3.36	3.86	4.96
0.6	4	150	280	2.64	3.04	3.64	4.14	5.24
0.7	4	175	280	2.64	3.04	3.64	4.14	5.24
0.8	5	160	280	2.92	3.32	3.92	4.42	5.52
0.9	5	180	280	2.92	3.32	3.92	4.42	5.52
1.0	6	167	280	3.20	3.60	4.20	4.70	5.80
1.1	7	158	280	3.48	3.88	4.48	4.98	6.08
1.2	7	172	280	3.48	3.88	4.48	4.98	6.08
1.3	8	163	280	3.76	4.16	4.76	5.26	6.36
1.4	8	175	280	3.76	4.16	4.76	5.26	6.36
1.5	9	167	280	4.04	4.44	5.04	5.54	6.64
1.6	9	178	280	4.04	4.44	5.04	5.54	6.64
1.7	10	170	280	4.32	4.72	5.32	5.82	6.92
1.8	10	180	280	4.32	4.72	5.32	5.82	6.92
1.9	11	173	280	4.60	5.00	5.60	6.10	7.20
2.0	12	167	280	4.88	5.28	5.88	6.38	7.48
2.1	12	175	280	4.88	5.28	5.88	6.38	7.48
2.2	13	170	280	5.16	5.56	6.16	6.66	7.76
2.3	13	177	280	5.16	5.56	6.16	6.66	7.76
2.4	14	172	280	5.44	5.84	6.44	6.94	8.04
2.5	14	179	280	5.44	5.84	6.44	6.94	8.04
2.6	15	174	280	5.72	6.12	6.72	7.22	8.32
2.7	15	180	280	5.72	6.12	6.72	7.22	8.32
2.8	16	175	280	6.00	6.40	7.00	7.50	8.60
2.9	17	171	280	6.28	6.68	7.28	7.78	8.88
3.0	17	177	280	6.28	6.68	7.28	7.78	8.88
3.1	18	173	280	6.56	6.96	7.56	8.06	9.16
3.2	18	178	280	6.56	6.96	7.56	8.06	9.16
3.3	19	174	280	6.84	7.24	7.84	8.34	9.44
3.4	19	179	280	6.84	7.24	7.84	8.34	9.44
3.5	20	175	280	7.12	7.52	8.12	8.62	9.72
3.6	20	180	280	7.12	7.52	8.12	8.62	9.72
3.7	21	177	280	7.40	7.80	8.40	8.90	10.00

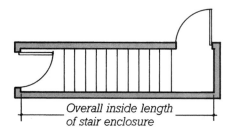

Overall inside length of stair enclosure

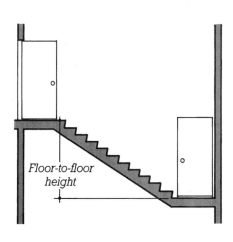

Floor-to-floor height

EXIT STAIRWAY DESIGN TABLES

TWO-FLIGHT STAIR: ENGLISH UNITS

Floor-to-Floor Height (ft-in.)	Number of Risers	Riser Height (in.)	Tread Depth (in.)	Overall Inside Length of Stair Enclosure (ft-in.)				
				36" Width	44" Width	56" Width	66" Width	88" Width
7-8*	14	6.57	11	11-6	12-10	14-10	16-6	20-2
8-0*	14	6.86	11	11-6	12-10	14-10	16-6	20-2
8-4	15	6.67	11	12-5	13-9	15-9	17-5	21-1
8-8	15	6.93	11	12-5	13-9	15-9	17-5	21-1
9-0	16	6.75	11	12-5	13-9	15-9	17-5	21-1
9-4	16	7.00	11	12-5	13-9	15-9	17-5	21-1
9-8	17	6.82	11	13-4	14-8	16-8	18-4	22-0
10-0	18	6.67	11	13-4	14-8	16-8	18-4	22-0
10-4	18	6.89	11	13-4	14-8	16-8	18-4	22-0
10-8	19	6.74	11	14-3	15-7	17-7	19-3	22-11
11-0	19	6.95	11	14-3	15-7	17-7	19-3	22-11
11-4	20	6.80	11	14-3	15-7	17-7	19-3	22-11
11-8	20	7.00	11	14-3	15-7	17-7	19-3	22-11
12-0	21	6.86	11	15-2	16-6	18-6	20-2	23-10
12-4	22	6.73	11	15-2	16-6	18-6	20-2	23-10
12-8	22	6.91	11	15-2	16-6	18-6	20-2	23-10
13-0	23	6.78	11	16-1	17-5	19-5	21-1	24-9
13-4	23	6.96	11	16-1	17-5	19-5	21-1	24-9
13-8	24	6.83	11	16-1	17-5	19-5	21-1	24-9
14-0	24	7.00	11	16-1	17-5	19-5	21-1	24-9
14-4	25	6.88	11	17-0	18-4	20-4	22-0	25-8
14-8	26	6.77	11	17-0	18-4	20-4	22-0	25-8
15-0	26	6.92	11	17-0	18-4	20-4	22-0	25-8
16-0	28	6.86	11	17-11	19-3	21-3	22-11	26-7
17-0	30	6.80	11	18-10	20-2	22-2	23-10	27-6
18-0	31	6.97	11	19-9	21-1	23-1	24-9	28-5
19-0	33	6.91	11	20-8	22-0	24-0	25-8	29-4
20-0	35	6.86	11	21-7	22-11	24-11	26-7	30-3
21-0	36	7.00	11	21-7	22-11	24-11	26-7	30-3
22-0	38	6.95	11	22-6	23-10	25-10	27-6	31-2
23-0	40	6.90	11	23-5	24-9	26-9	28-5	32-1
24-0	42	6.86	11	24-4	25-8	27-8	29-4	33-0

*The headroom in these stairs may be deficient, depending on the detailing of the stair structure.

Stairway widths may be determined rapidly by using the tables and graphs on pages 268–271 and 276–277.

EXIT STAIRWAY DESIGN TABLES

TWO-FLIGHT STAIR: METRIC UNITS (280-MM TREAD, MAXIMUM 180-MM RISER)

Floor-to-Floor Height (m)	Number of Risers	Riser Height (mm)	Tread Depth (mm)	Overall Inside Length of Stair Enclosure (m)				
				900-mm Width	1100-mm Width	1400-mm Width	1650-mm Width	2200-mm Width
2.3	13	177	280	3.48	3.88	4.48	4.98	6.08
2.4	14	172	280	3.48	3.88	4.48	4.98	6.08
2.5	14	179	280	3.48	3.88	4.48	4.98	6.08
2.6	15	174	280	3.76	4.16	4.76	5.26	6.36
2.7	15	180	280	3.76	4.16	4.76	5.26	6.36
2.8	16	175	280	3.76	4.16	4.76	5.26	6.36
2.9	17	171	280	4.04	4.44	5.04	5.54	6.64
3.0	17	177	280	4.04	4.44	5.04	5.54	6.64
3.1	18	173	280	4.04	4.44	5.04	5.54	6.64
3.2	18	178	280	4.04	4.44	5.04	5.54	6.64
3.3	19	174	280	4.32	4.72	5.32	5.82	6.92
3.4	19	179	280	4.32	4.72	5.32	5.82	6.92
3.5	20	175	280	4.32	4.72	5.32	5.82	6.92
3.6	20	180	280	4.32	4.72	5.32	5.82	6.92
3.7	21	177	280	4.60	5.00	5.60	6.10	7.20
3.8	22	173	280	4.60	5.00	5.60	6.10	7.20
3.9	22	178	280	4.60	5.00	5.60	6.10	7.20
4.0	23	174	280	4.88	5.28	5.88	6.38	7.48
4.1	23	179	280	4.88	5.28	5.88	6.38	7.48
4.2	24	175	280	4.88	5.28	5.88	6.38	7.48
4.3	24	180	280	4.88	5.28	5.88	6.38	7.48
4.4	25	176	280	5.16	5.56	6.16	6.66	7.76
4.5	25	180	280	5.16	5.56	6.16	6.66	7.76
4.8	27	178	280	5.44	5.84	6.44	6.94	8.04
5.1	29	176	280	5.72	6.12	6.72	7.22	8.32
5.4	30	180	280	5.72	6.12	6.72	7.22	8.32
5.7	32	179	280	6.00	6.40	7.00	7.50	8.60
6.0	34	177	280	6.28	6.68	7.28	7.78	8.88
6.3	35	180	280	6.56	6.96	7.56	8.06	9.16
6.6	37	179	280	6.84	7.24	7.84	8.34	9.44
6.9	39	177	280	7.12	7.52	8.12	8.62	9.72
7.2	40	180	280	7.12	7.52	8.12	8.62	9.72
7.4	42	177	280	7.40	7.80	8.40	8.90	100

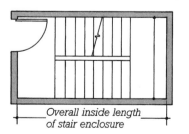

Overall inside length of stair enclosure

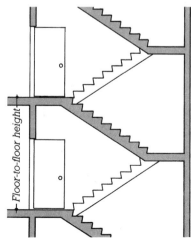

Floor-to-floor height

EXIT STAIRWAY DESIGN TABLES

THREE-FLIGHT STAIR: ENGLISH UNITS

Floor-to-Floor Height (ft-in.)	Number of Risers	Riser Height (in.)	Tread Depth (in.)	Overall Inside Length of Stair Enclosure (ft-in.)				
				36" Width	44" Width	56" Width	66" Width	88" Width
12-0	21	6.86	11	11-6	12-10	14-10	16-6	20-2
12-4	22	6.73	11	12-5	13-9	15-9	17-5	21-1
12-8	22	6.91	11	12-5	13-9	15-9	17-5	21-1
13-0	23	6.78	11	12-5	13-9	15-9	17-5	21-1
13-4	23	6.96	11	12-5	13-9	15-9	17-5	21-1
13-8	24	6.83	11	12-5	13-9	15-9	17-5	21-1
14-0	24	7.00	11	12-5	13-9	15-9	17-5	21-1
14-4	25	6.88	11	13-4	14-8	16-8	18-4	22-0
14-8	26	6.77	11	13-4	14-8	16-8	18-4	22-0
15-0	26	6.92	11	13-4	14-8	16-8	18-4	22-0
16-0	28	6.86	11	14-3	15-7	17-7	19-3	22-11
17-0	30	6.80	11	14-3	15-7	17-7	19-3	22-11
18-0	31	6.97	11	15-2	16-6	18-6	20-2	23-10
19-0	33	6.91	11	15-2	16-6	18-6	20-2	23-10
20-0	35	6.86	11	16-1	17-5	19-5	21-1	24-9
21-0	36	7.00	11	16-1	17-5	19-5	21-1	24-9
22-0	38	6.95	11	17-0	18-4	20-4	22-0	25-8
23-0	40	6.90	11	17-11	19-3	21-3	22-11	26-7
24-0	42	6.86	11	17-11	19-3	21-3	22-11	26-7

Stairway widths may be determined rapidly by using the tables and graphs on pages 268–271 and 276–277.

EXIT STAIRWAY DESIGN TABLES

THREE-FLIGHT STAIR: METRIC UNITS (280-MM TREAD, MAXIMUM 180-MM RISER)

Floor-to-Floor Height (m)	Number of Risers	Riser Height (mm)	Tread Depth (mm)	Overall Inside Length of Stair Enclosure (m)				
				900-mm Width	1100-mm Width	1400-mm Width	1650-mm Width	2200-mm Width
3.6	20	180	280	3.48	3.88	4.48	4.98	6.08
3.7	21	177	280	3.48	3.88	4.48	4.98	6.08
3.8	22	173	280	3.76	4.16	4.76	5.26	6.36
3.9	22	178	280	3.76	4.16	4.76	5.26	6.36
4.0	23	174	280	3.76	4.16	4.76	5.26	6.36
4.1	23	179	280	3.76	4.16	4.76	5.26	6.36
4.2	24	175	280	3.76	4.16	4.76	5.26	6.36
4.3	24	180	280	3.76	4.16	4.76	5.26	6.36
4.4	25	176	280	4.04	4.44	5.04	5.54	6.64
4.5	25	180	280	4.04	4.44	5.04	5.54	6.64
4.8	27	178	280	4.04	4.44	5.04	5.54	6.64
5.1	29	176	280	4.32	4.72	5.32	5.82	6.92
5.4	30	180	280	4.32	4.72	5.32	5.82	6.92
5.7	32	179	280	4.60	5.00	5.60	6.10	7.20
6.0	34	177	280	4.88	5.28	5.88	6.38	7.48
6.3	35	180	280	4.88	5.28	5.88	6.38	7.48
6.6	37	179	280	5.16	5.56	6.16	6.66	7.76
6.9	39	177	280	5.16	5.56	6.16	6.66	7.76
7.2	40	180	280	5.44	5.84	6.44	6.94	8.04
7.4	42	177	280	5.44	5.84	6.44	6.94	8.04

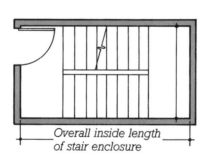

Overall inside length of stair enclosure

THREE-FLIGHT STAIR

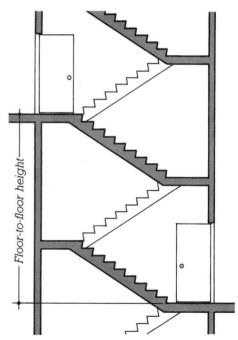

Floor-to-floor height

EXIT STAIRWAY DESIGN TABLES

FOUR-FLIGHT STAIR: ENGLISH UNITS

Floor-to-Floor Height (ft-in.)	Number of Risers	Riser Height (in.)	Tread Depth (in.)	Overall Inside Length of Stair Enclosure (ft-in.)				
				36" Width	44" Width	56" Width	66" Width	88" Width
16-0	28	6.86	11	11-6	12-10	14-10	16-6	20-2
17-0	30	6.80	11	12-5	13-9	15-9	17-5	21-1
18-0	31	6.97	11	12-5	13-9	15-9	17-5	21-1
19-0	33	6.91	11	13-4	14-8	16-8	18-4	22-0
20-0	35	6.86	11	13-4	14-8	16-8	18-4	22-0
21-0	36	7.00	11	13-4	14-8	16-8	18-4	22-0
22-0	38	6.95	11	14-3	15-7	17-7	19-3	22-11
23-0	40	6.90	11	14-3	15-7	17-7	19-3	22-11
24-0	42	6.86	11	15-2	16-6	18-6	20-2	23-10

Stairway widths may be determined rapidly by using the tables and graphs on pages 268–271 and 276–277.

EXIT STAIRWAY DESIGN TABLES

FOUR-FLIGHT STAIR: METRIC UNITS (280-MM TREAD, MAXIMUM 180-MM RISER)

Floor-to-Floor Height (m)	Number of Risers	Riser Height (mm)	Tread Depth (mm)	Overall Inside Length of Stair Enclosure (m)				
				900-mm Width	1100-mm Width	1400-mm Width	1650-mm Width	2200-mm Width
4.8	27	178	280	3.48	3.88	4.48	4.98	6.08
5.1	29	176	280	3.76	4.16	4.76	5.26	6.36
5.4	30	180	280	3.76	4.16	4.76	5.26	6.36
5.7	32	179	280	3.76	4.16	4.76	5.26	6.36
6.0	34	177	280	4.04	4.44	5.04	5.54	6.64
6.3	35	180	280	4.04	4.44	5.04	5.54	6.64
6.6	37	179	280	4.32	4.72	5.32	5.82	6.92
6.9	39	177	280	4.32	4.72	5.32	5.82	6.92
7.2	40	180	280	4.32	4.72	5.32	5.82	6.92
7.4	42	177	280	4.60	5.00	5.60	6.10	7.20

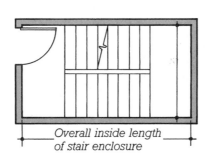

Overall inside length of stair enclosure

FOUR-FLIGHT STAIR

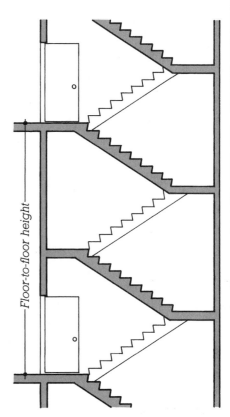

Floor-to-floor height

STAIRWAY AND RAMP DESIGN

291

EXIT STAIRWAY DESIGN TABLES

DOUGHNUT STAIR: ENGLISH UNITS

Floor-to-Floor Height (ft-in.)	Number of Risers	Riser Height (in.)	Tread Depth (in.)	36" Width	Overall Inside Length of Stair Enclosure (ft-in.)			
					44" Width	56" Width	66" Width	88" Width
7-8	14	6.57	11	7-10 × 8-9	9-2 × 10-1	11-2 × 12-1	12-10 × 13-9	16-6 × 17-5
8-0	14	6.86	11	7-10 × 8-9	9-2 × 10-1	11-2 × 12-1	12-10 × 13-9	16-6 × 17-5
8-4	15	6.67	11	8-9 × 8-9	10-1 × 10-1	12-1 × 12-1	13-9 × 13-9	17-5 × 17-5
8-8	15	6.93	11	8-9 × 8-9	10-1 × 10-1	12-1 × 12-1	13-9 × 13-9	17-5 × 17-5
9-0	16	6.75	11	8-9 × 8-9	10-1 × 10-1	12-1 × 12-1	13-9 × 13-9	17-5 × 17-5
9-4	16	7.00	11	8-9 × 8-9	10-1 × 10-1	12-1 × 12-1	13-9 × 13-9	17-5 × 17-5
9-8	17	6.82	11	8-9 × 9-8	10-1 × 11-0	12-1 × 13-0	13-9 × 14-8	17-5 × 18-4
10-0	18	6.67	11	8-9 × 9-8	10-1 × 11-0	12-1 × 13-0	13-9 × 14-8	17-5 × 18-4
10-4	18	6.89	11	8-9 × 9-8	10-1 × 11-0	12-1 × 13-0	13-9 × 14-8	17-5 × 18-4
10-8	19	6.74	11	9-8 × 9-8	11-0 × 11-0	13-0 × 13-0	14-8 × 14-8	18-4 × 18-4
11-0	19	6.95	11	9-8 × 9-8	11-0 × 11-0	13-0 × 13-0	14-8 × 14-8	18-4 × 18-4
11-4	20	6.80	11	9-8 × 9-8	11-0 × 11-0	13-0 × 13-0	14-8 × 14-8	18-4 × 18-4
11-8	20	7.00	11	9-8 × 9-8	11-0 × 11-0	13-0 × 13-0	14-8 × 14-8	18-4 × 18-4
12-0	21	6.86	11	9-8 × 10-7	11-0 × 11-11	13-0 × 13-11	14-8 × 15-7	18-4 × 19-3
12-4	22	6.73	11	9-8 × 10-7	11-0 × 11-11	13-0 × 13-11	14-8 × 15-7	18-4 × 19-3
12-8	22	6.91	11	9-8 × 10-7	11-0 × 11-11	13-0 × 13-11	14-8 × 15-7	18-4 × 19-3
13-0	23	6.78	11	10-7 × 10-7	11-11 × 11-11	13-11 × 13-11	15-7 × 15-7	19-3 × 19-3
13-4	23	6.96	11	10-7 × 10-7	11-11 × 11-11	13-11 × 13-11	15-7 × 15-7	19-3 × 19-3
13-8	24	6.83	11	10-7 × 10-7	11-11 × 11-11	13-11 × 13-11	15-7 × 15-7	19-3 × 19-3
14-0	24	7.00	11	10-7 × 10-7	11-11 × 11-11	13-11 × 13-11	15-7 × 15-7	19-3 × 19-3
14-4	25	6.88	11	10-7 × 11-6	11-11 × 12-10	13-11 × 14-10	15-7 × 16-6	19-3 × 20-2
14-8	26	6.77	11	10-7 × 11-6	11-11 × 12-10	13-11 × 14-10	15-7 × 16-6	19-3 × 20-2
15-0	26	6.92	11	10-7 × 11-6	11-11 × 12-10	13-11 × 14-10	15-7 × 16-6	19-3 × 20-2
16-0	28	6.86	11	11-6 × 11-6	12-10 × 12-10	14-10 × 14-10	16-6 × 16-6	20-2 × 20-2
17-0	30	6.80	11	11-6 × 12-5	12-10 × 13-9	14-10 × 15-9	16-6 × 17-5	20-2 × 21-1
18-0	31	6.97	11	12-5 × 12-5	13-9 × 13-9	15-9 × 15-9	17-5 × 17-5	21-1 × 21-1
19-0	33	6.91	11	12-5 × 13-4	13-9 × 14-8	15-9 × 16-8	17-5 × 18-4	21-1 × 22-0
20-0	35	6.86	11	13-4 × 13-4	14-8 × 14-8	16-8 × 16-8	18-4 × 18-4	22-0 × 22-0
21-0	36	7.00	11	13-4 × 13-4	14-8 × 14-8	16-8 × 16-8	18-4 × 18-4	22-0 × 22-0
22-0	38	6.95	11	13-4 × 14-3	14-8 × 15-7	16-8 × 17-7	18-4 × 19-3	22-0 × 22-11
23-0	40	6.90	11	14-3 × 14-3	15-7 × 15-7	17-7 × 17-7	19-3 × 19-3	22-11 × 22-11
24-0	42	6.86	11	14-3 × 15-2	15-7 × 16-6	17-7 × 18-6	19-3 × 20-2	22-11 × 23-10

Stairway widths may be determined rapidly by using the tables and graphs on pages 268–271 and 276–277.

EXIT STAIRWAY DESIGN TABLES

DOUGHNUT STAIR: METRIC UNITS (280-MM TREAD, 180-MM RISER)

Floor-to-Floor Height (m)	Number of Risers	Riser Height (mm)	Tread Depth (mm)	Overall Inside Length of Stair Enclosure (m)				
				900-mm Width	1100-mm Width	1400-mm Width	1650-mm Width	2200-mm Width
2.3	13	177	280	2.36 × 2.64	2.76 × 3.04	3.36 × 3.64	3.86 × 4.14	4.96 × 5.24
2.4	14	172	280	2.36 × 2.64	2.76 × 3.04	3.36 × 3.64	3.86 × 4.14	4.96 × 5.24
2.5	14	179	280	2.36 × 2.64	2.76 × 3.04	3.36 × 3.64	3.86 × 4.14	4.96 × 5.24
2.6	15	174	280	2.64 × 2.64	3.04 × 3.04	3.64 × 3.64	4.14 × 4.14	5.24 × 5.24
2.7	15	180	280	2.64 × 2.64	3.04 × 3.04	3.64 × 3.64	4.14 × 4.14	5.24 × 5.24
2.8	16	175	280	2.64 × 2.64	3.04 × 3.04	3.64 × 3.64	4.14 × 4.14	5.24 × 5.24
2.9	17	171	280	2.64 × 2.92	3.04 × 3.32	3.64 × 3.92	4.14 × 4.42	5.24 × 5.52
3.0	17	177	280	2.64 × 2.92	3.04 × 3.32	3.64 × 3.92	4.14 × 4.42	5.24 × 5.52
3.1	18	173	280	2.64 × 2.92	3.04 × 3.32	3.64 × 3.92	4.14 × 4.42	5.24 × 5.52
3.2	18	178	280	2.64 × 2.92	3.04 × 3.32	3.64 × 3.92	4.14 × 4.42	5.24 × 5.52
3.3	19	174	280	2.92 × 2.92	3.32 × 3.32	3.92 × 3.92	4.42 × 4.42	5.52 × 5.52
3.4	19	179	280	2.92 × 2.92	3.32 × 3.32	3.92 × 3.92	4.42 × 4.42	5.52 × 5.52
3.5	20	175	280	2.92 × 2.92	3.32 × 3.32	3.92 × 3.92	4.42 × 4.42	5.52 × 5.52
3.6	20	180	280	2.92 × 2.92	3.32 × 3.32	3.92 × 3.92	4.42 × 4.42	5.52 × 5.52
3.7	21	177	280	2.92 × 3.20	3.32 × 3.60	3.92 × 4.20	4.42 × 4.70	5.52 × 5.80
3.8	22	173	280	2.92 × 3.20	3.32 × 3.60	3.92 × 4.20	4.42 × 4.70	5.52 × 5.80
3.9	22	178	280	2.92 × 3.20	3.32 × 3.60	3.92 × 4.20	4.42 × 4.70	5.52 × 5.80
4.0	23	174	280	3.20 × 3.20	3.60 × 3.60	4.20 × 4.20	4.70 × 4.70	5.80 × 5.80
4.1	23	179	280	3.20 × 3.20	3.60 × 3.60	4.20 × 4.20	4.70 × 4.70	5.80 × 5.80
4.2	24	175	280	3.20 × 3.20	3.60 × 3.60	4.20 × 4.20	4.70 × 4.70	5.80 × 5.80
4.3	24	180	280	3.20 × 3.20	3.60 × 3.60	4.20 × 4.20	4.70 × 4.70	5.80 × 5.80
4.4	25	176	280	3.20 × 3.48	3.60 × 3.88	4.20 × 4.48	4.70 × 4.98	5.80 × 6.08
4.5	25	180	280	3.20 × 3.48	3.60 × 3.88	4.20 × 4.48	4.70 × 4.98	5.80 × 6.08
4.8	27	178	280	3.48 × 3.48	3.88 × 3.88	4.48 × 4.48	4.98 × 4.98	6.08 × 6.08
5.1	29	176	280	3.48 × 3.76	3.88 × 4.16	4.48 × 4.76	4.98 × 5.26	6.08 × 6.36
5.4	30	180	280	3.48 × 3.76	3.88 × 4.16	4.48 × 4.76	4.98 × 5.26	6.08 × 6.36
5.7	32	179	280	3.76 × 3.76	4.16 × 4.16	4.76 × 4.76	5.26 × 5.26	6.36 × 6.36
6.0	34	177	280	3.76 × 4.04	4.16 × 4.44	4.76 × 5.04	5.26 × 5.54	6.36 × 6.64
6.3	35	180	280	4.04 × 4.04	4.44 × 4.44	5.04 × 5.04	5.54 × 5.54	6.64 × 6.64
6.6	37	179	280	4.04 × 4.32	4.44 × 4.72	5.04 × 5.32	5.54 × 5.82	6.64 × 6.92
6.9	39	177	280	4.32 × 4.32	4.72 × 4.72	5.32 × 5.32	5.82 × 5.82	6.92 × 6.92
7.2	40	180	280	4.32 × 4.32	4.72 × 4.72	5.32 × 5.32	5.82 × 5.82	6.92 × 6.92
7.4	42	177	280	4.32 × 4.60	4.72 × 5.00	5.32 × 5.60	5.82 × 6.10	6.92 × 7.20

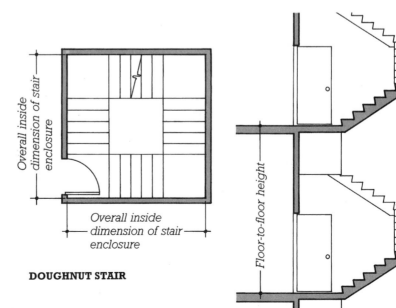

DOUGHNUT STAIR

DESIGNING WITH HEIGHT AND AREA LIMITATIONS

■■■■■■
HEIGHT
AND
AREA
LIMITATIONS

This section will help you determine which Construction Types are legally permitted for a building of a given height and area under the model building codes.

HEIGHT AND AREA LIMITATIONS

All building codes place limitations on building heights and areas in relation to the type of construction employed and the use or uses to which the building will be put. This is done in order to assure a minimum standard of fire safety for the occupants of the building and surrounding buildings. Height and area limitations, because they dictate the types of construction from which the designer may choose for a given building massing, have the largest impact on building design of any building code provisions. They often cause the designer to mass the building differently than might have been done otherwise, simply to enable it to be built using the most economical construction system possible.

Though similar in their approaches to limiting building height and area, the model building codes are different in detail. To the maximum extent possible, these differences have been minimized in the following height and area tables by presenting the data

Use these indexes to find the height and area limitations table for the building code and use group you are working with.

from the codes in a unified format, so that the designer may work as readily with one code as with the other. The authors have adopted the names "3-Hour," "2-Hour," and so on, for the Construction Types. These names· are based on the required fire resistance ratings of the structural loadbearing frame in each Type and are used to overcome inconsistencies in nomenclature between the codes. In addition, the adjustments permitted in each code for allowable area and height due to number of stories

and use of sprinklers have been precalculated for instant reference.

One difference between the codes that was not possible to resolve relates to the determination of allowable area. For the International Building Code, the tabulated values are for the *total area for all floors of the building combined.* For the National Building Code of Canada, the tabulated values are for the *area of any single floor.* When working with these tables, be sure to apply the indicated values appropriately.

INTERNATIONAL BUILDING CODE

See pages 7–10 for more information on Occupancy Groups in the International Building Code.

Each code has seemingly endless exceptions to its own basic height and area limitations. The most important exceptions deal with height and area increases permitted in exchange for approved automatic sprinkler systems and excess street frontage. The increases for sprinklered buildings have been incorporated fully into the tables, while the frontage increases are tabulated prominently in the accompanying notes. Other important exceptions have been noted in the text accompanying each table. A few exceptions are so complex that they could not reasonably be digested into these pages; for these you are directed to the code itself by notes accompanying the appropriate tables. Some exceptions were deemed by the authors to be so minor as not to warrant their inclusion here. For this reason, you must carry out a thorough investigation of the building code itself as a building design progresses into its developmental stage.

The following pages provide information on a number of topics closely related to determining the allowable height and area of a building. Pages 300–301 explain how the codes address buildings that contain more than one use. Page 302 discusses fire walls, which may be used to subdivide a large building into multiple smaller ones, each of which is considered a separate building. And page 303 provides guidelines for the incorporation of mezzanines and atriums into the height and area calculations for a building.

Listings of typical construction systems that satisfy the requirements for each Construction Type are presented on pages 304–315. These will be helpful in relating the information in the tables of height and area limitations to specific construction materials and framing systems.

NATIONAL BUILDING CODE OF CANADA

Occupancy Group	Page
A-1: Assembly, Theaters	376–377
A-2: Assembly, Miscellaneous	378–379
A-3: Assembly, Arenas	380–381
A-4: Assembly, Open-Air	382–383
B-1: Care or Detention, Restrained	384–385
B-2: Care or Detention, Unrestrained	386–387
C: Residential	388–389
D: Business and Personal Services	390–391
E: Mercantile	392–393
F-1: Industrial, High-Hazard	394–395
F-2: Industrial, Medium-Hazard	396–397
F-3: Industrial, Low-Hazard	398–399
F-3: Open-Air Garages	400–401

See pages 11–13 for more information about Occupancy Groups in the National Building Code of Canada.

A single project often incorporates more than one use—for example, retail space on the ground floor of an office building; restaurants, bars, and meeting rooms in a hotel; or parking garages beneath commercial or residential buildings. Use the following guidelines for preliminary design of such mixed-use buildings.

INTERNATIONAL BUILDING CODE

When two distinct uses are combined in one building, the International Building Code recognizes these mixed uses as either *Nonseparated* or *Separated*. In Nonseparated uses, there are no divisions between occupancies, and building height and area limitations are determined for the whole building by applying the requirements of the more restrictive occupancy. Within each use area, egress and other limitations are applied according to the requirements of that particular occupancy.

Separated uses are divided from one another by fire separations, which may include fire-resistant walls, fire doors or other rated openings, and fire-resistant floor/ceiling assemblies. The degree of fire resistance required for such separations may vary from 1 to 4 hours, depending on the relative hazard of the uses being separated and, in some cases, may be further modified based on the presence of a sprinkler system. For occupancies other than high-hazard industrial or storage uses, a 2-hour separation for nonsprinklered buildings, or 1-hour for sprinklered buildings, may be assumed for preliminary purposes. Certain specific mixed-use exceptions are also permitted without any separation, including:

• Commercial kitchens and the Group A-2 Assembly dining areas they serve

• Group A-3 Assembly areas less than 750 ft^2 (70 m^2) and any other adjacent use

• Group A-3 Assembly areas of any size accessory to an Educational use

• Group A-3 religious auditoriums and religious educational rooms

Other uses, such as H-1 High-Hazard, may not be mixed with other uses under any circumstances, and some uses may be mixed only in limited ways. For more information, consult the code.

In Separated Uses, each use area is required to conform to the height limitations for its occupancy classification. For example, in a 4-story building containing two Separated Uses, an occupancy type restricted to two floors in height may be located only on the first or second floors, whereas an occupancy permitted to be 4 stories in height can be located on any of the first through fourth floors. Where an entire floor contains only a single use, the floor area is limited by the area restrictions for that occupancy type. Where a floor shares two or more separated occupancies, floor area is limited through a proportional calculation of the combined areas as follows:

Step 1: For each use, divide the actual area by the area allowed by the code for that use to get a decimal fraction.

Step 2: Add the fractional results for all use areas on the floor plate.

Step 3: The sum total must not exceed 1.

For example, assume that one floor of a university science center has a 5000-sq-ft auditorium space classified as an Assembly A-3 occupancy, and 10,000 sq ft of classroom space classified as a Business B occupancy. For the proposed construction type, the code permits 11,550 sq ft for Group A-3 and 19,800 sq ft for Group B. For each use, we divide the actual area by the permitted area:

$$5000 \text{ ft}^2 / 11{,}500 \text{ ft}^2 = 0.43, \text{ and}$$
$$10{,}000 \text{ ft}^2 / 19{,}800 \text{ ft}^2 = 0.51$$

Then we sum the fractions:

$$0.43 + 0.51 = 0.94$$

Because 0.94 is less than 1, this combination of mixed-use areas is permitted.

In some cases, an occupancy that is minor in extent may be treated as an Accessory or Incidental use. A use area is considered Accessory when it occupies less than 10% of the area of any floor. In this case, the Accessory use need not be separated from the primary use, and building height, area, and egress restrictions are governed solely by the primary use. Certain occupancies, such as High-Hazard, may not be treated as Accessory.

Incidental uses are also considered minor in relation to some other use, but because of their higher degree of hazard, are required to maintain some measure of added fire protection or separation between the two uses. Except for the required protection or separation, all other restrictions are governed by the primary use. Examples of incidental uses include:

• Furnace and boiler rooms with equipment over a certain size

• Paint shops, laundry rooms, or storage rooms more than 100 sq ft (9 m^2)

• Laboratories or vocational shops located in Group E or I-2 occupancies

• Waste and linen collection rooms of more than 100 sq ft (9 m^2)

For a complete list of incidental uses and their requirements, consult the code.

MIXED-USE BUILDINGS

Parking Garages and Mixed-Use Occupancies

The International Building Code recognizes a number of circumstances in which parking occurring below other occupancies may be treated in unique ways, as summarized below. For more information, consult the code.

When a single-story enclosed parking garage used for the storage of private motor vehicles occurs below a Group A occupancy with an assembly space not exceeding an occupant load of 300, or under a Group B, M, or R occupancy, the two occupancies may be treated as separate buildings for the purposes of determining limitations in area, number of stories, type of construction, and placement of fire walls, provided that they are separated by a horizontal 3-hour fire assembly. Building height limitations are applied to the combined structure and are based on the least resistant construction type involved.

When a single-story enclosed parking garage used for the storage of private motor vehicles occurs below an open parking garage, the two garages may be treated as separate buildings for the purposes of determining construction type only, provided that the two uses are separated by a horizontal assembly with a fire-resistance rating equal to that required for a floor assembly in the enclosed garage, and the enclosed garage is of noncombustible construction with a fire-resistance rating equal to or greater than that of the open garage above. Building area limitations are determined as for a sep-

arated mixed-use occupancy (see page 300) and building height and story limitations are based on the height and area requirements for open parking garages (see pages 370–371).

When a single-story open or enclosed parking garage occurs below a Group R occupancy, the number of stories used to determine the required construction type of the Group R occupancy may be measured from the floor above the parking garage, provided that the two occupancies are separated by a horizontal assembly with a fire-resistance rating of at least 2 hours and at least equal to the floor assembly requirements for the parking garage construction type, and the garage is of 2-Hour or 3-Hour Noncombustible construction.

When an open parking garage occurs below a Group A, I, B, M, or R occupancy, the height and area limitations for the upper portion of the building should be read from the Height and Area Tables corresponding to the occupancy of that portion. The height of the building in both number of stories and feet is measured from the ground plane and includes both the garage and the upper occupancy. The height and area of the garage are limited according to the tables on pages 370–371. The two occupancies must be separated according to the code requirements for separate uses, and construction type should be determined for each occupancy separately according to the code requirements for that occupancy, except that structural members in the lower garage portion should be protected according to the more restrictive requirements of either occupancy.

NATIONAL BUILDING CODE OF CANADA

Under the National Building Code of Canada, multiple use areas within one building must generally be segregated from one another by fire separations, which may include fire-resistant walls, fire doors or other rated openings, and fire-resistant floor/ceiling assemblies. The degree of fire resistance required for such separations generally varies from 1 to 3 hours and must be determined by consulting the code. In multiple use buildings, the height and area requirements of the most restrictive occupancy are applied to the whole building. Certain mixtures of uses are not permitted under any circumstances. For example, a Group F-1 occupancy may not occur within a building with Group A, B, or C occupancies, and not more than one suite or residential occupancy can occur within a building with a Group F-2 occupancy.

In some cases, use areas of relatively small size may be treated as subsidiary to another occupancy. In buildings of 3 stories or fewer in height, having an area not exceeding 600 m² (6460 sq ft), and containing Group C, D, E, or F-3 occupancies, a use that does not exceed 10% of the total area of a given floor need not be considered as a separate use from the major use for the purpose of determining allowable building height and area.

Under the model building codes, each portion of a building separated from the remainder of the building by fire walls may be considered as a distinct building for purposes of calculating allowable heights and areas. This allows a building of virtually any Construction Type to be unlimited in horizontal extent so long as it is subdivided by fire walls into compartments that are each of a size that does not exceed the height and area limitations prescribed by the building code.

A fire wall must be constructed so that it will remain stable even if the construction on one side or the other of it collapses during a fire. It must extend through the roof to a parapet wall, except that in some instances a fire wall may terminate at the underside of a noncombustible roof. Fire walls may be built of masonry or concrete, or of gypsum plaster or gypsum wallboard supported by noncombustible framing. The required fire-resistance rating for a fire wall may be from one to four hours, depending on the occupancy of the building, the construction type, and the applicable building code.

Openings through a fire wall are restricted to a minor percentage of the length of the wall and must be protected with self-closing fire doors. Preliminary guidelines for fire wall fire-resistance rating requirements, see pages 304–307. For more detailed specifications for fire walls and their openings, consult the code. For purposes of showing a fire wall on preliminary design drawings, a wall thickness of 6 to 8 in. (150 to 200 mm) and a parapet height of 32 in. (800 mm) are generally sufficient.

MEZZANINES AND ATRIUMS

MEZZANINES

A mezzanine is an intermediate platform located between the floor and ceiling of a room. Under both model building codes, a mezzanine is not counted as a story and its area does not contribute toward floor area in determining the maximum allowable height in stories and area of the building. However, the area of the mezzanine is considered when calculating occupant loads. Although detailed requirements vary somewhat between the codes, a preliminary design for a mezzanine may be prepared according to the following simplified guidelines:

• Mezzanines must be mostly open to the room below within which they occur, without enclosing walls or partitions. An enclosed portion that does not exceed 10% of the mezzanine area and, in the case of the International Building Code, having an occupant load not exceeding 10 persons, is generally permitted.

• The International Building Code limits the mezzanine area to one-third of the room within which it is located. The National Building Code of Canada generally limits the area of a mezzanine to 500 m^2 (5380 sq ft) and 40% of the story on which it occurs. There may be more than one mezzanine on a single story as long as the aggregate total area does not exceed these limits.

• The International Building Code requires the fire resistance of the construction of a mezzanine to be consistent with that of the construction type of the floor on which it is located. In some cases, the National Building Code of Canada permits mezzanines with a lesser fire-resistance rating. See pages 306–307 for more information.

• Most mezzanines require two independent means of egress. These exits may be by way of open stairways.

ATRIUMS

An atrium is a roofed, occupied opening through three or more floor levels other than those provided for exit stairways, elevator hoistways, escalators, shafts, and the like.

International Building Code

Atriums constructed under the requirements of the International Building Code must conform to the following:

• A building containing an atrium must be sprinklered throughout, except that areas adjacent to or above the atrium need not be sprinklered if separated from the atrium by a 2-hour rated assembly.

• Atrium floor areas must be used for low-fire-hazard uses only, unless the atrium floor areas themselves are sprinklered.

• An atrium must be provided with a mechanical smoke control system designed to protect occupants from smoke and toxic gases during a fire emergency.

• In general, an atrium must be separated from adjacent spaces by 1-hour rated assemblies. Up to three adjacent floors may be open to an atrium, provided that the combined area of the atrium and open floors is included in the design of the required smoke control system. Walls separating atriums from adjacent spaces may also include windows or be constructed of glass, provided that the glass is protected by an automatic sprinkler system that will completely wet the surface of the glass when activated.

• Except at the lowest level, the portion of any exit access travel within an atrium is limited to 150 ft (46 m).

National Building Code of Canada

Under the National Building Code of Canada, atriums, referred to as *interconnected floor spaces,* must conform to the following requirements:

• Buildings with interconnected floor spaces must be sprinklered throughout and must be of noncombustible or heavy timber construction.

• Interconnected floor spaces must be separated from adjacent areas by fire separations with a fire-resistance rating not less than the rating required for floor assemblies.

• A mechanical smoke exhaust system serving the interconnected floor spaces is required.

• The quantities of combustible contents located in an interconnected floor space are limited. See the code for details.

• An interconnected floor space is exempt from the above requirements when serving the first floor of a building and only one adjacent floor above or below, is part of Occupancy Groups A-1, A-2, A-3, D, E, or F-3, is in a building not more than half the maximum area permitted by the code's height and area limitations, and the openings connecting the floors are limited to stairways, escalators, or moving walks only. An interconnected floor space in a Care or Detention, Restrained Group B-1 Occupancy connecting only two adjacent stories is also exempt from the above requirements. Sleeping areas part of a Group B-2 occupancy may not be part of an interconnected floor space.

CONSTRUCTION TYPES

INTERNATIONAL BUILDING CODE

This section summarizes the fire-resistance rating and construction requirements for Construction Types in the International Building Code. Once you have determined an appropriate Construction Type for a project, based on the Height and Area Tables on pages 320–373, use this section to relate this information to systems of construction. The table on these two facing pages consolidates and simplifies fire-resistance requirements for each Construction Type. The pages following this chart define each Construction Type in terms of specific structural systems, materials, and minimum thicknesses of components necessary to meet the required minimum fire-resistance rating. The values in the table below may be modified as follows:

• Sprinklers: Where sprinklers are not otherwise required by the code, they may be used to permit Unprotected Noncombustible or Combustible construction in lieu of 1-Hour construction. In this case, height and area requirements for the building are based on unsprinklered 1-Hour construction and assemblies are protected according to the requirements for Unprotected construction.

• Exterior Bearing Walls: Unprotected openings are permitted in rated exterior walls, depending on proximity to property lines or other buildings. See the code for details.

• Interior Bearing Walls: Interior bearing walls supporting roofs only may be 1-hour rated maximum.

• Fire Walls: Fire walls must be 4-hour rated when separating Group H-1 or H-2 occupancies, 2-hour rated for F-2, S-2, R-3, and R-4 occupancies, and 3-hour rated for all

CONSTRUCTION TYPE INTERNATIONAL BUILDING CODE NOMENCLATURE	Noncombustible			
	3-Hour (page 308)	2-Hour (page 309)	1-Hour (page 310)	Unprotected (page 311)
	Type I-A	Type I-B	Type II-A	Type II-B
STRUCTURAL FRAME INCLUDING COLUMNS, GIRDERS, TRUSSES	3	2	1	0
EXTERIOR BEARING WALLS	3	2	1	0
INTERIOR BEARING WALLS	3	2	1	0
FLOOR CONSTRUCTION	2	2	1	0
ROOF CONSTRUCTION	1½	1	1	0
PARTY WALLS AND FIRE WALLS	2–4	2–4	2–4	2–4
ENCLOSURES OF EXITS, EXIT HALLWAYS, EXIT STAIRWAYS, SHAFT ENCLOSURES	2	2	2 hours connecting 4 stories or more, 1 hour connecting fewer than 4 stories	
EXIT ACCESS CORRIDORS	0–1	0–1	0–1	0–1
TENANT SPACE SEPARATIONS	1	1	1	1
DWELLING UNIT AND GUEST ROOM SEPARATIONS	1	1	1	1
OTHER NONBEARING PARTITIONS	Noncombustible			

CONSTRUCTION TYPES

others. For more information see page 302.

• Roof Construction: Roof structures 20 ft (6 m) or more above the floor below may be unprotected construction in all occupancies except F-1, H, M, and S-1. Heavy timber construction is permitted wherever a 1-Hour Noncombustible or Combustible roof structure is required.

• Exit Enclosures: Exit enclosures are not required for dwelling unit stairways, stairways not required as exits, stairways in open parking garages, exits in Occupancy Group A-5 open arenas, and stairways serving only one adjacent floor and providing not more than 50% of the required egress. Horizontal passages that are part or an exit should match the fire-resistance rating of the stairway to which they connect.

• Corridors: Corridor separations must be 1-hour rated within all H-1, H-2, H-3, I-1, and I-3 occupancies, within all H-4 and H-5 occupancies when serving an occupant load greater than 30, within all R occupancies when serving an occupant load greater than 10, and within all A, B, E, F, M, S, and U occupancies when unsprinklered and serving an occupant load of greater than 30. Otherwise, corridor separations may be unrated. Corridor separations are not required to be rated within dwelling units or guest rooms, within open-air garages, within Group E occupancies when each classroom has direct exit access to the outside, or within certain subdivided areas within Occupancies I-1 and I-3.

• Dwelling Unit Separations: Dwelling Unit and Guest Room separations may be ½-hour rated in any Unprotected construction system, provided that the building is sprinklered throughout.

	Combustible					
	Mill (page 313)	Ordinary		Wood Light Frame		
		1-Hour (page 313)	Unprotected (page 312)	1-Hour (page 315)	Unprotected (page 315)	
CONSTRUCTION TYPE						
INTERNATIONAL BUILDING CODE NOMENCLATURE	Type IV-HT	Type III-A	Type III-B	Type V-A	Type V-B	
STRUCTURAL FRAME INCLUDING COLUMNS, GIRDERS, TRUSSES	Heavy Timber	1	0	1	0	
EXTERIOR BEARING WALLS	2	2	2	1	0	
INTERIOR BEARING WALLS	1 or Heavy Timber	1	0	1	0	
FLOOR CONSTRUCTION	Heavy Timber	1	0	1	0	
ROOF CONSTRUCTION	Heavy Timber	1	0	1	0	
PARTY WALLS AND FIRE WALLS	2–4	2–4	2–4	2–4	2–4	
ENCLOSURES OF EXITS, EXIT HALLWAYS, EXIT STAIRWAYS, SHAFT ENCLOSURES	2 hours connecting 4 stories or more, 1 hour connecting fewer than 4 stories					
EXIT ACCESS CORRIDORS	0–1	0–1	0–1	0–1	0–1	
TENANT SPACE SEPARATIONS	1	1	1	1	1	
DWELLING UNIT AND GUEST ROOM SEPARATIONS	1	1	1	1	1	
OTHER NONBEARING PARTITIONS	0	0	0	0	0	

HEIGHT AND AREA LIMITATIONS

NATIONAL BUILDING CODE OF CANADA

This section summarizes the fire-resistance rating and construction requirements for Construction Types in the National Building Code of Canada. Once you have determined an appropriate Construction Type for a project, based on the Height and Area Tables on pages 376–401, use this section to relate this information to systems of construction. The table on these two facing pages consolidates and simplifies fire-resistance requirements for each Construction Type. The pages following this chart define each Construction Type in terms of specific structural systems, materials, and minimum thicknesses of components necessary to meet the required minimum fire-resistance rating. The values in the table below may be modified as follows:

• Heavy Timber construction: Heavy Timber construction is an acceptable substitute for any building requiring Combustible ¾-Hour (or less) construction.

• Exterior Bearing Walls: Unprotected openings are permitted in rated exterior walls, depending on proximity to property lines or other buildings. See the code for details.

• Fire Walls: Fire walls must be of masonry or concrete. A 4-hour fire-resistance rating is required when separating Group E, F-1, or F-2 occupancies, and a 2-hour rating for other occupancies. In Group C Residential occupancy buildings 3 stories or less in height and not exceeding 600 m² (6460 sq ft) in area, party walls may be constructed as 1-hour rated fire separations. For more information see page 302.

• Loadbearing Columns, Walls, and Arches: In some cases, buildings classified as ¾-Hour Combustible construction for the purpose of determining height and area limitations must be constructed with noncombustible columns, walls, and arches. Consult the code for details.

• Roof Construction: Roofs supporting any occupancy must be con-

NATIONAL BUILDING CODE OF CANADA

CONSTRUCTION TYPE	Noncombustible			
	2-Hour (page 309)	1-Hour (page 310)	¾-Hour (page 314)	Unprotected (page 311)
LOADBEARING COLUMNS, WALLS AND ARCHES	2	1	¾	0
FLOOR CONSTRUCTION	2	1	¾	0
MEZZANINES	1	1	0	0
ROOF CONSTRUCTION	0–1	0–1	0–¾	0
PARTY WALLS AND FIRE WALLS	2–4	2–4	2–4	2–4
ENCLOSURES OF EXITS, EXIT HALLWAYS, EXIT STAIRWAYS	2	1	¾	¾
EXIT ACCESS CORRIDORS	1	1	¾	¾
SUITE SEPARATIONS	1	1	¾	¾
DWELLING UNIT AND GUEST ROOM SEPARATIONS	1	1	¾	¾
OTHER NONBEARING PARTITIONS	Noncombustible			

CONSTRUCTION TYPES

structed to the fire-resistance rating requirements for a floor assembly. Roofs of Heavy Timber construction are a permitted substitution for most buildings 1 or 2 stories in height, of any area, of any construction type, and sprinklered throughout. Arena roofs supporting only roof loads and 6 m (20 ft) or more above the floor may be Unprotected construction. Roof assembly rating requirements sometimes vary with area or height limitations.

• Corridors: Corridor separations may be unrated when the floor area is sprinklered throughout and the corridor does not serve a Group B Care and Detention, or Group C Residential occupancy. In buildings other than Group C Residential occupancy that are 3 stories or less in height and not exceeding 600 m² (6460 sq ft) in area, corridor separations may be unrated, provided that the floor area is sprinklered.

• Dwelling Unit Separations: Dwelling unit separations may have a 45-minute fire-resistance rating when the floor assembly above is permitted to have a rating of 45 minutes or less, or, if there is no floor assembly above, if the floor assembly below is permitted to have a rating of 45-minutes or less. In buildings 3 stories or fewer in height and not exceeding 600 m² (6460 sq ft) in area, no separation is required between floors within a dwelling unit.

Combustible				CONSTRUCTION TYPE
1-Hour (page 314)	Mill (page 312)	3/4-Hour (page 314)	Unprotected (page 315)	
2	Heavy Timber	¾	0	LOADBEARING COLUMNS, WALLS AND ARCHES
1	Heavy Timber	¾	0	FLOOR CONSTRUCTION
1	Heavy Timber	0–¾	0	MEZZANINES
0–1	Heavy Timber	0–¾	0	ROOF CONSTRUCTION
2–4	2–4	2–4	2–4	PARTY WALLS AND FIRE WALLS
1	¾	¾	¾	ENCLOSURES OF EXITS, EXIT HALLWAYS, EXIT STAIRWAYS
1	¾	¾	¾	EXIT ACCESS CORRIDORS
1	¾	¾	¾	SUITE SEPARATIONS
1	¾	¾	¾	DWELLING UNIT AND GUEST ROOM SEPARATIONS
0	0	0	0	OTHER NONBEARING PARTITIONS

3-HOUR NONCOMBUSTIBLE CONSTRUCTION

3-Hour Noncombustible construction requires a fire-resistance rating of 2 hours for floor construction and 3 hours for columns and bearing walls.

■ **Structural Steel** columns, beams, joists, and decking must be protected to these values with applied fireproofing materials or an appropriately fire-resistive ceiling of plaster, gypsum board, or fibrous panels (see pages 92–105).

■ **Reinforced Concrete** columns must be at least 12 in. (305 mm) in dimension, and loadbearing walls must be at least 6 in. (152 mm) thick. Floor slabs must be at least 5 in. (127 mm) thick. Concrete one-way and two-way joist systems (ribbed slabs and waffle slabs) with slabs thinner than 5 in. (127 mm) between joists require protection with applied fireproofing materials or an appropriately fire-resistive ceiling of plaster, gypsum board, or fibrous panels (see pages 107–123).

■ **Posttensioned Concrete** floor slabs must be at least 5 in. (127 mm) thick (see pages 114–123).

■ **Precast Concrete** columns must be at least 10 in. (254 mm) in dimension, and beams at least 7 in. (178 mm) wide. Loadbearing wall panels must be at least 6 (152 mm) thick. Solid slabs may not be less than 5 in. (127 mm) thick. Hollow core slabs must be at least 8 in. (203 mm) deep and may be used without a topping. Double and single tees require applied fireproofing materials or an appropriately fire-resistive ceiling of plaster, gypsum board, or fibrous panels, unless a concrete topping 3.25 in. (83 mm) is poured (see pages 125–135).

■ **Brick Masonry** loadbearing walls must be at least 6 in. (152 mm) thick. Vaults and domes must be at least 8 in. (203 mm) deep with a rise not less than one-twelfth the span (see pages 74–75).

■ **Concrete Masonry** loadbearing walls must be at least 8 in. (203 mm) thick. Depending on the composition and design of the masonry unit, applied plaster or stucco facings may also be required (see pages 82–83).

Fire-resistive requirements for non-loadbearing walls and partitions are summarized on pages 304–307.

CONSTRUCTION TYPES

2-HOUR NONCOMBUSTIBLE CONSTRUCTION

2-Hour Noncombustible construction requires a fire-resistance rating of 2 hours for floor construction, columns, and bearing walls.

■ **Structural Steel** columns, beams, joists, and decking must be protected to these values with applied fireproofing materials or an appropriately fire-resistive ceiling of plaster, gypsum board, or fibrous panels (see pages 92–105).

■ **Reinforced Concrete** columns must be at least 10 in. (254 mm) in dimension, and loadbearing walls must be at least 5 in. (127 mm) thick. Floor slabs must be at least 5 in. (127 mm) thick. Concrete one-way and two-way joist systems (ribbed slabs and waffle slabs) with slabs thinner than 5 in. (127 mm) between joists require protection with applied fireproofing materials or an appropriately fire-resistive ceiling of plaster, gypsum board, or fibrous panels (see pages 107–123).

■ **Posttensioned Concrete** floor slabs must be at least 5 in. (127 mm) thick (see pages 114–123).

■ **Precast Concrete** columns must be at least 8 in. (203 mm) in dimension, and beams at least 7 in. (178 mm) wide. Loadbearing wall panels must be at least 5 in. (127 mm) thick. Solid slabs may not be less than 5 in. (127 mm) thick. Hollow core slabs must be at least 8 in. (203 mm) deep and may be used without a topping. Double and single tees require applied fireproofing materials or an appropriately fire-resistive ceiling of plaster, gypsum board, or fibrous panels, unless a concrete topping 3.25 in. (83 mm) thick is poured (see pages 125–135).

■ **Brick Masonry** loadbearing walls must be at least 6 in. (152 mm) thick. Vaults and domes must be at least 8 in. (203 mm) deep with a rise not less than one-twelfth the span (see pages 74–75).

■ **Concrete Masonry** loadbearing walls must be at least 6 in. (152 mm) thick. Depending on the composition and design of the masonry unit, applied plaster or stucco facings may also be required (see pages 82–83).

Fire-resistive requirements for non-loadbearing walls and partitions are summarized on pages 304–307.

HEIGHT AND AREA LIMITATIONS

309

CONSTRUCTION TYPES

1-HOUR NONCOMBUSTIBLE CONSTRUCTION

1-Hour Noncombustible construction requires a fire-resistance rating of 1 hour for floor construction, columns, and bearing walls.

■ **Structural Steel** columns, beams, joists, and decking must be protected to these values with applied fireproofing materials or an appropriately fire-resistive ceiling of plaster, gypsum board, or fibrous panels (see pages 92–105).

■ **Light Gauge Steel** floor joists must be protected with a ceiling of two layers of ½-in. Type X gypsum board or its equivalent. Loadbearing walls framed with light gauge steel studs must be faced on both sides with single layers of ⅝-in. Type X gypsum board or its equivalent (see pages 88–91).

■ **Reinforced Concrete** columns must be at least 8 in. (203 mm) in dimension, and loadbearing walls must be at least 3.5 in. (89 mm) thick. Floor slabs must be at least 3.5 in. (89 mm) thick. Concrete one-way and two-way joist systems (ribbed slabs, skip-joist slabs, and waffle slabs) require protection with applied fireproofing materials or an appropriately fire-resistive ceiling of plaster, gypsum board, or acoustical panels unless the slab thickness is at least 3.5 in. between joists (see pages 107–123).

■ **Posttensioned Concrete** floor slabs must be at least 3.5 in. (89 mm) thick (see pages 114–123).

■ **Precast Concrete** columns must be at least 6 in. (152 mm) in dimension, and beams at least 4 in. (102 mm) wide. Loadbearing wall panels must be at least 3.5 (89 mm) thick. Solid slabs may not be less than 3.5 in. (89 mm) thick. Hollow core slabs must be at least 8 in. (203 mm) deep and may be used without a topping. Double and single tees require applied fireproofing materials or an appropriately fire-resistive ceiling of plaster, gypsum board, or acoustical panels unless a concrete topping 1.75 in. (44 mm) thick is poured (see pages 125–135).

■ **Brick Masonry** loadbearing walls must be at least 4 in. (102 mm) thick. Vaults and domes must be at least 4 in. (102 mm) deep with a rise not less than one-twelfth the span (see pages 74–75).

■ **Concrete Masonry** loadbearing walls must be at least 4 in. (102 mm) thick. Depending on the composition and design of the masonry unit, applied plaster or stucco facings may also be required (see pages 82–83).

Fire-resistive requirements for non-loadbearing walls and partitions are summarized on pages 304–307.

CONSTRUCTION TYPES

UNPROTECTED NONCOMBUSTIBLE CONSTRUCTION

Unprotected Noncombustible construction has no fire-resistive requirements for floor construction, columns, or bearing walls, except that they must be constructed of noncombustible materials.

■ **Structural Steel** columns, beams, joists, and decking may be used without applied fireproofing materials or fire-resistive ceilings (see pages 92–105).

■ **Light Gauge Steel Framing** may be used with minimum facings of gypsum board or its equivalent to brace the studs and joists against buckling (see pages 88–91).

■ **Reinforced Concrete** structures of all types may be designed to the minimum dimensions dictated by structural considerations, without need for applied fireproofing materials (see pages 107–123).

■ **Posttensioned Concrete** structures of all types may be designed to the minimum dimensions dictated by structural considerations, without need for applied fireproofing materials (see pages 114–123).

■ **Precast Concrete** structures of all types may be designed to the minimum dimensions dictated by structural considerations, without need for applied fireproofing materials (see pages 125–135).

■ **Masonry** structures of all types may be designed to the minimum dimensions dictated by structural considerations, without need for applied fireproofing materials (see pages 71–85).

Fire-resistive requirements for nonloadbearing walls and partitions are summarized on pages 304–307.

MILL CONSTRUCTION (HEAVY TIMBER)

Mill construction depends for its fire-resistive properties on timbers and decking whose thickness is such that they are slow to catch fire and burn. Either solid or glue laminated timbers and decking may be used. Thickness requirements vary slightly from code to code, but the following dimensions are appropriate for preliminary design purposes:

■ **Columns** supporting floor loads must be at least 8×8 nominal dimensions (7.5 × 7.5 in., or 184 × 184 mm). Columns supporting a roof and ceiling only may be no smaller than 6×8 (5.5 × 7.5 in., or 140 × 184 mm).

■ **Beams and Girders** supporting a floor must be at least 6×10 nominal dimensions (5.5 × 9.5 in., or 140 × 235 mm). If supporting a roof and ceiling only, they may be no smaller than 4×6 (3.5 × 5.5 in., or 89 × 140 mm).

■ **Trusses** must be made of members no smaller than 8×8 nominal dimensions (7.5 × 7.5 in., or 184 mm × 184 mm), except that roof trusses may be made up of members as small as 4×6 nominal dimensions (3.5 × 6.5 in., or 89 × 140 mm).

■ **Decking** for floors must consist nominally of 3-in, structural decking with a 1-in, finish floor laid at right angles on top (2.5 in. plus ¾ in., or 64 mm plus 19 mm). Roof decking may be nominally 2 in.

thick (actually 1.5 in., or 38 mm), or 1⅛-in. (29-mm) plywood.

■ **Exterior Walls** must be noncombustible; traditionally they have been made of loadbearing masonry. The degree of fire resistance required for exterior walls varies from zero to 4 hours depending on the occupancy of the building, the distance of the wall from the property line and adjacent buildings, and the applicable building code.

See pages 50–67 for structural information on the timber members of Mill construction and pages 71–85 for information on loadbearing walls. Fire-resistive requirements for nonloadbearing walls and partitions are summarized on pages 304–307.

ORDINARY CONSTRUCTION

So-called Ordinary construction consists of noncombustible exterior walls and an interior structure that is usually wood light framing but may be of metal or concrete.

■ **Interior Framing** members of wood may not be less than 2 in. nominal dimension (actual dimension 1.5 in., or 38 mm). Walls and partitions are framed with studs, floors with joists, and roofs with rafters or light trusses, usually at spacings of 16 or 24 in. (406 or 610 mm). In 1-Hour Ordinary construction, all roofs, loadbearing walls, and floors must have 1 hour of fire protection. In Unprotected Ordinary construction, no fire protection is required on these elements of the structure. One hour of protection may be provided on walls by applying ⅝-in. (16-mm) Type X gypsum board or its equivalent to each face of the studs. On ceilings, a layer of ⅝-in. Type X gypsum board or its equivalent is required for a 1-hour rating, assuming that the floor above consists of 1-in, nominal subflooring and 1-in. nominal finish flooring (actual dimensions ¾ in., or 19 mm, each).

■ **Exterior Walls** must be noncombustible; traditionally they have been made of loadbearing masonry. The degree of fire resistance required for exterior walls varies from zero to 4 hours depending on the occupancy of the building, the distance of the wall from the property line and adjacent buildings, and the applicable building code.

See pages 52–59 for structural information on the wood members of Ordinary construction and pages 71–85 for information on masonry loadbearing walls. Fire-resistive requirements for nonloadbearing walls and partitions are summarized on pages 304–307.

1-HOUR AND ¾-HOUR NONCOMBUSTIBLE OR COMBUSTIBLE CONSTRUCTION

1-Hour and ¾-Hour Noncombustible or Combustible construction are classifications established by the National Building Code of Canada. While the classifications are very broad, including any construction materials that will satisfy the requirements tabulated on pages 306–307, in practice they are most generally applied to light framing of wood or light gauge steel framing. Heavy Timber construction is also considered to be the equivalent of ¾-Hour construction under the National Building Code of Canada.

■ **Loadbearing Walls** framed with wood or light gauge steel studs may be given a 1-hour or ¾-hour fire-resistance rating by applying ⅝-in. (16-mm) Type X gypsum board or its equivalent to both faces of the framing, or by using ordinary ½-in, (13-mm) gypsum board or its equivalent on each face, and inserting a mineral fiber batt of certain minimum specifications in the cavity. Exterior walls framed with wood or steel studs and finished on the outside with wood sheathing and siding require an interior finish of ½-in (13-mm) gypsum board or its equivalent and the insertion of mineral fiber batts in the cavities.

■ **Ceilings below Floors and Roofs** framed with wood or metal require ⅝-in. (16-mm) Type X gypsum board or its equivalent to achieve a 1-hour or ¾-hour fire-resistance rating.

See pages 52–59 for structural information on wood light framing and pages 88–91 for information on light gauge steel framing. Fire-resistive requirements for nonload-bearing walls and partitions are summarized on pages 304–307.

CONSTRUCTION TYPES

WOOD LIGHT FRAME CONSTRUCTION

Floors, walls, and roofs of Wood Light Frame construction are framed with wood members not less than 2 in. in nominal thickness (actually 1.5 in., or 38 mm). These members are usually spaced at center-to-center distances of either 16 or 24 in. (406 or 610 mm) and covered with any of a very wide range of sheathing and finish materials.

■ **Unprotected Wood Light Frame Construction** allows the structure of the building to remain exposed or to be finished with materials that do not have a sufficient fire-resistance rating to satisfy a higher classification of construction, such as wood paneling or thin gypsum board.

■ **1-Hour Wood Light Frame Construction** requires that loadbearing walls and floors have 1-hour fire-resistance ratings. A 1-hour wall may be constructed of wood studs by applying ⅝-in. (16-mm) Type X gypsum board or its equivalent to each face of the studs. A floor with 1-in, nominal subflooring and finish flooring (actual dimensions ¾ in., or 19 mm each) has a 1-hour fire-resistance rating if it is finished below with a ceiling of ⅝-in. (16-mm) Type X gypsum board or its equivalent.

For structural information on Wood Light Frame construction, see pages 52–59. Fire-resistive requirements for nonloadbearing walls and partitions are summarized on pages 304–307.

HEIGHT AND AREA LIMITATIONS

315

▪▪▪▪▪▪▪▪
HEIGHT
AND
AREA
TABLES

This section provides simplified tables for determining the allowable building height and area for each Occupancy Group and model code.

HOW TO USE THE TABLES OF HEIGHT AND AREA LIMITATIONS FOR THE INTERNATIONAL BUILDING CODE

1. Be sure you are consulting the tables for the proper building code. If you are not sure which code you are working under, see pages 7, 12.

2. The Occupancy Group is given at the upper left-hand corner of the table. If you are not sure about the Occupancy Group into which your building falls, consult the indexes on pages 7–10.

3. Noncombustible Construction Types are tabulated on the left-hand page, combustible Construction Types on the right-hand page.

4. Each pair of columns represents one Construction Type. For specific information on the different materials and modes of construction that conform to that Construction Type, follow the page reference given here.

5. The paired columns tabulate height and area information for both sprinklered and unsprinklered buildings of each Construction Type.

6. The significance of the floor area numbers in the chart, which varies from one model code to another, is explained at the lower left-hand corner.

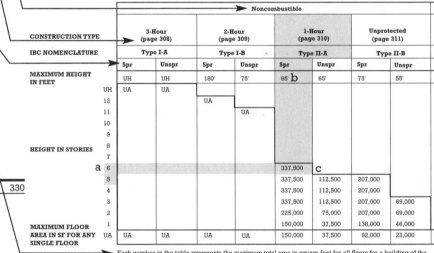

INTERNATIONAL BUILDING CODE

OCCUPANCY GROUP B: BUSINESS

Sprinklers

An approved sprinkler system is required for any Group B occupancy with:

• A floor having an occupant load of 30 or more located more than 55 ft (17 m) above grade

• Any story or basement greater than 1500 sq ft (139 m²) in area without openings to the exterior

• Most underground portions of the building where occupancy occurs more than 30 feet (9 m) below the lowest level of exit discharge

Unlimited Area Buildings

One- and two-story Occupancy B buildings may be of unlimited area when sprinklered throughout and surrounded on all sides by public ways or yards not less than 60 ft (18 m) in width.

Fire Walls

For multiplication of the allowable area by subdividing the building with fire walls, see page 302.

Basements

A single-story basement is not included in area calculations provided the basement area does not

exceed the area permitted for a one-story building.

Excess Frontage

If more than 25% of the building perimeter fronts on a street or open space at least 20 ft (6.1 m) wide that is accessible to firefighting vehicles, the tabulated area limitations below may be increased according to the following table. For example, for a building with half of its perimeter accessible to firefighting equipment via a space not less than 24 ft (7.3 m) wide, the allowable area increase is:

0.80% increase × 25% excess frontage = 20% total area increase.

OCCUPANCY GROUP B: BUSINESS

		Noncombustible						
CONSTRUCTION TYPE		3-Hour (page 308)		2-Hour (page 309)		1-Hour (page 310)		Unprotected (page 311)
IBC NOMENCLATURE		Type I-A		Type I-B		Type II-A		Type II-B
		Spr	Unspr	Spr	Unspr	Spr	Unspr	Spr	Unspr
MAXIMUM HEIGHT IN FEET		UH	UH	180'	75'	85' b	65'	75'	55'
	UH	UA	UA						
	12			UA					
	11				UA				
	10								
	9								
HEIGHT IN STORIES	8								
	7								
a	6					337,500			
	5					337,500	112,500	207,000	
	4					337,500	112,500	207,000	
	3					337,500	112,500	207,000	69,000
	2					225,000	75,000	207,000	69,000
	1					150,000	37,500	138,000	46,000
MAXIMUM FLOOR AREA IN SF FOR ANY SINGLE FLOOR	UA	UA	UA	UA	UA	150,000	37,500	92,000	23,000

Each number in the table represents the maximum total area in square feet for all floors for a building of the indicated story height.

Key to Abbreviations
UA	Unlimited area	Spr	With approved sprinkler system
UH	Unlimited height	Unspr	Without approved sprinkler system
NP	Not permitted		

330

INTERNATIONAL BUILDING CODE

INTERNATIONAL BUILDING CODE

Width of Frontage	Percent Area Increase for Each 1% of Frontage* in Excess of 25%
20' (6.1 m)	0.67%
22' (6.7 m)	0.73%
24' (7.3 m)	0.80%
26' (7.9 m)	0.87%
28' (8.5 m)	0.93%
30' (9.1 m) or wider	1.00%

*Intermediate values may be interpolated.

Measurements

Height is measured from the average finished ground level adjoining the building to the average level of the highest roof. Floor area is measured within exterior walls or exterior walls and fire walls, exclusive of courtyards.

Further Information

For information on Occupancy Group classifications, see page 7. For information on mixed-used buildings, see page 300. For information on which code to consult, see pages 7, 11.

Unit Conversions

1 ft = 304.8 mm, 1 sq ft = 0.0929 m².

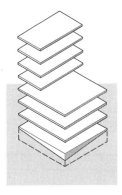

7. As an example of the use of this chart, a sprinklered building of Occupancy Group B, 1-Hour construction, under the International Building Code, may be no more than

a. 6 stories, or

b. 85 ft tall, whichever is less,

c. with a total floor area no larger than 337,500 sq ft.

8. As another example, if we wish to construct a 5-story unsprinklered building with 22,000 sq ft per floor, or 110,000 sq ft total area, we must use 1-Hour construction as a minimum. Looking to the right along the same row of the chart, we see that the addition of sprinklers would allow us to use Unprotected, Ordinary, or Mill construction. We also note that by slightly reducing the total building area to 108,000 sq ft, unsprinklered Mill construction would be permitted. By following the page references at the heads of these columns, we can determine exactly what each of these Construction Types is and proceed to preliminary configuration and sizing of the structural system we select.

Combustible										CONSTRUCTION TYPE
Ordinary				Mill		Wood Light Frame				
1-Hour (page 313)		Unprotected (page 313)		(page 312)		1-Hour (page 315)		Unprotected (page 315)		
Type III-A		Type III-B		Type IV-HT		Type V-A		Type V-B		IBC NOMENCLATURE
Spr	Unspr	Spr	Unspr	Spr	Unspr	Spr	Unspr	Spr	Unspr	
85'	65'	75'	55'	85'	65'	70'	50'	60'	40'	MAXIMUM HEIGHT IN FEET

Spr	Unspr	Spr	Unspr	Spr	Unspr	Spr	Unspr	Spr	Unspr	Stories
										UH
										12
										11
										10
										9
										8
										7
256,500				324,000						6
256,500	85,500	171,000		324,000	108,000					5
256,500	85,500	171,000	57,000	324,000	108,000	162,000				4
256,500	85,500	171,000	57,000	324,000	108,000	162,000	54,000	81,000		3
171,000	57,000	114,000	38,000	216,000	72,000	108,000	36,000	54,000	18,000	2
114,000	28,500	76,000	19,000	144,000	36,000	72,000	18,000	36,000	9,000	1
114,000	28,500	76,000	19,000	144,000	36,000	72,000	18,000	36,000	9,000	

HEIGHT IN STORIES

MAXIMUM FLOOR AREA IN SF FOR ANY SINGLE FLOOR

This table was compiled from information contained in the International Building Code 2000. It does not represent an official interpretation by the organization that issues this code.

OCCUPANCY GROUP A-1: ASSEMBLY, THEATERS

Sprinklers

An approved sprinkler system is required for Group A-1 occupancies when located on a floor other than the level of exit discharge, with floor area exceeding 12,000 sq ft (1115 m²), with an occupant load of 300 or more, or when containing multitheater complexes. A sprinkler system is also required for any A-1 occupancy with:

• A floor having an occupant load of 30 or more located more than 55 ft (17 m) above grade

• Any story or basement greater than 1500 square feet (139 m²) in area without openings to the exterior

• Most underground portions of the building where occupancy occurs more than 30 ft (9 m) below the lowest level of exit discharge

Unlimited Area Buildings

One-story motion picture theater buildings of Noncombustible 1-Hour, 2-Hour, or 3-Hour construction may be of unlimited area when sprinklered throughout and surrounded on all sides by public ways or yards not less than 60 ft (18 m) in width.

Fire Walls

For multiplication of the allowable area by subdividing the building with fire walls, see page 302.

Basements

A single-story basement is not included in area calculations, provided that the basement area does not exceed the area permitted for a one-story building.

Excess Frontage

If more than 25% of the building perimeter fronts on a street or open space at least 20 ft (6.1 m) wide that is accessible to firefighting vehicles, the tabulated area limitations below may be increased

OCCUPANCY GROUP A-1: ASSEMBLY, THEATERS

	Noncombustible							
CONSTRUCTION TYPE	3-Hour (page 308)		2-Hour (page 309)		1-Hour (page 310)		Unprotected (page 311)	
IBC NOMENCLATURE	Type I-A		Type I-B		Type II-A		Type II-B	
	Spr	Unspr	Spr	Unspr	Spr	Unspr	Spr	Unspr
MAXIMUM HEIGHT IN FEET	UH	75'	180'	160'	85'	65'	75'	55'
UH	UA	12,000/floor						
12		144,000						
11		132,000						
10		120,000						
9		108,000						
8		96,000						
7		84,000						
6		72,000	UA					
5		60,000		60,000				
4		48,000		48,000	139,500			
3		36,000		36,000	139,500	36,000	76,500	
2		24,000		24,000	93,000	24,000	51,000	17,000
1		12,000		12,000	62,000	12,000	34,000	8,500
MAXIMUM FLOOR AREA IN SF FOR ANY SINGLE FLOOR	UA	12,000	UA	12,000	62,000	12,000	34,000	8,500

Each number in the table represents the maximum total area in square feet for all floors for a building of the indicated story height.

Key to Abbreviations

UA	Unlimited area	Spr	With approved sprinkler system
UH	Unlimited height	Unspr	Without approved sprinkler system
NP	Not permitted		

according to the following table. For example, for a building with half of its perimeter accessible to firefighting equipment via a space not less than 24 ft (7.3 m) wide, the allowable area increase is:

0.80% increase × 25% excess frontage = 20% total area increase.

Width of Frontage*	Percent Area Increase for Each 1% of Frontage in Excess of 25%
20' (6.1 m)	0.67%
22' (6.7 m)	0.73%
24' (7.3 m)	0.80%
26' (7.9 m)	0.87%
28' (8.5 m)	0.93%
30' (9.1 m) or wider	1.00%

*Intermediate values may be interpolated.

Measurements

Height is measured from the average finished ground level adjoining the building to the average level of the highest roof. Floor area is measured within exterior walls or exterior walls and fire walls, exclusive of courtyards.

Further Information

For information on Occupancy Group classifications, see page 7. For information on mixed-use buildings, see page 300. For information on which code to consult, see pages 7, 11.

Unit Conversions

1 ft = 304.8 mm, 1 sq ft = 0.0929 m²

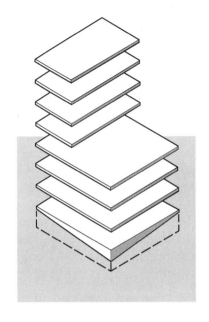

Combustible											
Ordinary				Mill (page 312)		Wood Light Frame					
1-Hour (page 313)		Unprotected (page 313)				1-Hour (page 315)		Unprotected (page 315)			CONSTRUCTION TYPE
Type III-A		Type III-B		Type IV-HT		Type V-A		Type V-B			IBC NOMENCLATURE
Spr	Unspr	Spr	Unspr	Spr	Unspr	Spr	Unspr	Spr	Unspr		
85'	65'	75'	55'	85'	65'	70'	50'	60'	40'		MAXIMUM HEIGHT IN FEET
										UH	
										12	
										11	
										10	
										9	HEIGHT IN STORIES
										8	
										7	
										6	
										5	
126,000				135,000						4	
126,000	36,000	76,500		135,000	36,000	103,500				3	
84,000	24,000	51,000	17,000	90,000	24,000	69,000	23,000	33,000		2	
56,000	12,000	34,000	8,500	60,000	12,000	46,000	11,500	22,000	5,500	1	MAXIMUM FLOOR AREA IN SF FOR ANY SINGLE FLOOR
56,000	12,000	34,000	8,500	60,000	12,000	46,000	11,500	22,000	5,500		

This table was compiled from information contained in the International Building Code 2000. It does not represent an official interpretation by the organization that issues this code.

HEIGHT AND AREA TABLES

321

OCCUPANCY GROUP A-2: ASSEMBLY, FOOD AND DRINK ESTABLISHMENTS

Sprinklers

An approved sprinkler system is required for Group A-2 occupancies when located on a floor other than the level of exit discharge, with floor area exceeding 5,000 sq ft (465 m²) or with an occupant load of 300 or more. A sprinkler system is also required for any A-2 occupancy with:

• A floor having an occupant load of 30 or more located more than 55 ft (17 m) above grade

• Any story or basement greater than 1500 sq ft (139 m²) in area without openings to the exterior

• Most underground portions of the building where occupancy occurs more than 30 feet (9 m) below the lowest level of exit discharge.

Fire Walls

For multiplication of the allowable area by subdividing the building with fire walls, see page 302.

Basements

A single-story basement is not included in area calculations, provided the basement area does not exceed area permitted for a one-story building.

Excess Frontage

If more than 25% of the building perimeter fronts on a street or open space at least 20 ft (6.1 m) wide that is accessible to firefighting vehicles, the tabulated area limitations below may be increased according to the following table. For example, for a building with half of its perimeter accessible to firefighting equipment via a space not less than 24 ft (7.3 m) wide, the allowable area increase is:

0.80% increase × 25% excess frontage = 20% total area increase.

OCCUPANCY GROUP A-2: ASSEMBLY, FOOD AND DRINK ESTABLISHMENTS

	Noncombustible							
CONSTRUCTION TYPE	**3-Hour** (page 308)		**2-Hour** (page 309)		**1-Hour** (page 310)		**Unprotected** (page 311)	
IBC NOMENCLATURE	Type I-A		Type I-B		Type II-A		Type II-B	
	Spr	Unspr	Spr	Unspr	Spr	Unspr	Spr	Unspr
MAXIMUM HEIGHT IN FEET	UH	75'	180'	75'	85'	65'	75'	55'
UH	UA	5,000/floor						
12		60,000	UA					
11		55,000		55,000				
10		50,000		50,000				
9		45,000		45,000				
8		40,000		40,000				
7		35,000		35,000				
6		30,000		30,000				
5		25,000		25,000				
4		20,000		20,000	139,500			
3		15,000		15,000	139,500	15,000	85,500	
2		10,000		10,000	93,000	10,000	57,000	10,000
1		5,000		5,000	62,000	5,000	38,000	5,000
MAXIMUM FLOOR AREA IN SF FOR ANY SINGLE FLOOR	UA	5,000	UA	5,000	62,000	5,000	38,000	5,000

Each number in the table represents the maximum total area in square feet for all floors for a building of the indicated story height.

Key to Abbreviations

UA	Unlimited area	Spr	With approved sprinkler system
UH	Unlimited height	Unspr	Without approved sprinkler system
NP	Not permitted		

322

Width of Frontage	Percent Area Increase for Each 1% of Frontage* in Excess of 25%
20' (6.1 m)	0.67%
22' (6.7 m)	0.73%
24' (7.3 m)	0.80%
26' (7.9 m)	0.87%
28' (8.5 m)	0.93%
30' (9.1 m) or wider	1.00%

*Intermediate values may be interpolated.

Measurements

Height is measured from the average finished ground level adjoining the building to the average level of the highest roof. Floor area is measured within exterior walls or exterior walls and fire walls, exclusive of courtyards.

Further Information

For information on Occupancy Group classifications, see page 7. For information on mixed-use buildings, see page 300. For information on which code to consult, see pages 7, 11.

Unit Conversions

1 ft 304.8 mm, 1 sq ft = 0.0929 in²

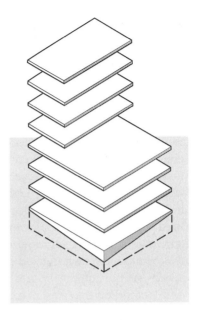

Combustible											
Ordinary						**Wood Light Frame**					
1-Hour (page 313)		**Unprotected** (page 313)		**Mill** (page 312)		**1-Hour** (page 315)		**Unprotected** (page 315)		**CONSTRUCTION TYPE**	
Type III-A		Type III-B		Type IV-HT		Type V-A		Type V-B		**IBC NOMENCLATURE**	
Spr	Unspr	Spr	Unspr	Spr	Unspr	Spr	Unspr	Spr	Unspr		
85'	65'	75'	55'	85'	65'	70'	50'	60'	40'	**MAXIMUM HEIGHT IN FEET**	
										UH	
										12	
										11	
										10	
										9	
										8	**HEIGHT IN STORIES**
										7	
										6	
										5	
126,000				135,000						4	
126,000	15,000	85,500		135,000	15,000	103,500				3	
84,000	10,000	57,000	10,000	90,000	10,000	69,000	10,000	36,000		2	
56,000	5,000	38,000	5,000	60,000	5,000	46,000	5,000	24,000	5,000	1	**MAXIMUM FLOOR AREA IN SF FOR ANY SINGLE FLOOR**
56,000	5,000	38,000	5,000	60,000	5,000	46,000	5,000	24,000	5,000		

HEIGHT AND AREA TABLES

323

This table was compiled from information contained in the International Building Code 2000. It does not represent an official interpretation by the organization that issues this code.

USE GROUP A-3: ASSEMBLY, MISCELLANEOUS

Sprinklers

An approved sprinkler system is required for Group A-3 occupancies when located on a floor other than the level of exit discharge, with floor area exceeding 12,000 sq ft (1115 m²) or with an occupant load of 300 or more. However, a sprinkler system is not required for A-3 occupancies when used exclusively as participant sports areas and located on the level of exit discharge, regardless of floor area or occupant load. A sprinkler system

is also required for any A-3 occupancy with:

- A floor having an occupant load of 30 or more located more than 55 ft (17 m) above grade

- Any story or basement greater than 1500 sq ft (139 m²) in area without openings to the exterior

- Most underground portions of the building where occupancy occurs more than 30 feet (9 m) below the lowest level of exit discharge

Fire Walls

For multiplication of the allowable area by subdividing the building with fire walls, see page 302.

Basements

A single-story basement is not included in area calculations, provided that the basement area does not exceed the area permitted for a one-story building.

Excess Frontage

If more than 25% of the building perimeter fronts on a street or open space at least 20 ft (6.1 m) wide that is accessible to firefighting vehicles, the tabulated area limitations below may be increased according to the following table. For example, for a building with half of its perimeter accessible to firefighting equipment via a space not less than 24 ft (7.3 m) wide, the allowable area increase is:

OCCUPANCY GROUP A-3: ASSEMBLY, MISCELLANEOUS

CONSTRUCTION TYPE		Noncombustible							
		3-Hour (page 308)		2-Hour (page 309)		1-Hour (page 310)		Unprotected (page 311)	
IBC NOMENCLATURE		Type I-A		Type I-B		Type II-A		Type II-B	
		Spr	Unspr	Spr	Unspr	Spr	Unspr	Spr	Unspr
MAXIMUM HEIGHT IN FEET		UH	75'	180'	75'	85'	65'	75'	55'
	UH	UA	12,000/floor						
	12		144,000	UA					
	11		132,000		132,000				
	10		120,000		120,000				
	9		108,000		108,000				
HEIGHT IN STORIES	8		96,000		96,000				
	7		84,000		84,000				
	6		72,000		72,000				
	5		60,000		60,000				
	4		48,000		48,000	139,500			
	3		36,000		36,000	139,500	36,000	85,500	
	2		24,000		24,000	93,000	24,000	57,000	19,000
	1		12,000		12,000	62,000	12,000	38,000	9,500
MAXIMUM FLOOR AREA IN SF FOR ANY SINGLE FLOOR		UA	12,000	UA	12,000	62,000	12,000	38,000	9,500

Each number in the table represents the maximum total area in square feet for all floors for a building of the indicated story height.

Key to Abbreviations

UA	Unlimited area	Spr	With approved sprinkler system
UH	Unlimited height	Unspr	Without approved sprinkler system
NP	Not permitted		

0.80% increase x 25% excess frontage = 20% total area increase.

Width of Frontage	Percent Area Increase for Each 1% of Frontage* in Excess of 25%
20' (6.1 m)	0.67%
22' (6.7 m)	0.73%
24' (7.3 m)	0.80%
26' (7.9 m)	0.87%
28' (8.5 m)	0.93%
30' (9.1 m) or wider	1.00%

*Intermediate values may be interpolated.

Measurements

Height is measured from the average finished ground level adjoining the building to the average level of the highest roof. Floor area is measured within exterior walls or exterior walls and fire walls, exclusive of courtyards.

Further Information

For information on Occupancy Group classifications, see page 7. For information on mixed-use buildings, see page 300. For information on which code to consult, see pages 7, 11.

Unit Conversions

1 ft = 304.8 mm, 1 sq ft = 0.0929 in^2

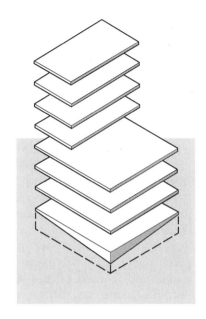

				Combustible						CONSTRUCTION TYPE
Ordinary						**Wood Light Frame**				
1-Hour (page 313)		**Unprotected** (page 313)		**Mill** (page 312)		**1-Hour** (page 315)		**Unprotected** (page 315)		
Type III-A		**Type III-B**		**Type IV-HT**		**Type V-A**		**Type V-B**		IBC NOMENCLATURE
Spr	Unspr	Spr	Unspr	Spr	Unspr	Spr	Unspr	Spr	Unspr	
85'	65'	75'	55'	85'	65'	70'	50'	60'	40'	MAXIMUM HEIGHT IN FEET

III-A Spr	III-A Unspr	III-B Spr	III-B Unspr	IV-HT Spr	IV-HT Unspr	V-A Spr	V-A Unspr	V-B Spr	V-B Unspr	Story
										UH
										12
										11
										10
										9
										8
										7
										6
										5
126,000				135,000						4
126,000	36,000	85,500		135,000	36,000	103,500				3
84,000	24,000	57,000	19,000	90,000	24,000	69,000	23,000	36,000		2
56,000	12,000	38,000	9,500	60,000	12,000	46,000	11,500	24,000	6,000	1
56,000	12,000	38,000	9,500	60,000	12,000	46,000	11,500	24,000	6,000	MAXIMUM FLOOR AREA IN SF FOR ANY SINGLE FLOOR

HEIGHT IN STORIES

HEIGHT AND AREA TABLES

325

This table was compiled from information contained in the International Building Code 2000. It does not represent an official interpretation by the organization that issues this code.

OCCUPANCY GROUP A-4: ASSEMBLY, INDOOR ARENAS

Sprinklers

An approved sprinkler system is required for Group A-4 occupancies when located on a floor other than the level of exit discharge, with floor area exceeding 12,000 sq ft (1115 m²) or with an occupant load of 300 or more. However, a sprinkler system is not required for A-4 occupancies when used exclusively as participant sports areas and located on the level of exit discharge, regardless of floor area or occupant load. A sprinkler system is also required for any A-4 occupancy with:

• A floor having an occupant load of 30 or more located more than 55 ft (17 m) above grade

• Any story or basement greater than 1500 square feet (139 m²) in area without openings to the exterior

• Most underground portions of the building where occupancy occurs more than 30 ft (9 m) below the lowest level of exit discharge

Unlimited Area Buildings

One-story Occupancy Group A-4 buildings may be of unlimited area when sprinklered throughout and surrounded on all sides by public ways or yards not less than 60 ft (18 m) in width. However, a sprinkler system is not required when such buildings are used exclusively for indoor participant sports, such as tennis, skating, swimming, and equestrian activities, provided that exit doors discharging directly to the outside are provided for the occupants and the building is equipped with an approved manual fire alarm system.

Fire Walls

For multiplication of the allowable area by subdividing the building with fire walls, see page 302.

Basements

A single-story basement is not included in area calculations, pro-

OCCUPANCY GROUP A-4: ASSEMBLY, INDOOR ARENAS

	Noncombustible							
CONSTRUCTION TYPE	**3-Hour** (page 308)		**2-Hour** (page 309)		**1-Hour** (page 310)		**Unprotected** (page 311)	
IBC NOMENCLATURE	Type I-A		Type I-B		Type II-A		Type II-B	
	Spr	Unspr	Spr	Unspr	Spr	Unspr	Spr	Unspr
MAXIMUM HEIGHT IN FEET	UH	75'	180'	75'	85'	65'	75'	55'
HEIGHT IN STORIES UH	UA	12,000/floor						
12		144,000	UA					
11		132,000		132,000				
10		120,000		120,000				
9		108,000		108,000				
8		96,000		96,000				
7		84,000		84,000				
6		72,000		72,000				
5		60,000		60,000				
4		48,000		48,000	139,500			
3		36,000		36,000	139,500	36,000	85,500	
2		24,000		24,000	93,000	24,000	57,000	19,000
1		12,000		12,000	62,000	12,000	38,000	9,500
MAXIMUM FLOOR AREA IN SF FOR ANY SINGLE FLOOR	UA	12,000	UA	12,000	62,000	12,000	38,000	9,500

Each number in the table represents the maximum total area in square feet for all floors for a building of the indicated story height.

Key to Abbreviations

UA	Unlimited area	Spr	With approved sprinkler system
UH	Unlimited height	Unspr	Without approved sprinkler system
NP	Not permitted		

vided that the basement area does not exceed the area permitted for a one-story building.

Excess Frontage

If more than 25% of the building perimeter fronts on a street or open space at least 20 ft (6.1 m) wide that is accessible to fire-fighting vehicles, the tabulated area limitations below may be increased according to the following table. For example, for a building with half of its perimeter accessible to firefighting equipment via a space not less than 24 ft (7.3 m) wide, the allowable area increase is:

0.80% increase × 25% excess frontage = 20% total area increase.

Width of Frontage	Percent Area Increase for Each 1% of Frontage* in Excess of 25%
20' (6.1 m)	0.67%
22' (6.7 m)	0.73%
24' (7.3 m)	0.80%
26' (7.9 m)	0.87%
28' (8.5 m)	0.93%
30' (9.1 m) or wider	1.00%

*Intermediate values may be interpolated.

Further Information

For information on Occupancy Group classifications, see page 7. For information on mixed-use buildings, see page 300. For information on which code to consult, see pages 7, 11.

Unit Conversions

1 ft = 304.8 mm, 1 sq ft = 0.0929 m².

Combustible												
Ordinary				Mill (page 312)		Wood Light Frame						
1-Hour (page 313)		Unprotected (page 313)				1-Hour (page 315)		Unprotected (page 315)				CONSTRUCTION TYPE
Type III-A		Type III-B		Type IV-HT		Type V-A		Type V-B				IBC NOMENCLATURE
Spr	Unspr	Spr	Unspr	Spr	Unspr	Spr	Unspr	Spr	Unspr			
85'	65'	75'	55'	85'	65'	70'	50'	60'	40'			MAXIMUM HEIGHT IN FEET
										UH		
										12		
										11		
										10		
										9		
										8		HEIGHT IN STORIES
										7		
										6		
										5		
126,000				135,000						4		
126,000	36,000	85,500		135,000	36,000	103,500				3		
84,000	24,000	57,000	19,000	90,000	24,000	69,000	23,000	36,000		2		
56,000	12,000	38,000	9,500	60,000	12,000	46,000	11,500	24,000	6,000	1		MAXIMUM FLOOR AREA IN SF FOR ANY SINGLE FLOOR
56,000	12,000	38,000	9,500	60,000	12,000	46,000	11,500	24,000	6,000			

This table was compiled from information contained in the International Building Code 2000. It does not represent an official interpretation by the organization that issues this code.

HEIGHT AND AREA TABLES

OCCUPANCY GROUP A-5: ASSEMBLY, OUTDOOR ARENAS

Sprinklers

In Occupancy Group A-5, an approved sprinkler system is required for concession stands, retail areas, press boxes, and other accessory use areas greater than 1000 sq ft (93 m²) in area.

Measurements

Height is measured from the average finished ground level adjoining the building to the average level of the highest roof. Floor area is measured within exterior walls or exterior walls and fire walls, exclusive of courtyards.

Further Information

For information on Occupancy Group classifications, see page 7.

For information on mixed-used buildings, see page 300. For information on which code to consult, see pages 7, 11.

Unit Conversions

1 ft = 304.8 mm, 1 sq ft = 0.0929 m².

OCCUPANCY GROUP A-5: ASSEMBLY, OUTDOOR ARENAS

CONSTRUCTION TYPE	Noncombustible							
	3-Hour (page 308)		2-Hour (page 309)		1-Hour (page 310)		Unprotected (page 311)	
IBC NOMENCLATURE	Type I-A		Type I-B		Type II-A		Type II-B	
	Spr	Unspr	Spr	Unspr	Spr	Unspr	Spr	Unspr
MAXIMUM HEIGHT IN FEET	UH	UH	180'	160'	85'	65'	75'	55'
UH	UA	UA	UA	UA	UA	UA	UA	UA
12								
11								
10								
9								
8								
7								
6								
5								
4								
3								
2								
MAXIMUM FLOOR AREA IN SF FOR ANY SINGLE FLOOR 1	UA	UA	UA	UA	UA	UA	UA	UA

Each number in the table represents the maximum total area in square feet for all floors for a building of the indicated story height.

Key to Abbreviations

UA Unlimited area   Spr   With approved sprinkler system
UH Unlimited height   Unspr Without approved sprinkler system
NP Not permitted

328

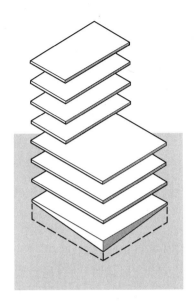

Combustible										
Ordinary				Mill (page 312)		Wood Light Frame				**CONSTRUCTION TYPE**
1-Hour (page 313)		Unprotected (page 313)				1-Hour (page 315)		Unprotected (page 315)		
Type III-A		Type III-B		Type IV-HT		Type V-A		Type V-B		**IBC NOMENCLATURE**
Spr	Unspr	Spr	Unspr	Spr	Unspr	Spr	Unspr	Spr	Unspr	
85'	65'	75'	55'	85'	65'	70'	50'	60'	40'	**MAXIMUM HEIGHT IN FEET**
UA	UA	UA	UA	UA	UA	UA	UA	UA	UA	UH
										12
										11
										10
										9
										8
										7
										6
										5
										4
										3
										2
										1
UA	UA	UA	UA	UA	UA	UA	UA	UA	UA	**MAXIMUM FLOOR AREA IN SF FOR ANY SINGLE FLOOR**

HEIGHT IN STORIES

HEIGHT AND AREA TABLES

329

This table was compiled from information contained in the International Building Code 2000. It does not represent an official interpretation by the organization that issues this code.

OCCUPANCY GROUP B: BUSINESS

Sprinklers

An approved sprinkler system is required for any Group B occupancy with:

• A floor having an occupant load of 30 or more located more than 55 ft (17 m) above grade

• Any story or basement greater than 1500 sq ft (139 m²) in area without openings to the exterior

• Most underground portions of the building where occupancy occurs more than 30 feet (9 m) below the lowest level of exit discharge

Unlimited Area Buildings

One- and two-story Occupancy B buildings may be of unlimited area when sprinklered throughout and surrounded on all sides by public ways or yards not less than 60 ft (18 m) in width.

Fire Walls

For multiplication of the allowable area by subdividing the building with fire walls, see page 302.

Basements

A single-story basement is not included in area calculations provided the basement area does not exceed the area permitted for a one-story building.

Excess Frontage

If more than 25% of the building perimeter fronts on a street or open space at least 20 ft (6.1 m) wide that is accessible to firefighting vehicles, the tabulated area limitations below may be increased according to the following table. For example, for a building with half of its perimeter accessible to firefighting equipment via a space not less than 24 ft (7.3 m) wide, the allowable area increase is:

0.80% increase × 25% excess frontage = 20% total area increase.

OCCUPANCY GROUP B: BUSINESS

	Noncombustible							
CONSTRUCTION TYPE	**3-Hour** (page 308)		**2-Hour** (page 309)		**1-Hour** (page 310)		**Unprotected** (page 311)	
IBC NOMENCLATURE	Type I-A		Type I-B		Type II-A		Type II-B	
	Spr	Unspr	Spr	Unspr	Spr	Unspr	Spr	Unspr
MAXIMUM HEIGHT IN FEET	UH	UH	180'	75'	85'	65'	75'	55'
HEIGHT IN STORIES UH	UA	UA						
12			UA					
11				UA				
10								
9								
8								
7								
6					337,500			
5					337,500	112,500	207,000	
4					337,500	112,500	207,000	
3					337,500	112,500	207,000	69,000
2					225,000	75,000	207,000	69,000
1					150,000	37,500	138,000	46,000
MAXIMUM FLOOR AREA IN SF FOR ANY SINGLE FLOOR UA	UA	UA	UA	UA	150,000	37,500	92,000	23,000

Each number in the table represents the maximum total area in square feet for all floors for a building of the indicated story height.

Key to Abbreviations

UA Unlimited area Spr With approved sprinkler system
UH Unlimited height Unspr Without approved sprinkler system
NP Not permitted

Width of Frontage	Percent Area Increase for Each 1% of Frontage* in Excess of 25%
20' (6.1 m)	0.67%
22' (6.7 m)	0.73%
24' (7.3 m)	0.80%
26' (7.9 m)	0.87%
28' (8.5 m)	0.93%
30' (9.1 m) or wider	1.00%

*Intermediate values may be interpolated.

Measurements

Height is measured from the average finished ground level adjoining the building to the average level of the highest roof. Floor area is measured within exterior walls or exterior walls and fire walls, exclusive of courtyards.

Further Information

For information on Occupancy Group classifications, see page 7. For information on mixed-used buildings, see page 300. For information on which code to consult, see pages 7, 11.

Unit Conversions

1 ft = 304.8 mm, 1 sq ft = 0.0929 m^2.

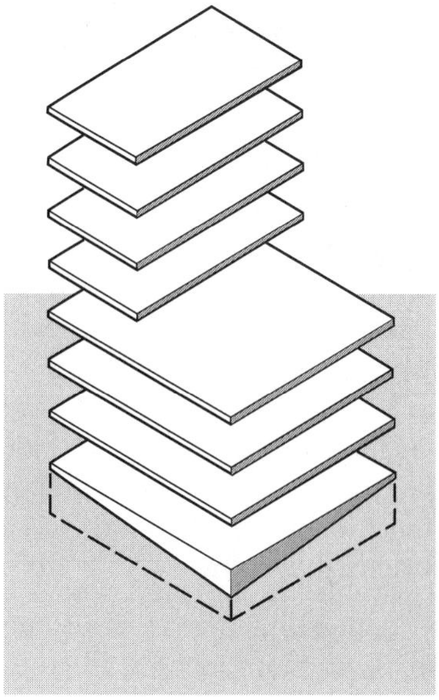

Combustible											
Ordinary						Wood Light Frame					
1-Hour (page 313)		Unprotected (page 313)		Mill (page 312)		1-Hour (page 315)		Unprotected (page 315)			CONSTRUCTION TYPE
Type III-A		Type III-B		Type IV-HT		Type V-A		Type V-B			IBC NOMENCLATURE
Spr	Unspr	Spr	Unspr	Spr	Unspr	Spr	Unspr	Spr	Unspr		
85'	65'	75'	55'	85'	65'	70'	50'	60'	40'		MAXIMUM HEIGHT IN FEET
										UH	
										12	
										11	
										10	
										9	
										8	HEIGHT IN STORIES
										7	
256,500				324,000						6	
256,500	85,500	171,000		324,000	108,000					5	
256,500	85,500	171,000	57,000	324,000	108,000	162,000				4	
256,500	85,500	171,000	57,000	324,000	108,000	162,000	54,000	81,000		3	
171,000	57,000	114,000	38,000	216,000	72,000	108,000	36,000	54,000	18,000	2	
114,000	28,500	76,000	19,000	144,000	36,000	72,000	18,000	36,000	9,000	1	
114,000	28,500	76,000	19,000	144,000	36,000	72,000	18,000	36,000	9,000		MAXIMUM FLOOR AREA IN SF FOR ANY SINGLE FLOOR

This table was compiled from information contained in the International Building Code 2000. It does not represent an official interpretation by the organization that issues this code.

OCCUPANCY GROUP E: EDUCATIONAL

Sprinklers

An approved sprinkler system is required for Group E occupancies when located on a floor below the level of exit discharge, or with floor area exceeding 20,000 sq ft (1858 m²), except where each classroom has at least one exterior exit door at ground level. A sprinkler system is also required for any Group E occupancy with:

• A floor having an occupant load of 30 or more located more than 55 ft (17 m) above grade

• Any story or basement greater than 1500 sq ft (139 m²) in area

without openings to the exterior

• Most underground portions of the building where occupancy occurs more than 30 feet (9 m) below the lowest level of exit discharge

Unlimited Area Buildings

Occupancy E buildings of Noncombustible construction of any rating, or of Ordinary 1-hour or Mill construction, may be of unlimited area when sprinklered throughout, surrounded on all sides by public ways or yards not less than 60 ft (18 m) in width, and where each classroom has at least two means of egress, one of which discharges directly to the exterior.

Fire Walls

For multiplication of the allowable area by subdividing the building with fire walls, see page 302.

Basements

A single-story basement is not included in area calculations, provided that the basement area does not exceed the area permitted for a one-story building.

Excess Frontage

If more than 25% of the building perimeter fronts on a street or open space at least 20 ft (6.1 m) wide that is accessible to firefighting vehicles, the tabulated area limitations below may be increased according to the following table. For example,

OCCUPANCY GROUP E: EDUCATIONAL

	Noncombustible							
CONSTRUCTION TYPE	**3-Hour** (page 308)		**2-Hour** (page 309)		**1-Hour** (page 310)		**Unprotected** (page 311)	
IBC NOMENCLATURE	Type I-A		Type I-B		Type II-A		Type II-B	
	Spr	Unspr	Spr	Unspr	Spr	Unspr	Spr	Unspr
MAXIMUM HEIGHT IN FEET	UH	75'	180'	75'	85'	65'	75'	55'
HEIGHT IN STORIES UH	UA	UA						
12								
11								
10								
9								
8								
7								
6			UA					
5				UA				
4					238,500			
3					238,500	79,500	130,500	
2					159,000	53,000	87,000	29,000
1					106,000	26,500	58,000	14,500
MAXIMUM FLOOR AREA IN SF FOR ANY SINGLE FLOOR	UA	UA	UA	UA	106,000	26,500	58,000	14,500

Each number in the table represents the maximum total area in square feet for all floors for a building of the indicated story height.

Key to Abbreviations

UA	Unlimited area	Spr	With approved sprinkler system
UH	Unlimited height	Unspr	Without approved sprinkler system
NP	Not permitted		

for a building with half of its perimeter accessible to firefighting equipment via a space not less than 24 ft (7.3 m) wide, the allowable area increase is:

0.80% increase × 25% excess frontage = 20% total area increase.

Width of Frontage*	Percent Area Increase for Each 1% of Frontage* in Excess of 25%
20' (6.1 m)	0.67%
22' (6.7 m)	0.73%
24' (7.3 m)	0.80%
26' (7.9 m)	0.87%
28' (8.5 m)	0.93%
30' (9.1 m) or wider	1.00%

*Intermediate values may be interpolated.

Measurements

Height is measured from the average finished ground level adjoining the building to the average level of the highest roof. Floor area is measured within exterior walls or exterior walls and fire walls, exclusive of courtyards.

Further Information

For information on Occupancy Group classifications, see page 7. For information on mixed-used buildings, see page 300. For information on which code to consult, see pages 7, 11.

Unit Conversions

1 ft = 304.8 mm, 1 sq ft = 0.0929 m².

	Combustible											CONSTRUCTION TYPE
	Ordinary						Wood Light Frame					
	1-Hour (page 313)		Unprotected (page 313)		Mill (page 312)		1-Hour (page 315)		Unprotected (page 315)			
	Type III-A		Type III-B		Type IV-HT		Type V-A		Type V-B			IBC NOMENCLATURE
	Spr	Unspr	Spr	Unspr	Spr	Unspr	Spr	Unspr	Spr	Unspr		
	85'	65'	75'	55'	85'	65'	70'	50'	60'	40'		MAXIMUM HEIGHT IN FEET
UH												
12												
11												
10												
9												
8												HEIGHT IN STORIES
7												
6												
5												
4	211,500				229,500							
3	211,500	70,500	130,500		229,500	76,500	166,500					
2	141,000	47,000	87,000	29,000	153,000	51,000	111,000	37,000	57,000			
1	94,000	23,500	58,000	14,500	102,000	25,500	74,000	18,500	38,000	9,500		MAXIMUM FLOOR AREA IN SF FOR ANY SINGLE FLOOR
	94,000	23,500	58,000	14,500	102,000	25,500	74,000	18,500	38,000	9,500		

HEIGHT AND AREA TABLES

333

This table was compiled from information contained in the International Building Code 2000. It does not represent an official interpretation by the organization that issues this code.

OCCUPANCY GROUP F-1: FACTORY, MODERATE HAZARD

Sprinklers

An approved sprinkler system is required for Group F-1 occupancies with floor area exceeding 12,000 sq ft (1115 m²), where more than 3 stories in height, or where the combined area of all floors and mezzanines exceeds 24,000 sq ft (2230 m²). A sprinkler system is required for woodworking operations involving finely divided combustible waste or materials greater than 2500 sq ft (232 m²) in area. A sprinkler system is also required for any F-1 occupancy with:

• A floor having an occupant load of 30 or more located more than 55 ft (17 m) above grade

• Any story or basement greater than 1500 sq ft (139 m²) in area without openings to the exterior

• Most underground portions of the building where occupancy occurs more than 30 feet (9 m) below the lowest level of exit discharge

Unlimited Area Buildings

One- and two-story Occupancy F-1 buildings may be of unlimited area when sprinklered throughout and surrounded on all sides by public ways or yards not less than 60 ft (18 m) in width.

Fire Walls

For multiplication of the allowable area by subdividing the building with fire walls, see page 302.

Basements

A single-story basement is not included in area calculations, provided that the basement area does not exceed the area permitted for a one-story building.

Excess Frontage

If more than 25% of the building perimeter fronts on a street or open space at least 20 ft (6.1 m) wide that is accessible to firefighting vehicles, the tabulated area limitations below may be increased according to the following table.

OCCUPANCY GROUP F-1: FACTORY, MODERATE HAZARD

	Noncombustible							
CONSTRUCTION TYPE	3-Hour (page 308)		2-Hour (page 309)		1-Hour (page 310)		Unprotected (page 311)	
IBC NOMENCLATURE	Type I-A		Type I-B		Type II-A		Type II-B	
	Spr	Unspr	Spr	Unspr	Spr	Unspr	Spr	Unspr
MAXIMUM HEIGHT IN FEET	UH	75'	180'	75'	85'	65'	75'	55'
HEIGHT IN STORIES — UH	UA							
12			UA					
11								
10								
9								
8								
7								
6								
5					225,000			
4					225,000			
3		24,000		24,000	225,000	24,000	139,500	
2		24,000		24,000	150,000	24,000	93,000	24,000
1		12,000		12,000	100,000	12,000	62,000	12,000
MAXIMUM FLOOR AREA IN SF FOR ANY SINGLE FLOOR	UA	12,000	UA	12,000	100,000	12,000	62,000	12,000

Each number in the table represents the maximum total area in square feet for all floors for a building of the indicated story height.

Key to Abbreviations

UA	Unlimited area	Spr	With approved sprinkler system
UH	Unlimited height	Unspr	Without approved sprinkler system
NP	Not permitted		

INTERNATIONAL BUILDING CODE

For example, for a building with half of its perimeter accessible to firefighting equipment via a space not less than 24 ft (7.3 m) wide, the allowable area increase is:

0.80% increase × 25% excess frontage = 20% total area increase.

Width of Frontage*	Percent Area Increase for Each 1% of Frontage* in Excess of 25%
20' (6.1 m)	0.67%
22' (6.7 m)	0.73%
24' (7.3 m)	0.80%
26' (7.9 m)	0.87%
28' (8.5 m)	0.93%
30' (9.1 m) or wider	1.00%

*Intermediate values may be interpolated.

Measurements

Height is measured from the average finished ground level adjoining the building to the average level of the highest roof. Floor area is measured within exterior walls or exterior walls and fire walls, exclusive of courtyards.

Further Information

For information on Occupancy Group classifications, see page 7. For information on mixed-used buildings, see page 300. For information on which code to consult, see pages 7, 11.

Unit Conversions

1 ft = 304.8 mm, 1 sq ft = 0.0929 m².

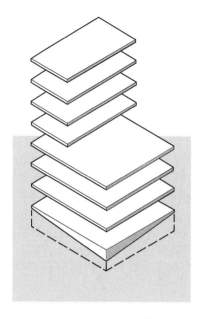

	Combustible										
	Ordinary					Wood Light Frame					
	1-Hour (page 313)		Unprotected (page 313)		Mill (page 312)		1-Hour (page 315)		Unprotected (page 315)		**CONSTRUCTION TYPE**
	Type III-A		Type III-B		Type IV-HT		Type V-A		Type V-B		**IBC NOMENCLATURE**
	Spr	Unspr	Spr	Unspr	Spr	Unspr	Spr	Unspr	Spr	Unspr	
	85'	65'	75'	55'	85'	65'	70'	50'	60'	40'	**MAXIMUM HEIGHT IN FEET**
UH											
12											
11											
10											
9											
8											**HEIGHT IN STORIES**
7											
6											
5					301,500						
4	171,000				301,500						
3	171,000	24,000	108,000		301,500	24,000	12,600				
2	114,000	24,000	72,000	24,000	201,000	24,000	8,400	2,800	51,000		
1	76,000	12,000	48,000	12,000	134,000	12,000	5,600	1,400	34,000	8,500	**MAXIMUM FLOOR**
	76,000	12,000	48,000	12,000	134,000	12,000	5,600	1,400	34,000	8,500	**AREA IN SF FOR ANY SINGLE FLOOR**

This table was compiled from information contained in the International Building Code 2000. It does not represent an official interpretation by the organization that issues this code.

OCCUPANCY GROUP F-2: FACTORY, LOW HAZARD

Sprinklers

An approved sprinkler system is required for any Group F-2 occupancy with:

• Any story or basement greater than 1500 sq ft (139 m²) in area without openings to the exterior

• Most underground portions of the building where occupancy occurs more than 30 feet (9 m) below the lowest level of exit discharge

Some low-hazard industrial processes requiring unusually large areas or high building heights, such as rolling mills, power distribution plants, foundries, and fabrication plants, may be exempt from the height and area limitations shown here. Consult the code and local regulatory authorities for more details.

Unlimited Area Buildings

One-story Occupancy F-2 buildings, sprinklered or unsprinklered, and two-story Occupancy F-2 buildings, sprinklered throughout, may be of unlimited area when surrounded on all sides by public ways or yards not less than 60 ft (18 m) in width.

Fire Walls

For multiplication of the allowable area by subdividing the building with fire walls, see page 302.

Basements

A single-story basement is not included in area calculations, provided that the basement area does not exceed the area permitted for a one-story building.

Excess Frontage

If more than 25% of the building perimeter fronts on a street or open space at least 20 ft (6.1 m) wide that is accessible to firefighting vehicles, the tabulated area limitations below may be increased according to the

OCCUPANCY GROUP F-2: FACTORY, LOW HAZARD

	Noncombustible							
CONSTRUCTION TYPE	3-Hour (page 308)		2-Hour (page 309)		1-Hour (page 310)		Unprotected (page 311)	
IBC NOMENCLATURE	Type I-A		Type I-B		Type II-A		Type II-B	
	Spr	Unspr	Spr	Unspr	Spr	Unspr	Spr	Unspr
MAXIMUM HEIGHT IN FEET	UH	75'	180'	75'	85'	65'	75'	55'
UH	UA	UA						
12			UA					
11				UA				
10								
9								
8								
7								
6					337,500			
5					337,500	112,500		
4					337,500	112,500	207,000	
3					337,500	112,500	207,000	69,000
2					225,000	75,000	138,000	46,000
1					150,000	37,500	92,000	23,000
MAXIMUM FLOOR AREA IN SF FOR ANY SINGLE FLOOR	UA	UA	UA	UA	150,000	37,500	92,000	23,000

Each number in the table represents the maximum total area in square feet for all floors for a building of the indicated story height.

Key to Abbreviations

UA	Unlimited area	Spr	With approved sprinkler system
UH	Unlimited height	Unspr	Without approved sprinkler system
NP	Not permitted		

INTERNATIONAL BUILDING CODE

following table. For example, for a building with half of its perimeter accessible to firefighting equipment via a space not less than 24 ft (7.3 m) wide, the allowable area increase is:

0.80% increase × 25% excess frontage = 20% total area increase.

Width of Frontage*	Percent Area Increase for Each 1% of Frontage* in Excess of 25%
20' (6.1 m)	0.67%
22' (6.7 m)	0.73%
24' (7.3 m)	0.80%
26' (7.9 m)	0.87%
28' (8.5 m)	0.93%
30' (9.1 m) or wider	1.00%

*Intermediate values may be interpolated.

Measurements

Height is measured from the average finished ground level adjoining the building to the average level of the highest roof. Floor area is measured within exterior walls or exterior walls and fire walls, exclusive of courtyards.

Further Information

For information on Occupancy Group classifications, see page 7. For information on mixed-used buildings, see page 300. For information on which code to consult, see pages 7, 11.

Unit Conversions

1 ft = 304.8 mm, 1 sq ft = 0.0929 m².

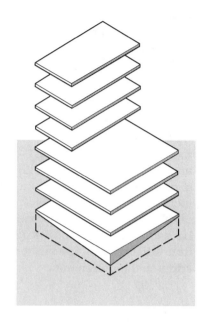

Combustible											
Ordinary				Mill		Wood Light Frame					CONSTRUCTION TYPE
1-Hour (page 313)		Unprotected (page 313)		(page 312)		1-Hour (page 315)		Unprotected (page 315)			
Type III-A		Type III-B		Type IV-HT		Type V-A		Type V-B			IBC NOMENCLATURE
Spr	Unspr	Spr	Unspr	Spr	Unspr	Spr	Unspr	Spr	Unspr		
85'	65'	75'	55'	85'	65'	70'	50'	60'	40'		MAXIMUM HEIGHT IN FEET
										UH	
										12	
										11	
										10	
										9	
										8	HEIGHT IN STORIES
										7	
				454,500						6	
256,500				454,500	151,500					5	
256,500	85,500	162,000		454,500	151,500	189,000				4	
256,500	85,500	162,000	54,000	454,500	151,500	189,000	63,000	117,000		3	
171,000	57,000	108,000	36,000	303,000	101,000	126,000	42,000	78,000	26,000	2	
114,000	28,500	72,000	18,000	202,000	50,500	84,000	21,000	52,000	13,000	1	MAXIMUM FLOOR AREA IN SF FOR ANY SINGLE FLOOR
114,000	28,500	72,000	18,000	202,000	50,500	84,000	21,000	52,000	13,000		

HEIGHT AND AREA TABLES

337

This table was compiled from information contained in the International Building Code 2000. It does not represent an official interpretation by the organization that issues this code.

OCCUPANCY GROUP H-1: HIGH HAZARD, DETONATION HAZARD

Special Requirements

All Group H-1 occupancy buildings must be used solely for the H-1 use, must be sprinklered, may not exceed one story in height, may not include basements, crawl spaces, or other underfloor areas, and must be set back at least 75 ft (23 m) from adjacent lots. See the code for additional requirements.

Excess Frontage

If more than 25% of the building perimeter fronts on a street or open space at least 20 ft (6.1 m) wide that is accessible to firefighting vehicles, the tabulated area limitations below may be increased according to the following table. For example, for a building with half of its perimeter accessible to firefighting equipment via a space not less than 24 ft (7.3 m) wide, the allowable area increase is:

0.80% increase × 25% excess frontage = 20% total area increase.

Width of Frontage*	Percent Area Increase for Each 1% of Frontage* in Excess of 25%
20' (6.1 m)	0.67%
22' (6.7 m)	0.73%
24' (7.3 m)	0.80%
26' (7.9 m)	0.87%
28' (8.5 m)	0.93%
30' (9.1 m) or wider	1.00%

*Intermediate values may be interpolated.

OCCUPANCY GROUP H-1: HIGH-HAZARD, DETONATION HAZARD

CONSTRUCTION TYPE	Noncombustible							
	3-Hour (page 308)		2-Hour (page 309)		1-Hour (page 310)		Unprotected (page 311)	
IBC NOMENCLATURE	Type I-A		Type I-B		Type II-A		Type II-B	
	Spr	Unspr	Spr	Unspr	Spr	Unspr	Spr	Unspr
MAXIMUM HEIGHT IN FEET	UH		180'		85'		75'	

HEIGHT IN STORIES: UH, 12, 11, 10, 9, 8, 7, 6, 5, 4, 3, 2, 1

MAXIMUM FLOOR AREA IN SF FOR ANY SINGLE FLOOR	Spr	Unspr	Spr	Unspr	Spr	Unspr	Spr	Unspr
1	21,000	NP	16,500	NP	11,000	NP	7,000	NP
	21,000	NP	16,500	NP	11,000	NP	7,000	NP

Each number in the table represents the maximum total area in square feet for all floors for a building of the indicated story height.

Key to Abbreviations

UA	Unlimited area	Spr	With approved sprinkler system
UH	Unlimited height	Unspr	Without approved sprinkler system
NP	Not permitted		

INTERNATIONAL BUILDING CODE

Measurements

Height is measured from the average finished ground level adjoining the building to the average level of the highest roof. Floor area is measured within exterior walls or exterior walls and fire walls, exclusive of courtyards.

Further Information

For information on Occupancy Group classifications, see page 7. For information on mixed-used buildings, see page 300. For information on which code to consult, see pages 7, 11.

Unit Conversions

1 ft = 304.8 mm, 1 sq ft = 0.0929 m².

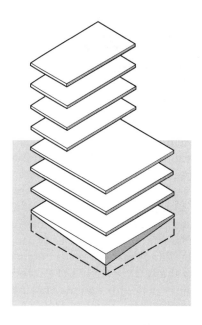

Combustible									
Ordinary						**Wood Light Frame**			
1-Hour (page 313)		Unprotected (page 313)		Mill (page 312)		1-Hour (page 315)		Unprotected (page 315)	
Type III-A		Type III-B		Type IV-HT		Type V-A		Type V-B	
Spr	Unspr	Spr	Unspr	Spr	Unspr	Spr	Unspr	Spr	Unspr
85'		75'		85'		70'			
9,500	NP	7,000	NP	10,500	NP	7,500	NP	NP	NP
9,500	NP	7,000	NP	10,500	NP	7,500	NP	NP	NP

CONSTRUCTION TYPE

IBC NOMENCLATURE

MAXIMUM HEIGHT IN FEET

UH
12
11
10
9
8 **HEIGHT IN STORIES**
7
6
5
4
3
2
1 **MAXIMUM FLOOR AREA IN SF FOR ANY SINGLE FLOOR**

HEIGHT AND AREA TABLES

339

This table was compiled from information contained in the International Building Code 2000. It does not represent an official interpretation by the organization that issues this code.

OCCUPANCY GROUP H-2: HIGH HAZARD, ACCELERATED BURNING HAZARD

Special Requirements

All occupancy Group H-2 buildings must be sprinklered, and when greater than 1,000 sq ft (93 m²) in area, must be set back at least 30 ft (23 m) from adjacent lots. Depending on the quantities of hazardous materials stored, H-2 occupancy buildings may be restricted to solely the H-2 use, may not exceed one story in height, and may not include basements, crawlspaces, or other underfloor areas. In some cases H-2 occupancies must be detached from other uses or buildings and must be set back at least 50 ft (15 m) from adjacent lots. When an H-2 occupancy is part of a mixed-use building, at least 25% of its perimeter must be an exterior wall. Grain elevators and similar structures of Noncombustible construction of any rating may be of unlimited height, or if of Mill construction, may be 65 ft to 85 ft (20 m to 26 m) in height, depending on location and degree of isolation from other buildings. In some cases, an H-2 occupancy of limited area may be permitted in an unlimited area building of F or S occupancy. See the code for additional requirements.

Fire Walls

For multiplication of the allowable area by subdividing the building with fire walls, see page 302.

Basements

A single-story basement is not included in area calculations, provided that the basement area does not exceed the area permitted for a one-story building.

Excess Frontage

If more than 25% of the building perimeter fronts on a street or open space at least 20 ft (6.1 m) wide that is accessible to firefighting vehicles, the tabulated area limitations below may be increased according to the

OCCUPANCY GROUP H-2: HIGH-HAZARD, ACCELERATED BURNING HAZARD

Noncombustible								
CONSTRUCTION TYPE	3-Hour (page 308)		2-Hour (page 309)		1-Hour (page 310)		Unprotected (page 311)	
IBC NOMENCLATURE	Type I-A		Type I-B		Type II-A		Type II-B	
	Spr	Unspr	Spr	Unspr	Spr	Unspr	Spr	Unspr
MAXIMUM HEIGHT IN FEET	UH		180'		85'		75'	
UH	63,000							
12	63,000							
11	63,000							
10	63,000							
9	63,000							
8	63,000							
7	63,000							
6	63,000							
5	63,000							
4	63,000							
3	63,000		49,500					
2	42,000		33,000		22,000			
1	21,000	NP	16,500	NP	11,000	NP	7,000	NP
MAXIMUM FLOOR AREA IN SF FOR ANY SINGLE FLOOR	21,000	NP	16,500	NP	11,000	NP	7,000	NP

Each number in the table represents the maximum total area in square feet for all floors for a building of the indicated story height.

Key to Abbreviations

UA	Unlimited area	Spr	With approved sprinkler system
UH	Unlimited height	Unspr	Without approved sprinkler system
NP	Not permitted		

INTERNATIONAL BUILDING CODE

following table. For example, for a building with half of its perimeter accessible to firefighting equipment via a space not less than 24 ft (7.3 m) wide, the allowable area increase is:

0.80% increase × 25% excess frontage = 20% total area increase.

Width of Frontage*	Percent Area Increase for Each 1% of Frontage* in Excess of 25%
20' (6.1 m)	0.67%
22' (6.7 m)	0.73%
24' (7.3 m)	0.80%
26' (7.9 m)	0.87%
28' (8.5 m)	0.93%
30' (9.1 m) or wider	1.00%

*Intermediate values may be interpolated.

Measurements

Height is measured from the average finished ground level adjoining the building to the average level of the highest roof. Floor area is measured within exterior walls or exterior walls and fire walls, exclusive of courtyards.

Further Information

For information on Occupancy Group classifications, see page 7. For information on mixed-used buildings, see page 300. For information on which code to consult, see pages 7, 11.

Unit Conversions

1 ft = 304.8 mm, 1 sq ft = 0.0929 m².

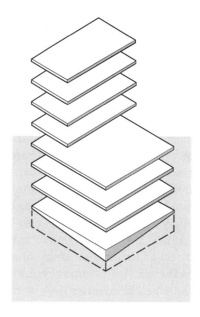

	Combustible												
	Ordinary						Wood Light Frame						
	1-Hour (page 313)		Unprotected (page 313)		Mill (page 312)		1-Hour (page 315)		Unprotected (page 315)				
	Type III-A		Type III-B		Type IV-HT		Type V-A		Type V-B				CONSTRUCTION TYPE
													IBC NOMENCLATURE
	Spr	Unspr	Spr	Unspr	Spr	Unspr	Spr	Unspr	Spr	Unspr			
	85'		75'		85'		70'		60'				MAXIMUM HEIGHT IN FEET
UH													
12													
11													
10													
9													
8													HEIGHT IN STORIES
7													
6													
5													
4													
3													
2	19,000				21,000								
1	9,500	NP	7,000	NP	10,500	NP	7,500	NP	3,000	NP			MAXIMUM FLOOR AREA IN SF FOR ANY SINGLE FLOOR
	9,500	NP	7,000	NP	10,500	NP	7,500	NP	3,000	NP			

HEIGHT AND AREA TABLES

341

This table was compiled from information contained in the International Building Code 2000. It does not represent an official interpretation by the organization that issues this code.

OCCUPANCY GROUP H-3: HIGH HAZARD, COMBUSTIBLES

Special Requirements

All occupancy Group H-3 buildings must be sprinklered. Depending on the quantities of hazardous materials stored, H-3 occupancy buildings may be restricted to solely H-3 use, may not exceed one story in height, and may not include basements, crawl spaces, or other underfloor areas. In some cases an H-3 occupancy must be detached from other uses or buildings, and must be set back at least 50 ft (15 m) from adjacent lots. When an H-3 occupancy is part of a mixed-use building, at least 25% of its perimeter must be an exterior wall. In some cases, an H-3 occupancy of limited area may be permitted in an unlimited area building of F or S occupancy. See the code for additional requirements.

Fire Walls

For multiplication of the allowable area by subdividing the building with fire walls, see page 302.

Basements

A single-story basement is not included in area calculations, provided that the basement area does not exceed the area permitted for a one-story building.

Excess Frontage

If more than 25% of the building perimeter fronts on a street or open space at least 20 ft (6.1 m) wide that is accessible to firefighting vehicles, the tabulated area limitations below may be increased according to the following table. For example, for a building with half of its perimeter accessible to firefighting equipment via a space not less than 24 ft (7.3 m) wide, the allowable area increase is:

0.80% increase × 25% excess frontage = 20% total area increase.

OCCUPANCY GROUP H-3: HIGH-HAZARD, COMBUSTIBLES

	Noncombustible							
CONSTRUCTION TYPE	**3-Hour (page 308)**		**2-Hour (page 309)**		**1-Hour (page 310)**		**Unprotected (page 311)**	
IBC NOMENCLATURE	**Type I-A**		**Type I-B**		**Type II-A**		**Type II-B**	
	Spr	Unspr	Spr	Unspr	Spr	Unspr	Spr	Unspr
MAXIMUM HEIGHT IN FEET	UH		180'		85'		75'	
HEIGHT IN STORIES UH	UA							
12								
11								
10								
9								
8								
7								
6			180,000					
5			180,000					
4			180,000		79,500			
3			180,000		79,500			
2			120,000		53,000		28,000	
1		NP	60,000	NP	26,500	NP	14,000	NP
MAXIMUM FLOOR AREA IN SF FOR ANY SINGLE FLOOR	UA	NP	60,000	NP	26,500	NP	14,000	NP

Each number in the table represents the maximum total area in square feet for all floors for a building of the indicated story height.

Key to Abbreviations

UA	Unlimited area	Spr	With approved sprinkler system
UH	Unlimited height	Unspr	Without approved sprinkler system
NP	Not permitted		

342

INTERNATIONAL BUILDING CODE

Width of Frontage*	Percent Area Increase for Each 1% of Frontage* in Excess of 25%
20' (6.1 m)	0.67%
22' (6.7 m)	0.73%
24' (7.3 m)	0.80%
26' (7.9 m)	0.87%
28' (8.5 m)	0.93%
30' (9.1 m) or wider	1.00%

*Intermediate values may be interpolated.

Measurements

Height is measured from the average finished ground level adjoining the building to the average level of the highest roof. Floor area is measured within exterior walls or exterior walls and fire walls, exclusive of courtyards.

Further Information

For information on Occupancy Group classifications, see page 7. For information on mixed-used buildings, see page 300. For information on which code to consult, see pages 7, 11.

Unit Conversions

1 ft = 304.8 mm, 1 sq ft = 0.0929 m².

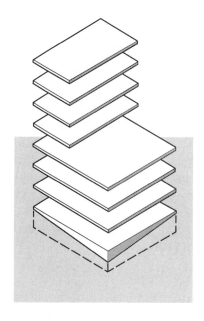

Combustible											
Ordinary				Mill (page 312)		Wood Light Frame					CONSTRUCTION TYPE
1-Hour (page 313)		Unprotected (page 313)				1-Hour (page 315)		Unprotected (page 315)			
Type III-A		Type III-B		Type IV-HT		Type V-A		Type V-B			IBC NOMENCLATURE
Spr	Unspr	Spr	Unspr	Spr	Unspr	Spr	Unspr	Spr	Unspr		
85'		75'		85'		70'		60'			MAXIMUM HEIGHT IN FEET
										UH	
										12	
										11	
										10	
										9	
										8	HEIGHT IN STORIES
										7	
										6	
										5	
52,500				76,500						4	
52,500				76,500						3	
35,000		26,000		51,000		20,000				2	
17,500	NP	13,000	NP	25,500	NP	10,000	NP	5,000	NP	1	MAXIMUM FLOOR AREA IN SF FOR ANY SINGLE FLOOR
17,500	NP	13,000	NP	25,500	NP	10,000	NP	5,000	NP		

This table was compiled from information contained in the International Building Code 2000. It does not represent an official interpretation by the organization that issues this code.

HEIGHT AND AREA TABLES

343

OCCUPANCY GROUP H-4: HIGH HAZARD, CORROSIVES AND TOXICS

Special Requirements

All occupancy Group H-4 buildings must be sprinklered. In some cases, an H-4 occupancy of limited area may be permitted in an unlimited area building of F or S occupancy. See the code for additional requirements.

Fire Walls

For multiplication of the allowable area by subdividing the building with fire walls, see page 302.

Basements

A single-story basement is not included in area calculations, provided that the basement area does not exceed the area permitted for a one-story building.

Excess Frontage

If more than 25% of the building perimeter fronts on a street or open space at least 20 ft (6.1 m) wide that is accessible to firefighting vehicles, the tabulated area limitations below may be increased according to the following table. For example, for a building with half of its perimeter accessible to firefighting equipment via a space not less than 24 ft (7.3 m) wide, the allowable area increase is:

0.80% increase × 25% excess frontage = 20% total area increase.

Width of Frontage*	Percent Area Increase for Each 1% of Frontage* in Excess of 25%
20' (6.1 m)	0.67%
22' (6.7 m)	0.73%
24' (7.3 m)	0.80%
26' (7.9 m)	0.87%
28' (8.5 m)	0.93%
30' (9.1 m) or wider	1.00%

*Intermediate values may be interpolated.

OCCUPANCY GROUP H-4: HIGH-HAZARD, CORROSIVES AND TOXICS

CONSTRUCTION TYPE		Noncombustible							
		3-Hour (page 308)		2-Hour (page 309)		1-Hour (page 310)		Unprotected (page 311)	
IBC NOMENCLATURE		Type I-A		Type I-B		Type II-A		Type II-B	
		Spr	Unspr	Spr	Unspr	Spr	Unspr	Spr	Unspr
MAXIMUM HEIGHT IN FEET		UH		180'		85'		75'	
HEIGHT IN STORIES	UH	UA							
	12								
	11								
	10								
	9								
	8			UA					
	7								
	6					337,500			
	5					337,500			
	4					337,500		157,500	
	3					337,500		157,500	
	2					225,000		105,000	
	1		NP		NP	150,000	NP	70,000	NP
MAXIMUM FLOOR AREA IN SF FOR ANY SINGLE FLOOR		UA	NP	UA	NP	150,000	NP	70,000	NP

Each number in the table represents the maximum total area in square feet for all floors for a building of the indicated story height.

Key to Abbreviations

UA	Unlimited area	Spr	With approved sprinkler system
UH	Unlimited height	Unspr	Without approved sprinkler system
NP	Not permitted		

INTERNATIONAL BUILDING CODE

Measurements

Height is measured from the average finished ground level adjoining the building to the average level of the highest roof. Floor area is measured within exterior walls or exterior walls and fire walls, exclusive of courtyards.

Further Information

For information on Occupancy Group classifications, see page 7. For information on mixed-used buildings, see page 300. For information on which code to consult, see pages 7, 11.

Unit Conversions

1 ft = 304.8 mm, 1 sq ft = 0.0929 m².

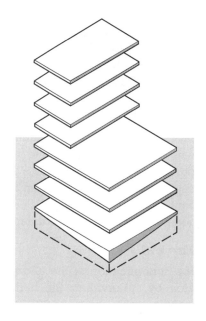

Combustible											
Ordinary						Wood Light Frame					
1-Hour (page 313)		Unprotected (page 313)		Mill (page 312)		1-Hour (page 315)		Unprotected (page 315)		**CONSTRUCTION TYPE**	
Type III-A		Type III-B		Type IV-HT		Type V-A		Type V-B		**IBC NOMENCLATURE**	
Spr	Unspr	Spr	Unspr	Spr	Unspr	Spr	Unspr	Spr	Unspr		
85'		75'		85'		70'		60'		**MAXIMUM HEIGHT IN FEET**	

										Stories	
										UH	
										12	
										11	
										10	
										9	
										8	**HEIGHT IN STORIES**
										7	
				324,000						6	
256,500				324,000						5	
256,500		157,500		324,000		162,000				4	
256,500		157,500		324,000		162,000		58,500		3	
171,000		105,000		216,000		108,000		39,000		2	
114,000	NP	70,000	NP	144,000	NP	72,000	NP	26,000	NP	1	
114,000	NP	70,000	NP	144,000	NP	72,000	NP	26,000	NP		**MAXIMUM FLOOR AREA IN SF FOR ANY SINGLE FLOOR**

This table was compiled from information contained in the International Building Code 2000. It does not represent an official interpretation by the organization that issues this code.

OCCUPANCY GROUP H-5: HIGH-HAZARD, HAZARDOUS PRODUCTION FACILITIES

Special Requirements

All Occupancy Group H-5 buildings must be sprinklered. In some cases, portions of H-5 occupancies must be at least 30 ft (9.1 m) from adjacent lots and public ways. See the code for additional requirements.

Fire Walls

For multiplication of the allowable area by subdividing the building with fire walls, see page 302.

Basements

A single-story basement is not included in area calculations, provided that the basement area does not exceed the area permitted for a one-story building.

Excess Frontage

If more than 25% of the building perimeter fronts on a street or open space at least 20 ft (6.1 m) wide that is accessible to firefighting vehicles, the tabulated area limitations below may be increased according to the following table. For example, for a building with half of its perimeter accessible to firefighting equipment via a space not less than 24 ft (7.3 m) wide, the allowable area increase is:

0.80% increase × 25% excess frontage = 20% total area increase.

Width of Frontage*	Percent Area Increase for Each 1% of Frontage* in Excess of 25%
20' (6.1 m)	0.67%
22' (6.7 m)	0.73%
24' (7.3 m)	0.80%
26' (7.9 m)	0.87%
28' (8.5 m)	0.93%
30' (9.1 m) or wider	1.00%

*Intermediate values may be interpolated.

OCCUPANCY GROUP H-5: HIGH-HAZARD, HAZARDOUS PRODUCTION FACILITIES

	Noncombustible							
CONSTRUCTION TYPE	3-Hour (page 308)		2-Hour (page 309)		1-Hour (page 310)		Unprotected (page 311)	
IBC NOMENCLATURE	Type I-A		Type I-B		Type II-A		Type II-B	
	Spr	Unspr	Spr	Unspr	Spr	Unspr	Spr	Unspr
MAXIMUM HEIGHT IN FEET	UH		180'		85'		75'	
HEIGHT IN STORIES UH 12 11 10 9 8 7 6 5 4 3 2 1	UA	NP	UA	NP	337,500 225,000 150,000	NP	207,000 138,000 92,000	NP
MAXIMUM FLOOR AREA IN SF FOR ANY SINGLE FLOOR	UA	NP	UA	NP	150,000	NP	92,000	NP

Each number in the table represents the maximum total area in square feet for all floors for a building of the indicated story height.

Key to Abbreviations

UA	Unlimited area	Spr	With approved sprinkler system
UH	Unlimited height	Unspr	Without approved sprinkler system
NP	Not permitted		

INTERNATIONAL BUILDING CODE

Measurements

Height is measured from the average finished ground level adjoining the building to the average level of the highest roof. Floor area is measured within exterior walls or exterior walls and fire walls, exclusive of courtyards.

Further Information

For information on Occupancy Group classifications, see page 7. For information on mixed-used buildings, see page 300. For information on which code to consult, see pages 7, 11.

Unit Conversions

1 ft = 304.8 mm, 1 sq ft = 0.0929 m².

					Combustible						
	Ordinary							**Wood Light Frame**			**CONSTRUCTION TYPE**
1-Hour (page 313)		**Unprotected** (page 313)		**Mill** (page 312)		**1-Hour** (page 315)		**Unprotected** (page 315)			
Type III-A		**Type III-B**		**Type IV-HT**		**Type V-A**		**Type V-B**			**IBC NOMENCLATURE**
Spr	Unspr	Spr	Unspr	Spr	Unspr	Spr	Unspr	Spr	Unspr		
85'		75'		85'		70'		60'			**MAXIMUM HEIGHT IN FEET**
										UH	
										12	
										11	
										10	
										9	
										8	**HEIGHT IN STORIES**
										7	
										6	
										5	
										4	
256,500		171,000		324,000		162,000				3	
171,000		114,000		216,000		108,000		54,000		2	
114,000	NP	76,000	NP	144,000	NP	72,000	NP	36,000	NP	1	
114,000	NP	76,000	NP	144,000	NP	72,000	NP	36,000	NP		**MAXIMUM FLOOR AREA IN SF FOR ANY SINGLE FLOOR**

HEIGHT AND AREA TABLES

347

This table was compiled from information contained in the International Building Code 2000. It does not represent an official interpretation by the organization that issues this code.

OCCUPANCY GROUP I-1: INSTITUTIONAL, RESIDENTIAL CARE

Sprinklers

An approved sprinkler system is required for all Group I-1 occupancies. A residential class NFPA 13R or 13D sprinkler system is also permitted, with the modified height and area limitations as indicated in the table columns labeled "Residential Spr."

Fire Walls

For multiplication of the allowable area by subdividing the building with fire walls, see page 302.

Basements

A single-story basement is not included in area calculations, provided that the basement area does not exceed the area permitted for a one-story building.

Excess Frontage

If more than 25% of the building perimeter fronts on a street or open space at least 20 ft (6.1 m) wide that is accessible to firefighting vehicles, the tabulated area limitations below may be increased according to the following table. For example, for a building with half of its perimeter accessible to firefighting equipment via a space not less than 24 ft (7.3 m) wide, the allowable area increase is:

0.80% increase × 25% excess frontage = 20% total area increase.

Width of Frontage*	Percent Area Increase for Each 1% of Frontage* in Excess of 25%
20' (6.1 m)	0.67%
22' (6.7 m)	0.73%
24' (7.3 m)	0.80%
26' (7.9 m)	0.87%
28' (8.5 m)	0.93%
30' (9.1 m) or wider	1.00%

*Intermediate values may be interpolated.

OCCUPANCY GROUP I-1: INSTITUTIONAL, RESIDENTIAL CARE

		Noncombustible						
CONSTRUCTION TYPE		3-Hour (page 308)		2-Hour (page 309)		1-Hour (page 310)		Unprotected (page 311)	
IBC NOMENCLATURE		Type I-A		Type I-B		Type II-A		Type II-B	
		Spr	*Residential Spr	Spr	*Residential Spr	Spr	*Residential Spr	Spr	*Residential Spr
MAXIMUM HEIGHT IN FEET		UH	75'	180'	75'	85'	65'	75'	60'
HEIGHT IN STORIES	UH	UA							
	12								
	11								
	10			660,000					
	9			660,000					
	8			660,000					
	7			660,000					
	6			660,000					
	5			660,000		171,000			
	4		UA	660,000	165,000	171,000	57,000	90,000	
	3			660,000	165,000	171,000	57,000	90,000	30,000
	2			330,000	110,000	114,000	38,000	60,000	20,000
	1			220,000	55,000	76,000	19,000	40,000	10,000
MAXIMUM FLOOR AREA IN SF FOR ANY SINGLE FLOOR		UA	UA	220,000	55,000	76,000	19,000	40,000	10,000

Each number in the table represents the maximum total area in square feet for all floors for a building of the indicated story height.

*Residential grade sprinkler system NFPA 13D or NFPA 13R.

**NFPA 13R only.

Key to Abbreviations

UA	Unlimited area	Spr	With approved sprinkler system
UH	Unlimited height	Unspr	Without approved sprinkler system
NP	Not permitted		

INTERNATIONAL BUILDING CODE

Measurements

Height is measured from the average finished ground level adjoining the building to the average level of the highest roof. Floor area is measured within exterior walls or exterior walls and fire walls, exclusive of courtyards.

Further Information

For information on Occupancy Group classifications, see page 7. For information on mixed-used buildings, see page 300. For information on which code to consult, see pages 7, 11.

Unit Conversions

1 ft = 304.8 mm, 1 sq ft = 0.0929 m².

Combustible												
Ordinary					Mill (page 312)		Wood Light Frame					**CONSTRUCTION TYPE**
1-Hour (page 313)		Unprotected (page 313)					1-Hour (page 315)		Unprotected (page 315)			
Type III-A		Type III-B		Type IV-HT			Type V-A		Type V-B			**IBC NOMENCLATURE**
Spr	*Residential Spr	Spr	*Residential Spr	Spr	*Residential Spr	Spr	*Residential Spr	Spr	*Residential Spr			
85'	65'	75'	60'	85'	65'	70'	60'	60'	60'			**MAXIMUM HEIGHT IN FEET**
										UH		
										12		
										11		
										10		
										9		
										8		**HEIGHT IN STORIES**
										7		
										6		
148,500				162,000						5		
148,500	49,500	90,000		162,000	54,000	94,500	**31,500			4		
148,500	49,500	90,000	30,000	162,000	54,000	94,500	31,500	40,500	**13,500	3		
99,000	33,000	60,000	20,000	108,000	36,000	63,000	21,000	27,000	9,000	2		
66,000	16,500	40,000	10,000	72,000	18,000	42,000	10,500	18,000	4,500	1		**MAXIMUM FLOOR AREA IN SF FOR ANY SINGLE FLOOR**
66,000	16,500	40,000	10,000	72,000	18,000	42,000	10,500	18,000	4,500			

This table was compiled from information contained in the International Building Code 2000. It does not represent an official interpretation by the organization that issues this code.

HEIGHT AND AREA TABLES

349

OCCUPANCY GROUP I-2: INSTITUTIONAL, MEDICAL CARE

Special Requirements

An approved sprinkler system is required for all Group I-2 occupancies. Floors with an occupant load greater than 50 or any floor used by patients for sleeping or treatment must be subdivided by a smoke barrier into at least two separate areas with independent means of egress. See the code for additional special requirements.

Fire Walls

For multiplication of the allowable area by subdividing the building with fire walls, see page 302.

Basements

A single-story basement is not included in area calculations, provided that the basement area does not exceed the area permitted for a one-story building.

Excess Frontage

If more than 25% of the building perimeter fronts on a street or open space at least 20 ft (6.1 m) wide that is accessible to firefighting vehicles, the tabulated area limitations below may be increased according to the following table. For example, for a building with half of its perimeter accessible to firefighting equipment via a space not less than 24 ft (7.3 m) wide, the allowable area increase is:

0.80% increase × 25% excess frontage = 20% total area increase.

OCCUPANCY GROUP I-2: INSTITUTIONAL, MEDICAL CARE

	Noncombustible							
CONSTRUCTION TYPE	**3-Hour** (page 308)		**2-Hour** (page 309)		**1-Hour** (page 310)		**Unprotected** (page 311)	
IBC NOMENCLATURE	Type I-A		Type I-B		Type II-A		Type II-B	
	Spr	Unspr	Spr	Unspr	Spr	Unspr	Spr	Unspr
MAXIMUM HEIGHT IN FEET	UH		180'		85'		75'	
HEIGHT IN STORIES / **MAXIMUM FLOOR AREA IN SF FOR ANY SINGLE FLOOR**	UA	NP	UA	NP	135,000 (3) / 90,000 (2) / 60,000 (1)	NP	44,000	NP
	UA	NP	UA	NP	60,000	NP	44,000	NP

Each number in the table represents the maximum total area in square feet for all floors for a building of the indicated story height.

Key to Abbreviations

UA	Unlimited area	Spr	With approved sprinkler system
UH	Unlimited height	Unspr	Without approved sprinkler system
NP	Not permitted		

INTERNATIONAL BUILDING CODE

Width of Frontage*	Percent Area Increase for Each 1% of Frontage* in Excess of 25%
20' (6.1 m)	0.67%
22' (6.7 m)	0.73%
24' (7.3 m)	0.80%
26' (7.9 m)	0.87%
28' (8.5 m)	0.93%
30' (9.1 m) or wider	1.00%

*Intermediate values may be interpolated.

Measurements

Height is measured from the average finished ground level adjoining the building to the average level of the highest roof. Floor area is measured within exterior walls or exterior walls and fire walls, exclusive of courtyards.

Further Information

For information on Occupancy Group classifications, see page 7. For information on mixed-used buildings, see page 300. For information on which code to consult, see pages 7, 11.

Unit Conversions

1 ft = 304.8 mm, 1 sq ft = 0.0929 m².

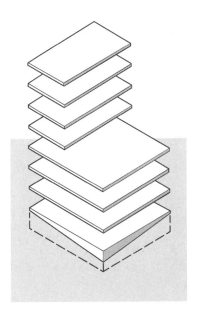

			Combustible									
Ordinary				Wood Light Frame								
1-Hour (page 313)		Unprotected (page 313)		Mill (page 312)		1-Hour (page 315)		Unprotected (page 315)				CONSTRUCTION TYPE
Type III-A		Type III-B		Type IV-HT		Type V-A		Type V-B				IBC NOMENCLATURE
Spr	Unspr	Spr	Unspr	Spr	Unspr	Spr	Unspr	Spr	Unspr			
85'				85'		70'		'				MAXIMUM HEIGHT IN FEET
										UH		
										12		
										11		
										10		
										9		
										8		HEIGHT IN STORIES
										7		
										6		
										5		
										4		
										3		
										2		
48,000	NP	NP	NP	48,000	NP	38,000	NP	NP	NP	1		MAXIMUM FLOOR AREA IN SF FOR ANY SINGLE FLOOR
48,000	NP	NP	NP	48,000	NP	38,000	NP	NP	NP			

This table was compiled from information contained in the International Building Code 2000. It does not represent an official interpretation by the organization that issues this code.

HEIGHT AND AREA TABLES

351

OCCUPANCY GROUP I-3: INSTITUTIONAL, RESTRAINED

Special Requirements

An approved sprinkler system is required for all Group I-3 occupancies. Floors with an occupant load greater than 50 and any floor used by residents for sleeping must be subdivided by a smoke barrier into at least two separate areas with independent means of egress, or, alternatively, residents must have direct exit access to a public way, separated building, or secured yard or court. See the code for additional special requirements.

Fire Walls

For multiplication of the allowable area by subdividing the building with fire walls, see page 302.

Basements

A single-story basement is not included in area calculations, provided that the basement area does not exceed the area permitted for a one-story building.

Excess Frontage

If more than 25% of the building perimeter fronts on a street or open space at least 20 ft (6.1 m) wide that is accessible to firefighting vehicles, the tabulated area limitations below may be increased according to the following table. For example, for a building with half of its perimeter accessible to firefighting equipment via a space not less than 24 ft (7.3 m) wide, the allowable area increase is:

0.80% increase $\times$ 25% excess frontage = 20% total area increase.

OCCUPANCY GROUP I-3: INSTITUTIONAL, MEDICAL CARE

	Noncombustible							
CONSTRUCTION TYPE	3-Hour (page 308)		2-Hour (page 309)		1-Hour (page 310)		Unprotected (page 311)	
IBC NOMENCLATURE	Type I-A		Type I-B		Type II-A		Type II-B	
	Spr	Unspr	Spr	Unspr	Spr	Unspr	Spr	Unspr
MAXIMUM HEIGHT IN FEET	UH		180'		85'		75'	
HEIGHT IN STORIES / UH	UA							
3					135,000			
2					90,000		60,000	
5			UA					
1		NP		NP	60,000	NP	40,000	NP
MAXIMUM FLOOR AREA IN SF FOR ANY SINGLE FLOOR	UA	NP	UA	NP	60,000	NP	40,000	NP

Each number in the table represents the maximum total area in square feet for all floors for a building of the indicated story height.

Key to Abbreviations

UA	Unlimited area	Spr	With approved sprinkler system
UH	Unlimited height	Unspr	Without approved sprinkler system
NP	Not permitted		

INTERNATIONAL BUILDING CODE

Width of Frontage*	Percent Area Increase for Each 1% of Frontage* in Excess of 25%
20' (6.1 m)	0.67%
22' (6.7 m)	0.73%
24' (7.3 m)	0.80%
26' (7.9 m)	0.87%
28' (8.5 m)	0.93%
30' (9.1 m) or wider	1.00%

*Intermediate values may be interpolated.

Measurements

Height is measured from the average finished ground level adjoining the building to the average level of the highest roof. Floor area is measured within exterior walls or exterior walls and fire walls, exclusive of courtyards.

Further Information

For information on Occupancy Group classifications, see page 7. For information on mixed-used buildings, see page 300. For information on which code to consult, see pages 7, 11.

Unit Conversions

1 ft = 304.8 mm, 1 sq ft = 0.0929 m².

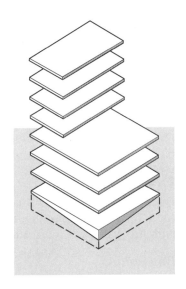

Combustible											
Ordinary				Mill (page 312)		Wood Light Frame					CONSTRUCTION TYPE
1-Hour (page 313)		Unprotected (page 313)				1-Hour (page 315)		Unprotected (page 315)			
Type III-A		Type III-B		Type IV-HT		Type V-A		Type V-B			IBC NOMENCLATURE
Spr	Unspr	Spr	Unspr	Spr	Unspr	Spr	Unspr	Spr	Unspr		
85'		75'		85'		70'		60'			MAXIMUM HEIGHT IN FEET
										UH	
										12	
										11	
										10	
										9	
										8	
										7	HEIGHT IN STORIES
										6	
										5	
										4	
94,500				108,000		67,500				3	
63,000		45,000		72,000		45,000		30,000		2	
42,000	NP	30,000	NP	48,000	NP	30,000	NP	20,000	NP	1	MAXIMUM FLOOR AREA IN SF FOR ANY SINGLE FLOOR
42,000	NP	30,000	NP	48,000	NP	30,000	NP	20,000	NP		

This table was compiled from information contained in the International Building Code 2000. It does not represent an official interpretation by the organization that issues this code.

HEIGHT AND AREA TABLES

353

OCCUPANCY GROUP I-4: INSTITUTIONAL, DAY CARE

Sprinklers

An approved sprinkler system is required for all Group I-4 occupancies.

Fire Walls

For multiplication of the allowable area by subdividing the building with fire walls, see page 302.

Basements

A single-story basement is not included in area calculations, pro-vided that the basement area does not exceed the area permitted for a one-story building.

Excess Frontage

If more than 25% of the building perimeter fronts on a street or open space at least 20 ft (6.1 m) wide that is accessible to firefighting vehicles, the tabulated area limitations below may be increased according to the following table. For example, for a building with half of its perimeter accessible to firefighting equipment via a space not less than 24 ft (7.3 m) wide, the allowable area increase is:

0.80% increase × 25% excess frontage = 20% total area increase.

Width of Frontage*	Percent Area Increase for Each 1% of Frontage* in Excess of 25%
20' (6.1 m)	0.67%
22' (6.7 m)	0.73%
24' (7.3 m)	0.80%
26' (7.9 m)	0.87%
28' (8.5 m)	0.93%
30' (9.1 m) or wider	1.00%

*Intermediate values may be interpolated.

Measurements

Height is measured from the average finished ground level adjoining the building to the average level of the highest roof. Floor area

OCCUPANCY GROUP I-4: INSTITUTIONAL, DAY CARE

CONSTRUCTION TYPE	Noncombustible							
	3-Hour (page 308)		2-Hour (page 309)		1-Hour (page 310)		Unprotected (page 311)	
IBC NOMENCLATURE	Type I-A		Type I-B		Type II-A		Type II-B	
	Spr	Unspr	Spr	Unspr	Spr	Unspr	Spr	Unspr
MAXIMUM HEIGHT IN FEET	UH		180'		85'		75'	
HEIGHT IN STORIES UH	UA							
12								
11								
10								
9								
8								
7								
6			544,500					
5			544,500					
4			544,500		238,500			
3			544,500		238,500		117,000	
2			363,000		159,000		78,000	
1		NP	242,000	NP	106,000	NP	52,000	NP
MAXIMUM FLOOR AREA IN SF FOR ANY SINGLE FLOOR	UA	NP	242,000	NP	106,000	NP	52,000	NP

Each number in the table represents the maximum total area in square feet for all floors for a building of the indicated story height.

Key to Abbreviations

UA	Unlimited area	Spr	With approved sprinkler system
UH	Unlimited height	Unspr	Without approved sprinkler system
NP	Not permitted		

INTERNATIONAL BUILDING CODE

is measured within exterior walls or exterior walls and fire walls, exclusive of courtyards.

Further Information

For information on Occupancy Group classifications, see page 7. For information on mixed-used buildings, see page 300. For information on which code to consult, see pages 7, 11.

Unit Conversions

1 ft = 304.8 mm, 1 sq ft = 0.0929 m².

Combustible										
Ordinary				Mill (page 312)		Wood Light Frame				CONSTRUCTION TYPE
1-Hour (page 313)		Unprotected (page 313)				1-Hour (page 315)		Unprotected (page 315)		
Type III-A		Type III-B		Type IV-HT		Type V-A		Type V-B		IBC NOMENCLATURE
Spr	Unspr	Spr	Unspr	Spr	Unspr	Spr	Unspr	Spr	Unspr	
85'		75'		85'		70'		60'		MAXIMUM HEIGHT IN FEET
										UH
										12
										11
										10
										9
										8
										7 HEIGHT IN STORIES
										6
										5
211,500				211,500						4
211,500		117,000		211,500						3
141,000		78,000		141,000		111,000		54,000		2
94,000	NP	52,000	NP	94,000	NP	74,000	NP	36,000	NP	1
94,000	NP	52,000	NP	94,000	NP	74,000	NP	36,000	NP	MAXIMUM FLOOR AREA IN SF FOR ANY SINGLE FLOOR

This table was compiled from information contained in the International Building Code 2000. It does not represent an official interpretation by the organization that issues this code.

OCCUPANCY GROUP M: MERCANTILE

Sprinklers

An approved sprinkler system is required for Group M occupancies with floor area exceeding 12,000 sq ft (1115 m²), of more than three stories in height, where the combined area of all floors and mezzanines exceeds 24,000 sq ft (2230 m²), or where storage or merchandise is in high-piled or rack storage arrays. A sprinkler system is also required for any M occupancy with:

• A floor having an occupant load of 30 or more located more than 55 ft (17 m) above grade

• Any story or basement greater than 1500 sq ft (139 m2) in area without openings to the exterior

• Most underground portions of the building where occupancy occurs more than 30 feet (9 m) below the lowest level of exit discharge

Unlimited Area Buildings

One- and two-story Occupancy M buildings may be of unlimited area when sprinklered throughout and surrounded on all sides by public ways or yards not less than 60 ft (18 m) in width. Unlimited area Occupancy M buildings of noncombustible construction used for rack storage facilities and that do not have access by the public may be of any height.

Covered Mall Buildings

Covered malls, consisting of a single building enclosing multiple retail, entertainment, passenger transportation, and other similar facilities, are subject to a number of special provisions under the International Building Code. Covered mall buildings must be fully sprinklered. If constructed with any type except Wood Light Frame, covered malls may be of unlimited area, provided that they are surrounded on all sides by permanent open space not less than 60 feet (18 m) in width. See the code for additional requirements.

Fire Walls

For multiplication of the allowable area by subdividing the building with fire walls, see page 302.

OCCUPANCY GROUP M: MERCANTILE

	Noncombustible							
CONSTRUCTION TYPE	3-Hour (page 308)		2-Hour (page 309)		1-Hour (page 310)		Unprotected (page 311)	
IBC NOMENCLATURE	Type I-A		Type I-B		Type II-A		Type II-B	
	Spr	Unspr	Spr	Unspr	Spr	Unspr	Spr	Unspr
MAXIMUM HEIGHT IN FEET	UH	75'	180'	75'	85'	65'	75'	55'
HEIGHT IN STORIES UH	UA	UA						
12			UA					
11				UA				
10								
9								
8								
7								
6								
5					193,500		112,500	
4					193,500	64,500	112,500	37,500
3					193,500	64,500	112,500	37,500
2					129,000	43,000	75,000	25,000
1					86,000	21,500	50,000	12,500
MAXIMUM FLOOR AREA IN SF FOR ANY SINGLE FLOOR	UA	UA	UA	UA	86,000	21,500	50,000	12,500

Each number in the table represents the maximum total area in square feet for all floors for a building of the indicated story height.

Key to Abbreviations

UA	Unlimited area	Spr	With approved sprinkler system
UH	Unlimited height	Unspr	Without approved sprinkler system
NP	Not permitted		

INTERNATIONAL BUILDING CODE

Basements

A single-story basement is not included in area calculations, provided that the basement area does not exceed the area permitted for a one-story building.

Excess Frontage

If more than 25% of the building perimeter fronts on a street or open space at least 20 ft (6.1 m) wide that is accessible to firefighting vehicles, the tabulated area limitations below may be increased according to the following table. For example, for a building with half of its perimeter accessible to firefighting equipment via a space not less than 24 ft (7.3 m) wide, the allowable area increase is:

0.80% increase × 25% excess frontage = 20% total area increase.

Width of Frontage*	Percent Area Increase for Each 1% of Frontage* in Excess of 25%
20' (6.1 m)	0.67%
22' (6.7 m)	0.73%
24' (7.3 m)	0.80%
26' (7.9 m)	0.87%
28' (8.5 m)	0.93%
30' (9.1 m) or wider	1.00%

*Intermediate values may be interpolated.

Measurements

Height is measured from the average finished ground level adjoining the building to the average level of the highest roof. Floor area is measured within exterior walls or exterior walls and fire walls, exclusive of courtyards.

Further Information

For information on Occupancy Group classifications, see page 7. For information on mixed-used buildings, see page 300. For information on which code to consult, see pages 7, 11.

Unit Conversions

1 ft = 304.8 mm, 1 sq ft = 0.0929 m².

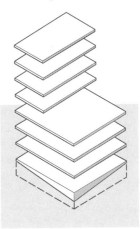

				Combustible							CONSTRUCTION TYPE
Ordinary						Wood Light Frame					
1-Hour (page 313)		Unprotected (page 313)		Mill (page 312)		1-Hour (page 315)		Unprotected (page 315)			
Type III-A		Type III-B		Type IV-HT		Type V-A		Type V-B			IBC NOMENCLATURE
Spr	Unspr	Spr	Unspr	Spr	Unspr	Spr	Unspr	Spr	Unspr		
85'	65'	75'	55'	85'	65'	70'	50'	60'	40'		MAXIMUM HEIGHT IN FEET
										UH	
										12	
										11	
										10	
										9	
										8	HEIGHT IN STORIES
										7	
										6	
166,500		112,500		184,500						5	
166,500	55,500	112,500	37,500	184,500	61,500	126,000				4	
166,500	55,500	112,500	37,500	184,500	61,500	126,000	42,000			3	
111,000	37,000	75,000	25,000	123,000	41,000	84,000	28,000	54,000		2	
74,000	18,500	50,000	12,500	82,000	20,500	56,000	14,000	36,000	9,000	1	MAXIMUM FLOOR AREA IN SF FOR ANY SINGLE FLOOR
74,000	18,500	50,000	12,500	82,000	20,500	56,000	14,000	36,000	9,000		

This table was compiled from information contained in the International Building Code 2000. It does not represent an official interpretation by the organization that issues this code.

OCCUPANCY GROUP R-1: RESIDENTIAL, HOTELS AND MOTELS

Sprinklers

An approved sprinkler system is required for all Group R-1 occupancies. A residential class NFPA 13R sprinkler system is also permitted with R-1 occupancies. In this case, height and area limitations from the "Residential Spr" column of the table on these two facing pages should be used. Sprinklers may be omitted entirely from a Group R-1 occupancy where guest rooms are not more than three stories above the lowest level of exit discharge and each guest room has at least one door leading directly to an exterior exit access. In this case, height and area limitations should be read from the "Residential Spr" columns of the table, with the added restriction that the number of stories permitted for buildings of Wood Light Frame construction must be reduced by one from the values shown in those columns.

A sprinkler system is also required for any R-1 occupancy with:

- Any story or basement greater than 1500 sq ft (139 m^2) in area without openings to the exterior

- Most underground portions of the building where occupancy occurs more than 30 feet (9 m) below the lowest level of exit discharge

Fire Walls

For multiplication of the allowable area by subdividing the building with fire walls, see page 302.

Basements

A single-story basement is not included in area calculations, provided that the basement area does not exceed the area permitted for a one-story building.

Excess Frontage

If more than 25% of the building perimeter fronts on a street or open space at least 20 ft (6.1 m) wide that is accessible to firefighting vehicles, the tabulated area limitations below may be increased according to the following table. For example, for a

OCCUPANCY GROUP R-1: RESIDENTIAL, HOTELS AND MOTELS

	Noncombustible							
CONSTRUCTION TYPE	3-Hour (page 308)		2-Hour (page 309)		1-Hour (page 310)		Unprotected (page 311)	
IBC NOMENCLATURE	Type I-A		Type I-B		Type II-A		Type II-B	
	Spr	*Residential Spr	Spr	*Residential Spr	Spr	*Residential Spr	Spr	*Residential Spr
MAXIMUM HEIGHT IN FEET	UH	60'	180'	60'	85'	60'	75'	60'
HEIGHT IN STORIES UH	UA							
12			UA					
11								
10								
9								
8								
7								
6								
5					216,000		144,000	
4		UA		UA	216,000	72,000	144,000	48,000
3					216,000	72,000	144,000	48,000
2					144,000	48,000	96,000	32,000
1					96,000	24,000	64,000	16,000
MAXIMUM FLOOR AREA IN SF FOR ANY SINGLE FLOOR	UA	UA	UA	UA	96,000	24,000	64,000	16,000

Each number in the table represents the maximum total area in square feet for all floors for a building of the indicated story height.

*Residential grade sprinkler system NFPA 13R.

Key to Abbreviations

UA	Unlimited area	Spr	With approved sprinkler system
UH	Unlimited height	Unspr	Without approved sprinkler system
NP	Not permitted		

building with half of its perimeter accessible to firefighting equipment via a space not less than 24 ft (7.3 m) wide, the allowable area increase is:

0.80% increase × 25% excess frontage = 20% total area increase.

Width of Frontage*	Percent Area Increase for Each 1% of Frontage* in Excess of 25%
20' (6.1 m)	0.67%
22' (6.7 m)	0.73%
24' (7.3 m)	0.80%
26' (7.9 m)	0.87%
28' (8.5 m)	0.93%
30' (9.1 m) or wider	1.00%

*Intermediate values may be interpolated.

Measurements

Height is measured from the average finished ground level adjoining the building to the average level of the highest roof. Floor area is measured within exterior walls or exterior walls and fire walls, exclusive of courtyards.

Further Information

For information on Occupancy Group classifications, see page 7. For information on mixed-used buildings, see page 300. For information on which code to consult, see pages 7, 11.

Unit Conversions

1 ft = 304.8 mm, 1 sq ft = 0.0929 m².

	Combustible									
	Ordinary				Mill (page 312)		Wood Light Frame			
Stories	1-Hour (page 313)		Unprotected (page 313)				1-Hour (page 315)		Unprotected (page 315)	
	Type III-A		Type III-B		Type IV-HT		Type V-A		Type V-B	
	Spr	*Residential Spr	Spr	*Residential Spr	Spr	*Residential Spr	Spr	*Residential Spr	Spr	*Residential Spr
Max Height (ft)	85'	60'	75'	60'	85'	60'	70'	60'	60'	60'
5	216,000		144,000		184,500					
4	216,000	72,000	144,000	48,000	184,500	61,500	108,000	36,000		
3	216000	72,000	144,000	48,000	184,500	61,500	108,000	36,000	63,000	21,000
2	144,000	48,000	96,000	32,000	123,000	41,000	72,000	24,000	42,000	14,000
1	96,000	24,000	64,000	16,000	82,000	20,500	48,000	12,000	28,000	7,000
	96,000	24,000	64,000	16,000	82,000	20,500	48,000	12,000	28,000	7,000

CONSTRUCTION TYPE

IBC NOMENCLATURE

MAXIMUM HEIGHT IN FEET

HEIGHT IN STORIES

MAXIMUM FLOOR AREA IN SF FOR ANY SINGLE FLOOR

HEIGHT AND AREA TABLES

359

This table was compiled from information contained in the International Building Code 2000. It does not represent an official interpretation by the organization that issues this code.

OCCUPANCY GROUP R-2: RESIDENTIAL, MULTIFAMILY

Special Requirements

An approved sprinkler system is required for all Group R-2 occupancies. A residential class NFPA 13R sprinkler system is also permitted with R-2 occupancies. In this case, height and area limitations from the "Residential Spr" column of the table on these two facing pages should be used. Sprinklers may be omitted entirely from a Group R-2 occupancy not more than two stories in height (including basements with R-2 occupancy) and not having more than 16 dwelling units. In this case, height and area limitations should be read from the "Residential Spr" columns of the table, from the rows for one- and two-story heights only.

A sprinkler system is also required for any R-2 occupancy with:

• Any story or basement greater than 1500 sq ft (139 m²) in area without openings to the exterior

The height of R-2 occupancies of sprinklered 1-Hour Ordinary construction may be increased to six stories where the floor construction above the basement has a fire-resistance rating of not less than 3 hours and floors are subdivided by 2-hour rated fire walls into areas not larger than 3000 sq ft (279 m²). The height of R-2 occupancies of sprinklered 1-Hour Noncombustible construction may be increased to nine stories and 100 ft (30 m) where floor construction above the basement has a fire-resistance rating of 1½ hours, the building is separated by not less than 50 ft (15 m) from other buildings and property lines, and exits are protected by 2-hour rated enclosures.

Fire Walls

For multiplication of the allowable area by subdividing the building with fire walls, see page 302.

Basements

A single-story basement is not

OCCUPANCY GROUP R-2: RESIDENTIAL, MULTIFAMILY

	Noncombustible							
CONSTRUCTION TYPE	**3-Hour (page 308)**		**2-Hour (page 309)**		**1-Hour (page 310)**		**Unprotected (page 311)**	
IBC NOMENCLATURE	**Type I-A**		**Type I-B**		**Type II-A**		**Type II-B**	
	Spr	*Residential Spr	Spr	*Residential Spr	Spr	*Residential Spr	Spr	*Residential Spr
MAXIMUM HEIGHT IN FEET	UH	60'	180'	60'	85'	60'	75'	60'
UH	UA							
12			UA					
11								
10								
9								
8								
7								
6								
5					216,000		144,000	
4		UA		UA	216,000	72,000	144,000	48,000
3					216,000	72,000	144,000	48,000
2					144,000	48,000	96,000	32,000
1					96,000	24,000	64,000	16,000
MAXIMUM FLOOR AREA IN SF FOR ANY SINGLE FLOOR	UA	UA	UA	UA	96,000	24,000	64,000	16,000

Each number in the table represents the maximum total area in square feet for all floors for a building of the indicated story height.

*Residential grade sprinkler system NFPA 13R.

Key to Abbreviations

UA	Unlimited area	Spr	With approved sprinkler system
UH	Unlimited height	Unspr	Without approved sprinkler system
NP	Not permitted		

INTERNATIONAL BUILDING CODE

included in area calculations, provided that the basement area does not exceed the area permitted for a one-story building.

Excess Frontage

If more than 25% of the building perimeter fronts on a street or open space at least 20 ft (6.1 m) wide that is accessible to firefighting vehicles, the tabulated area limitations below may be increased according to the following table. For example, for a building with half of its perimeter accessible to firefighting equipment via a space not less than 24 ft (7.3 m) wide, the allowable area increase is:

0.80% increase × 25% excess frontage = 20% total area increase.

Width of Frontage*	Percent Area Increase for Each 1% of Frontage* in Excess of 25%
20' (6.1 m)	0.67%
22' (6.7 m)	0.73%
24' (7.3 m)	0.80%
26' (7.9 m)7	0.87%
28' (8.5 m)	0.93%
30' (9.1 m) or wider	1.00%

*Intermediate values may be interpolated.

Measurements

Height is measured from the average finished ground level adjoining the building to the average level of the highest roof. Floor area is measured within exterior walls or exterior walls and fire walls, exclusive of courtyards.

Further Information

For information on Occupancy Group classifications, see page 7. For information on mixed-used buildings, see page 300. For information on which code to consult, see pages 7, 11.

Unit Conversions

1 ft = 304.8 mm, 1 sq ft = 0.0929 m².

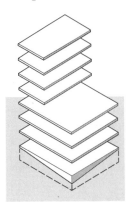

	Combustible											
	Ordinary					**Wood Light Frame**						CONSTRUCTION TYPE
	1-Hour (page 313)		Unprotected (page 313)		Mill (page 312)		1-Hour (page 315)		Unprotected (page 315)			
	Type III-A		Type III-B		Type IV-HT		Type V-A		Type V-B			IBC NOMENCLATURE
	Spr	*Residential Spr	Spr	*Residential Spr	Spr	*Residential Spr	—	*Residential Spr	Spr	*Residential Spr		
	85'	60'	75'	60'	85'	60'	70'	60'	60'	60'		MAXIMUM HEIGHT IN FEET
UH												
12												
11												
10												
9												
8												HEIGHT IN STORIES
7												
6												
5	216,000		144,000		184,500							
4	216,000	72,000	144,000	48,000	184,500	61,500	108,000	36,000				
3	216,000	72,000	144,000	48,000	184,500	61,500	108,000	36,000	63,000	21,000		
2	144,000	48,000	96,000	32,000	123,000	41,000	72,000	24,000	42,000	14,000		
1	96,000	24,000	64,000	16,000	82,000	20,500	48,000	12,000	28,000	7,000		
	96,000	24,000	64,000	16,000	82,000	20,500	48,000	12,000	28,000	7,000		MAXIMUM FLOOR AREA IN SF FOR ANY SINGLE FLOOR

This table was compiled from information contained in the International Building Code 2000. It does not represent an official interpretation by the organization that issues this code.

HEIGHT AND AREA TABLES

361

OCCUPANCY GROUP R-3: RESIDENTIAL, ONE- AND TWO-FAMILY

International Residential Code

Residential one- and two-family dwellings not more than three stories in height and with separate means of egress are governed by the requirements of the *International Residential Code,* a separate but related code developed by the International Code Council for buildings of this type. For buildings such as these, use the following preliminary guidelines:

• Building height is limited to three stories.

• Adjoining units in two-family dwellings must be separated by 1-hour rated wall and ceiling/floor assemblies,

• Exterior walls of separate buildings facing within 3 ft (0.9 m) of each other must be 1-hour rated, and free of openings.

• Common walls separating adjoining townhouses must be 2-hour rated and free of plumbing and mechanical services.

• Local building department regulations should be consulted for sprinkler requirements, if any.

International Building Code

Residential one- and two-family dwellings greater than three stories in height or with shared means of egress are governed by the requirements of the International Building Code. For these buildings, use the table on these two facing pages to determine height and area limitations.

In Group R-3 Residential buildings, a residential class NFPA 13D sprinkler system is permitted. In this case, read from the columns in the table for unsprinklered systems. For Construction Types limited to less than 4 stories in height, the story height may be increased by one from that shown. Maximum building height may also be increased up to 60' (18 m) where indicated as less in the table. A residential class NFPA 13R sprinkler

OCCUPANCY GROUP R-3: RESIDENTIAL, ONE- AND TWO-FAMILY

	Noncombustible							
CONSTRUCTION TYPE	3-Hour (page 308)		2-Hour (page 309)		1-Hour (page 310)		Unprotected (page 311)	
IBC NOMENCLATURE	Type I-A		Type I-B		Type II-A		Type II-B	
	Spr	Unspr	Spr	Unspr	Spr	Unspr	Spr	Unspr
MAXIMUM HEIGHT IN FEET	UH	75'	180'	75'	85'	65'	75'	55'
HEIGHT IN STORIES	UA	UA	UA	UA	UA	UA	UA	UA
MAXIMUM FLOOR AREA IN SF FOR ANY SINGLE FLOOR	UA	UA	UA	UA	UA	UA	UA	UA

Each number in the table represents the maximum total area in square feet for all floors for a building of the indicated story height.

Key to Abbreviations

UA	Unlimited area	Spr	With approved sprinkler system
UH	Unlimited height	Unspr	Without approved sprinkler system
NP	Not permitted		

INTERNATIONAL BUILDING CODE

system is also permitted in Group R-3 Residential buildings. In this case, read from the table for unsprinklered systems, without modification.

For separation of dwelling units and adjacent buildings, use the following preliminary guidelines:

• Adjoining units in two-family dwellings must be separated by 1-hour rated wall and ceiling/floor assemblies.

• Exterior walls of separate buildings facing within 10 ft (3 m) of each other must be 1-hour rated, and free of openings.

• Common walls separating adjoining townhouses must be 2-hour

rated and free of plumbing and mechanical services.

Measurements

Height is measured from the average finished ground level adjoining the building to the average level of the highest roof. Floor area is measured within exterior walls or exterior walls and fire walls, exclusive of courtyards.

Further Information

For information on Occupancy Group classifications, see page 7. For information on mixed-used buildings, see page 300. For information on which code to consult, see pages 7, 11.

Unit Conversions

1 ft = 304.8 mm, 1 sq ft = 0.0929 m².

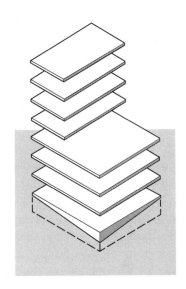

Combustible											
Ordinary				Mill (page 312)		Wood Light Frame					CONSTRUCTION TYPE
1-Hour (page 313)		Unprotected (page 313)				1-Hour (page 315)		Unprotected (page 315)			
Type III-A		Type III-B		Type IV-HT		Type V-A		Type V-B			IBC NOMENCLATURE
Spr	Unspr	Spr	Unspr	Spr	Unspr	Spr	Unspr	Spr	Unspr		
55'	65'	75'	55'	85'	65'	70'	50'	60'	40'		MAXIMUM HEIGHT IN FEET

UH
12
11
10
9
8   HEIGHT IN STORIES
7
6
5
4
3
2
1

MAXIMUM FLOOR AREA IN SF FOR ANY SINGLE FLOOR

HEIGHT AND AREA TABLES

363

This table was compiled from information contained in the International Building Code 2000. It does not represent an official interpretation by the organization that issues this code.

OCCUPANCY GROUP R-4: RESIDENTIAL, ASSISTED LIVING

Sprinklers

An approved sprinkler system is required for all Group R-4 occupancies with 8 or more occupants. A sprinkler system is also required for any R-4 occupancy with:

• Any story or basement greater than 1500 sq ft (139 m²) in area without openings to the exterior

• Most underground portions of the building where occupancy occurs more than 30 ft (9 m) below the lowest level of exit discharge

In Group R-4 Residential buildings, a residential class NFPA 13D sprinkler system is permitted. In this case, read from the columns in the table for unsprinklered systems. For Construction Types limited to less than 4 stories in the table, the story height may be increased by one from that shown. Maximum building height may be also increased up to 60 ft (18 m) where indicated as less in the table. A residential class NFPA 13R sprinkler system is also permitted in Group R-4 Residential buildings. In this case, read from the table for unsprinklered systems, without modification.

Fire Walls

For multiplication of the allowable area by subdividing the building with fire walls, see page 302.

Basements

A single-story basement is not included in area calculations, provided that the basement area does not exceed the area permitted for a one-story building.

Excess Frontage

If more than 25% of the building perimeter fronts on a street or open space at least 20 ft (6.1 m) wide that is accessible to firefighting vehicles, the tabulated area limitations below may be increased according to the following table. For example,

OCCUPANCY GROUP R-4: RESIDENTIAL, ASSISTED LIVING

	Noncombustible							
CONSTRUCTION TYPE	3-Hour (page 308)		2-Hour (page 309)		1-Hour (page 310)		Unprotected (page 311)	
IBC NOMENCLATURE	Type I-A		Type I-B		Type II-A		Type II-B	
	Spr	*Unspr	Spr	*Unspr	Spr	*Unspr	Spr	*Unspr
MAXIMUM HEIGHT IN FEET	UH	75'	180'	75'	85'	65'	75'	55'
HEIGHT IN STORIES UH	UA	UA						
12			UA					
11				UA				
10								
9								
8								
7								
6								
5					216,000		144,000	
4					216,000	72,000	144,000	48,000
3					216,000	72,000	144,000	48,000
2					144,000	48,000	96,000	32,000
1					96,000	24,000	64,000	16,000
MAXIMUM FLOOR AREA IN SF FOR ANY SINGLE FLOOR	UA	UA	UA	UA	96,000	24,000	64,000	16,000

Each number in the table represents the maximum total area in square feet for all floors for a building of the indicated story height.

*See "Sprinklers" above.

Key to Abbreviations

UA	Unlimited area	Spr	With approved sprinkler system
UH	Unlimited height	Unspr	Without approved sprinkler system
NP	Not permitted		

for a building with half of its perimeter accessible to firefighting equipment via a space not less than 24 ft (7.3 m) wide, the allowable area increase is:

0.80% increase × 25% excess frontage = 20% total area increase.

Width of Frontage*	Percent Area Increase for Each 1% of Frontage* in Excess of 25%
20' (6.1 m)	0.67%
22' (6.7 m)	0.73%
24' (7.3 m)	0.80%
26' (7.9 m)	0.87%
28' (8.5 m)	0.93%
30' (9.1 m) or wider	1.00%

*Intermediate values may be interpolated.

Measurements

Height is measured from the average finished ground level adjoining the building to the average level of the highest roof. Floor area is measured within exterior walls or exterior walls and fire walls, exclusive of courtyards.

Further Information

For information on Occupancy Group classifications, see page 7. For information on mixed-used buildings, see page 300. For information on which code to consult, see pages 7, 11.

Unit Conversions

1 ft = 304.8 mm, 1 sq ft = 0.0929 m².

CONSTRUCTION TYPE

IBC NOMENCLATURE

MAXIMUM HEIGHT IN FEET

HEIGHT IN STORIES

MAXIMUM FLOOR AREA IN SF FOR ANY SINGLE FLOOR

HEIGHT AND AREA TABLES

365

Combustible									
Ordinary				Mill (page 312)		Wood Light Frame			
1-Hour (page 313)		Unprotected (page 313)				1-Hour (page 315)		Unprotected (page 315)	
Type III-A		Type III-B		Type IV-HT		Type V-A		Type V-B	
Spr	*Unspr	Spr	*Unspr	Spr	*Unspr	Spr	*Unspr	Spr	*Unspr
85'	65'	75'	55'	85'	65'	70'	50'	60'	40'

Type III-A Spr	Type III-A *Unspr	Type III-B Spr	Type III-B *Unspr	Type IV-HT Spr	Type IV-HT *Unspr	Type V-A Spr	Type V-A *Unspr	Type V-B Spr	Type V-B *Unspr	Stories
										UH
										12
										11
										10
										9
										8
										7
										6
216,000		144,000		184,500						5
216,000	72,000	144,000	48,000	184,500	61,500	108,000				4
216,000	72,000	144,000	48,000	184,500	61,500	108,000	36,000	63,000		3
144,000	48,000	96,000	32,000	123,000	41,000	72,000	24,000	42,000	14,000	2
96,000	24,000	64,000	16,000	82,000	20,500	48,000	12,000	28,000	7,000	1
96,000	24,000	64,000	16,000	82,000	20,500	48,000	12,000	28,000	7,000	

This table was compiled from information contained in the International Building Code 2000. It does not represent an official interpretation by the organization that issues this code.

INTERNATIONAL BUILDING CODE

OCCUPANCY GROUP S-1: STORAGE, MODERATE HAZARD

Sprinklers

An approved sprinkler system is required for Group S-1 occupancies with any floor exceeding 12,000 sq ft (1115 m²) in area, where more than three stories in height, or where the combined area of all floors and mezzanines exceeds 24,000 sq ft (2230 m²). A sprinkler system is required for repair garages two or more stories in height (including basements with S-1 occupancy) and greater than 10,000 sq ft (939 m²) in area, for one-story repair garages more than 12,000 sq ft (1115 m²) in area, for any repair garage occurring in a base-ment, and for any building with bulk storage of tires greater than 20,0000 cu ft (566 m³) in volume. A sprinkler system is also required for any S-1 occupancy with:

- A floor having an occupant load of 30 or more located more than 55 ft (17 m) above grade
- Any story or basement greater than 1500 sq ft (139 m²) in area without openings to the exterior
- Most underground portions of the building where occupancy occurs more than 30 ft (9 m) below the lowest level of exit discharge.

Unlimited Area Buildings

One- and two-story Occupancy S-2 buildings, sprinklered throughout, may be of unlimited area when sur-rounded on all sides by public ways or yards not less than 60 ft (18 m) in width.

Fire Walls

For multiplication of the allowable area by subdividing the building with fire walls, see page 302.

Basements

A single-story basement is not included in area calculations, pro-vided that the basement area does not exceed the area permitted for a one-story building.

Excess Frontage

If more than 25% of the building perimeter fronts on a street or open space at least 20 ft (6.1 m) wide that is accessible to firefighting vehi-cles, the tabulated area limitations

OCCUPANCY GROUP S-1: STORAGE, MODERATE HAZARD

CONSTRUCTION TYPE	Noncombustible							
	3-Hour (page 308)		2-Hour (page 309)		1-Hour (page 310)		Unprotected (page 311)	
IBC NOMENCLATURE	Type I-A		Type I-B		Type II-A		Type II-B	
	Spr	Unspr	Spr	Unspr	Spr	Unspr	Spr	Unspr
MAXIMUM HEIGHT IN FEET	UH	75'	180'	75'	85'	65'	75'	55'
UH	UA							
12			432,000					
11			432,000					
10			432,000					
9			432,000					
8			432,000					
7			432,000					
6			432,000					
5			432,000		234,000			
4			432,000		234,000		157,500	
3		UA	432,000	24,000	234,000	24,000	157,500	24,000
2			288,000	24,000	156,000	24,000	105,000	24,000
1			192,000	12,000	104,000	12,000	70,000	12,000
MAXIMUM FLOOR AREA IN SF FOR ANY SINGLE FLOOR	UA	UA	192,000	12,000	104,000	12,000	70,000	12,000

Each number in the table represents the maximum total area in square feet for all floors for a building of the indicated story height.

Key to Abbreviations

UA	Unlimited area	Spr	With approved sprinkler system
UH	Unlimited height	Unspr	Without approved sprinkler system
NP	Not permitted		

INTERNATIONAL BUILDING CODE

below may be increased according to the following table. For example, for a building with half of its perimeter accessible to firefighting equipment via a space not less than 24 ft (7.3 m) wide, the allowable area increase is:

0.80% increase × 25% excess frontage = 20% total area increase.

Width of Frontage*	Percent Area Increase for Each 1% of Frontage* in Excess of 25%
20' (6.1 m)	0.67%
22' (6.7 m)	0.73%
24' (7.3 m)	0.80%
26' (7.9 m)	0.87%
28' (8.5 m)	0.93%
30' (9.1 m) or wider	1.00%

*Intermediate values may be interpolated.

Measurements

Height is measured from the average finished ground level adjoining the building to the average level of the highest roof. Floor area is measured within exterior walls or exterior walls and fire walls, exclusive of courtyards.

Further Information

For information on Occupancy Group classifications, see page 7. For information on mixed-used buildings, see page 300. For information on which code to consult, see pages 7, 11.

Unit Conversions

1 ft = 304.8 mm, 1 sq ft = 0.0929 m².

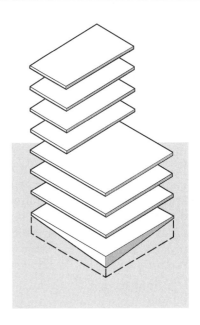

				Combustible							
Ordinary						Wood Light Frame					CONSTRUCTION TYPE
1-Hour (page 313)		Unprotected (page 313)		Mill (page 312)		1-Hour (page 315)		Unprotected (page 315)			
Type III-A		Type III-B		Type IV-HT		Type V-A		Type V-B			IBC NOMENCLATURE
Spr	Unspr	Spr	Unspr	Spr	Unspr	Spr	Unspr	Spr	Unspr		
85'	65'	75'	55'	85'	65'	70'	50'	60'	40'		MAXIMUM HEIGHT IN FEET
										UH	
										12	
										11	
										10	
										9	
										8	HEIGHT IN STORIES
										7	
										6	
				229,500						5	
234,000		157,500		229,500		126,000				4	
234,000	24,000	157,500	24,000	229,500	24,000	126,000	24,000			3	
156,000	24,000	105,000	24,000	153,000	24,000	84,000	24,000	54,000		2	
104,000	12,000	70,000	12,000	102,000	12,000	56,000	12,000	36,000	9,000	1	MAXIMUM FLOOR AREA IN SF FOR ANY SINGLE FLOOR
104,000	12,000	70,000	12,000	102,000	12,000	56,000	12,000	36,000	9,000		

This table was compiled from information contained in the International Building Code 2000. It does not represent an official interpretation by the organization that issues this code.

HEIGHT AND AREA TABLES

367

OCCUPANCY GROUP S-2: STORAGE, LOW HAZARD

Sprinklers

An approved sprinkler system is required for all enclosed parking garages located beneath other occupancy groups, except when located beneath Group R-3 occupancies not exceeding three stories in height. A sprinkler system is required for commercial truck or bus storage areas exceeding 5000 sq ft (464 m^2) in area. A sprinkler system is also required for any S-2 occupancy with:

• A floor having an occupant load of 30 or more located more than 55 ft (17 m) above grade

• Any story or basement greater than 1500 sq ft (139 m^2) in area without openings to the exterior

• Most underground portions of buildings where occupancy occurs more than 30 ft (9 m) below the lowest level of exit discharge

Unlimited Area Buildings

One-story occupancy S-2 buildings, sprinklered or unsprinklered, and two-story Occupancy S-2 buildings, sprinklered throughout, may be of unlimited area when surrounded on all sides by public ways or yards not less than 60 ft (18 m) in width.

Parking Garages

For enclosed garages, which rely on mechanical ventilation to prevent the accumulation of exhaust gasses, use the height and area table on these two facing pages. For open garages, which rely on natural ventilation, use the table on the next two facing pages. For more information about Parking Garages and mixed-use occupancies, see page 301.

Fire Walls

For multiplication of the allowable area by subdividing the building with fire walls, see page 302.

Basements

A single-story basement is not included in area calculations, provided that the basement area does not exceed the area permitted for a one-story building.

Excess Frontage

If more than 25% of the building perimeter fronts on a street or open space at least 20 ft (6.1 m) wide that is accessible to firefighting vehicles, the tabulated area limitations

OCCUPANCY GROUP S-2: STORAGE, LOW HAZARD

	Noncombustible							
CONSTRUCTION TYPE	3-Hour (page 308)		2-Hour (page 309)		1-Hour (page 310)		Unprotected (page 311)	
IBC NOMENCLATURE	Type I-A		Type I-B		Type II-A		Type II-B	
	Spr	Unspr	Spr	Unspr	Spr	Unspr	Spr	Unspr
MAXIMUM HEIGHT IN FEET	UH	75'	180'	75'	85'	65'	75'	55'
UH	UA	UA						
12			711,000					
11			711,000	237,000				
10			711,000	237,000				
9			711,000	237,000				
8			711,000	237,000				
7			711,000	237,000				
6			711,000	237,000	351,000			
5			711,000	237,000	351,000	117,000	234,000	
4			711,000	237,000	351,000	117,000	234,000	78,000
3			711,000	237,000	351,000	117,000	234,000	78,000
2			474,000	158,000	234,000	78,000	156,000	52,000
1			316,000	79,000	156,000	39,000	104,000	26,000
MAXIMUM FLOOR AREA IN SF FOR ANY SINGLE FLOOR	UA	UA	316,000	79,000	156,000	39,000	104,000	26,000

Height in Stories labels appear in left column (UH, 12, 11, 10, 9, 8, 7, 6, 5, 4, 3, 2, 1) under **HEIGHT IN STORIES**.

Each number in the table represents the maximum total area in square feet for all floors for a building of the indicated story height.

368

Key to Abbreviations

UA	Unlimited area	Spr	With approved sprinkler system
UH	Unlimited height	Unspr	Without approved sprinkler system
NP	Not permitted		

INTERNATIONAL BUILDING CODE

below may be increased according to the following table. For example, for a building with half of its perimeter accessible to firefighting equipment via a space not less than 24 ft (7.3 m) wide, the allowable area increase is:

0.80% increase × 25% excess frontage = 20% total area increase.

Width of Frontage*	Percent Area Increase for Each 1% of Frontage* in Excess of 25%
20' (6.1 m)	0.67%
22' (6.7 m)	0.73%
24' (7.3 m)	0.80%
26' (7.9 m)	0.87%
28' (8.5 m)	0.93%
30' (9.1 m) or wider	1.00%

*Intermediate values may be interpolated.

Measurements

Height is measured from the average finished ground level adjoining the building to the average level of the highest roof. Floor area is measured within exterior walls or exterior walls and fire walls, exclusive of courtyards.

Further Information

For information on Occupancy Group classifications, see page 7. For information on mixed-used buildings, see page 300. For information on which code to consult, see pages 7, 11.

Unit Conversions

1 ft = 304.8 mm, 1 sq ft = 0.0929 m².

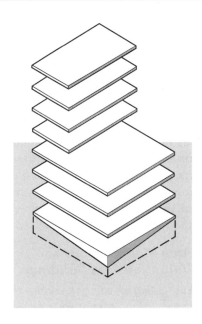

	Combustible										CONSTRUCTION TYPE
	Ordinary						Wood Light Frame				
	1-Hour (page 313)		Unprotected (page 313)		Mill (page 312)		1-Hour (page 315)		Unprotected (page 315)		
	Type III-A		Type III-B		Type IV-HT		Type V-A		Type V-B		IBC NOMENCLATURE
	Spr	Unspr	Spr	Unspr	Spr	Unspr	Spr	Unspr	Spr	Unspr	
	85'	65'	75'	55'	85'	65'	70'	50'	60'	40'	MAXIMUM HEIGHT IN FEET

Type III-A Spr	Type III-A Unspr	Type III-B Spr	Type III-B Unspr	Type IV-HT Spr	Type IV-HT Unspr	Type V-A Spr	Type V-A Unspr	Type V-B Spr	Type V-B Unspr	Stories
										UH
										12
										11
										10
										9
										8
										7
				346,500						6
351,000		234,000		346,500	115,500	189,000				5
351,000	117,000	234,000	78,000	346,500	115,500	189,000	63,000			4
351,000	117,000	234,000	78,000	346,500	115,500	189,000	63,000	121,500		3
234,000	78,000	156,000	52,000	231,000	77,000	126,000	42,000	81,000	27,000	2
156,000	39,000	104,000	26,000	154,000	38,500	84,000	21,000	54,000	13,500	1
156,000	39,000	104,000	26,000	154,000	38,500	84,000	21,000	54,000	13,500	MAXIMUM FLOOR AREA IN SF FOR ANY SINGLE FLOOR

HEIGHT IN STORIES

This table was compiled from information contained in the International Building Code 2000. It does not represent an official interpretation by the organization that issues this code.

OCCUPANCY GROUP S-2: OPEN PARKING GARAGES

Definition

To qualify as an open parking garage, two or more sides of the structure must be substantially open to the passage of air and the garage must be used for the parking or storage of private automobiles only. Parking is permitted on the roof of the structure.

Area Modifications and Unlimited Area Buildings

For garages using parking machines, lifts, elevators, or other mechanical devices to move vehicles to and from the street level, and in which the public does not have access above the street level, garage heights may be increased to 12 floors for Unprotected Noncombustible construction, 15 floors for 1-Hour Noncombustible construction, and 18 floors for 2-hour Noncombustible construction.

Garages open on 75% of the exterior may be larger in area by 25% and higher by one floor than otherwise indicated in the table on these two facing pages. Garages open on all four sides may be larger in area by 50% and higher by one floor. For garages of maximum allowable area, but less than the maximum allowable height, at least three sides of the garage must have open walls, and no point on any floor may be more than 200 ft (61 m) from an open wall. Garages of 1-Hour and Unprotected Noncombustible construction may be unlimited in area if not higher than 75 ft (23 m), open on all four sides, and the distance from any point on a floor is no more than 200 ft (61 m) from any open wall.

Open Garages and Mixed-Use Occupancies

For more information about Parking Garages and mixed-use occupancies, see page 301.

Fire Walls

For multiplication of the allowable area by subdividing the building with fire walls, see page 302.

Excess Frontage

If more than 25% of the building perimeter fronts on a street or open space at least 20 ft (6.1 m) wide that

OCCUPANCY GROUP S-2: OPEN PARKING GARAGES

CONSTRUCTION TYPE	Noncombustible							
	3-Hour (page 308)		2-Hour (page 309)		1-Hour (page 310)		Unprotected (page 311)	
IBC NOMENCLATURE	Type I-A		Type I-B		Type II-A		Type II-B	
	Spr	Unspr	Spr	Unspr	Spr	Unspr	Spr	Unspr
MAXIMUM HEIGHT IN FEET	UH	UH	180'	160'	85'	65'	75'	55'
HEIGHT IN STORIES UH	UA	UA						
12			UA	UA				
11								
10					500,000	500,000		
9					500,000	500,000		
8					500,000	500,000	400,000	400,000
7					500,000	500,000	400,000	400,000
6					500,000	500,000	400,000	400,000
5					500,000	500,000	400,000	400,000
4					500,000	500,000	400,000	400,000
3					500,000	500,000	400,000	400,000
2					500,000	500,000	400,000	400,000
1					500,000	500,000	400,000	400,000
MAXIMUM FLOOR AREA IN SF FOR ANY SINGLE FLOOR	UA	UA	UA	UA	500,000	500,000	400,000	400,000

Each number in the table represents the maximum total area in square feet for all floors for a building of the indicated story height.

370

Key to Abbreviations

UA Unlimited area Spr With approved sprinkler system
UH Unlimited height Unspr Without approved sprinkler system
NP Not permitted

is accessible to firefighting vehicles, the tabulated area limitations below may be increased according to the following table. For example, for a building with half of its perimeter accessible to firefighting equipment via a space not less than 24 ft (7.3 m) wide, the allowable area increase is:

0.80% increase × 25% excess frontage = 20% total area increase.

Width of Frontage*	Percent Area Increase for 1% of Frontage* Each in Excess of 25%
20' (6.1 m)	0.67%
22' (6.7 m)	0.73%
24' (7.3 m)	0.80%
26' (7.9 m)	0.87%
28' (8.5 m)	0.93%
30' (9.1 m) or wider	1.00%

*Intermediate values may be interpolated.

Measurements

Height is measured from the average finished ground level adjoining the building to the average level of the highest roof. Floor area is measured within exterior walls or exterior walls and fire walls, exclusive of courtyards.

Further Information

For information on Occupancy Group classifications, see page 7. For information on mixed-used buildings, see page 300. For information on which code to consult, see pages 7, 11.

Unit Conversions

1 ft = 304.8 mm, 1 sq ft = 0.0929 m².

				Combustible							
Ordinary						**Wood Light Frame**					**CONSTRUCTION TYPE**
1-Hour (page 313)		Unprotected (page 313)		Mill (page 312)		1-Hour (page 315)		Unprotected (page 315)			
Type III-A		Type III-B		Type IV-HT		Type V-A		Type V-B			**IBC NOMENCLATURE**
Spr	Unspr	Spr	Unspr	Spr	Unspr	Spr	Unspr	Spr	Unspr		
				85'	65'						**MAXIMUM HEIGHT IN FEET**
										UH	
										12	
										11	
										10	
										9	
										8	**HEIGHT IN STORIES**
										7	
										6	
										5	
				200,000	200,000					4	
				200,000	200,000					3	
				200,000	200,000					2	
NP	NP	NP	NP	200,000	200,000	NP	NP	NP	NP	1	**MAXIMUM FLOOR AREA IN SF FOR ANY SINGLE FLOOR**
NP	NP	NP	NP	200,000	200,000	NP	NP	NP	NP		

HEIGHT AND AREA TABLES

371

This table was compiled from information contained in the International Building Code 2000. It does not represent an official interpretation by the organization that issues this code.

OCCUPANCY GROUP U: UTILITY

Sprinklers

An approved sprinkler system is required for any Group U occupancy with:

• Most underground portions of the building where occupancy occurs more than 30 ft (9 m) below the lowest level of exit discharge

Private Garages

Occupancy Group U private garages and carports are limited to 1000 sq ft (93 m^2) in area and one story in height. If constructed with exterior walls and opening protectives as required for Group R-1 or R-2 occupancies, or if part of a mixed-occupancy building (such as an apartment house and a private parking garage) and constructed with exterior walls and opening protectives as required for the major occupancy, private garages may be 3000 sq ft (279 m^2) in area. Multiple Occupancy Group U private garage areas may be aggregated in one building by separating each area with fire walls. Height and area limitations for mixed-use occupancies including Group U private garages should be determined according to the major occupancy. For private garages exceeding these limits, the use should be reassigned to Group S-2 or other appropriate occupancy that permits greater heights and areas.

Residential private garages must be separated from a residence by a minimum of ½-in. gypsum board applied on the garage side of the separation wall and/or ceiling assemblies, and solid doors in any openings. Carports fully open on at least two sides and with no enclosed space above do not require separation from a residence. Openings from a garage or carport directly into a room used for sleeping are not permitted.

Fire Walls

For multiplication of the allowable area by subdividing the building with fire walls, see page 302.

OCCUPANCY GROUP U: UTILITY

CONSTRUCTION TYPE	Noncombustible							
	3-Hour (page 308)		2-Hour (page 309)		1-Hour (page 310)		Unprotected (page 311)	
IBC NOMENCLATURE	Type I-A		Type I-B		Type II-A		Type II-B	
	Spr	Unspr	Spr	Unspr	Spr	Unspr	Spr	Unspr
MAXIMUM HEIGHT IN FEET	UH	75'	180'	75'	85'	65'	75'	55'
UH	UA	UA						
12								
11								
10								
9								
8								
7			319,500					
6			319,500	106,500				
5			319,500	106,500	171,000			
4			319,500	106,500	171,000	57,000		
3			319,500	106,500	171,000	57,000	76,500	
2			213,000	71,000	114,000	38,000	51,000	17,000
1			142,000	35,500	76,000	19,000	34,000	8,500
MAXIMUM FLOOR AREA IN SF FOR ANY SINGLE FLOOR	UA	UA	142,000	35,500	76,000	19,000	34,000	8,500

Each number in the table represents the maximum total area in square feet for all floors for a building of the indicated story height.

Key to Abbreviations

UA	Unlimited area	Spr	With approved sprinkler system
UH	Unlimited height	Unspr	Without approved sprinkler system
NP	Not permitted		

INTERNATIONAL BUILDING CODE

Basements

A single-story basement is not included in area calculations, provided that the basement area does not exceed the area permitted for a one-story building.

Excess Frontage

If more than 25% of the building perimeter fronts on a street or open space at least 20 ft (6.1 m) wide that is accessible to firefighting vehicles, the tabulated area limitations below may be increased according to the following table. For example, for a building with half of its perimeter accessible to firefighting equipment via a space not less than 24 ft (7.3 m) wide, the allowable area increase is:

0.80% increase × 25% excess frontage = 20% total area increase.

Width of Frontage*	Percent Area Increase for 1% of Frontage* Each in Excess of 25%
20' (6.1 m)	0.67%
22' (6.7 m)	0.73%
24' (7.3 m)	0.80%
26' (7.9 m)	0.87%
28' (8.5 m)	0.93%
30' (9.1 m) or wider	1.00%

*Intermediate values may be interpolated.

Measurements

Height is measured from the average finished ground level adjoining the building to the average level of the highest roof. Floor area is measured within exterior walls or exterior walls and fire walls, exclusive of courtyards.

Further Information

For information on Occupancy Group classifications, see page 7. For information on mixed-used buildings, see page 300. For information on which code to consult, see pages 7, 11.

Unit Conversions

1 ft = 304.8 mm, 1 sq ft = 0.0929 m².

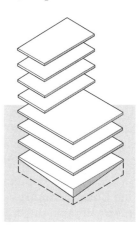

Combustible											CONSTRUCTION TYPE
Ordinary				Mill (page 312)		Wood Light Frame					
1-Hour (page 313)		Unprotected (page 313)				1-Hour (page 315)		Unprotected (page 315)			
Type III-A		Type III-B		Type IV-HT		Type V-A		Type V-B			IBC NOMENCLATURE
Spr	Unspr	Spr	Unspr	Spr	Unspr	Spr	Unspr	Spr	Unspr		
85'	65'	75'	55'	85'	65'	70'	50'	60'	40'		MAXIMUM HEIGHT IN FEET
										UH	
										12	
										11	
										10	
										9	
										8	HEIGHT IN STORIES
										7	
										6	
				162,000						5	
126,000				162,000	54,000					4	
126,000	42,000	76,500		162,000	54,000	81,000				3	
84,000	28,000	51,000	17,000	108,000	36,000	54,000	18,000	33,000		2	
56,000	14,000	34,000	8,500	72,000	18,000	36,000	9,000	22,000	5,500	1	
56,000	14,000	34,000	8,500	72,000	18,000	36,000	9,000	22,000	5,500		MAXIMUM FLOOR AREA IN SF FOR ANY SINGLE FLOOR

This table was compiled from information contained in the International Building Code 2000. It does not represent an official interpretation by the organization that issues this code.

HOW TO USE THE TABLES OF HEIGHT AND AREA LIMITATIONS FOR THE NATIONAL BUILDING CODE OF CANADA

1. Be sure you are consulting the tables for the proper building code. If you are not sure which code you are working under, see pages 7, 11.

2. The Occupancy Group is given at the upper left-hand corner of the table. If you are not sure about the Occupancy Group into which your building falls, consult the index of Occupancy Groups on pages 11–13.

3. Noncombustible Construction Types are tabulated on the left-hand page, and combustible Construction Types are tabulated on the right-hand page.

4. Each pair of columns repre-sents one Construction Type. For specific information on the different materials and modes of construction that conform to that Construction Type, follow the page reference given here.

5. The paired columns tabulate height and area information for both sprinklered and unsprin-klered buildings of each Construction Type.

6. The significance of the floor area numbers in the chart, which varies from one model code to another, is explained at the lower left-hand corner.

NATIONAL BUILDING CODE OF CANADA

OCCUPANCY GROUP D: BUSINESS AND PERSONAL USES

Basements
Basements must be fully sprinklered, or subdivided by fire separations into areas not more than 600 m² (6460 sq ft). A fire separation is also required between a basement and the floor above, and if there is more than one story below grade, between every below-grade story.

Excess Frontage
For unsprinklered buildings, except as noted in the table, the tabulated areas shown below may be increased by 25% if the building faces at least two streets, and by 50% if facing at least three.

Fire Walls
For multiplication of the allowable area by subdividing the building with fire walls, see page 302.

Measurements
Area is measured as the greatest horizontal area of a building above grade within the outside surfaces of the exterior walls, or between the outside surfaces of the exterior walls and the center line of a fire wall.

Further Information
For information on Occupancy Group classifications, see page 11. For information on mixed-use buildings, see page 301. For information on which code to consult, see pages 7, 11.

Unit Conversion
1 m² = 10.76 sq ft.

OCCUPANCY GROUP D: BUSINESS AND PERSONAL SERVICES

CONSTRUCTION TYPE		Noncombustible							
		2-Hour (page 309)		1-Hour (page 310)		¼-Hour (page 314)		Unprotected (page 311)	
HEIGHT IN STORIES, AND MAXIMUM AREA PER FLOOR IN M.²ᵧ		Spr	Unspr	Spr	Unspr	Spr	Unspr	Spr	Unspr
	UH	UA							
	6		2,400	7,200	2,400				
	5		2,880	8,640	2,880				
	4		3,600	10,800	3,600				
	3		4,800	14,400	4,800	4,800	1,600	4,800	1,600
	2		*7,200	UA	*7,200	7,200	2,400	7,200	2,400
	1		UA	UA	UA	14,400	4,800	14,400	4,800

Each number in the table represents the maximum area per floor in square meters for every floor of a building of that story height.

*For a building facing at least two streets, building area is unlimited.

390

Key to Abbreviations
UA   Unlimited area
UH   Unlimited height
NP   Not permitted
Spr   With approved sprinkler system
Unspr Without approved sprinkler system

NATIONAL BUILDING CODE OF CANADA

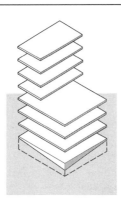

7. As an example of the use of this chart, a sprinklered building of Occupancy Group D, 1-Hour Noncombustible construction, under the National Building Code of Canada, may be no more than six stories tall, with no floor larger in area than 7200 m².

8. As another example, if we wish to construct a three-story unsprinklered building with 3150 m² per floor, we must use 1-Hour Noncombustible construction as a minimum. Looking to the right along the same row of the chart, we see that the addition of sprinklers would allow us to use Mill or 1-Hour or ¾-Hour Noncombustible or Combustible construction. By following the page references at the heads of these columns, we can determine exactly what each of these Construction Types is, and proceed to preliminary configuration and sizing of the structural system we select.

Combustible									
1-Hour (page 314)		Mill (page 312)		¾-Hour (page 314)		Unprotected (page 315)			CONSTRUCTION TYPE
Spr	Unspr	Spr	Unspr	Spr	Unspr	Spr	Unspr		
								UH	HEIGHT IN STORIES, AND MAXIMUM AREA PER FLOOR IN M²$_V$
								6	
								5	
3,600								4	
3,600	1,600	4,800	1,600	4,800	1,600			3	
3,600	2,400	7,200	2,400	7,200	2,400			2	
3,600	4,800	14,400	4,800	14,400	4,800	NP	NP	1	

This table was compiled from information contained in the National Building Code of Canada 1995. It does not represent an official interpretation by the organization that issues this code.

The reference tables appearing on pages 376–401 are for preliminary purposes only. They represent the authors' interpretation of certain major provisions of the National Building Code of Canada 1995. No official interpretation has been sought from or granted by the National Research Council of Canada. For design development work and final preparation of building plans, you must consult the *National Building Code of Canada,* copyright 1995, National Research Council of Canada, Ottawa, Ontario K1A OR6.

USE GROUP A-1: ASSEMBLY, THEATERS

Unlimited Area Buildings

Occupancy Group A-1 one-story buildings of at least ¾-Hour Combustible or Noncombustible construction, with an auditorium occupant load no greater than 300, may be unlimited in area.

Basements

Basements must be fully sprinklered, or subdivided by fire-separations into areas of not more than 600 m² (6460 sq ft). A fire separation is also required between a basement and the floor above, and if there is more than one story below grade, between every below-grade story.

Fire Walls

For multiplication of the allowable area by subdividing the building with fire walls, see page 302.

Measurements

Area is measured as the greatest horizontal area of a building above grade within the outside surfaces of the exterior walls, or between the outside surfaces of the exterior walls and the center line of a fire wall.

Further Information

For information on Occupancy Group classifications, see page 11. For information on mixed-use buildings, see page 301. For information on which code to consult, see pages 7, 11.

Unit Conversion

1 m² = 10.76 sq ft.

OCCUPANCY GROUP A-1: ASSEMBLY, THEATERS

CONSTRUCTION TYPE	Noncombustible							
	2-Hour (page 309)		1-Hour (page 310)		¾-Hour (page 314)		Unprotected (page 311)	
HEIGHT IN STORIES, AND MAXIMUM AREA PER FLOOR IN M²	Spr	Unspr	Spr	Unspr	Spr	Unspr	Spr	Unspr
UH	UA							
12								
11								
10								
9								
8								
7								
6								
5								
4								
3								
2			*600		*600			
1		NP	*600	NP	*600	NP	NP	NP

Each number in the table represents the maximum area per floor in square meters for every floor of a building of the indicated story height.

*The occupant load of the building may not exceed 600. In two-story buildings, the second story may not exceed 40% of the area of the first story.

Key to Abbreviations

UA	Unlimited area
UH	Unlimited height
NP	Not permitted
Spr	With approved sprinkler system
Unspr	Without approved sprinkler system

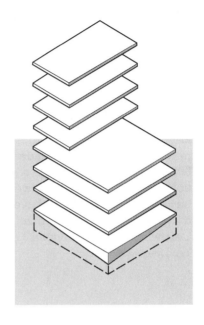

Combustible								
1-Hour **(page 314)**		**Mill** **(page 312)**		**¾-Hour** **(page 314)**		**Unprotected** **(page 315)**		
Spr	**Unspr**	**Spr**	**Unspr**	**Spr**	**Unspr**	**Spr**	**Unspr**	
								UH
								12
								11
								10
								9
								8
								7
								6
								5
								4
								3
*600		*600		*600				2
*600	NP	*600	NP	*600	NP	NP	NP	1

CONSTRUCTION TYPE

**HEIGHT IN STORIES,
AND MAXIMUM AREA
PER FLOOR IN M²**

This table was compiled from information contained in the National Building Code of Canada 1995. It does not represent an official interpretation by the organization that issues this code.

HEIGHT AND AREA TABLES

USE GROUP A-2: ASSEMBLY, MISCELLANEOUS

Basements

Basements must be fully sprinklered, or subdivided by fire separations into areas of not more than 600 m² (6460 sq ft). A fire separation is also required between a basement and the floor above, and if there is more than one story below grade, between every below-grade story.

Excess Frontage

For unsprinklered buildings, the tabulated areas shown below may be increased by 25% if the building faces at least two streets, and by 50% if facing at least three.

Fire Walls

For multiplication of the allowable area by subdividing the building with fire walls, see page 302.

Measurements

Area is measured as the greatest horizontal area of a building above grade within the outside surfaces of the exterior walls, or between the outside surfaces of the exterior walls and the center line of a fire wall.

Further Information

For information on Occupancy Group classifications, see page 11. For information on mixed-use buildings, see page 301. For information on which code to consult, see pages 7, 11.

Unit Conversion

1 m² = 10.76 sq ft.

OCCUPANCY GROUP A-2: ASSEMBLY, MISCELLANEOUS

CONSTRUCTION TYPE	Noncombustible							
	2-Hour (page 309)		1-Hour (page 310)		¾-Hour (page 314)		Unprotected (page 311)	
HEIGHT IN STORIES, AND MAXIMUM AREA PER FLOOR IN M²	Spr	Unspr	Spr	Unspr	Spr	Unspr	Spr	Unspr
UH	UA							
6			UA					
5								
4								
3								
2		800		800	2,400	800	2,400	800
1		1,600		1,600	4,800	1,600	4,800	1,600

Each number in the table represents the maximum area per floor in square meters for every floor of a building of that story height

*One-story buildings with no basement may be 2400 m² in area.

Key to Abbreviations

UA	Unlimited area
UH	Unlimited height
NP	Not permitted
Spr	With approved sprinkler system
Unspr	Without approved sprinkler system

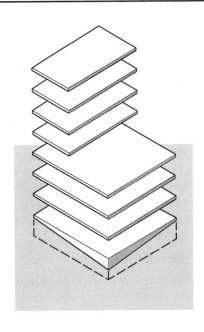

Combustible									
1-Hour (page 314)		Mill (page 312)		¾-Hour (page 314)		Unprotected (page 315)			
Spr	Unspr	Spr	Unspr	Spr	Unspr	Spr	Unspr		
								UH	**CONSTRUCTION TYPE**
								6	**HEIGHT IN STORIES, AND MAXIMUM AREA PER FLOOR IN M²**
								5	
								4	
								3	
2,400	800	2,400	800	2,400	800	600		2	
4,800	1,600	4,800	1,600	4,800	1,600	*1200	400	1	

This table was compiled from information contained in the National Building Code of Canada 1995. It does not represent an official interpretation by the organization that issues this code.

OCCUPANCY GROUP A-3: ASSEMBLY, ARENAS

Basements

Basements must be fully sprinklered, or subdivided by fire separations into areas of not more than 600 m² (6460 sq ft). A fire separation is also required between a basement and the floor above, and if there is more than one story below grade, between every below-grade story.

Excess Frontage

For unsprinklered buildings, the tabulated areas shown below may be increased by 25% if the building faces at least two streets, and by 50% if facing at least three.

Fire Walls

For multiplication of the allowable area by subdividing the building with fire walls, see page 302.

Measurements

Area is measured as the greatest horizontal area of a building above grade within the outside surfaces of the exterior walls, or between the outside surfaces of the exterior walls and the center line of a fire wall.

Further Information

For information on Occupancy Group classifications, see page 11. For information on mixed-use buildings, see page 301. For information on which code to consult, see pages 7, 11.

Unit Conversion

1 m² = 10.76 sq ft.

OCCUPANCY GROUP A-3: ASSEMBLY, ARENAS

CONSTRUCTION TYPE		Noncombustible							
		2-Hour (page 309)		1-Hour (page 310)		¾-Hour (page 314)		Unprotected (page 311)	
		Spr	Unspr	Spr	Unspr	Spr	Unspr	Spr	Unspr
HEIGHT IN STORIES, AND MAXIMUM AREA PER FLOOR IN M²	UH	UA							
	6								
	5								
	4								
	3								
	2		2,000	6,000	2,000				
	1		4,000	12,000	4,000	7,200	2,400	7,200	2,400

Each number in the table represents the maximum area per floor in square meters for every floor of a building of the indicated story height.

Key to Abbreviations

UA	Unlimited area
UH	Unlimited height
NP	Not permitted
Spr	With approved sprinkler system
Unspr	Without approved sprinkler system

NATIONAL BUILDING CODE OF CANADA

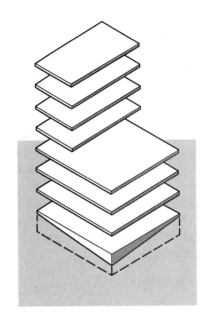

Combustible									CONSTRUCTION TYPE
1-Hour (page 314)		Mill (page 312)		¾-Hour (page 314)		Unprotected (page 315)			
Spr	Unspr	Spr	Unspr	Spr	Unspr	Spr	Unspr		
								UH	HEIGHT IN STORIES, AND MAXIMUM AREA PER FLOOR IN M²
								6	
								5	
								4	
								3	
								2	
7,200	2,400	7,200	2,400	7,200	2,400	7,200	1,000	1	

This table was compiled from information contained in the National Building Code of Canada 1995. It does not represent an official interpretation by the organization that issues this code.

OCCUPANCY GROUP A-4: ASSEMBLY, OPEN-AIR

Special Conditions

Occupancy A-4 buildings may have roof assemblies of Heavy Timber construction. All occupied spaces below seating tiers must be sprinklered. Buildings of Combustible construction are limited to less than 1500 occupants, and exposed building faces must be at least 6 m (20 ft) from adjacent property lines or buildings.

Basements

Basements must be fully sprinklered, or subdivided by fire separations into areas of not more than 600 m² (6460 sq ft). A fire separation is also required between a basement and the floor above, and if there is more than one story below grade, between every below-grade story.

Fire Walls

For multiplication of the allowable area by subdividing the building with fire walls, see page 302.

Measurements

Area is measured as the greatest horizontal area of a building above grade within the outside surfaces of the exterior walls, or between the outside surfaces of the exterior walls and the center line of a fire wall.

Further Information

For information on Occupancy Group classifications, see page 11. For information on mixed-use buildings, see page 301. For information on which code to consult, see pages 7, 11.

Unit Conversion

1 m² = 10.76 sq ft.

OCCUPANCY GROUP A-4: ASSEMBLY, OPEN-AIR

CONSTRUCTION TYPE		Noncombustible							
		2-Hour (page 309)		1-Hour (page 310)		¾-Hour (page 314)		Unprotected (page 311)	
		Spr	Unspr	Spr	Unspr	Spr	Unspr	Spr	Unspr
HEIGHT IN STORIES, AND MAXIMUM AREA PER FLOOR IN M²	UH	UA		UA		UA		UA	
	12								
	11								
	10								
	9								
	8								
	7								
	6								
	5								
	4								
	3								
	2								
	1		NP		NP		NP		NP

Each number in the table represents the maximum area per floor in square meters for every floor of the indicated story height.

*See Special Conditions on this page for more information.

Key to Abbreviations

UA   Unlimited area
UH   Unlimited height
NP   Not permitted
Spr   With approved sprinkler system
Unspr Without approved sprinkler system

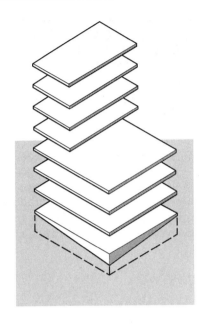

Combustible									
1-Hour (page 314)		Mill (page 312)		¾-Hour (page 314)		Unprotected (page 315)			**CONSTRUCTION TYPE**
Spr	Unspr	Spr	Unspr	Spr	Unspr	Spr	Unspr		
*UA		*UA		*UA		*UA		UH	**HEIGHT IN STORIES, AND MAXIMUM AREA PER FLOOR IN M²**
								12	
								11	
								10	
								9	
								8	
								7	
								6	
								5	
								4	
								3	
								2	
	NP		NP		NP		NP	1	

This table was compiled from information contained in the National Building Code of Canada 1995. It does not represent an official interpretation by the organization that issues this code.

HEIGHT AND AREA TABLES

383

OCCUPANCY GROUP B-1: CARE OR DETENTION, RESTRAINED

Basements

Basements must be fully sprinklered, or subdivided by fire separations into areas of not more than 600 m² (6460 sq ft). A fire separation is also required between a basement and the floor above, and if there is more than one story below grade, between every below-grade story.

Fire Walls

For multiplication of the allowable area by subdividing the building with fire walls, see page 302.

Measurements

Area is measured as the greatest horizontal area of a building above grade within the outside surfaces of the exterior walls, or between the outside surfaces of the exterior walls and the center line of a fire wall.

Further Information

For information on Occupancy Group classifications, see page 11. For information on mixed-use buildings, see page 301. For information on which code to consult, see pages 7, 11.

Unit Conversion

1 m² = 10.76 sq ft.

OCCUPANCY GROUP B-1: CARE OR DETENTION, RESTRAINED

CONSTRUCTION TYPE		Noncombustible							
		2-Hour (page 309)		1-Hour (page 310)		¾-Hour (page 314)		Unprotected (page 311)	
		Spr	Unspr	Spr	Unspr	Spr	Unspr	Spr	Unspr
HEIGHT IN STORIES, AND MAXIMUM AREA PER FLOOR IN M²	UH	UA							
	6								
	5								
	4								
	3			8,000					
	2			12,000					
	1		NP	UA	NP	NP	NP	NP	NP

Each number in the table represents the maximum area per floor in square meters for every floor of a building of that story height.

Key to Abbreviations

UA	Unlimited area
UH	Unlimited height
NP	Not permitted
Spr	With approved sprinkler system
Unspr	Without approved sprinkler system

CONSTRUCTION TYPE

HEIGHT IN STORIES, AND MAXIMUM AREA PER FLOOR IN M²

Combustible								UH
1-Hour (page 314)		Mill (page 312)		¾-Hour (page 314)		Unprotected (page 315)		
Spr	Unspr	Spr	Unspr	Spr	Unspr	Spr	Unspr	
								6
								5
								4
								3
								2
NP	NP	NP	NP	NP	NP	NP	NP	1

This table was compiled from information contained in the National Building Code of Canada 1995. It does not represent an official interpretation by the organization that issues this code.

HEIGHT AND AREA TABLES

385

OCCUPANCY GROUP B-2: CARE OR DETENTION, UNRESTRAINED

Basements

Basements must be fully sprinklered, or subdivided by fire separations into areas of not more than 600 m² (6460 sq ft). A fire separation is also required between a basement and floor above, and if there is more than one story below grade, between every below-grade story.

Fire Walls

For multiplication of the allowable area by subdividing the building with fire walls, see page 302.

Measurements

Area is measured as the greatest horizontal area of a building above grade within the outside surfaces of the exterior walls, or between the outside surfaces of the exterior walls and the center line of a fire wall.

Further Information

For information on Occupancy Group classifications, see page 11. For information on mixed-use buildings, see page 301. For information on which code to consult, see pages 7, 11.

Unit Conversion

1 m² = 10.76 sq ft.

OCCUPANCY GROUP B-2: CARE OR DETENTION, UNRESTRAINED

CONSTRUCTION TYPE		Noncombustible							
		2-Hour (page 309)		1-Hour (page 310)		¾-Hour (page 314)		Unprotected (page 315)	
		Spr	Unspr	Spr	Unspr	Spr	Unspr	Spr	Unspr
HEIGHT IN STORIES, AND MAXIMUM AREA PER FLOOR IN M²	UH	UA							
	6								
	5								
	4								
	3			8,000					
	2			12,000		1,600			
	1		NP	UA	NP	2,400	NP	500	NP

Each number in the table represents the maximum area per floor in square meters for every floor of a building of that story height.

Key to Abbreviations

UA	Unlimited area
UH	Unlimited height
NP	Not permitted
Spr	With approved sprinkler system
Unspr	Without approved sprinkler system

Combustible									
1-Hour **(page 314)**		**Mill** **(page 312)**		**¾-Hour** **(page 314)**		**Unprotected** **(page 315)**			
Spr	Unspr	Spr	Unspr	Spr	Unspr	Spr	Unspr		
								UH	
								6	
								5	
								4	
								3	
1,600		1,600		1,600				2	
2,400	NP	2,400	NP	2,400	NP	500	NP	1	

CONSTRUCTION TYPE

HEIGHT IN STORIES, AND MAXIMUM AREA PER FLOOR IN M^2

This table was compiled from information contained in the National Building Code of Canada 1995. It does not represent an official interpretation by the organization that issues this code.

HEIGHT AND AREA TABLES

387

OCCUPANCY GROUP C: RESIDENTIAL

Basements

In residential occupancies that are not otherwise required to be sprinklered, basements containing only residential occupancies and providing at least one access door or window for each 15 m (49 ft) of wall in at least one wall facing a street are not required to be sprinklered. Other basements must be fully sprinklered, or subdivided by fire separations into areas of not more than 600 m² (6460 sq ft). A fire separation is also required between a basement and the floor above, and if there is more than one story below grade, between every below-grade story.

Fire Separations

In Occupancy C Residential buildings of 2-Hour Noncombustible construction, floor assemblies entirely within one dwelling unit may have a 1-Hour fire-resistance rating. In buildings of ¾-Hour Noncombustible construction, or 1-Hour or ¾-Hour Combustible construction, where no residential units occur above or below other units, floor assemblies entirely within any unit are not required to be fire-rated.

A fire separation is not required between a dwelling unit and a garage, provided that the dwelling unit and garage are separated from other dwelling units, the construction and openings between the dwelling unit and garage provide effective barriers to the passage of gas and exhaust fumes, and that doors from the garage do not open directly into rooms intended for sleeping. A separation between a dwelling unit and a garage is not required to be rated, provided that the garage contains not more than five vehicles, the dwelling unit and garage are sprinklered, the dwelling unit and garage are separated from other dwelling units, the construction and openings between the dwelling unit and the garage provide effective barriers to the passage of gas and exhaust fumes, and that doors from the garage do not open directly into rooms intended for sleeping.

OCCUPANCY GROUP C: RESIDENTIAL

CONSTRUCTION TYPE	Noncombustible							
	2-Hour (page 309)		1-Hour (page 310)		¾-Hour (page 314)		Unprotected (page 311)	
	Spr	Unspr	Spr	Unspr	Spr	Unspr	Spr	Unspr
HEIGHT IN STORIES, AND MAXIMUM AREA PER FLOOR IN M² UH	UA							
6			6,000					
5			7,200					
4			9,000					
3		4,000	12,000	4,000	1,800	600	**600	**600
2		*6,000	UA	*6,000	2,700	900	**600	**600
1		UA	UA	UA	5,400	1,800	**600	**600

Each number in the table represents the maximum area per floor in square meters for every floor of a building of that story height.

*For a building facing at least two streets, building area is unlimited.

**Dwelling units only, when one unit does not occur above or below another unit or other occupancy. No area increases permitted for excess frontage.

Key to Abbreviations

UA	Unlimited area
UH	Unlimited height
NP	Not permitted
Spr	With approved sprinkler system
Unspr	Without approved sprinkler system

Excess Frontage

For unsprinklered buildings, except as noted in the table, the tabulated areas shown below may be increased by 25% if the building faces at least two streets, and by 50% if facing at least three.

Fire Walls

For multiplication of the allowable area by subdividing the building with fire walls, see page 302.

Measurements

Area is measured as the greatest horizontal area of a building above grade within the outside surfaces of the exterior walls, or between the outside surfaces of the exterior walls and the center line of a fire wall.

Further Information

For information on Occupancy Group classifications, see page 11. For information on mixed-use buildings, see page 301. For information on which code to consult, see pages 7, 11.

Unit Conversion

$1 \text{ m}^2 = 10.76 \text{ sq ft.}$

| Combustible | | | | | | | | | | CONSTRUCTION TYPE |
| 1-Hour (page 314) | | Mill (page 312) | | ¾-Hour (page 314) | | Unprotected (page 315) | | | | |
Spr	Unspr	Spr	Unspr	Spr	Unspr	Spr	Unspr			
								UH		HEIGHT IN STORIES, AND MAXIMUM AREA PER FLOOR IN M²
								6		
								5		
1,800								4		
2,400	800	1,800	600	1,800	600	**600	**600	3		
3,600	1,200	2,700	900	2,700	900	**600	**600	2		
7,200	2,400	5,400	1,800	5,400	1,800	**600	**600	1		

This table was compiled from information contained in the National Building Code of Canada 1995. It does not represent an official interpretation by the organization that issues this code.

HEIGHT AND AREA TABLES

OCCUPANCY GROUP D: BUSINESS AND PERSONAL USES

Basements

Basements must be fully sprinklered, or subdivided by fire separations into areas not more than 600 m² (6460 sq ft). A fire separation is also required between a basement and the floor above, and if there is more than one story below grade, between every below-grade story.

Excess Frontage

For unsprinklered buildings, except as noted in the table, the tabulated areas shown below may be increased by 25% if the building faces at least two streets, and by 50% if facing at least three.

Fire Walls

For multiplication of the allowable area by subdividing the building with fire walls, see page 302.

Measurements

Area is measured as the greatest horizontal area of a building above grade within the outside surfaces of the exterior walls, or between the outside surfaces of the exterior walls and the center line of a fire wall.

Further Information

For information on Occupancy Group classifications, see page 11. For information on mixed-use buildings, see page 301. For information on which code to consult, see pages 7, 11.

Unit Conversion

1 m² = 10.76 sq ft.

OCCUPANCY GROUP D: BUSINESS AND PERSONAL SERVICES

CONSTRUCTION TYPE		Noncombustible							
		2-Hour (page 309)		1-Hour (page 310)		¾-Hour (page 314)		Unprotected (page 311)	
HEIGHT IN STORIES, AND MAXIMUM AREA PER FLOOR IN M²		Spr	Unspr	Spr	Unspr	Spr	Unspr	Spr	Unspr
UH		UA							
6			2,400	7,200	2,400				
5			2,880	8,640	2,880				
4			3,600	10,800	3,600				
3			4,800	14,400	4,800	4,800	1,600	4,800	1,600
2			*7,200	UA	*7,200	7,200	2,400	7,200	2,400
1			UA	UA	UA	14,400	4,800	14,400	4,800

Each number in the table represents the maximum area per floor in square meters for every floor of a building of that story height.

*For a building facing at least two streets, building area is unlimited.

Key to Abbreviations

UA Unlimited area
UH Unlimited height
NP Not permitted
Spr With approved sprinkler system
Unspr Without approved sprinkler system

Combustible										
1-Hour (page 314)		Mill (page 312)		¾-Hour (page 314)		Unprotected (page 315)				**CONSTRUCTION TYPE**
Spr	Unspr	Spr	Unspr	Spr	Unspr	Spr	Unspr			
								UH		**HEIGHT IN STORIES, AND MAXIMUM AREA PER FLOOR IN M²**
								6		
								5		
3,600								4		
3,600	1,600	4,800	1,600	4,800	1,600			3		
3,600	2,400	7,200	2,400	7,200	2,400			2		
3,600	4,800	14,400	4,800	14,400	4,800	NP	NP	1		

This table was compiled from information contained in the National Building Code of Canada 1995. It does not represent an official interpretation by the organization that issues this code.

OCCUPANCY GROUP E: MERCANTILE

Basements

Basements must be fully sprinklered, or subdivided by fire separations into areas not more than 600 m² (6460 sq ft). A fire separation is also required between a basement and the floor above, and if there is more than one story below grade, between every below-grade story.

Fire Walls

For multiplication of the allowable area by subdividing the building with fire walls, see page 302.

Measurements

Area is measured as the greatest horizontal area of a building above grade within the outside surfaces of the exterior walls, or between the outside surfaces of the exterior walls and the center line of a fire wall.

Further Information

For information on Occupancy Group classifications, see page 11. For information on mixed-use buildings, see page 301. For information on which code to consult, see pages 7, 11.

Unit Conversion

1 m² = 10.76 sq ft.

OCCUPANCY GROUP E: MERCANTILE

CONSTRUCTION TYPE		Noncombustible							
		2-Hour (page 309)		1-Hour (page 310)		¼-Hour (page 314)		Unprotected (page 311)	
		Spr	Unspr	Spr	Unspr	Spr	Unspr	Spr	Unspr
HEIGHT IN STORIES, AND MAXIMUM AREA PER FLOOR IN M²	UH	UA							
	6								
	5								
	4			1,800					
	3	***800	1,800	***800		2,400	***800		
	2	**1,200	1,800	**1,200		3,600	**1,200		
	1	*1,500	1,800	*1,500		7,200	*1,500	NP	NP

Each number in the table represents the maximum area per floor in square meters for every floor of a building of that story height.

*No area increase for excess frontage.

**For a building facing two or more streets, increase allowable area by 25%.

***For a building facing two streets, allowable area is 1000 m², for a building facing at least three streets, 1500 m².

Key to Abbreviations

UA	Unlimited area
UH	Unlimited height
NP	Not permitted
Spr	With approved sprinkler system
Unspr	Without approved sprinkler system

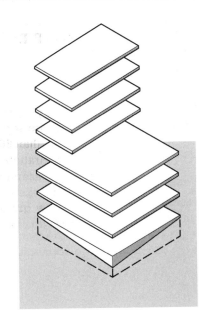

CONSTRUCTION TYPE

Combustible								
1-Hour (page 314)		Mill (page 312)		¾-Hour (page 314)		Unprotected (page 315)		
Spr	Unspr	Spr	Unspr	Spr	Unspr	Spr	Unspr	
								UH
								6
								5
1,800								4
1,800	***800	2,400	***800	2,400	***800			3
1,800	**1,200	3,600	**1,200	3,600	**1,200			2
1,800	*1,500	7,200	*1,500	7,200	*1,500	NP	NP	1

HEIGHT IN STORIES, AND MAXIMUM AREA PER FLOOR IN M²

This table was compiled from information contained in the National Building Code of Canada 1995. It does not represent an official interpretation by the organization that issues this code.

HEIGHT AND AREA TABLES

OCCUPANCY GROUP F-1: INDUSTRIAL, HIGH HAZARD

Sprinklers

Provincial or local laws may require sprinklering of buildings in this Occupancy Group.

Basements

Basements must be fully sprinklered, or subdivided by fire separations into areas not more than 600 m² (6460 sq ft). A fire separation is also required between a basement and the floor above, and if there is more than one story below grade, between every below-grade story.

Fire Walls

For multiplication of the allowable area by subdividing the building with fire walls, see page 302.

Measurements

Area is measured as the greatest horizontal area of a building above grade within the outside surfaces of the exterior walls, or between the outside surfaces of the exterior walls and the center line of a fire wall.

Further Information

For information on Occupancy Group classifications, see page 11. For information on mixed-use buildings, see page 301. For information on which code to consult, see pages 7, 11.

Unit Conversion

1 m² = 10.76 sq ft.

OCCUPANCY GROUP F-1: FACTORY, HIGH HAZARD

CONSTRUCTION TYPE	Noncombustible							
	2-Hour (page 309)		1-Hour (page 310)		¾-Hour (page 314)		Unprotected (page 311)	
HEIGHT IN STORIES, AND MAXIMUM AREA PER FLOOR IN M²	Spr	Unspr	Spr	Unspr	Spr	Unspr	Spr	Unspr
UH								
6								
5								
4	2,250							
3	3,000		1,200		1,200			
2	4,500		1,800		1,800		1,200	
1	9,000	800	3,600	800	3,600	800	2,400	800

Each number in the table represents the maximum area per floor in square meters for every floor of a building of that story height.

Key to Abbreviations

UA	Unlimited area
UH	Unlimited height
NP	Not permitted
Spr	With approved sprinkler system
Unspr	Without approved sprinkler system

NATIONAL BUILDING CODE OF CANADA

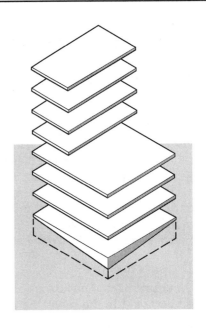

Combustible									
1-Hour **(page 314)**		**Mill** **(page 312)**		**¾-Hour** **(page 314)**		**Unprotected** **(page 315)**			
Spr	**Unspr**	**Spr**	**Unspr**	**Spr**	**Unspr**	**Spr**	**Unspr**		
								UH	
								6	
								5	
								4	
		1,200						3	
1,200		1,800		1,200				2	
2,400	800	3,600	800	2,400	800	800	800	1	

CONSTRUCTION TYPE

HEIGHT IN STORIES,
AND MAXIMUM AREA
PER FLOOR IN M²

This table was compiled from information contained in the National Building Code of Canada 1995. It does not represent an official interpretation by the organization that issues this code.

HEIGHT AND AREA TABLES

395

OCCUPANCY GROUP F-2: INDUSTRIAL, MEDIUM HAZARD

Basements

Basements must be fully sprinklered, or subdivided by fire separations into areas not more than 600 m² (6460 sq ft). A fire separation is also required between a basement and the floor above, and if there is more than one story below grade, between every below-grade story.

Excess Frontage

For unsprinklered buildings, excepted as noted in the table, the tabulated areas shown below may be increased by 25% if the building faces at least two streets, and by 50% if facing at least three.

Fire Walls

For multiplication of the allowable area by subdividing the building with fire walls, see page 302.

Measurements

Area is measured as the greatest horizontal area of a building above grade within the outside surfaces of the exterior walls, or between the outside surfaces of the exterior walls and the center line of a fire wall.

Further Information

For information on Occupancy Group classifications, see page 11. For information on mixed-use buildings, see page 301. For information on which code to consult, see pages 7, 11.

Unit Conversion

1 m² = 10.76 sq ft.

OCCUPANCY GROUP F-2: FACTORY, MEDIUM-HAZARD

CONSTRUCTION TYPE		Noncombustible							
		2-Hour (page 309)		1-Hour (page 310)		¾-Hour (page 314)		Unprotected (page 311)	
		Spr	Unspr	Spr	Unspr	Spr	Unspr	Spr	Unspr
HEIGHT IN STORIES, AND MAXIMUM AREA PER FLOOR IN M²	UH	UA							
	6								
	5								
	4			4,500		2,400			
	3		**1,070	6,000	**1,070	3,200	**1,070		
	2		*1,500	9,000	*1,500	4,800	*1,500	1,800	600
	1		*1,500	18,000	*1,500	9,600	*1,500	4,500	1,000

Each number in the table represents the maximum area per floor in square meters for every floor of a building of that story height.

*No area increase for excess frontage.

**For buildings facing two streets, increase allowable area to 1340 m²; for buildings facing at least three streets, increase allowable area to 1500 m².

Key to Abbreviations

UA	Unlimited area
UH	Unlimited height
NP	Not permitted
Spr	With approved sprinkler system
Unspr	Without approved sprinkler system

NATIONAL BUILDING CODE OF CANADA

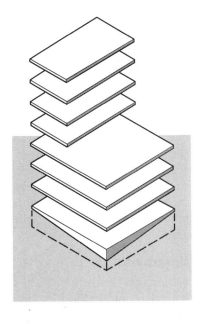

Combustible									HEIGHT IN STORIES, AND MAXIMUM AREA PER FLOOR IN M²
1-Hour (page 314)		Mill (page 312)		¾-Hour (page 314)		Unprotected (page 315)			
Spr	Unspr	Spr	Unspr	Spr	Unspr	Spr	Unspr		
								UH	
								6	
								5	
2,400		2,400		2,400				4	
3,200	**1,070	3,200	**1,070	3,200	**1,070			3	
4,800	*1,500	4,800	*1,500	4,800	*1,500			2	
9,600	*1,500	9,600	*1,500	9,600	*1,500	NP	NP	1	

This table was compiled from information contained in the National Building Code of Canada 1995. It does not represent an official interpretation by the organization that issues this code.

OCCUPANCY GROUP F-3: INDUSTRIAL, LOW HAZARD

Unlimited Area Buildings

Occupancy Group F-3 buildings, one story in height, of Noncombustible construction, and used solely for low fire load occupancies such as power generating plants or the manufacture of noncombustible materials, may be unlimited in area.

Basements

Basements must be fully sprinklered, or subdivided by fire separations into areas not more than 600 m² (6460 sq ft). A fire separation is also required between a basement and the floor above, and if there is more than one story below grade, between every below-grade story.

Parking Garages

A basement used as a parking garage may be considered as a separate building from a different use above, provided that the basement level is separated from the use above by masonry or concrete walls and floor/ceiling assemblies of not less than a 2-hour fire-resistance rating. Garage exterior walls may have unprotected openings if the garage is sprinklered throughout and separation between the two uses is maintained with horizontal projections over openings and setbacks of walls above. See the code for more information.

Excess Frontage

For unsprinklered buildings, the tabulated areas shown below may be increased by 25% if the building faces at least two streets, and by 50% if facing at least three.

Fire Walls

For multiplication of the allowable area by subdividing the building with fire walls, see page 302.

Measurements

Area is measured as the greatest horizontal area of a building above grade within the outside surfaces of the exterior walls, or between the outside surfaces of the exterior walls and the center line of a fire wall.

Further Information

For information on Occupancy Group classifications, see page 11. For information on mixed-use buildings, see page 301. For information on which code to consult, see pages 7, 11.

Unit Conversion

1 m² = 10.76 sq ft.

OCCUPANCY GROUP F-3: FACTORY, LOW HAZARD

CONSTRUCTION TYPE		Noncombustible							
		2-Hour (page 309)		1-Hour (page 310)		¾-Hour (page 314)		Unprotected (page 311)	
		Spr	Unspr	Spr	Unspr	Spr	Unspr	Spr	Unspr
HEIGHT IN STORIES, AND MAXIMUM AREA PER FLOOR IN M²	UH	UA							
	6		2,400	7,200	2,400				
	5		2,880	8,640	2,880				
	4		3,660	10,800	3,660	3,600	1,200	3,600	1,200
	3		4,800	14,400	4,800	4,800	1,600	4,800	1,600
	2		7,200	21,600	7,200	7,200	2,400	7,200	2,400
	1		UA	UA	UA	14,400	4,800	14,400	4,800

Each number in the table represents the maximum area per floor in square meters for every floor of a building of that story height.

Key to Abbreviations

UA	Unlimited area
UH	Unlimited height
NP	Not permitted
Spr	With approved sprinkler system
Unspr	Without approved sprinkler system

Combustible										
1-Hour **(page 314)**		**Mill** **(page 312)**		**¾-Hour** **(page 314)**		**Unprotected** **(page 315)**				
Spr	Unspr	Spr	Unspr	Spr	Unspr	Spr	Unspr			
								UH		**CONSTRUCTION TYPE**
								6		**HEIGHT IN STORIES,**
								5		**AND MAXIMUM AREA**
3,600	1,200	3,600	1,200	3,600	1,200			4		**PER FLOOR IN M²**
4,800	1,600	4,800	1,600	4,800	1,600			3		
7,200	2,400	7,200	2,400	7,200	2,400			2		
14,400	4,800	14,400	4,800	14,400	4,800	16,800	5,600	1		

This table was compiled from information contained in the National Building Code of Canada 1995. It does not represent an official interpretation by the organization that issues this code.

OCCUPANCY GROUP F-3: OPEN-AIR GARAGES

Special Requirements

Garages as shown in the table below must have at least 25% of their perimeter open in a manner that provides cross ventilation to the entirety of each floor, may not be more than 22 m (72 ft) high, may have no other occupancy above, and may have no point on any floor more than 60 m (197 ft) from an exterior wall opening. For garages not meeting these criteria, see the height and area requirements for Occupancy F-3, Industrial, Low Hazard, pages 398–399.

Fire Walls

For multiplication of the allowable area by subdividing the building with fire walls, see page 302.

Measurements

Area is measured as the greatest horizontal area of a building above grade within the outside surfaces of the exterior walls, or between the outside surfaces of the exterior walls and the center line of a fire wall.

Further Information

For information on Occupancy Group classifications, see page 11. For information on mixed-use buildings, see page 301. For information on which code to consult, see pages 7, 11.

OCCUPANCY GROUP F-3: OPEN-AIR GARAGES

CONSTRUCTION TYPE		Noncombustible							
		2-Hour (page 309)		1-Hour (page 310)		¾-Hour (page 314)		Unprotected (page 311)	
		Spr	Unspr	Spr	Unspr	Spr	Unspr	Spr	Unspr
HEIGHT IN STORIES, AND MAXIMUM AREA PER FLOOR IN M²	UH	10,000	10,000	10,000	10,000	10,000	10,000	10,000	10,000
	6	10,000	10,000	10,000	10,000	10,000	10,000	10,000	10,000
	5	10,000	10,000	10,000	10,000	10,000	10,000	10,000	10,000
	4	10,000	10,000	10,000	10,000	10,000	10,000	10,000	10,000
	3	10,000	10,000	10,000	10,000	10,000	10,000	10,000	10,000
	2	10,000	10,000	10,000	10,000	10,000	10,000	10,000	10,000
	1	10,000	10,000	10,000	10,000	10,000	10,000	10,000	10,000

Each number in the table represents the maximum area per floor in square meters for every floor of a building of that story height.

Key to Abbreviations

UA	Unlimited area
UH	Unlimited height
NP	Not permitted
Spr	With approved sprinkler system
Unspr	Without approved sprinkler system

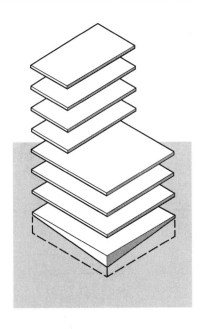

CONSTRUCTION TYPE

Combustible							
1-Hour (page 314)		Mill (page 312)		¾-Hour (page 314)		Unprotected (page 315)	
Spr	Unspr	Spr	Unspr	Spr	Unspr	Spr	Unspr
NP	NP	NP	NP	NP	NP	NP	NP

UH
6
5
4
3
2
1

HEIGHT IN STORIES, AND MAXIMUM AREA PER FLOOR IN M^2

This table was compiled from information contained in the National Building Code of Canada 1995. It does not represent an official interpretation by the organization that issues this code.

APPENDIX A
UNITS OF CONVERSION

ENGLISH	METRIC	METRIC	ENGLISH
1 in.	25.4 mm	1 mm	0.0394 in.
1 ft	304.8 mm	1 m	39.37 in.
1 ft	0.3048 m	1 m	3.2808 ft
1 lb	0.454 kg	1 kg	2.205 lb
1 ft^2	0.0929 m^2	1 m^2	10.76 ft^2
1 psi	6.89 kPa	1 kPa	0.145 psi
1 lb/ft^2	4.884 kg/m^2	1 kg/m^2	0.205 lb/ft^2
1 lb/ft^3	16.019 kg/m^3	1 kg/m^3	0.0624 lb/ft^3
1 ft/min	0.0051 m/sec	1 m/sec	196.85 ft/min
1 cfm	0.0005 m^3/sec	1 m^3/sec	2119 cfm
1 BTU	1.055 kJ	1 kJ	0.9479 BTU
1 BTU	3.9683 kcal	1 kcal	0.252 BTU
1 BTUH	0.2928 W	1 W	3.412 BTUH

$$1 \text{ Pa} = 0.102 \text{ kg/m}^2$$
$$1 \text{ kg/m}^2 = 9.80 \text{ Pa}$$

APPENDIX B
BIBLIOGRAPHY

These references are recommended as starting points if you need additional information. For those books that are not commonly available in bookstores, the publishers' mailing addresses are given.

DESIGNING THE STRUCTURE

For a more comprehensive treatment of structural design and analysis: Schodek, Daniel L. *Structures.* Englewood Cliffs, NJ, Prentice-Hall, Inc., 2000.

For a comprehensive discussion of construction materials and methods: Allen, Edward. *Fundamentals of Building Construction* (3rd ed.). New York, John Wiley & Sons, Inc., 1999.

For Heavy Timber construction: American Institute of Timber Construction. *Timber Construction Manual* (4th ed.). New York, John Wiley & Sons, Inc., 1994.

For Wood Light Frame construction: American Wood Council. *Span Tables for Joists and Rafters.* Washington, 1993. (Address: 1111 19th St., N.W., Suite 800, Washington, DC 20036.) Also highly recommended is the literature published by the APA, The Engineered Wood, P.O. Box 11700, Tacoma, WA 98411.

For brick masonry construction: Brick Institute of America. *Technical Notes on Brick Construction.* Reston, VA, various dates. (Address: 11490 Commerce Park Drive, Reston, VA 28191.)

For concrete masonry construction: National Concrete Masonry Association. *A Manual of Facts on Concrete Masonry.* Herndon, VA, various dates. (Address: 2302 Horse Pen Road, Herndon, VA 20171.)

For structural steel: American Institute of Steel Construction. *LRFD Manual of Steel Construction* (2nd ed.). Chicago, American Institute of Steel Construction. (Address: One East Wacker Drive, Suite 3100, Chicago, IL 60601.)

For sitecast concrete: Concrete Reinforcing Steel Institute. *CRSI Handbook 1996* (8th ed.). Schaumburg, Illinois, Concrete Reinforcing Steel Institute, 1996. (Address: 933 North Plum Grove Road, Schaumburg, IL 60173.)

For precast concrete: Precast/Prestressed Concrete Institute. *PCI Design Handbook: Precast and Prestressed Concrete* (5th ed.). Precast/Prestressed Concrete Institute, 1999. (Address: 209 West Jackson Boulevard, Chicago, IL 60606.)

DESIGNING SPACES FOR MECHANICAL AND ELECTRICAL SERVICES

American Society of Heating, Refrigerating, and Air-Conditioning Engineers. *ASHRAE Handbook,* in four volumes entitled *Fundamentals, HVAC Applications, HVAC Systems and Equipment,* and *Refrigeration.* Atlanta, ASHRAE, various dates. (Address: 1791 Tullie Circle, NE, Atlanta, GA 30329.)

Stein, Benjamin, and John S. Reynolds. Mechanical and Electrical Equipment for *Buildings* (9th ed). New York, John Wiley & Sons, 2001.

DESIGNING FOR DAYLIGHTING

Baker, N. V., A. Fanchiottie, and K. Steemers. *Daylighting in Architecture: A European Reference Book.* London, James & James Science Publishers, Limited, 1997.

Moore, Fuller. *Environmental Control Systems: Heating, Cooling, Lighting.* New York, McGraw-Hill College Division, 1992.

Guzowski, Mary. *Daylighting for Sustainable Design.* New York, The McGraw-Hill Companies, 1999.

DESIGNING FOR EGRESS

National Fire Protection Agency. *NFPA 101 Life Safety Code 2000.* Quincy, MA, NFPA, 2000. (Address: 1 Batterymarch Park, PO Box 9101, Quincy, MA 02269.)

BUILDING CODES

International Code Council. *International Building Code 2000.* Falls Church, VA, International Code Council, 2000. (Address: 5203 Leesburg Pike, Suite 708, Falls Church, VA 22041.)

Institute for Research in Construction, National Research Council of Canada. *National Building Code of Canada 1995.* Ottawa, Canada, 1995. (Address: Ottawa, Ontario, K1A 0R6.)

INDEX

INDEX